William F. P. Noble

1776-1876 - a Century of Gospel-Work

a history of the growth of evangelical religion in the United States, containing full descriptions of the great revivals of the century, personal sketches of eminent clergymen

William F. P. Noble

1776-1876 - a Century of Gospel-Work
a history of the growth of evangelical religion in the United States, containing full descriptions of the great revivals of the century, personal sketches of eminent clergymen

ISBN/EAN: 9783337266523

Printed in Europe, USA, Canada, Australia, Japan

Cover: Foto ©Lupo / pixelio.de

More available books at **www.hansebooks.com**

EVSEBIANA

ESSAYS ON

THE ECCLESIASTICAL HISTORY OF

EUSEBIUS

BISHOP OF CAESAREA

BY

HUGH JACKSON LAWLOR, D.D.

CANON AND PRECENTOR OF ST. PATRICK'S AND BERESFORD
PROFESSOR OF ECCLESIASTICAL HISTORY
IN THE UNIVERSITY OF DUBLIN

OXFORD
AT THE CLARENDON PRESS
MDCCCCXII

HENRY FROWDE, M.A.
PUBLISHER TO THE UNIVERSITY OF OXFORD
LONDON, EDINBURGH, NEW YORK
TORONTO AND MELBOURNE

VIRO
DOCTO · VENERABILI · ILLVSTRI
IOHANNI GWYNN
SACRAE THEOLOGIAE PROFESSORI REGIO
MAGISTRO DISCIPVLVS
AMICO AMICVS
D.D.D.

PREFACE

It has been my habit for some years to give occasional courses of lectures on the *Ecclesiastical History* of Eusebius. The following Essays are based on material collected for that purpose.

I have to thank the editors of the *Journal of Theological Studies* and *Hermathena* for permission to make use of articles published in those journals. The Essays on the *Hypomnemata* of Hegesippus and on the Use of Volumes of Tracts by Eusebius are expansions of two notes which appeared in *Hermathena* nine years ago (1902). With the former has now been incorporated an article entitled 'Hegesippus and the Apocalypse', printed in the *Journal of Theological Studies* for April 1907. The Essay on the Heresy of the Phrygians is reproduced from the latter journal (July 1908), and that on the Chronology of the *Martyrs of Palestine* from *Hermathena* (1908)—in both cases after careful revision, and with some additions.

In passing the present volume through the press I have received much help and encouragement from my friends. Among these I would specially mention Dr. L. C. Purser, who contributed the note on the Rate of March of a Roman Army which is printed as an Appendix to the fifth Essay; the Lord Bishop of Ossory, who, while he was still my colleague at St. Patrick's Cathedral and in the University, was kind enough to read the Essays before they were printed; Professor Newport J. D. White, who performed a similar office with the proof; Mr. H. Montgomery Miller, who examined a rare book for me in the British Museum; and my former pupil, the Rev. E. G. Sullivan, who pointed out a serious mistake in the Essay on the *Martyrs of Palestine*, all trace of which is now, I hope, removed. To all these, and to others, to whom my obligations are recorded in footnotes, I desire to express my gratitude.

My thanks are also due to the Delegates of the Clarendon Press for undertaking the publication of my book.

H. J. LAWLOR.

Trinity College,
   Dublin.
Conversion of St. Paul, 1912.

CONTENTS

ESSAY I

PAGE

THE *Hypomnemata* OF HEGESIPPUS 1
APPENDIX: The Remaining Fragments of the *Hypomnemata* 98

ESSAY II

THE HERESY OF THE PHRYGIANS . . . 108

ESSAY III

ON THE USE BY EUSEBIUS OF VOLUMES OF TRACTS . 136

ESSAY IV

THE CHRONOLOGY OF EUSEBIUS'S *Martyrs of Palestine* 179

ESSAY V

THE CHRONOLOGY OF THE NINTH BOOK OF THE *Ecclesiastical History* 211

APPENDIX I. The Rate of March of a Roman Army, by L. C. PURSER, Litt.D. . . . 235

APPENDIX II. The Authorship of the *De Mortibus Persecutorum* 237

ESSAY VI

THE EARLIER FORMS OF THE *Ecclesiastical History*   243

INDEX OF PASSAGES OF EARLY WRITERS QUOTED
OR REFERRED TO 292

GENERAL INDEX 299

THE *HYPOMNEMATA* OF HEGESIPPUS

By some writers Hegesippus has been styled the 'Father of Church History'. Others, anxious to reserve this honourable title for Eusebius, have drawn attention to the fact that the last of his five *Memoirs*[1] contained an account of so early an event as the martyrdom of James the Just, and from this infer that his work was 'nothing more than a collection of reminiscences', and 'quite without chronological order and historical completeness'.[2] On both sides it seems to be tacitly assumed that Hegesippus composed what at least aimed at being a history of the Church. And this was the opinion of St. Jerome. 'Hegesippus', he writes, 'vicinus apostolicorum temporum et omnes a passione Domini usque ad suam aetatem ecclesiasticorum actuum texens historias, multaque ad utilitatem legentium pertinentia hinc inde congregans, quinque libros composuit sermone simplici.'[3] But Jerome gives no evidence, except in this sentence, that he knew more of Hegesippus than we ourselves may learn from the work which in so many cases appears to have been his only source of information as to early Christian writers, the *Ecclesiastical History* of Eusebius.

---

[1] It is only in recent times, I believe, that this word has come to be used as the equivalent of ὑπομνήματα, which it appears to me to represent very inadequately. But, as it has received the sanction of such high authorities as Lightfoot, Hort, and Westcott, I have thought it convenient to retain it.

[2] McGiffert, in *Nicene and Post-Nicene Fathers*, vol. i, pp. 81, 198.

[3] *De Vir. Ill.* 22.

And the remark which has been quoted seems to have been only an expansion, quite after Jerome's manner, of the words of Eusebius, 'In five treatises he composed memoirs (ὑπομνηματισάμενος),[1] in a very simple style of writing, containing the uncorrupt tradition of the apostolic doctrine (κηρύγματος),' in which there is nothing which necessarily implies a historical work. Let us see, then, what Eusebius really tells us as to the nature of the book which Hegesippus wrote. His most important statement occurs in the immediate vicinity of that now referred to, forming the closing sentence of *II. E.* iv. 7 and the opening words of the next chapter. After giving some account of Saturninus and Basilides, and of Carpocrates, 'the father of the Gnostics,' he proceeds : 'Nevertheless, in the time of the heretics just mentioned, the truth again called to her aid many champions of her own, who made war against the godless heresies, not only by viva voce refutations, but also by written demonstrations. Among these (ἐν τούτοις) flourished Hegesippus.' After a few sentences devoted to him, Eusebius passes on to Justin Martyr. This description leaves no doubt that the work of Hegesippus was not primarily a history. It was a defence of the Faith against the attacks of heretics, and specially of the Gnostics. But it was more than this. That Hegesippus, like his elder contemporary Justin, argued against heathens, as well as against heretics, may, I think, be safely inferred from a sentence quoted incidentally by Eusebius, with a view to fixing the date of the

[1] *II. E.* iv. 8. 2. Valois translates παράδοσιν ὑπομνηματισάμενος by 'historiam complexus', which is quite arbitrary. I should add that 'vicinus apostolicorum temporum' appears to represent ἐπὶ τῆς πρώτης τῶν ἀποστόλων γενόμενος διαδοχῆς (*II. E.* ii. 23. 3), which Rufinus renders 'qui post ipsas statim primas apostolorum successiones fuit'. Perhaps the words should be translated 'who *was born* in the period immediately following the age of the Apostles'.

writer. He writes thus concerning those who at the first set up idols : 'To whom they erected cenotaphs and temples, as is done up to the present time; among whom is also Antinous, the slave of Hadrian Caesar,' &c.[1] And in the course of his argument he gave an exposition of primitive apostolic teaching to which he himself steadfastly adhered.[2]

The *Memoirs* then were an Apology for the Faith against unbelievers, for orthodoxy against misbelievers. Now, in disputing with the Greeks, if our writer used the arguments which form the stock-in-trade of the second-century apologists, he would not draw much upon ecclesiastical history. Against the Gnostics also there was much to be said which was purely theological, though here there was a historical argument, upon which Hegesippus, like other controversialists of his age, laid stress. The non-historical portion of the *Memoirs*, in fact, must have included the greater part of the work. Let us suppose that the argument based on the early history of the Church was only reached in the fifth *Memoir*,[3] and we have at once an explanation of the facts that Eusebius does not expressly refer to the first four, and that the martyrdom of St. James was narrated in the closing division of the work. We may thus defend Hegesippus from the charges which have been made against him, of want of method and arrangement. It is true that our defence obliges us to give up speaking of him as a historian, and as the 'Father of Church History'; but to do this is only to cease calling him what he did not, as it

---

[1] *H. E.* iv. 8. 2.
[2] *H. E.* iv. 22. 1. 'He has left a very full account of his own opinions.'
[3] That in the fifth *Memoir* Hegesippus contended against Gnostics, and that the argument was not *wholly* historical, may be gathered from Photius, *Bibl.* 232. See Appendix VI.

seems, claim to be, and what no one who had seen his work claimed for him.[1]

Our thesis, then, is that the first four *Memoirs* contained few, if any, allusions to the history of the Church. This will become a highly probable supposition if we can show that the historical passages quoted by Eusebius, the exact source of which is not stated, are, for the most part, drawn from the fifth division of Hegesippus's work. This, I think, will be found to be the case. We can, as I believe, reconstruct nearly the whole of two long passages of the fifth *Memoir*, the greater part of which Eusebius, after his manner, has cut up into fragments, and inserted where it suited him in his *History*,[2] and which include all the extant fragments of the writings of our author which have a direct bearing on Ecclesiastical History.

I

The earliest extract from Hegesippus is found in *H. E.* ii. 23, and contains the account of the martyrdom of James the Just, first bishop of Jerusalem. It is printed in the Appendix to this Essay.[3] This is the only passage quoted by Eusebius of the position of which in the work of Hegesippus he gives us explicit information. It is expressly stated that it came from the fifth *Memoir*.

In the passage as given by Eusebius there are many repetitions which suggest either that he took it from a

[1] Eusebius distinctly states (*H. E.* i. 1. 3) : πρῶτοι νῦν τῆς ὑποθέσεως ἐπιβάντες οἷά τινα ἐρήμην καὶ ἀτριβῆ ἰέναι ὁδὸν ἐπιχειροῦμεν. On the other hand, the title 'Ηγησίππου ἱστορία, which occurs in the sixteenth century, was probably taken from a manuscript copy of the *Memoirs*. See Zahn, *Forschungen zur Geschichte des neutest. Kanons u. der altkirchl. Literatur*, vi. Teil, Leipzig, 1900, p. 249, note.

[2] So he quotes nearly an entire chapter of Tertullian (*Apol.* 5), *H. E.* ii. 2. 25; iii. 20; v. 5.

[3] Appendix III c–e.

THE *HYPOMNEMATA* OF HEGESIPPUS 5

manuscript containing a corrupt text, or that Hegesippus was a very unskilful writer.[1] But it has all the appearance of having been transcribed in its entirety. There is no evident indication that Eusebius has omitted any part of it. We shall find, nevertheless, when we consult another writer who knew and read the *Memoirs*, Epiphanius, bishop of Constantia, that this appearance is delusive. For he brings to our knowledge some sentences which must have belonged to this passage, and of which Eusebius takes no notice.

Before attempting to prove this it is necessary to assure ourselves that Epiphanius had direct knowledge of the *Memoirs* of Hegesippus, or at any rate that for what he knew of them he was not entirely dependent on Eusebius. This fact—for that it is a fact I hope to show—cannot be established beyond controversy from any express statement in his writings; for he never mentions Hegesippus, and though it is highly probable that he more than once refers to the *Memoirs* by name, in doing so he gives them a title which is not assigned to them by other writers.

It is quite certain, however, that several passages of his *Panarion* are based on portions of the *Memoirs* quoted verbatim by Eusebius; and a careful examination of those passages gives us reason to believe that in writing them Epiphanius used a text of the *Memoirs* which differed considerably from that which was known to Eusebius. He has, for example, in *Haer*. 78. 7 a description of James the Just which is plainly borrowed from the fragment now before us. This will be obvious to any one who compares the two together.[2] It is only necessary to call attention to one clause in which his indebtedness to Hegesippus is less evident than elsewhere. He writes

[1] See the notes in Schwartz's edition of the *History*.
[2] See Appendix III c, e.

that James 'was a Nazoraean, which being interpreted is holy'. Now in the *Memoirs* as quoted by Eusebius the word 'Nazoraean' does not occur. What according to him Hegesippus said was, ' He was holy from his mother's womb, he drank not wine and strong drink, neither did he eat flesh, a razor did not touch his head, he did not anoint himself with oil, and he did not use a bath.' That the greater part of this sentence might be fairly epitomized in the statement that James was a Nazoraean (i. e. Nazirite) many will agree. That Epiphanius thought so is clear. For in another place, after quoting part of it almost as it stands in Eusebius—'In a bath he never washed, he partook not of flesh'—he adds the comment, 'If the sons of Joseph knew the order of virginity and *the work of Nazoraeans*, how much more did the old and honourable man (*sc.* Joseph the father of James) know how to keep a virgin pure, and to honour the vessel wherein, so to speak, dwelt the salvation of men?'[1] Now it will be observed that in Epiphanius the information that James was called *Oblias* is given near the beginning of the passage, immediately before this reference to his asceticism. In Eusebius it is lower down, after the account of his prayers.[2]

Let us glance at the statement as it appears in Eusebius's text. It runs thus: διά γέ τοι τὴν ὑπερβολὴν τῆς δικαιοσύνης αὐτοῦ ἐκαλεῖτο ὁ δίκαιος καὶ ὠβλίας, ὅ ἐστιν ἑλληνιστὶ περιοχὴ τοῦ λαοῦ, καὶ δικαιοσύνη, ὡς οἱ προφῆται δηλοῦσιν περὶ αὐτοῦ. Several facts rouse the suspicion that the text is corrupt in this place. That James was named ' the Just' was already said, and enlarged upon, only two

---

[1] *Haer.* 78. 14 εἰ γὰρ οἱ παῖδες τοῦ Ἰωσὴφ ᾔδεισαν παρθενίας τάξιν καὶ Ναζωραίων τὸ ἔργον, πόσῳ γε μᾶλλον ὁ πρεσβύτης καὶ τίμιος ἀνὴρ ᾔδει φυλάττειν παρθένον ἁγνὴν καὶ τιμᾶν τὸ σκεῦος, ἔνθα που ἐνεδήμησεν ἡ τῶν ἀνθρώπων σωτηρία ;

[2] § 7. See Appendix III e.

THE *HYPOMNEMATA* OF HEGESIPPUS 7

sentences higher up; the explanation of the title here given is mere tautology.[1]—he was called righteous because of his righteousness; further on, the word δικαιοσύνη, whether it be taken as another name of James, as Schwartz's punctuation seems to suggest, or as a second translation of *Oblias*, is almost certainly wrong; and finally no satisfactory explanation of the allusion to the prophets in the last clause has ever been offered. Now in Epiphanius, *Haer*. 78. 14, there is a passage which is, at any rate in part, a paraphrase of the opening sentences of our fragment.[2] In it we find the words δι' ὑπερβολὴν εὐλαβείας. They evidently correspond to διά γέ τοι τὴν ὑπερβολὴν τῆς δικαιοσύνης αὐτοῦ in the sentence just quoted; for the two phrases are not only strikingly similar, they occur also in the same position, immediately after the notice of James's habit of prayer. But Epiphanius differs from Eusebius in two respects. He reads εὐλαβείας instead of δικαιοσύνης, and he connects the clause, not with the statement that James received the name of 'the Just', but with the assertion that he was a man of prayer. So taken it yields admirable sense. James prayed unceasingly[3] because he was a man of much piety. There can be little doubt that here Epiphanius had access to a better text of Hegesippus than Eusebius. We can give a good account of the difficulties raised by the remainder of the sentence as read by Eusebius if we follow him in other matters.

We may suppose the passage, as Epiphanius knew it, to have run somewhat as follows: (§ 4) οὗτος ἐκαλεῖτο ὠβλίας, ὅ ἐστιν ἑλληνιστὶ περιοχή, ὡς οἱ προφῆται δηλοῦσιν περὶ αὐτοῦ,

---

[1] Eusebius avoided the tautology by paraphrasing (*Dem. Ev.* iii. 5, p. 116), διὰ τὰ τῆς ἀρετῆς πλεονεκτήματα.
[2] Appendix III c–e.
[3] Perhaps we should rather say, for a reason that will appear later, 'with prevailing power'.

καὶ ὠνομάσθη ὑπὸ πάντων δίκαιος ... (§ 6) καὶ μόνος εἰσήρχετο εἰς τὸν ναὸν ηὑρίσκετό τε κείμενος ... ὡς ἀπεσκληκέναι τὰ γόνατα ... διὰ τὸ ... αἰτεῖσθαι ἄφεσιν τῷ λαῷ (§ 7) διὰ τὴν ὑπερβολὴν τῆς εὐλαβείας αὐτοῦ. If some of the words here given from § 4 were transferred to the end of those taken from § 7, and others repeated at the same place, the passage would assume the form ὁ ὀνομασθεὶς ὑπὸ πάντων δίκαιος ... διὰ τὴν ὑπερβολὴν τῆς εὐλαβείας αὐτοῦ. ἐκαλεῖτο ὠβλίας, ὅ ἐστιν ἑλληνιστὶ περιοχή, ὡς οἱ προφῆται κτλ., καὶ δίκαιος. The change of εὐλαβείας into δικαιοσύνης, and the connexion of the clause in which the word occurs with what follows (leading to the insertion of γέ τοι), are now easily explained. The further removal of δίκαιος to an earlier place, and the insertion of δικαιοσύνη, are no doubt attempts of scribes to improve the logical nexus of the sentence.

One other point must be noticed. Epiphanius explains *Oblias* as meaning τεῖχος, which is equivalent to περιοχή. Thus he vouches for the genuineness of the latter word. But he omits the words τοῦ λαοῦ which follow it in Eusebius's text, and which thereby fall under suspicion. They were probably the gloss of a reader who took ὠβλίας to be a transliteration of עֹפֶל עָם.[1] Assuming that they are a later addition to the text, the passage of the prophets referred to by Hegesippus was probably regarded by him merely as an illustration of the application of the word περιοχή to James. It may be suggested that he had in view Isaiah xxxiii. 15 f. in the version of Symmachus: πορευόμενος ἐν δικαιοσύνῃ ... αὐτὸς ἐν ὑψηλοῖς κατασκηνώσει, ὡς περιοχαὶ πετρῶν τὸ ὕψος αὐτοῦ.[2]

[1] Reading perhaps ὠβλίαμ.
[2] There is nothing chronologically impossible in the use of the version of Symmachus by Hegesippus. That one who quoted the Gospel of the Hebrews (Eus. *H. E.* iv. 22. 8) should also refer to a translation of the Old Testament by an Ebionite is within the bounds

THE *HYPOMNEMATA* OF HEGESIPPUS 9

It is perhaps already clear that the text used by Epiphanius differed considerably from that quoted by Eusebius in this passage, and was freer from corrupt readings. It may be added, as a further proof of its comparative excellence, that it presents a more satisfactory arrangement of the clauses. In Eusebius the order is: James was called 'the Just', he was an ascetic, he had priestly privileges and was constant in prayer, he was called 'the Just' and *Oblias*. In Epiphanius, on the other hand, the names by which he was known are first fully dealt with, and thus the way is opened for a description of his character, which proceeds without interruption.

Now it is evident that if Epiphanius used a better text of the *Memoirs* than that which is preserved in Eusebius's extracts, he cannot have depended on Eusebius for his knowledge of them. He must have had either another series of excerpts, or more probably a complete copy of the work itself.

Two other passages which point to the same conclusion must now be examined.[1]

In *Haer.* 27. 6 Epiphanius discusses the chronological difficulty involved in the statement that Clement was appointed bishop of Rome by the Apostles Peter and Paul, though he was not first but third in the succession. His explanation is that Clement resigned the bishopric, and resumed it after the episcopate of Linus and Anencletus; and in the course of his argument he appeals to a passage in Clement's Epistle to the Corinthians: 'He

---

of probability. Compare *Dict. of Christ. Biog.* iv. 748 f., s.v. Symmachus (2).

[1] On them see Lightfoot, *St. Clement of Rome*, i. 328 ff.; Harnack, in *Sitzungsberichte d. k. preuss. Akad. d. Wissensch.* 1892, pp. 639 ff. (reprinted in his *Chronologie*, i. 180 ff.); Zahn, *Forschungen zur Gesch. d. NTlichen Kanons*, vi. 258 ff.

himself says in one of his letters, I withdraw, I will depart, let the people of God remain at peace.' And Epiphanius adds, 'For I have found this in certain memoirs' (ἔν τισι ὑπομνηματισμοῖς).[1] Epiphanius therefore did not quote Clement at first hand. From what source then did he take this excerpt? When we bear in mind that perhaps Hegesippus himself,[2] and certainly Eusebius,[3] called our *Memoirs* by the title ὑπομνήματα, and that the latter applies to them the cognate verb ὑπομνηματίζεσθαι,[4] Lightfoot's suggestion that the same work is here designated by the word ὑπομνηματισμοί is very probable. And its probability is increased when we remember that Hegesippus certainly gave some account of Clement's Epistle in his *Memoirs*.[5]

In a subsequent passage [6] Epiphanius writes of James the Just, ' For he was Joseph's eldest born and consecrated [as such]. Moreover, we have found that he exercised a priestly office according to the old priesthood. Wherefore it was permitted to him to enter once a year into the Holy of Holies, as the law enjoined the high priests in accordance with the Scriptures. For so it is recorded concerning him by many before us, Eusebius and Clement and others. Nay, he was allowed to wear the (high priest's) mitre on his head as the afore-mentioned trustworthy persons have testified in the same memoirs ' (ὑπομνηματισμοῖς).

Now of the various statements here made about James, only two—that he was ' consecrated '[7] and that he was permitted to enter the Holy of Holies—can be traced to

---

[1] The translation of this and the next passage quoted from Epiphanius is that given by Lightfoot, l. c.
[2] *H. E.* ii. 23. 8. See Appendix III e.
[3] *H. E.* iii. 23. 3; iv. 22. 1. See Appendix V d.
[4] *H. E.* iv. 8. 2.   [5] *H. E.* iv. 22. 1. See Appendix V a.
[6] *Haer.* 29. 4. See Appendix III c.
[7] ἡγιασμένος, equivalent to ἅγιος in *H. E.* ii. 23. 5.

THE *HYPOMNEMATA* OF HEGESIPPUS 11

the *Ecclesiastical History* of Eusebius, and both of them appear there in an extract from Hegesippus.[1] None of them are found in the extant writings of Clement of Alexandria. And independent evidence will be produced presently that all of them came from the *Memoirs* of Hegesippus. This is in fact antecedently probable, since Hegesippus is named by Eusebius as his main authority for St. James,[2] and is also used by him as supplying information about other relatives of our Lord.[3] And the word ὑπομνηματισμοί once more suggests a veiled reference to that work.

The special importance of these two passages lies in the fact that, if they have been correctly interpreted, at least in the former Epiphanius claims first-hand knowledge of the *Memoirs*. It will soon appear that the second of them has a direct bearing on the extract from the *Memoirs* with which we are now concerned.

If it be admitted, as a result of the foregoing argument, that Epiphanius had before him the *Memoirs* or a catena of passages extracted therefrom, independent of Eusebius, we can with the help of his *Panarion* considerably extend our knowledge of Hegesippus's work. If we find Epiphanius making statements obviously borrowed from fragments of the *Memoirs* embedded in the *Ecclesiastical History* of Eusebius, and in the same context making other statements intimately associated with them, though not vouched for by extracts in Eusebius, we are entitled to conclude, with such reserve as may be necessary, that the authority for the latter is a portion of the *Memoirs* not otherwise known. Let us take some examples.

In *Haer.* 78. 7 we have two passages, one of which we have already shown to be founded on the excerpt now

[1] Appendix III c, d. [2] *H. E.* ii. 23. 3.
[3] *H. E.* iii. 11 ; 20; iv. 22. 4. See Appendix III g-i, IV f, h, k.

before us,[1] while the other will hereafter be proved to be borrowed from a later section of the *Memoirs*.[2] The latter of these is immediately followed by a sentence about the first wife of Joseph and her children,[3] which leads up to and is immediately followed by the former. It may reasonably be inferred that this sentence, like the two between which it stands, is taken from the *Memoirs*. It is true indeed that elsewhere in this chapter Epiphanius gleans information from the apocryphal *Protevangelium of James*; but from it the information given in this sentence could not have been derived. It records that Joseph's wife was of the tribe of Judah and that she had six children, facts which are not mentioned in the *Protevangelium*.

To the description of James succeeds an argumentative passage, which occupies the remainder of the chapter, and then comes (*Haer*. 78. 8)[4] an enumeration of the children of Joseph by his first wife and other particulars not contained in the *Protevangelium*. These may on similar grounds, but with less confidence, be referred to the *Memoirs*.

The description of James in *Haer*. 78. 7 begins with words to which nothing corresponds in the text as given by Eusebius: 'He (Joseph) had therefore as his first-born James.' For like reasons this clause may be considered as borrowed from the *Memoirs*. The inference is confirmed by the passage already quoted, which claims for the statement the authority of the ὑπομνηματισμοί of Eusebius, Clement, and others.[5] It is there associated with the statement that James was 'sanctified' (ἡγιασμένος), which corresponds with Hegesippus's 'he was holy (ἅγιος) from his mother's womb'.

[1] Appendix III c. [2] Appendix III j; see below, p. 35.
[3] Appendix III a. [4] Appendix III b.
[5] Above, p. 10. Appendix III c, d.

THE *HYPOMNEMATA* OF HEGESIPPUS 13

In *Haer.* 78. 14[1] we are told that James wore the mitre —a statement which the passage just referred to has already led us to ascribe to Hegesippus—and that in answer to his prayer rain descended in a time of dearth; and these statements are followed by information, evidently drawn from Hegesippus, that he did not wear woollen garments, that by his constant prayers his knees had been hardened like the knees of camels, that he was called 'the Just', and that he did not partake of flesh. This is succeeded by the observation, not found elsewhere, that he did not wear sandals.[2] The inference suggests itself that the first two and the last of these sentences came from the same source as the others, the *Memoirs* of Hegesippus. It is confirmed by the fact that in the same chapter there is an account of the martyrdom of James taken from Hegesippus.

Elsewhere (*Haer.* 78. 13)[3] Hegesippus's enumeration of the ascetic practices of James is reproduced, upon which a few sentences follow mainly taken up with statements to the effect that the sons of Zebedee adopted a similar mode of life, and that James was called the brother of our Lord because he was the son of Joseph, who became the husband of Mary under compulsion,[4] and then the remark, in part agreeing with words in the same context given by Eusebius, 'only to this James was it permitted to enter once a year into the Holy of Holies, because he was a Nazoraean, and *took part in the office of the priesthood*' (μεμίχθαι τῇ ἱερωσύνῃ). This points to the fact that in the *Memoirs* mention was made of the exercise of sacerdotal functions by James. In a passage already quoted[5] the ὑπομνηματισμοί are given as the authority for this.

[1] Appendix III c–e.
[2] Ibid.
[3] Appendix III c, d.
[4] This is from the *Protevangelium*.
[5] Page 10.

We have now reasons of varying force for believing that we have recovered from the *Panarion* of Epiphanius no less than seven passages not quoted by Eusebius. They contain the following statements:—

1. That by his first wife, who was of the tribe of Judah, Joseph had four sons and two daughters.

2. His sons were James, born when he was about forty years old, Jose, Symeon, and Judas, and his daughters Mary and Salome. After a widowhood of many years he took Mary when he was about eighty years of age.

3. James was his first-born.

4. James did not wear sandals.

5. He exercised priestly functions.

6. He wore the mitre.

7. At his prayer the heaven gave rain.

To these we may perhaps add

8. That he was appointed first bishop by the Lord.

Now it is plain that we shall hold the opinion that these statements came from Hegesippus with more confidence if it can be shown that they may be placed in contexts with which they obviously cohere, that they do not interrupt the continuity of Hegesippus's periods.

Of the first two little need be said. They evidently serve suitably enough as an introduction to the whole passage in connexion with which they appear in Epiphanius. From the nature of their contents no. 2 may be assumed to follow rather than to precede no. 1. No. 3 of course gives no fresh information. But it may be regarded as a separate assertion of Hegesippus, not only because it appears twice in Epiphanius, the word πρωτότοκος being used in each case, but also because it is connected with no. 1 in *Haer*. 78. 7 by the particle οὖν, and closely linked with the description of James's mode of life both there and in *Haer*. 29. 4. The argument seems to be: James

THE *HYPOMNEMATA* OF HEGESIPPUS 15

was the eldest son of Joseph; being therefore the firstborn of such a household he was, as we might expect. a man of holiness.

The omission of no. 4 by Eusebius may be due to the corrupt state of the text of his exemplar. It fits in well with the details that are given of James's asceticism.

Nos. 5 and 6 are naturally taken together. They might well introduce the statement that James had access to the Holy of Holies, with which they are expressly connected by Epiphanius.[1]

Epiphanius puts no. 7 after the notice of the wearing of the mitre by James and before the statement that he wore linen garments. That may be very nearly its true place. But perhaps it stands most fitly after the statement that he asked forgiveness for the people. If we insert it there, as an example of the efficacy of his prayer, and suppose that it was followed by the words διὰ τὴν ὑπερβολὴν τῆς εὐλαβείας αὐτοῦ, which almost certainly had their place at the end of the section. we have a most interesting parallel to Heb. v. 7, he was 'heard for his godly fear'.[2]

As to no. 8. It seems likely that Hegesippus, who gives further on a full account of the election of Symeon to the bishopric, would have told something about the appointment of James. And an examination of the opening words of the section relating to him quoted by Eusebius lends colour to the supposition that something of the kind was recorded immediately before them, which has been omitted. To the words διαδέχεται τὴν ἐκκλησίαν, indeed, I have observed no exact parallel elsewhere. In similar connexions the most common formula in Irenaeus,[3]

---

[1] *Haer.* 29. 4 διὸ καί.
[2] ὃς ... δεήσεις τε καὶ ἱκετηρίας ... προσενέγκας καὶ εἰσακουσθεὶς ἀπὸ τῆς εὐλαβείας. [3] Three times, ap. Eus. *H. E.* v. 6. 2, 4.

the anonymous writer against the Montanists,[1] and Eusebius[2] is διαδέχεταί (διεδέξατό)[3] τίς τινα, the person who last held the office or privilege referred to being in the accusative. But another construction occurs frequently in which the office is in the accusative, the name of the previous incumbent being given in an earlier clause, e. g. διαδέχεται τὴν ἐπισκοπὴν Δόμνος.[4] The word ἐκκλησία does not of course denote an office ; but since Hegesippus certainly regarded James as the first bishop of Jerusalem, we seem justified in taking it here as a rough equivalent of ἡ ἐπισκοπὴ τῆς ἐκκλησίας or ὁ θρόνος τῆς ἐκκλησίας. In all the passages referred to above διαδέχεσθαι involves the notion of succession ; it does not denote merely receiving office. And the predecessor is always named. Hence we may translate ' The brother of the Lord, James, succeeds to the oversight of the Church '. But who was his predecessor ? He need not,[5] and cannot, have been a bishop. Epiphanius says, quite distinctly, and apparently on the authority of Hegesippus, that he was the Lord himself, and that by Him James was appointed to the episcopate.[6] The addition of a few words to the text of Hegesippus, as Eusebius gives it, would be

[1] Once, ap. Eus. *H. E.* v. 17. 4 τοὺς ἀπὸ Μοιτανοῦ ... τίνες ... διεδέξαντο.

[2] Thirty-two times, *H. E.* i. 7. 3 ; ii. 8. 1 ; iii. 13 (*bis*) ; 14 ; 15 ; 21 (*bis*) ; 26. 1 ; iv. 4 ; 5. 5 ; 14. 10 ; 19 ; v. Praef. 1 ; 22. 1 ; vi. 6 ; 8. 7 ; 10 ; 21. 1, 2 ; 23. 3 ; 26 ; 28 ; 29. 1 ; 39. 1 ; vii. 1 ; 27. 1 ; 28. 3 ; 32. 1, 2, 24, 30. And so Africanus ap. *H. E.* i. 7. 12.

[3] The aorist is found in Iren. ap. Eus. *H. E.* v. 6. 4 ; Anon. l. c.; and Eus. *H. E.* i. 7. 3 ; iii. 26. 1 ; vi. 6 ; vii. 32. 2.

[4] *H. E.* vii. 14. I have noted twenty-one examples : i. 9. 1 ; ii. 24 ; iii. 35 ; iv. 3 ; 5. 5 ; 10 ; 20 ; v. 5. 8 ; vi. 11. 4 ; 21. 2 ; 29. 1, 4 (*bis*) ; 34 ; 39. 1 ; vii. 10. 1 ; 14 (*bis*) ; 32. 4, 29, 31.

[5] *H. E.* ii. 24 πρῶτος μετὰ Μάρκον ... τῆς ἐν Ἀλεξανδρείᾳ παροικίας Ἀννιανὸς τὴν λειτουργίαν διαδέχεται. Annianus was first bishop, iii. 14.

[6] *Haer.* 78. 7. See Appendix III c. Cp. the Menology quoted below, p. 44, note.

THE *HYPOMNEMATA* OF HEGESIPPUS 17

sufficient to convey both these pieces of information.[1] But if Hegesippus wrote this Eusebius would probably have regarded his statements as unhistorical, if not blasphemous. Hence we can readily account for the fact that he never refers to Hegesippus as a source of information in regard to the appointment of James. For this he prefers to depend on Clement of Alexandria, according to whom James was elected bishop by the Apostles Peter, James, and John, who did not claim this glory for themselves.[2] But this statement is at variance with the intimation of Hegesippus that James exercised co-ordinate authority with the apostles.[3] If we abandon the supposition that Hegesippus said what Epiphanius seems to impute to him, we must, I believe, accept the alternative theory that he said nothing on the subject of James's appointment, which does not commend itself as probable. And it is at any rate certain that Eusebius was not ignorant of the view that James was appointed bishop by the Lord. In one place he describes him as 'having received the episcopate of the Church of Jerusalem at the hands of the Saviour himself and the apostles'.[4] Is he not here making

---

[1] Cp. *H. E.* i. 9. 1 ἐκ διαθηκῶν Ἡρῴδου τοῦ πατρός, ἐπικρίσεώς τε Καίσαρος Αὐγούστου, τὴν κατὰ Ἰουδαίων βασιλείαν διεδέξατο [ὁ Ἀρχέλαος].

[2] *H. E.* ii. 1. 2 f. See also ii. 23. 1, where Eusebius is clearly not relying on Hegesippus.

[3] *H. E.* ii. 23. 4. See Appendix III c. By the way of parallel compare such passages as *H. E.* iv. 14. 10 Μάρκος . . . σὺν καὶ Λουκίῳ ἀδελφῷ διαδέχεται. The fact that Hegesippus describes James as ruling 'with the apostles' appears to me fatal to Zahn's contention (pp. 271 ff.) that Clement derived his statement from Hegesippus. It may be added that, if he did, it is hard to understand why Eusebius should have quoted Clement rather than Hegesippus as his authority.

[4] *H. E.* vii. 19 τὸν γὰρ Ἰακώβου θρόνον, τοῦ πρώτου τῆς Ἱεροσολύμων ἐκκλησίας τὴν ἐπισκοπὴν πρὸς τοῦ σωτῆρος καὶ τῶν ἀποστόλων ὑποδεξαμένου κτλ. My attention has been called to this passage by Mr. C. H. Turner, *Journ. of Theol. Studies*, i. (1900) 535 f., where reference is also made

an attempt to combine the statements of Hegesippus and Clement?

II

We turn next to another passage which Eusebius states that he transcribed from Hegesippus, and the opening sentences of which run thus (*H. E.* iv. 22. 4):[1]

'And after James the Just had borne witness (μαρτυρῆ-σαι), as did also the Lord, for the same reason, again (πάλιν) the son of his paternal uncle, Symeon the son of Clopas, is appointed (καθίσταται) bishop; whom all put forward as second [bishop] since he was a cousin of the Lord. On this account they called the Church a virgin; for (γάρ) it was not yet corrupted by vain teachings.'

The text of this passage presents features which suggest that Eusebius has not transcribed his source correctly, or that he has tacitly omitted some sentences which were essential to a full understanding of those which he has preserved.

We notice first the statement that 'again' (πάλιν) Symeon was appointed bishop. Since it cannot be supposed that Symeon was made bishop twice the word 'again' must, if the text is sound, refer to the appointment of James the Just. But if his appointment was mentioned at all by Hegesippus it must have been in a much earlier part of his narrative—so far back, it would seem, that the word 'again' would not naturally be used in reference to it.[2] Indeed we have found reason to suppose that Hege-

---

to *Clem. Recog.* i. 43 as stating (probably after Hegesippus) that James was appointed bishop by Christ.

[1] For the Greek see Appendix III g–i, l.

[2] Rufinus and the Syriac translator seem to have felt the difficulty of πάλιν, for both of them omit it. The clause has been rendered so as to mean that again one was appointed bishop who was a cousin of the Lord, a translation which is sufficiently disposed of by Lightfoot

THE *HYPOMNEMATA* OF HEGESIPPUS 19

sippus represented the designation of James as so entirely different in its character from the designation of Symeon that the two could hardly be connected by the word πάλιν. According to him, if we are right, he was promoted to the episcopate not as the result of an election, but by the personal act of the Lord. We may suspect then that some words have here fallen out of the text, among them being the verb with which πάλιν was connected.

The next sentence also causes considerable difficulty. The phrase 'on this account' hangs in the air; for the mere fact that Symeon was unanimously elected to the episcopate cannot account for the Church being called a virgin. Zahn, it is true, will not admit this. The unanimous election he holds to have been the outward sign of the unity of the Church, and that unity to have been the justification to Hegesippus of the title ' virgin '.[1] But to interpret thus, I venture to think, is to read into the final clause of the first sentence what must have been clearly expressed if the phrase 'on this account' had reference to it. Moreover Symeon was not elected to the bishopric by the unanimous vote *of the Church* ; but this will be made clear in the sequel. Valois cuts the knot by emending to μέχρι τούτου. Heinichen prefers to follow Stroth, and talks of the badness of Hegesippus's style,

---

(*Galatians*[?], p. 277) and Zahn (p. 237). Lightfoot himself translates πάλιν 'next', which is not satisfactory. Zahn thinks that πάλιν may introduce the second of two events which are not identical in their circumstances, but merely resemble one another, citing as examples Matt. iv. 8, Rom. xv. 12, Mark xv. 13 (see vv. 3, 11), Mark iii. 1. The resemblance between the appointments of James and Symeon was that both were relatives of the Lord, the one a brother and the other a cousin. But, apart from other objections, this seems to assume that James, like Symeon, was appointed because of his kinship to Christ, of which there seems to be no indication.

[1] Op. cit., p. 237.

which is perhaps hardly fair. But a solution lies close at hand, so obvious that I can scarcely imagine that no one has hitherto suggested it. What is to hinder us from supposing that Eusebius has omitted a passage, not relevant to his immediate purpose, before the words 'on this account'?

We seem then to have some ground for supposing that in the quotation now before us Eusebius omitted two portions of the text of Hegesippus. It may be urged, indeed, that this would not be in accordance with his usual method of citation. When he quotes two passages from an early writer which are not consecutive, he usually introduces the second with some such phrase as τούτους δὲ μεθ' ἕτερα ἐπιφέρει λέγων. But this is not an overwhelming difficulty.[1] Nor is it unreasonable to suppose that Eusebius was guilty of so quoting Hegesippus as to leave his expressions without meaning. He does the same thing with other writers.[2] But our conjecture will be made much more probable if we can supply, from other parts of the *History*, the passages, or a considerable part of them, which we suppose Eusebius to have here omitted. This we shall now endeavour to do.

It is first necessary to rescue for Hegesippus two fragments which are not obviously his. I begin by translating two closely connected chapters of the *Ecclesiastical History* (iii. 11, 12):[3]

---

[1] In his quotation from Clement of Alexandria, in *H. E.* v. 11, he, in like manner, omits a sentence. And it is at least possible that some of the passages which we have added to Hegesippus's account of St. James were omitted of set purpose. Cp. also *H. E.* i. 2. 3, 15; x. 4. 30, 32, 48, 49 ff., 71.

[2] See, for example, his quotation from Dionysius of Alexandria, *H. E.* iii. 28. 4 f., which can only be understood when read with its context in *H. E.* vii. 25. 1-5.

[3] For the Greek see Appendix III g-j, IV a.

THE *HYPOMNEMATA* OF HEGESIPPUS 21

'(c. 11) A record preserves the following story (λόγος κατέχει): After the witness (μαρτυρίαν) of James and the capture of Jerusalem which immediately followed it, such of the apostles and the disciples of the Lord as still remained alive came together from every direction to the same place, together with those who were of the same race, according to the flesh, as the Lord—for many even of these were still living—and all of them took counsel together whom they should adjudge worthy to succeed James. And then with one mind all of them approved of Symeon the son of Clopas, of whom the passage of the Gospel makes mention, as worthy of the seat of the community there, since he was, if report is to be believed (ὥς γέ φασι), a cousin of the Saviour. For, in fact, Clopas was brother to Joseph : so Hegesippus relates ('Ηγήσιππος ἱστορεῖ). (c. 12) And besides these things [the authority cited adds] (καὶ ἐπὶ τούτοις): Vespasian after the capture of Jerusalem commanded that all who were of the race of David should be sought out, to the end that there might not be left among the Jews any of those who belonged to the royal tribe ; and from this cause a very great persecution was again stirred up against the Jews.'

Before entering upon a discussion of this important passage something must be said in justification of the translation which has been given of the introductory words, λόγος κατέχει. This phrase has been often assumed to indicate no more than an oral tradition, and so in the latest, and I believe the best, English translation of the *History*[1] it is rendered 'it is said'. But this is incorrect. As Lightfoot has observed, the expression λόγος κατέχει 'is not confined to oral tradition, but may include contemporary written authorities, and implies authentic and trustworthy information'.[2] I have myself collected a number of instances of the use of this and similar phrases from the *History*, which completely corroborate this

---

[1] That of Mr. McGiffert, in *Nicene and Post-Nicene Fathers*, vol. i.
[2] *Ignatius*, vol. i. pp. 58, 238. Cp. Harnack, *Chron.* i. 128, n.

remark. In the majority of cases where Eusebius introduces a narrative with the words λόγος (κατ)έχει, the document on which he relies is either indicated in the immediate context,[1] or may be discovered by a search through the passages from previous writers scattered over his pages.[2] Only a few instances of the phrase remain, in which it does not seem possible to name the document referred to,[3] and in none of these is the use of documentary evidence excluded, or improbable. It may be regarded therefore as much more likely than not that in our passage the use of the phrase implies that Eusebius

[1] H. E. ii. 7 ; 17. 6, 19 ; 22. 2 (see §§ 3-7) ; iii. 19 ; 32. 1 (see § 2) ; 36. 3 (see § 7 : the passage cited does not, of course, prove that Ignatius was actually martyred, though, judging from H. E. iv. 16, it is not impossible that Eusebius thought otherwise) ; iv. 5. 1 (see § 2 : the statement that the bishops were short-lived may be an inference from the number of names in the written lists—the διαδοχαί of v. 12; but see below, p. 92); iv. 23 (see 29. 3); v. 5. 1, 2 (see §§ 3-7) ; vi. 28.

[2] H. E. iii. 37. 1 (see v. 17. 3) ; v. 10. 1 (see vi. 19. 13, where, however, it is not stated that Pantaenus was a Stoic. Observe that λόγος έχει is here, as it seems, contrasted with φασί). In H. E. iii. 24. 5 we have the statement, depending on λόγος κατέχει, that Matthew and John wrote their Gospels 'of necessity' (ἐπάναγκες). It is possible that Eusebius intended λόγος κατέχει to cover only his assertion about St. Matthew. For when in §§ 7 ff. he recounts a story of the origin of St. John's Gospel, for which no earlier authority is known, he refers, and apparently with some emphasis, to common report as the evidence for what he tells (φασί, §§ 7 bis, 11). His assertion about St. Matthew is scarcely more than a fair inference from extracts which he gives elsewhere from Papias (iii. 39. 16), Irenaeus (v. 8. 2), and Origen (vi. 25. 4). That it was made by Papias in so many words, in the passage of which no more than the two concluding sentences are now preserved (iii. 39. 16), is far from incredible.

[3] H. E. i. 12. 3 ; ii. 17. 1 ; vi. 4. 3 (perhaps referring to a letter of Origen, as in the next sentence, ὥς που φησὶν αὐτός) ; vii. 12 ; 32. 6 ; viii. 6. 6 (cp. below, p. 268); App. 1. In ii. 1. 13 reference is, no doubt, made to Irenaeus, Adv. Haer. iii. 12. 8, while for the statement in v. 19. 1 there can be no question that a written list of bishops of Antioch was the voucher. H. E. iii. 18. 1 ; 20. 9 will be discussed below.

THE *HYPOMNEMATA* OF HEGESIPPUS 23

is not merely reporting a current tradition, but paraphrasing a document.

If this be granted, several arguments, which taken together amount to practical demonstration, may be urged in proof of the conclusion that the document which lay before Eusebius was in fact the *Memoirs* of Hegesippus.[1]

The first is based on the evidence supplied by the text of the passage itself. It consists of five distinct statements, three in chapter 11 and two in chapter 12, in the *oratio obliqua*, the subject in each case being in the accusative and the verb in the infinitive, and each statement depending on λόγος κατέχει or 'Ηγήσιππος ἱστορεῖ. Confining ourselves for the present to chapter 11, it is obvious that λόγος κατέχει controls the first statement. But the first and second statements are so closely connected that it is impossible to suppose that they were derived from different sources. Hence the 'record' must have contained all that is told in chapter 11, with the possible exception of the last clause, which might also have been regarded as controlled by λόγος κατέχει if the words 'Ηγήσιππος ἱστορεῖ had not followed it. Now the word ἱστορεῖ could scarcely be used of such a simple statement as that Clopas was Joseph's brother: it almost always implies a narrative, however brief.[2] Hence 'Ηγήσιππος ἱστορεῖ must include the second statement, and therefore also the first, as well as the third. The conclusion is plain that λόγος κατέχει and 'Ηγήσιππος ἱστορεῖ are in the present instance equivalent statements. One of the two is redundant, since Hegesippus was actually the author of the 'record'. We may suppose that by the time Eusebius reached the end of chapter 11 he had forgotten that

[1] Cp. Hort, *Judaistic Christianity*, p. 170.
[2] Many passages might be cited in support of this statement. But on the other hand see *H. E.* ii. 17. 2; iv. 22. 7.

he had introduced his indirect quotation with the former phrase, and so came to repeat it in another form. An exact parallel for this grammatical confusion is not perhaps to be found elsewhere in the *History*. But something like it occurs a little further on (iii. 19),[1] where to an indirect quotation from Hegesippus the words παλαιὸς κατέχει λόγος are prefixed, after which a direct quotation immediately follows, prefaced with 'These things Hegesippus makes plain, speaking as follows'.[2]

But again the note of time in the very first clause of chap. 11 is distinctly Hegesippean. The assembly of the apostles and disciples is said to have taken place after the martyrdom of James '*and the capture of Jerusalem which immediately followed it*'. Now Eusebius follows two main authorities for the martyrdom, Josephus and Hegesippus. The former dates it between the death of Festus and the arrival of his successor Albinus,[3] i. e. A.D. 61–2. This date Eusebius adopts in his *Chronica*, where he assigns the murder to An. Ab. 2077 = 7 Nero.[4] But Hegesippus puts it immediately before either the Jewish war or the siege of Jerusalem.[5] This is the date given in the passage before us.

[1] See Appendix IV c, f.
[2] Compare iii. 32. 1 f. τὸν καθ' ἡμῶν κατέχει λόγος ἀνακινηθῆναι διωγμόν ... καὶ τούτου μάρτυς αὐτὸς ἐκεῖνος ... Ἡγήσιππος.
[3] *H. E.* ii. 23. 21 ff. = Joseph. *Ant.* xx. 9. 1.
[4] See also *H. E.* ii. 23. 2. See C. H. Turner in *Journal of Theological Studies*, i (1900), p. 533.
[5] Ap. *H. E.* ii. 23. 18. See Appendix III e. Zahn (p. 234) adduces strong reasons for the view that in the words καὶ εὐθὺς Οὐεσπασιανὸς πολιορκεῖ αὐτούς Hegesippus is alluding to the war, not to the siege. In that case the date indicated by Hegesippus would be Passover 66, a month before the uproar in Jerusalem mentioned by Josephus (*B. J.* ii. 15. 2), which took place in May and may be regarded as the beginning of the war. But Eusebius certainly understood the words to refer to the siege, which began shortly before Passover 70; for he immediately afterwards

And lastly, when we place chapter 11 beside the passage translated above,[1] which is expressly stated to have been from the pen of Hegesippus, we discover that a great part of the first sentence of the latter appears in slightly altered form in the former. There are, it is true, three important additions in the passage now before us: the mention of the siege of Jerusalem, the account of the assembling of the apostles and relatives of the Lord, and the remark that Clopas was Joseph's brother. But the last two of these occur at the very places where we have already found reason to suspect omissions in the quotation first considered, one preceding and the other following the statement that Symeon was unanimously elected. And now that the substance of the omitted sentences is known to us we can easily understand why Eusebius passed them over in his transcript in *II. E.* iv. 22. 4. For his purpose there was to give an account of the introduction of heretical teaching into the Church; and to that purpose the details of the election and the exact relationship of Symeon to the Lord were not pertinent. The remainder of the passage, however—standing now as the first sentence of the direct quotation—was necessary to fix the date, and to explain the allusion to the heresiarch Thebuthis which immediately follows.[2] For no doubt it was the intention of Eusebius to convey that Thebuthis was proposed as a rival candidate for the bishopric when Symeon was elected. Anyhow it is very probable that this actually took place. He was a convert from one of the Jewish sects, and the majority of such converts were won through the influence of James the Just.[3] He belonged, it would therefore seem, to a later and perhaps less conservative generation

paraphrases them thus: τῆς παραχρῆμα μετὰ τὸ μαρτύριον αὐτοῦ πολιορκίας τῆς Ἱερουσαλήμ.   [1] Page 18.
[2] See Appendix III l.   [3] *II. E.* ii. 23. 9. See Appendix III e.

of believers. It is quite likely that when the bishopric became vacant they would propose a candidate of their own in opposition to the candidate favoured by those who survived from the period which closed some forty years earlier. It appears certain therefore that *H. E.* iii. 11 is a paraphrase of the earlier part of the passage of the *Memoirs* from which we have in *II. E.* iv. 22. 4 a series of extracts.

It is not unimportant to observe that on the hypothesis that Thebuthis was a rival of Symeon, the electors of the latter were not the general body of the faithful, as we might have expected, but the surviving apostles and disciples—i. e. those who had believed on Christ before the Ascension—and His relatives. Their unanimity was therefore not an indication of the unity of the Church of Jerusalem. It only showed that the followers of Thebuthis, if he had any, were not included among the privileged persons who had the final voice in the election of the bishop. Thus Zahn's explanation of the puzzling words διὰ τοῦτο [1] can hardly be maintained.

It has been debated whether the indirect quotation in chapter 12 depends on λόγος κατέχει at the beginning, or on Ἡγήσιππος ἱστορεῖ at the end of chapter 11.[2] For us the question is purely syntactic, or even without meaning. If our reasoning has been correct it is certainly derived from Hegesippus. But it must be remarked that the opening phrase καὶ ἐπὶ τούτοις seems to mark it as not continuous with the passage paraphrased in chapter 11.[3]

[1] See above, p. 19.
[2] The third alternative suggested by Zahn (p. 238), that the construction depends on ὥς γέ φασι (which he regards as a resumption of λόγος κατέχει), seems highly improbable. The meaning of ὥς γέ φασι will be discussed below.
[3] Cp. *H. E.* i. 8. 16; ii. 1. 14; 6. 7, 8; iii. 32. 7; vii. 25. 6, &c. But see also iv. 15. 15. Compare Heinichen ad loc.

THE *HYPOMNEMATA* OF HEGESIPPUS

We may now attempt to fix the position in the *Memoirs* of the passage represented by *H. E.* iv. 22. 4 and iii. 11. It began, as we have seen, with some such words as 'And after James the Just had borne witness . . . and Jerusalem had immediately afterwards been captured'. This seems to imply that a narrative of the martyrdom of James had preceded it; and if so there can be little question that the narrative referred to was that which Eusebius has quoted from the *Memoirs*.[1] If the whole of that section is summarized in the words 'after James the Just had borne witness', its closing words, καὶ εὐθὺς Οὐεσπασιανὸς πολιορκεῖ αὐτούς, are recalled by the succeeding allusion to the sack of Jerusalem. But while it seems plain that the passage now under consideration followed the account of the martyrdom of St. James, it is less easy to decide whether it followed it immediately or was separated from it by another passage. On the one hand, the abrupt close of the story of the martyrdom with the sentence just quoted certainly suggests that some account of the Jewish war followed.[2] And the inference is supported by the first sentence of our passage. Would Hegesippus have resumed his narrative in so elaborate a fashion if nothing had intervened between the close of the section about St. James and the beginning of that about Symeon? But on the other hand it is difficult to believe that if Hegesippus had enlarged on this subject Eusebius would have failed to quote him. For the war the historian depends wholly on Josephus, though when he comes to the murder of St. James he places his account side by side with that of the Christian writer. Had Hegesippus dealt with the subject of the war at any length he would certainly have told much that would have been of interest to Eusebius, and

[1] *H. E.* ii. 23. 4–18. See Appendix III c–c.
[2] Compare Zahn, p. 236.

of no little importance in regard to the history of the Church in Palestine.¹ On the whole it seems most probable that our passage was introduced by a short section concerning the war, which however did not tell its story in such detail as to call for comparison with the fuller narrative of Josephus.

Now Zahn ² holds the opinion that Hegesippus included in his *Memoirs* a notice of the flight of the Christians of Jerusalem to Pella, immediately before the siege. The arguments by which this hypothesis is supported may be stated as follows. Epiphanius has three short narratives of the flight. The first two occur in successive chapters of the *Panarion*, in the first of which he treats of the origin of the Nazoraeans, and in the second, in similar fashion, of that of the Ebionites (*Haer*. 29. 7; 30. 2); the third is found in his treatise De *Mensuris et Ponderibus* (c. 15).³ And the three accounts are characterized by remarkable similarities of phraseology. Thus in *Haer*. 29 the flight is ἡ ἀπὸ τῶν Ἱεροσολύμων μετάστασις, and in *De Mens*. 15 we are told that the Christians were enjoined μεταστῆναι ἀπὸ τῆς πόλεως. In *Haer*. 30 they are described as μετανaστάντων, and in *De Mens*. 15 as μετανάσται γενόμενοι. The fugitives are 'all the apostles'⁴ in *Haer*. 29, 'all the disciples' in *De Mens*. 15, and in *Haer*. 30 'all

¹ It may be added that if Hegesippus intended to date the martyrdom of James immediately before the outbreak of the war (i. e. April 66) Eusebius could not have misunderstood him and dated it immediately before the siege (i. e. Spring 70) if Hegesippus had given an account of the military operations between the former and the latter date. See above, p. 24.

² Op. cit., p. 269 f.

³ These passages are printed in Appendix III f.

⁴ So Dindorf with the Venetian MS. But the reading is rendered suspicious by Eusebius's implication (see below, p. 33 f.) that the apostles did not go to Pella. The older editors read μαθηταί, which would make the agreement between *Haer*. 29 and *De Mens*. 15 yet closer.

THE *HYPOMNEMATA* OF HEGESIPPUS   29

who believed in Christ'. In *Haer.* 29 we have the phrase ἐν Πέλλῃ ᾠκηκότων, and in *De Mens.* 15 ᾤκησαν ἐν Πέλλῃ. In *Haer.* 29 we find the words τὴν Περαίαν οἰκήσαντες ἐκεῖσε ... διέτριβον, which are matched by τὴν Περαίαν ... κατῴκησαν ... καὶ ἐκεῖσε διατριβόντων in *Haer.* 30. In *Haer.* 29 it is said that Jerusalem ἤμελλε πάσχειν πολιορκίαν; *Haer.* 30 does not mention the impending siege, but in *De Mens.* 15 it is alluded to in the expression ἔμελλε ἁλίσκεσθαι κτλ. and μελλούσης ἄρδην ἀπόλλυσθαι. The word ἅλωσις for the capture of the city in *Haer.* 30 is balanced by the use of the cognate verb ἁλίσκεσθαι with the same reference in *De Mens.* 15. And finally Pella is said both in *Haer.* 30 and *De Mens.* 15 to have been a city of the Decapolis,[1] a coincidence all the more remarkable because the name 'Decapolis' was obsolete in Epiphanius's day. This fact he plainly intimates, in one case by observing that the Decapolis is mentioned in the Gospel, and in the other by his disclaimer of first-hand knowledge—' the city *is said* to belong to the Decapolis.'

The greater number of these words and phrases may be supposed to have come from the source from which Epiphanius derived his knowledge of the flight, especially since it is known that the composition of the treatise about weights and measures was separated from that of the *Panarion* by an interval of fifteen years or more. Can we discover what that source was? We turn naturally to the only extant account of the flight of earlier date than Epiphanius, that which is given by Eusebius.[2] It is evident, however, that Epiphanius did not depend on it. for he states definitely that the Christians left Jerusalem

---

[1] So also in *Haer.* 29. 7, in the sentence immediately preceding the passage given in Appendix III f., the Nazoraeans are said to have dwelt ἐν τῇ Δεκαπόλει περὶ τὰ τῆς Πέλλης μέρη and elsewhere.

[2] *H. E.* iii. 5. 2 f. See Appendix III f.

in obedience to a command of Christ (*Haer.* 29) which was conveyed by an angel (*De Mens.* 15), while Eusebius merely says that they had 'some sort of (τινὰ) divine intimation (χρησμόν) granted by revelation'. And several of the phrases quoted above do not occur in Eusebius. Nevertheless between Eusebius and Epiphanius there is no contradiction, and there are many points of contact. If according to Eusebius the Christians received a χρησμός, in *De Mens.* 15 it is said προεχρηματίσθησαν. We have in Eusebius the phrase μεταναστῆναι τῆς πόλεως corresponding to μεταστῆναι ἀπὸ τῆς πόλεως in *De Mens.* 15, and reminding us of ἀπὸ τῶν Ἱεροσολύμων μετάστασις in *Haer.* 29, μεταναστάντες in *Haer.* 30, and μετανάσται in *De Mens.* 15. Jerusalem is ἡ πόλις in Eusebius and *De Mens.* 15, and Pella is τις πόλις in Eusebius and *Haer.* 30. The verb οἰκεῖν is used in relation to Pella in Eusebius exactly as in the three passages of Epiphanius, οἱ εἰς Χριστὸν πεπιστευκότες as in *Haer.* 30, ἄρδην of the destruction of Jerusalem as in *De Mens.* 15, Χριστοῦ φήσαντος as in *Haer.* 29, though in a different connexion. We may also note that πόλιν ... Πέλλαν αὐτὴν ὀνομάζουσιν in Eusebius and Πέλλῃ ... πόλει καλουμένῃ in *Haer.* 30 read very like different paraphrases of the same words.

All these facts lead to the conclusion that Eusebius and Epiphanius relied on a common document for the flight to Pella. What was it? In the earlier part of the long sentence in which Eusebius mentions the flight an indirect reference is made to Hegesippus, when the death of James the Just is said to have been 'already recounted'; and Epiphanius, in that part of the *Panarion* in which occur his first two accounts of the same incident, is probably depending on the *Memoirs* for some of his statements about other things.[1] It is not rash to infer that both

[1] See above, p. 10.

THE *HYPOMNEMATA* OF HEGESIPPUS 31

writers learned also what they knew of the flight to Pella from that work.

This reasoning, no doubt, does not compel assent. But it is materially strengthened when we take account of another consideration. If Hegesippus alluded at all to the flight, it is obvious that in his work the narrative of it would most naturally follow that of the martyrdom of James, and thus, if we have argued correctly, precede the story of the election of Symeon. Let us then try the experiment of putting the story which lies behind the four passages of Eusebius and Epiphanius into that place, and see whether it fits comfortably into the niche which has been provided for it. We shall find, if I am not mistaken, that it harmonizes admirably with its surroundings.

In the first place, it satisfies the expectation raised by the closing sentence of the narrative of the martyrdom of St. James, that Hegesippus had something to say about the Jewish war, and said it in a passage immediately following, which Eusebius has not quoted. The Pella narrative, moreover, can have been of no great length. A sentence suffices for a summary of it in three of our passages, and little more than a sentence in the fourth. This also is in accordance with our anticipation. We can understand too why Eusebius does not compare it with the history of the war which he extracts from Josephus; for the only incident with which it is concerned is not recorded by Josephus at all. And it is quite in keeping with what we know of the design of the *Memoirs* that Hegesippus should restrict his notice of the war to this one event. For he was not at all concerned with the misfortunes of the Jewish people as such, or with the sack of the city for its own sake, but only with these things in their relation to the Church of Jerusalem. The war, in fact, caused a lacuna in the history of the Church of that place. Hegesippus had only to explain how this happened, and how the total destruction of the Church was avoided; and that is fully done in the Pella story.

Then again, we have already observed that Eusebius introduces his account of the flight with a reference to the *Memoirs*. It is not without significance that the passage to which he alludes is that which, on our hypothesis, immediately preceded the Pella story as told by Hegesippus. Again, Hegesippus closes his account of St. James with the words καὶ εὐθὺς Οὐεσπασιανὸς πολιορκεῖ αὐτούς:[1] we are reminded of it by the remark in *Haer.* 29 that Jerusalem ἤμελλε πάσχειν πολιορκίαν. Again in *Haer.* 30 we meet with the phrase, μετὰ τὴν τῶν Ἱεροσολύμων ἅλωσιν: it occurs again with trifling variations in Eusebius's paraphrase of the first sentence of the section of the *Memoirs* about Symeon, μετὰ ... τὴν αὐτίκα γενομένην ἅλωσιν τῆς Ἱερουσαλήμ.[2]

But further, a close examination of the account of Symeon's election seems to reveal the fact that it was introduced by a notice of the departure of the Christians from Jerusalem. We have seen that the portion of this passage which followed the introductory clauses is represented in the direct quotation by the single word πάλιν: and we have learned from the paraphrase that its

[1] It is not altogether impossible that these words may really belong to the Pella story. We have seen that Eusebius is quite capable of tacitly omitting part of a passage in quotation; and there is force in Schwartz's remark, though perhaps he expresses himself rather too dogmatically, that this and the preceding sentences are alternative endings to the narrative, both of which cannot have stood in the original text. However, it must be remembered that wherever the words were in Eusebius's copy of the *Memoirs* they must have been in sufficiently close connexion with the martyrdom to convince him that the latter took place immediately before the siege.

[2] *H. E.* iii. 11. See Appendix III g.

THE *HYPOMNEMATA* OF HEGESIPPUS 33

substance was that as many of the apostles, disciples, and relatives of the Lord as survived assembled from all quarters to elect a bishop to succeed James the Just. Eusebius also informs us that Symeon was elected bishop of the Church in *Jerusalem*,[1] a statement which he probably derived from the portion of Hegesippus's *Memoirs* now under consideration. It seems to imply that the Christians had returned thither on the conclusion of the siege. These facts determine with high probability the verb with which πάλιν was connected in the text of Hegesippus. We can scarcely doubt that it was συνέρχονται, or an equivalent, represented by συνελθεῖν in the paraphrase. But the phrase πάλιν συνέρχονται —'they assemble once more'—involves a scattering recounted in the preceding context. Thus our hypothesis that the flight to Pella was recorded before the election of Symeon is confirmed.

It does not follow of course that this was the record of which Eusebius and Epiphanius made use. But now we must notice another fact. Hegesippus stated, if we are to believe Eusebius, that those who elected Symeon 'came together from all directions' (πανταχόθεν). We might have expected him to say 'from Pella', or at any rate 'from Peraea'. Again, the electors are divided into three classes—apostles, disciples who had heard the teaching of the Lord, the kindred of Christ. But the first class is evidently comprehended in the second. Why then are they treated as distinct? Various reasons might be suggested; but let us turn to Eusebius's account of the flight. There too there is the same sharp distinction between apostles and disciples. Both left Jerusalem, and both, as we see when we read Eusebius and Epiphanius together, in obedience to a command of Christ.

[1] *H. E.* iii. 32. 1.

But the former obeyed the command of St. Matthew xxviii. 19; they went to preach the Gospel 'to all the nations': the latter obeyed a command given at the time; they sought safety by going to Pella and the neighbouring district. And so after the siege the former came to Jerusalem from all directions, only the latter from Peraea. And further it would seem that in the original narrative the second of the three classes of electors was distinguished from the general body of the faithful, though neither Eusebius nor Epiphanius has caught the point. The whole body might very well be represented by the word μαθηταί, used in *Haer.* 29 (?)[1] and *De Mens.* 15; but οἱ εἰς Χριστὸν πεπιστευκότες, the phrase which takes its place in Eusebius and *Haer.* 30, may have indicated the smaller company who had followed the Lord during His public ministry. Thus we find not a few indications that the passage about Symeon and the narrative of the flight from Jerusalem which Eusebius and Epiphanius consulted are of a piece. And on the whole I see no reason to doubt that it was taken from the *Memoirs*, and in them immediately followed the story of the martyrdom of James.

This long discussion of the story of the migration to Pella, though it has in some directions illustrated the narrative of the election of Symeon, has nevertheless withdrawn our attention from it. To it we must now return. It appears from Eusebius's paraphrase that Hegesippus not only stated that Symeon was chosen as bishop because he was a cousin of the Lord, but also added the explanation, which is omitted in the direct quotation, that Symeon's father Clopas was Joseph's brother. Of the contents of the passage of Hegesippus thus summarized we gain fuller knowledge from another source.

It will be remembered that we have already shown

[1] See above, p. 28, note.

THE *HYPOMNEMATA* OF HEGESIPPUS 35

that a description of James the Just given by Epiphanius, *Haer.* 78. 7, is founded on a passage of Hegesippus of which his knowledge, if not direct, was at least independent of Eusebius.[1] In the earlier part of the same paragraph he maintains the opinion that Mary was only the nominal wife of Joseph. He professes to base his argument on the tradition of the Jews (κατὰ τὴν ἀκολουθίαν ἐκ τῆς τῶν 'Ιουδαίων παραδόσεως), and then proceeds to make some statements which could not have been derived from such a source, and are, in fact, in the main based on the *Protevangelium of James*. But he immediately adds that Joseph was the brother of Clopas, both being sons of one James, surnamed Panther. Afterwards he gives the names of Joseph's children, and speaks more at length about the eldest of them, James the Just, in the passage just referred to. It would seem to have been these latter particulars, or some of them, and especially the assertion that Joseph and Clopas were sons of James Panther, that Epiphanius or his authority connected with Jewish tradition. Now it is quite impossible that Epiphanius could have gathered his material from Jewish tradition; but, on the other hand, it is certain that Hegesippus, whom he follows closely in certain parts of this very passage, did make use of it. This is the direct statement of Eusebius.[2] The inference at once becomes highly probable that Epiphanius is here reproducing the earlier Christian writing. Its probability is enhanced when we observe the striking similarity between the words of Epiphanius, οὗτος μὲν γὰρ ὁ 'Ιωσὴφ ἀδελφὸς γίνεται τοῦ Κλωπᾶ, and Eusebius's paraphrase of Hegesippus, Κλωπᾶν ἀδελφὸν τοῦ 'Ιωσήφ.[3]

But there is more to be said. Epiphanius implies that

[1] See above, pp. 5 ff. [2] *H. E.* iv. 22. 8.
[3] In this paragraph I have closely followed Zahn, pp. 265 ff.

the writer of whom he made use professed to have drawn his information about the relationship between Joseph and Clopas from Jewish tradition, and Eusebius makes Hegesippus say the same thing—ἀνεψιόν, ὥς γέ φασι, γεγονότα τοῦ σωτῆρος. The words ὥς γέ φασι are not to be understood as an addition by Eusebius. Still less are they a mere variation of λόγος κατέχει.[1] They represent something that stood in the text of the *Memoirs*. And they may very well be a paraphrase of a clause nearly identical with the κατὰ τὴν ἀκολουθίαν ἐκ τῆς τῶν Ἰουδαίων παραδόσεως of Epiphanius, since φασί is a favourite word of Eusebius for unwritten report.[2]

Thus there is little reason to doubt that Eusebius and Epiphanius had the same passage of the *Memoirs* before them, and that it contained the statement, which Eusebius passes over, that James, surnamed Panther, was the father of Joseph and Clopas.

Two further remarks may be made. If I am right, Eusebius has deliberately omitted the name of the father of these two men. This is not to be wondered at; we shall presently come across another passage in which he

[1] As Zahn holds, p. 238.

[2] I have noticed only one passage in which Eusebius uses the word φασί as equivalent to λόγος κατέχει, *H. E.* vii. 12. He sometimes indicates by it information derived from written records, e.g. *H. E* i. 12. 1, 3 (cf. 13. 10); ii. 2. 2. On the other hand it appears to be contrasted with λόγος κατέχει (implying documentary evidence) in *H. E.* ii. 16. 1; 17. 1; iii. 24. 5, 7, 11. Eusebius tells us that he gathered material for his account of Origen partly from Origen's own epistles and partly from the oral testimony of elders who had known him (*H. E.* vi. 2. 1; 33. 4). Facts related on the evidence of the latter are sparingly given, and are introduced by φασί in *H. E.* vi. 2. 11; 3. 7; 5. 2; 36. 1. The word is not apparently used of information derived from the epistles. For other instances of the application of φασί to oral tradition see *H. E.* ii. 15. 2; iv. 29. 6; 30. 2; v. 10. 2; vii. 17 (a narrative of the surviving friends of Astyrius); 32. 6, 8; and perhaps vi. 29. 2.

THE *HYPOMNEMATA* OF HEGESIPPUS 37

omits names that were before him in the *Memoirs*.[1] But it is to be observed that in the present case he had a special motive for the omission on account of the hideous fables that the Jews had made to centre round the name of Panther.

And again, if ὥς γέ φασι and κατὰ ἀκολουθίαν ἐκ τῆς τῶν Ἰουδαίων παραδόσεως are independent paraphrases of words used by Hegesippus, it is worthy of note that the former in Eusebius does not appear in immediate connexion with the assertion that Joseph and Clopas were brothers. It is in the previous clause, in which Symeon is said to have been a cousin of the Lord. Thus these two clauses are bound together and must have been originally parts of the same context. It is most unlikely that the latter of the two was taken from another part of the *Memoirs*, as might perhaps have been thought probable if Eusebius's *History* had been our only source of information.

Now this conclusion is very much to our purpose. For it goes to show that in the direct quotation there is a lacuna, as we have already had reason to suspect, before the words 'on this account they called the Church a virgin'. But the omitted portion must have included more than the clause concerning Clopas; for the words 'on this account' still remain without justification. In other words, we have not yet found the concluding portion of the omitted passage. But if the omission is once granted it is not far to seek. Eusebius tells that Hegesippus, when narrating the events of the times of Trajan and his predecessors,[2] relates 'that until the times then present the Church remained a virgin pure and uncorrupt, since those, if there were any in existence, who were

---

[1] See below, p. 78, and Appendix IV g.

[2] Τὰ κατὰ τοὺς δηλουμένους. Trajan has just been mentioned; Nero and Domitian are spoken of in an earlier part of the chapter.

seeking to corrupt the sound rule of the saving doctrine were still at that time in obscure darkness somewhere, as it were hiding'.

'But', he proceeds, 'when the sacred company of the apostles attained, each in his own way, the end of life, and that generation of those who had been counted worthy to hear with their own ears the divine ($\grave{\epsilon}\nu\theta\acute{\epsilon}ov$) wisdom had passed away, then the conspiracy of atheistic ($\grave{a}\theta\acute{\epsilon}ov$) error took its origin through the deceitfulness of the teachers of strange doctrines, who also, now that none of the apostles any longer remained, henceforth with naked head were attempting to proclaim the knowledge falsely so called in opposition to the proclamation of the truth.'[1]

A hasty reader might assume that all this was a paraphrase of Hegesippus. But Zahn[2] points out that the *oratio obliqua* is confined to the first sentence: and it must be added that the second sentence reminds one rather of the ornate periods of Eusebius than of the 'very simple style' of the earlier writer. If it is ultimately based on Hegesippus it must have been entirely recast by Eusebius. But this is unlikely. The 'Church' which according to Hegesippus was styled 'a virgin' was the Church of Jerusalem,[3] while the Church referred to in the second sentence is clearly the Universal Church. What would give increased courage to the heretics at Jerusalem would not be the death of the last of the apostles at Ephesus, but the withdrawal from their neighbourhood of those who had elected Symeon. On the whole, therefore, it seems that while the first sentence is an indirect quotation from Hegesippus, the second is Eusebius's commentary. And the commentary appears to be based

[1] *H. E.* iii. 32. 7 f. For the Greek of the first sentence see Appendix III k.   [2] p. 241.

[3] See Heg. ap. *H. E.* iv. 22. 5 f. (Appendix III l.) That Eusebius understood the passage to refer to the Church universal is clear from the preceding context, §§ 1-4.

THE *HYPOMNEMATA* OF HEGESIPPUS 39

on a misunderstanding. Eusebius supposed that Hegesippus was speaking of the origin of heresy in the Church as a whole, and he probably interpreted a reference to the departure of the apostles from Jerusalem as indicating their death.[1]

Now the first sentence of the quotation, which is certainly from Hegesippus, may with some confidence be regarded as the passage of which we are in search. It would be a very suitable introduction to the following:—

'On this account they called the Church a virgin; for it was not yet corrupted by vain teachings. But Thebuthis, because he was not himself made bishop, begins to corrupt it from the seven heresies among the people—to which he himself belonged . . . Each [of the heretical teachers] severally and in different ways introduced their several opinions. From these came false Christs, false prophets, false apostles, men who divided the unity of the Church with corrupt words against God and against His Christ.'[2]

In other words, the first sentence of the quotation is the close of the portion omitted by Eusebius in his transcript of the passage of Hegesippus which leads up to that which is here translated. Whether it immediately followed the statement that Clopas was Joseph's brother is not capable of confident determination. Some sentences may perhaps have intervened; but it must be added that there is no obvious reason for thinking so.

But however that may be, it is easy to fix upon the passage which followed that which has just been quoted, since Eusebius himself helps us to find it. 'Hegesippus', he

---

[1] Valois seems to regard the whole passage as a paraphrase of that which is quoted next. But this cannot be. On the other hand, Zahn's view (p. 241), that at least the first sentence is based on a passage in which the substance of the latter was repeated in a different connexion, seems to me unsupported by evidence, and *a priori* not very probable.

[2] *H. E.* iv. 22. 4 ff. See Appendix III 1.

says,[1] 'in his narrative about certain heretics goes on to state that by these at that time the above-mentioned person [Symeon] was subjected to accusation, and after being tortured for many days in various manners as being a Christian, and very greatly astonishing the judge and his attendants, won as his reward a death which resembled the passion of the Lord.' The first words of this sentence plainly allude to the passage quoted above. The allusion would have been more obvious if the list of heresies and false teachers which it contains had not been omitted in our translation. The succeeding clause will be at once recognized as a condensed paraphrase of the following:—

'Certain of these (namely the heretics) accuse Simon the son of Clopas as being a descendant of David and a Christian. And so he bears witness at the age of 120 years under Trajan Caesar and the proconsul Atticus.'[2]

The parenthesis 'namely the heretics' is clearly an addition of Eusebius. It is necessary when the sentence is quoted, as it is by him, apart from its context, but needless when it is led up to by the section dealing with 'the heretics'. It will be found hereafter that the remainder of the sentence, about the sufferings of Symeon, corresponds to another extract from Hegesippus preserved by the historian.

III

We have now placed a considerable number of passages from the *Memoirs* in their proper sequence. We have in fact before us, either in the *ipsissima verba* of Hegesippus or in the paraphrase of Eusebius, the whole of a section of his work which dealt with the history of the Church of Jerusalem during the later years of the episcopate of

---

[1] *H. E.* iii. 32. 2. See Appendix III l, m; IV l.
[2] *H. E.* iii. 32. 3. See Appendix III m.

THE *HYPOMNEMATA* OF HEGESIPPUS 41

James the Just, and that of his successor Symeon, with the possible exception of some sentences here and there not quoted by Eusebius. Our main difficulty in regard to this group of extracts has been the discovery of the order in which they stood in the *Memoirs*. In the case of the series next to be considered the arrangement of the fragments will give us less trouble, and with three exceptions the determination of the passages which belong to it is easy, since they are expressly stated by Eusebius to have come from the pen of Hegesippus.

To the task of setting forth the evidence for the Hegesippean authorship of the three anonymous fragments referred to we must now address ourselves.

By way of preliminary two passages must be exhibited side by side. The first is reproduced, with some omissions, from Eusebius's *Ecclesiastical History*, Book III, chapters xvii–xx. 5. This I designate by the letter *E*. The second has been edited from the Paris MS. 1555 A by J. A. Cramer in his *Anecdota Graeca e codd. manuscriptis Bibliothecae Regiae Parisiensis*, Oxford, 1839, ii. 88, and from the Bodleian MS. Barocc. 142 by C. de Boor in *Texte und Untersuchungen*, v. 2. 169. I call it *C*, and indicate the four sentences of which it consists by numerals. Words which are common to the two are underlined.

E

xvii Πολλήν γε μὴν εἰς πολλοὺς ἐπιδειξάμενος ὁ Δομετιανὸς ὠμότητα, οὐκ ὀλίγον τε τῶν ἐπὶ Ῥώμης εὐπατριδῶν τε καὶ ἐπισήμων ἀνδρῶν πλῆθος οὐ μετ' εὐλόγου κρίσεως κτείνας, μυρίους τε ἄλλους ἐπιφανεῖς ἄνδρας ταῖς ὑπὲρ τὴν ἐνορίαν ζημιώσας φυγαῖς καὶ ταῖς τῶν οὐσιῶν ἀποβολαῖς ἀναιτίως, τελευ-

C

1 Δομετιανὸς υἱὸς Οὐεσπασιανοῦ πολλὰ κακὰ εἰς τοὺς ἐν τέλει Ῥωμαίους ἐνδειξάμενος

E

τῶν τῆς Νέρωνος θεοεχθρίας τε καὶ θεομαχίας διάδοχον ἑαυτὸν κατεστήσατο. Δεύτερος δῆτα τὸν καθ' ἡμῶν ἀνεκίνει διωγμόν, καίπερ τοῦ πατρὸς αὐτῷ Οὐεσπασιανοῦ μηδὲν καθ' ἡμῶν ἄτοπον ἐπινοήσαντος.

xviii. 1 Ἐν τούτῳ κατέχει λόγος τὸν ἀπόστολον ἅμα καὶ εὐαγγελιστὴν Ἰωάννην ἔτι τῷ βίῳ ἐνδιατρίβοντα, τῆς εἰς τὸν θεῖον λόγον ἕνεκεν μαρτυρίας Πάτμον οἰκεῖν καταδικασθῆναι τὴν νῆσον ...

xix ... Ταῦτα δὲ δηλοῖ κατὰ λέξιν ὡδέ πως λέγων ὁ Ἡγήσιππος.

xx. 1 Ἔτι δὲ περιῆσαν οἱ ἀπὸ γένους τοῦ Κυρίου υἱωνοὶ Ἰούδα, τοῦ κατὰ σάρκα λεγομένου αὐτοῦ ἀδελφοῦ· οὓς ἐδηλατόρευσαν ὡς ἐκ γένους ὄντας Δαυίδ ...

5 ἐφ' οἷς μηδὲν αὐτῶν κατεγνωκότα τὸν Δομετιανόν, ἀλλὰ καὶ ὡς εὐτελῶν καταφρονήσαντα, ἐλευθέρους μὲν αὐτοὺς ἀνεῖναι, καταπαῦσαι δὲ διὰ προστάγματος τὸν κατὰ τῆς ἐκκλησίας διωγμόν ...

7 Ταῦτα μὲν ὁ Ἡγήσιππος.

C

τὴν Νέρωνος νικήσας ὠμότητα

δεύτερος κατὰ Χριστιανῶν διωγμὸν ἐποίησεν.

2 καθ' ὃν καὶ τὸν ἀπόστολον καὶ εὐαγγελιστὴν Ἰωάννην ἐν Πάτμῳ περιώρισεν.

3 συντυχὼν δὲ Δομετιανὸς τοῖς υἱοῖς Ἰούδα τοῦ ἀδελφοῦ τοῦ Κυρίου,

καὶ γνοὺς τὴν ἀρετὴν τῶν ἀνδρῶν

τοῦ καθ' ἡμῶν ἐπαύσατο διωγμοῦ.

4 Ἀναφέρει δὲ ὁ Ἡγήσιππος καὶ τὰ ὀνόματα αὐτῶν, καί φησιν ὅτι ὁ μὲν ἐκαλεῖτο Ζωκήρ, ὁ δὲ Ἰάκωβος. [Ἱστορεῖ δὲ καὶ ἄλλα ἀναγκαῖα.]

A comparison of these two passages clearly proves that there is a literary connexion between them. But it is manifestly impossible that E is a mere expansion of C. May we then suppose that C was derived from E by way of abridgement? This is certainly a possible hypothesis.

THE *HYPOMNEMATA* OF HEGESIPPUS 43

But it appears to me to be improbable for several reasons. In the first place we are informed in *C* 4 that the names of the sons, or as *E* calls them grandsons, of Jude were Zocer and James. This fact the writer cannot have learnt from *E*; for it is not recorded there. And he expressly tells us that he bases his statement on the authority of Hegesippus. Now it is *a priori* probable that *C* 1-3 is immediately derived from the same source as *C* 4. And, indeed, this seems to be indicated by the very phrase of the epitomizer: 'Αναφέρει δὲ ὁ 'Ηγήσιππος καὶ τὰ ὀνόματα αὐτῶν. *C*, then, may fairly be assumed to be founded not on *E*, but on the *Memoirs* of Hegesippus. And this is the work from which, as Eusebius himself says, *E* xx. 1-6 is a quotation. Thus we are led to the conclusion that from the *Memoirs E* and *C* are alike derived as their common source.

And this conclusion is confirmed by other considerations. There is nothing in *C* to correspond to *E* xviii. 2-4. Now on the supposition that *C* is an epitome of *E* this omission is not easy to explain. For the latter part of *E* xviii gives information which is both important and interesting. In §§ 2, 3 evidence is given as to the date of the Apocalypse; § 4 records the banishment of Flavia Domitilla. Why should such things have been passed over by one who undertook to give a summary, however brief, of *E*? On the other hand, on the theory which is here advocated, their absence from *C* is accounted for without difficulty. For §§ 2, 3 are a quotation from Irenaeus; and § 4 is based, as we are told, on τοὺς ἄποθεν τοῦ καθ' ἡμᾶς λόγου συγγραφεῖς. Whatever the latter phrase may mean, it is at least certain that Hegesippus cannot be among the writers whom it includes; and it is abundantly evident from the parallel passage in the *Chronicle*[1] that Bruttius, or Bret-

[1] Ed. Schoene, ii. 160, 163. Cp. Lightfoot, *Clement of Rome*, i. 46 ff.

tius, was the principal, if not the only, authority on whom Eusebius relied for his account of Flavia Domitilla. Thus on the supposition that the writer of C had before him not E, but the *Memoirs* of Hegesippus, it was impossible for him to include in his summary the facts recorded in E xviii. 2-4.

But again, according to the narrative of E, quoted verbatim from Hegesippus, the persons who were brought before Domitian were the grandsons (υἰωνοί) of Jude. And that this is the true reading of Eusebius's text is manifest, for he himself paraphrases it by the word ἀπόγονοι.[1] But according to both the manuscripts of C they were the sons (υἱοί) of Jude. This might be set down to mere clerical error. But that would be a too hasty conclusion. Two other authorities have been found for the names James and Zocer,[2] and both call them sons of Jude.[3]

[1] *H. E.* iii. 19. See Appendix IV f.
[2] A Menology quoted by C. F. Matthaei, *Evangelium sec. Matthaeum*, Rigae, 1778, p. 138, and the monk Epiphanius, *Life of Mary*, 14. I owe the references to Zahn, p. 240.
[3] Matthaei's Menology has the following at 26 May: Ὁ ἅγιος ἀπόστολος Ἰούδας, ὁ καὶ Ἀλφαῖος, εἰς τῶν ιβ̄ ἀποστόλων τῶν μεγάλων. οὗτος υἱὸς ἦν Ἰωσὴφ τοῦ μνηστῆρος, ὡς εἶναι καὶ αὐτὸν ἀδελφὸν τοῦ κυρίου. οὗτος ἔσχε δύο υἱούς, Ἰάκωβον τὸν ἀπόστολον, ὄντα εἰς τοὺς ιβ̄, ὃς λέγεται Ἰάκωβος Ἀλφαίου, διὰ τὸν πατέρα Ἀλφαῖον. ὁ δὲ τούτου ἀδελφὸς ἤκουε (sic) Ζωκήρ. γέγονε δὲ τρίτος ἐπίσκοπος Ἱεροσολύμων. πρῶτος γὰρ ἐπίσκοπος Ἱεροσολύμων ἦν ὁ τούτου ἀδελφὸς Ἰάκωβος, ὁ ἀδελφόθεος, δεύτερος Συμεὼν ὁ υἱὸς Κλεόπα, τρίτος δὲ Ἰούδας ἔτη ζ̄. And again at 23 October: Ὁ ἅγιος ἀπόστολος Ἰάκωβος ὁ ἀδελφόθεος. οὗτος ὁ ἅγιος ἀπόστολος ἱερομάρτυς Ἰάκωβος, ὁ ἀδελφὸς τοῦ κυρίου, ἦν υἱὸς Ἰωσὴφ ἀδελφὸς δὲ τοῦ κυρίου διὰ τὴν τοῦ Ἰωσὴφ πρὸς τὴν ἁγίαν θεοτόκον μνηστείαν. ἐκαλεῖτο δὲ πρότερον ὀβλίας, ὃ ἑρμηνεύεται περιοχὴ παθῶν. Ἰάκωβος δὲ πτερνιστής. ἐχειροτονήθη ὑπὸ τοῦ κυρίου ἐπίσκοπος Ἱεροσολύμων, μήτε οἶνον μήτε σίκερα πεπωκώς, μήτε ἔμψυχόν τι φαγών, μήτε ἐλαίῳ μήτε βαλανείῳ ἀπολούσας τὸ σῶμα. οὗτος ἐνομοθέτει τὰ ἔθνη κτλ. τοῦτον οἱ Ἰουδαῖοι ἀπὸ τοῦ πτερυγίου τοῦ ἱεροῦ ὥσαντες κάτω καὶ ξύλῳ κναφείῳ κατὰ τῆς κεφαλῆς πατάξαντες τέλος αὐτῷ ἐπέθηκαν. And again: ἰοβλίας λέγεται ὀφθαλμὸς λεῖα βλέπων. In Epiphanius Monachus, *De vita B. Virg.* 14 (*P. G.* cxx. 204), we read:

THE *HYPOMNEMATA* OF HEGESIPPUS 45

Moreover, they exhibit, in addition to the names, traces of the influence of Hegesippus which are obviously independent of Eusebius. There seems to be no escape from the inference that υἱοί was a variant for υἰωνοί in some manuscripts of the *Memoirs*, and that C follows a text different from that used by Eusebius. It might even be contended that υἱοί is the correct reading, for the sons of Jude are more likely than his grandsons to have been contemporary with his cousin Symeon and the Apostle John. But, however that may be, if C is based on a different text of Hegesippus from that used in E it cannot be a mere epitome of E.

Assuming then the correctness of our hypothesis as to the relation between C and E, we can now form a pretty accurate conception of the method of work of the compiler to whom we are indebted for C. For E xx. 1-6 is a quotation, in part direct, in part indirect, from Hegesippus. We have in it, in great measure, the very words of the passage of which C 3 is a summary. Comparing the two

Καὶ ἔλαβεν τὴν θυγατέρα Μαρίαν ὁ ἀδελφὸς αὐτῶν (sc. τοῦ Ἰωσὴφ καὶ τῆς θεοτόκου) Κλωπᾶς γυναῖκα ἑαυτῷ· Κλεόπας δὲ ὁ ἀδελφὸς αὐτοῦ Ἰακὼβ (l. Ἰωσὴφ) ὁμοπάτριος ἐκ τοῦ Ἰακώβ, καὶ ἐγέννησεν ἐξ αὐτῆς τὸν Συμεῶνα. οὗτος δὲ ὁ Συμεὼν μετὰ Ἰάκωβον τὸν ἀδελφὸν τοῦ κυρίου ἐπίσκοπος γίγονεν εἰς Ἱεροσόλυμα· καὶ ἐπὶ Δομετιανοῦ βασιλέως Ῥώμης μετὰ πολλὰς βασάνους ὕστερον ἐσταυρώθη, ὧν ἐτῶν ρκ΄. Ἰάκωβος δὲ ὁ υἱὸς Ἰωσήφ, ὥς φασίν τινες, ἔσχεν αὐτῷ γυναῖκα ἐπὶ ἔτη δύο· καὶ τελευτησάσης αὐτῆς ἑτέραν οὐκ ἔσχεν. Ἰούδας δὲ ὁ ἀδελφὸς αὐτοῦ ἐποίησεν δύο υἱούς, Ζωκὴρ καὶ Ἰάκωβον, οὕτω προσαγορευομένους. οὗτοι παραστάντες Δομετιανῷ βασιλεῖ Ῥώμης διὰ τὴν ἀρετὴν αὐτῶν καὶ σοφίαν τὴν κατὰ τῶν Χριστιανῶν ἐπαύσαντο διωγμόν.

It will be observed that in the Menology two interpretations of ὠβλίας are given—περιοχὴ παθῶν and ὀφθαλμὸς λεῖα βλέπων—neither of which is in Eusebius. And James is said to have been appointed bishop by the Lord. Epiphanius Monachus, in the story of the sons of Jude, agrees with C (see p. 42) in using ἐπαύσα(ν)το where Eusebius has καταπαῦσαι, and in speaking of the ἀρετή of the brothers. He has also the phrase κατὰ Χριστιανῶν διωγμός, which occurs in C in a different connexion (Appendix IV b), but not in this section of Eusebius.

together we observe, in the first place, that the writer of
C has much reduced the length of his original : C 3 contains only twenty-one words, E xx. 1-5 contains 200.
But we notice also that he has been careful to preserve,
as far as possible, the phrases of Hegesippus. Of his
twenty-one words, thirteen are found in E. In fact, it
would scarcely be untrue to say that he never departs from
the words of Hegesippus except for the purpose of abbreviation. Thus συντυχών sums up the series of events recounted in E xx. 1ᵇ—the laying of an information against
the sons of Jude, and their appearance before the emperor
in charge of the evocatus; while τὴν ἀρετὴν τῶν ἀνδρῶν
indicates by a single word their hard-working honesty
and faith, described in detail in E xx. 2-4.

Now we find that the relation between C 1, 2 and E
xvii, xviii. 1 is similar to that which exists between C 3
and E xx. 1-5, though the disparity in length between the
passages to be compared is not so marked in the former
case as in the latter. In E xvii there are seventy words;
in C 1 twenty, of which thirteen are in E. And E xviii. 1
has twenty-six words, six of which are found among the
eleven of which C 2 consists. Moreover, as indicating
anxiety on the part of the writer of C to retain the words
of his source, we may mention the strange phrase, πολλὰ
κακὰ εἰς τοὺς ... Ῥωμαίους ἐνδειξάμενος: we can understand it when we remember that E has πολλὴν ... εἰς
πολλοὺς ἐπιδειξάμενος ... ὠμότητα.

It is true that some words are found here in C which do
not occur in E. Such are κακά, τοὺς ἐν τέλει, νικήσας,
Χριστιανῶν, ἐποίησεν, περιώρισεν. Most of them may be
accounted for as arising from the desire of the compiler to
be brief. In all but two cases (Χριστιανῶν and ἐποίησεν)
they are in truth shorter equivalents of phrases in E. But
another fact has to be kept in view. We are here com-

THE *HYPOMNEMATA* OF HEGESIPPUS 47

paring *C*, not with the text of Eusebius's source, but with Eusebius's presentation of the source in his own language. Now we can form some idea of the way in which Eusebius dealt with Hegesippus when he made use of his *Memoirs* without actually transcribing them; for in two places we are able to compare the text of the earlier writer with a paraphrase which the historian gives, not in the immediate context of his direct quotation.[1]

The passages transcribed from the *Memoirs* contain together about 80 words, the paraphrases almost exactly the same number; and there are common to the two about 30 words. We conclude that in paraphrasing Eusebius does not abridge, but that he deals with the phraseology pretty freely.[2] In the passages referred to not half of the words of Hegesippus remain. Hence it might be expected that if the compiler of *C* worked directly on the *Memoirs* he would preserve in his summary not a few words of the original which Eusebius has not retained in his paraphrase. Such may be the words Χριστιανῶν for ἡμῶν, ἐποίησεν for ἀνεκίνει, and others of those mentioned above. Such also may be ἡμῶν for τῆς ἐκκλησίας and ἀρετήν in *C* 3.[3]

The obvious inference from these facts seems to be that *E* xvii, xviii. 1 adheres pretty closely to Hegesippus. And we may, at any rate, feel confident that the expressions which are common to *E* xvii. xviii, 1 and *C* 1, 2 were also used by him.

If it were possible to leave the matter at this point, a good many of my readers would perhaps concede that the

[1] *H. E.* iii. 32. 6 (= iii. 20. 6; 32. 2) and iv. 22. 4 (= iii. 11). See Appendix III g, i; IV k.
[2] He omits phrases here and there, but makes up for this by substituting for others more wordy equivalents: e.g. καθίσταται ἐπίσκοπος becomes τοῦ τῆς αὐτόθι παροικίας θρόνον ἄξιον εἶναι δοκιμάσαι.
[3] Compare above, p. 45, note.

hypothesis here suggested has a reasonable degree of probability. But it now becomes my duty to mention some facts, which, though I do not regard them as destroying the validity of my argument, must be regarded as in some degree mitigating its force.

The passage which I have called C is, in the Bodleian manuscript from which C. de Boor extracted it, one of a series extending from f. 212 to f. 216. At the beginning of the series stands this title, Συναγωγὴ ἱστοριῶν διαφόρων ἀπὸ τῆς κατὰ σάρκα γεννήσεως τοῦ κυρίου καὶ ἐξῆς τὴν ἀρχὴν ἔχουσα ἀπὸ τοῦ πρώτου λόγου τῆς ἐκκλησιαστικῆς ἱστορίας Εὐσεβίου τοῦ Παμφίλου. At the end is the note, ἕως τούτων ἱστορεῖ ὁ Εὐσέβιος. It is thus clearly intimated that the whole series of passages is a collection of excerpts from Eusebius's *Ecclesiastical History*. Moreover, the passages are arranged in groups, each group having a heading indicating the book of the *History* from which the excerpts in it are taken.[1]

Now it appears that these notes so far agree with the phenomena of the passages to which they refer, that the large majority of them have a manifest connexion with the text of Eusebius, if they cannot in all cases be reckoned as summaries of it. It may be asked, Does not all this directly contradict the theory that C is an excerpt not from Eusebius, but from the source which Eusebius used? And, that being so, is not the theory untenable?

Several considerations forbid us to give with confidence an affirmative answer to this question. For it must be remarked that the notes to which our attention is directed are not in complete accordance with the facts. Several of the passages in the manuscript are not, as they stand, mere epitomes of Eusebius. There is, for example, a

[1] C. de Boor in *Zeitsch. f. Kirchengesch.* vi. 486, *Texte u. Untersuch.* v. 2. 168.

reference to Nestorius, in connexion with Paul of Samosata. There is also a citation from St. Chrysostom. And there is a passage about the later kings of the Jews which could not have been compiled from Eusebius alone. And besides these there are seven pieces, the earlier part of each of which *may* be a summary of a passage in Eusebius, while the latter part is certainly taken from the writer whom Eusebius happened to be using at the moment —Papias, Hegesippus, Origen, or Pierius—but from a passage which he does not quote.[1] Since the notes in the Bodleian MS. are not strictly accurate, it is legitimate to inquire with regard to each of these seven, whether the compiler has been content to follow Eusebius as far as he went, or whether he did not resort in each case for the whole of his summary, and not only for its closing sentences, to Eusebius's source.

But, further, these notes are peculiar to the manuscript used by C. de Boor. We have therefore no right to assume that they were in the collection of excerpts from which both it and Cramer's Paris manuscript were ultimately derived. It is at least conceivable that they are due to an editorially-minded scribe—the writer of the Oxford manuscript, or of an exemplar from which it is descended. In that case they have no more authority as a description of the procedure of the original compiler, though they doubtless agree more closely with the facts, than the note which appears in the Paris copy as the title of the series, Εὐσταθίου Ἐπιφανέως Συρίας ἐπιτομὴ τῆς ἀρχαιολογίας Ἰωσήπου.

---

[1] *Texte u. Untersuch.* v. 2. 168 ff. One of these passages is, of course, that with which we are immediately concerned. At least one of the others occurs also in the Paris MS., but without the passage of Eusebius (*H. E.* iii. 25) which precedes it in the Oxford MS. In the Paris MS. it immediately follows our extract from Hegesippus. See Cramer, ii. 88.

But whatever weight the objections drawn from the notes in the Oxford manuscript may seem to have against the argument with which it and its companion manuscript at Paris supply us, our original conclusion may be reached by an entirely different process of reasoning which they do not affect. This I shall now proceed to show.

In passing from the tenth to the eleventh chapter of the third book of the *Ecclesiastical History* we experience one of those jolts to which readers of Eusebius soon become accustomed. Chapters v–x have dealt with the siege of Jerusalem and its historian Josephus, and they have been entirely based on his writings.[1] Chapters xi–xxiii are a fairly consecutive narrative, dealing for the most part with the history of the Christian Church, and covering the period from Vespasian to Trajan. Eusebius leaves the impression that for it he had recourse to many authorities, from one to another of which he passes rapidly. I shall here set out a table of the contents of chapters xi–xx, stating under each head the authority which Eusebius consulted. In doing so, however, I omit the records of the successions of emperors and bishops which, according to his wont, he inserts here and there in his narrative.

> Chap. xi. The election of Symeon as bishop of Jerusalem: λόγος κατέχει = Hegesippus.[2]
>
> Chap. xii. Vespasian's proceedings against the descendants of David: λόγος κατέχει = Hegesippus.[3]
>
> Chap. xvi. Digression on the Epistle of Clement. For the disturbance at Corinth which gave occasion to it reference is made to Hegesippus.
>
> Chap. xvii. The persecution of Domitian. No authority given.

---

[1] Except the part of chap. v which mentions the flight to Pella.
[2] See above, p. 23.   [3] See above, p. 26.

Chap. xviii. § 1. St. John's banishment: κατέχει λόγος.
  § 2. The date of the Apocalypse: Irenaeus.
  § 4. The banishment of Flavia Domitilla: οἱ ἄποθεν τοῦ καθ' ἡμᾶς λόγου συγγραφεῖς.
Chap. xix. Summary account of Domitian's proceedings against the grandsons of Jude: παλαιὸς κατέχει λόγος.
Chap. xx. § 1. More detailed account of the same: Hegesippus.
  § 7. General account of Domitian's reign: Tertullian.
  § 8. Nerva's reversal of Domitian's policy: οἱ γραφῇ τὰ κατὰ τοὺς χρόνους παραδόντες.
  § 9. Return of St. John to Ephesus: ὁ τῶν παρ' ἡμῖν ἀρχαίων παραδίδωσι λόγος.

An examination of this table reveals the fact that for four of the twelve sections into which chapters xi-xx may be divided Hegesippus was used as an authority by Eusebius, while statements are introduced by the formula κατέχει λόγος or an equivalent four or five times, in all but two of which the λόγος referred to is the *Memoirs* of Hegesippus. And the phrase κατέχει λόγος seems everywhere to imply a written document.[1] It is natural to assume that throughout the narrative which we are considering it always refers to the same authoritative writing. And further, few will read together chapter xviii. § 1 and chapter xx. § 9 without being convinced that they are based on a single document. It would be arbitrary in the extreme to postulate one source for the statement that St. John went to Patmos, and another for the statement that he left it. There is a minimum of assumption in the further inference that that document is the same as that from which Eusebius

[1] See above, p. 21 f.

drew the information contained in the two or three remaining paragraphs in which he uses the words κατέχει λόγος. The assumption is made, if possible, less formidable when we remember that elsewhere in his third book Eusebius uses the same formula for the *Memoirs*. In chapter xxxii. §§ 1, 2, he writes, 'A record contains the information (κατέχει λόγος) that after Nero and Domitian, under him of whose time we are now treating, in various places and different cities persecution was stirred up against us by risings of the people, in which . . . we have ascertained that Symeon ended his life by martyrdom. And the witness for this fact is . . . Hegesippus.' And then he proceeds to paraphrase the account of the martyrdom of Symeon with which we are already familiar.[1]

Eusebius gives us no hint as to the source from which he borrowed his general account of the reign of Domitian in chapter xvii. But its closing words fit in most appropriately with chapter xii. Vespasian, says Eusebius in chapter xii, attempted to extirpate the house of David, and in consequence *the Jews* were persecuted. The very same policy, he says in chapter xvii, led Domitian further than his father had gone: he persecuted *the Christians*. The antithesis may appear to suggest that these two chapters were founded on passages which lay not far apart in the same treatise. But chapter xii certainly, as we have seen, came ultimately from Hegesippus. And it will be remembered that Hegesippus was in the mind of Eusebius, if the *Memoirs* were not actually open before him, when he began to write chapter xvii. For chapter xvi ends with a reference to that work. And finally it may be added, by way of confirmation, that Rufinus believed that

[1] See above, p. 40, and Appendix III 1, m.

chapter xvii was a quotation from Hegesippus. For he renders the closing sentence of chapter xvi thus: 'Verum de seditione facta apud Corinthios ac dissensione plebis testis valde fidelis Hegesippus indicat, *hoc modo dicens*.' Rufinus, it is of course admitted, was mistaken in supposing that the sentences which follow make any allusion to the affairs of the Church of Corinth.

Let us assume, then, that all the passages of Eus. *H. E.* iii. 11-20 which we have examined were taken from the *Memoirs*. On that hypothesis we find ourselves able to give a reasonable account of the construction of this part of the *Ecclesiastical History*. Eusebius acted, it would seem, exactly as we might expect that a historian would act whose design was to give a narrative of a series of events, which should practically consist of extracts from earlier writers. He took as his basis Hegesippus, who gave the fullest account known to him of the history of the Church during the period with which he was concerned. And here and there he added to his Hegesippean narrative illustrations from other authorities— Irenaeus, Tertullian, Brettius, and the rest.

Thus by a completely different path we have arrived once more at our former conclusion, that Eusebius drew from Hegesippus the account of Domitian in chapter xvii and the statement of chapter xviii that the Apostle St. John was banished under Domitian to Patmos; and we have extended it by tracing to the same source the further statement in chapter xx that the apostle returned to Ephesus in the reign of Nerva.

We are now in a position to collect the passages which form the second series of extracts from the *Memoirs*. I give a brief summary of each, prefixing to it the reference to the place at which it may be found in Eusebius's *History*, and a letter indicating its position in

54 THE *HYPOMNEMATA* OF HEGESIPPUS

Appendix IV. The summaries are arranged in the order in which, as I believe, the passages appeared in the *Memoirs*.

H. E. iii. 12. (*a*) Vespasian ordered members of the family of David to be sought out. A second persecution of the Jews ensued.

H. E. iii. 17. (*b*) Description of the cruelty of Domitian, resulting in a second persecution of the Christians.

H. E. iii. 19. (*c*) Domitian ordered the descendants of David to be slain.

H. E. iii. 18. 1. (*d*) At this time St. John was banished.

H. E. iii. 20. 9. (*e*) He returned to Ephesus under Nerva.

H. E. iii. 20. 1. (*f*) Under the above order (*c*) the grandsons of Jude were arraigned.

Cramer and de Boor, ll. cc. (*g*) Their names were Zocer and James.

H. E. iii. 20. 2–4. (*h*) They were examined by Domitian.

H. E. iii. 20. 5 f. (*i*) After further examination they were dismissed and the persecution was stayed.

H. E. iii. 32. 6. (*k*) The grandsons of Jude presided over every Church and lived until Trajan's reign.

H. E. iii. 32. 6. (*l*) Under Trajan Symeon was accused, tortured for many days, and crucified.

H. E. iii. 32. 4. (*m*) His accusers were slain as being of the Jewish royal family.

The reasons by which the order of the fragments here epitomized has been determined must now be stated. We may confine our attention for the moment to the group *b*–*m*, the consideration of *a* being postponed to a later stage of the inquiry.

In *H. E.* iii. 20 *f*, *h*, *i* form a continuous narrative, the former part of which is quoted from Hegesippus in the *oratio recta* and the latter part in the *oratio obliqua*, including as its closing section a paraphrase of *k*. Eusebius has here, in fact, treated a portion of the *Memoirs* precisely as in *H. E.* iv. 15 he treated the letter of the Smyrnaeans, reproducing it in the manner partly of direct and partly of indirect quotation. There can be no doubt, therefore, that *f, h, i, k* stood in the *Memoirs* in the order which we have assigned them. Again, that *l* followed *k* is manifest since they are consecutive parts of a passage transcribed from the *Memoirs* in *H. E.* iii. 32. 6. Further, the epitome quoted above from Cramer and de Boor summarizes *b, d, h, i* in this order. Thus the order of the fragments *b–m* is fixed with the exception of *c, e, g, m*.

The clause *g* is known to us from the Cramer-de Boor epitome only, and there, though it follows *i*, its position in the *Memoirs* is obviously undetermined. But it is evidently connected with the narrative in *f, h, i*, and I have inserted it after *f* as the place at which the names of the grandsons of Jude would most probably be given.

If the method of Hegesippus had been strictly chronological the return of St. John from Patmos in the reign of Nerva (*e*) would have followed *i* or perhaps *k*. But it is not easy to find room for it there. And in fact Hegesippus does not arrange his material chronologically. The narrative of the election of Symeon to the episcopate in or shortly after A.D. 70 is followed by a short account of his martyrdom under Trajan.[1] Just in the same way it may be supposed that he passed immediately from his notice of the banishment of St. John to Patmos, to a statement that he left the island some years later. Hence *e* has been placed after *d*.

In *H. E.* iii. 19 *c* is immediately followed by a paraphrase of *f*; and apart from this evidence it is obvious

---

[1] See Appendix III g–m.

that Hegesippus must have mentioned the decree under which proceedings were taken against the descendants of David before recording the trial of Zocer and James which presupposed it. But c need not have immediately preceded f if this trial was not the first of the kind mentioned. It is probable, however, that it came after rather than before the general description of Domitian's policy in b. Hence in regard to its position it has only to be determined whether it preceded or followed d, e. Now it is fairly certain that St. John was nearly related to Christ,[1] and was therefore a descendant of David and liable to be proceeded against under the edict referred to in c. We may suppose then without improbability that he was banished in accordance with its provisions, and that Hegesippus said so, though the summaries of his statements about St. John which are in our hands do not inform us of the fact. If we make this assumption and place c before d the whole passage acquires a logical coherence which it otherwise lacks. Domitian issues the edict against the descendants of David. Under it John is banished, and Zocer and James are brought before the Emperor.

As to the position of m I do not feel so confident. It certainly followed one of the two accounts given by Hegesippus of the martyrdom of Symeon. Eusebius seems[2] to connect it with the earlier of the two.[3] But on the other hand the incident occurred under Trajan, and would naturally find place in the record of the events of that reign. Moreover, the later account of the martyrdom is fuller than the earlier, and the fate of the accusers of Symeon is just such a thing as might be

---

[1] See Westcott on St. John xix. 25.
[2] *H. E.* iii. 32. 3 f.
[3] *H. E.* iii. 32. 3. See Appendix III m.

THE *HYPOMNEMATA* OF HEGESIPPUS 57

passed over in the more succinct and related in the more detailed narrative. For these reasons I have put it after *l*. A few words must here be said about the statement made by Eusebius, in a passage in which he is paraphrasing Hegesippus, that Symeon 'attained an end like to the suffering of the Lord'.[1] Of this clause Lightfoot remarks[2] that it is 'apparently in the words or at least according to the sentiment' of Hegesippus, and one is tempted to assume that it is a comment by that writer on the fact that Symeon was crucified. But, though it is certainly in Hegesippus's manner,[3] it is also in the manner of many of the early martyrologists, not excepting Eusebius himself, as Lightfoot has shown.[4] And what appears to me conclusive against the claim of this clause to represent otherwise unknown words of Hegesippus is the fact that Eusebius elsewhere, in a precisely similar connexion, uses a phrase almost, if not entirely, identical with it. Of the Apostle Peter he is represented by an early Syriac translator as saying, 'In the likeness of the suffering of our Lord he suffered'.[5] The underlying Greek perhaps only differed from our clause in one word. In the one place as in the other we have a more

[1] *H. E.* iii. 32. 2. See Appendix IV l.
[2] *Ignatius*, vol. i, p. 596.
[3] See *H. E.* ii. 23. 10, 11, 16, and Lightfoot, l. c.
[4] Lightfoot quotes *M. P.* (Grk.) 6. 5, to which may be added ib. 8. 10, 11; 11. 1, 24. It is remarkable, however, that in paraphrasing documents Eusebius sometimes omits comparisons between the sufferings of the martyrs and the passion of Christ. Cp. *H. E.* iv. 15. 11 f. with *Mar. Pol.* 6 f., and note that in his paraphrase (*H. E.* iii. 11) of the passage quoted from Hegesippus in *H. E.* iv. 22. 4 he takes no notice of the words ὡς καὶ ὁ κύριος ἐπὶ τῷ αὐτῷ λόγῳ : see Appendix III g.
[5] *M. P.* (Syr.) Pref. (Cureton, p. ܀) ܀ ܀ ܀ ܀ ܀. In the immediately preceding words ܀ ܀ ܀ we have perhaps an attempt to bring out the force of ἀπηνέγκατο τέλος. Cp. Cureton, p. 44.

periphrasis of Eusebius for the statement of the source used that the martyr was put to death by crucifixion.

We are now able to regard the whole group *b-m* as a series of consecutive, or nearly consecutive, passages from the *Memoirs* of Hegesippus. In what relation does this group stand to that with which we were concerned at an earlier stage, and which ended with the shorter account of the martyrdom of Symeon? It is evident that the arrangement of each group is roughly, though not exactly, chronological. That this arrangement was deliberate is implied in the formal introduction to the reign of Domitian in the second group, which I have marked *b*. But if so the inference is near at hand that the group which on the whole deals with the later period followed that which deals with the earlier; or, in other words, that *b-m* had a place in the *Memoirs* subsequent rather than anterior to the first group.

That this was the case will further appear from a passage which has been already quoted. According to Eusebius[1] 'Hegesippus in his narrative about certain heretics goes on to state that the above-mentioned [Symeon], having at this time been charged by these, and having suffered many and various tortures as a Christian for very many days, and very greatly astonished the judge himself and his attendants, attained an end similar to the passion of the Lord'.

It has been pointed out that the first clause of this sentence refers to the passage in which Hegesippus speaks of Thebuthis as the earliest propagator of heresy in the Church of Jerusalem.[2] There are, it is true, other references in the extant fragments to heretics,[3] but an

---

[1] *H. E.* iii. 32. 2.
[2] *H. E.* iv. 22. 5. See Appendix III 1.
[3] *H. E.* ii. 23. 8; iii. 19; iv. 22. 7. See Appendix II, III e, IV f.

inspection of the passages will satisfy the reader that none of them could have introduced an account of the martyrdom of Symeon. The second clause couples with it the shorter notice of the death of Symeon.[1] That notice is quoted by Eusebius immediately after the sentence which we are considering; and it accounts for the statement that Symeon suffered torture because he was a Christian, though it does not fully justify it, since it makes his descent from David the primary charge. The statement could not have been founded upon anything in the second narrative of the martyrdom, nor upon any of the other fragments of the *Memoirs*. But from this second narrative the remainder of the sentence is plainly drawn. It alone mentions the prolonged torture of Symeon, the amazement of the judge and others who were present, and the precise manner of his death. And the second narrative is actually transcribed lower down in the same chapter of the *History*.[2] Thus in one sentence Eusebius alludes to three distinct fragments of the *Memoirs*; and the probability is that he alludes to them in the order in which they followed one another in that work. Hence we conclude that in it the fuller account of the martyrdom, and along with it the whole group of passages to which it belongs, followed the shorter, though not necessarily in immediate sequence.

The order of the two groups of extracts from the *Memoirs* having been determined it becomes possible to discuss the question, To which of these two groups does the passage about Vespasian (*a*) belong, if indeed it is to be reckoned with either? And what was its place in the *Memoirs*?

If Hegesippus had adopted a strictly chronological

---

[1] *H. E.* iii. 32. 3. See Appendix III m.
[2] Ibid. § 6. See Appendix IV l.

arrangement, it manifestly ought to have been assigned to the first group. But it is exceedingly difficult to find a place for it there. Chronologically it might be put after the notice of the election of Symeon, but in such a position it would cohere very imperfectly with the context. And we have seen that Eusebius seems to imply that it did not immediately follow that section of the *Memoirs*.[1] We may conclude that it is not to be placed before the first notice of the martyrdom of Symeon.

On the other hand, it has a remarkable feature characteristic of the second group. In the passages belonging to that group special prominence is given to kinship to Christ or descent from David as a ground of accusation before the magistrates. This is first alluded to at the end of the first group as the main reason for the condemnation of Symeon.[2] It is explicitly mentioned as the charge made against the grandsons of Jude.[3] And it was because they were said to be of the Jewish royal family that the accusers of Symeon were put to death.[4] Moreover, as we have seen, it is not improbable that it was alleged as the reason of St. John's exile at Patmos. All this is in keeping with the information given in *a* that Vespasian ordered the descendants of David to be sought for. Such a statement may very well have followed immediately, or at no long interval, after the end of the first group, and as an introduction to the second. We may suppose the sequence of thought to have been of this kind. Hegesippus gave an account of the episcopate of Symeon, ending with a short statement of the issue of the malice of the heretical informers. This involved the assertion that the principal charge against him was his connexion with the family of David.

[1] See above, p. 26. [2] Appendix III m.
[3] Appendix IV f. [4] Appendix IV m.

Now this was a charge which many of his readers might not understand. It was probably unique in the annals of martyrdom that a Christian should be put to death on such a pretext. It was necessary therefore for Hegesippus to show that his narrative was not encumbered with an improbability. He had to find other cases in which trials took place on the charge of relationship to the Jewish royal family. The first of his precedents is the persecution of the Jews, based on the principle that the descendants of David ought not to be permitted to live, and inaugurated by an order that inquisition should be made for them. He passes on to Domitian's persecution of the Christians. It also began with a similar order. As a result St. John, the Lord's kinsman, was sent into exile, and the two grandsons of Jude were dragged before the Emperor himself. It was nothing wonderful if Symeon was arraigned before Trajan's proconsul on a similar charge.[1] And so he returns once more to the incidents of the martyrdom.

That we have found the true position of the reference to Vespasian is confirmed by a fact which has been already mentioned for a somewhat different purpose.[2] This passage is continuous with what we regard as its following context, not only because it is the first of a series of precedents, but because it stands in a relation of antithesis to the passage which comes immediately after it in our arrangement.[3] The review of the policy of Domitian

---

[1] ἐπὶ τῷ αὐτῷ λόγῳ. This phrase indicates the real significance of the narrative about the grandsons of Jude. Valois takes it to mean 'quod Christi fidem praedicaret'; but I do not think his reference to the use of the same words in a wholly different context (*H. E.* iv. 22. 4) will carry conviction. It appears obviously to signify here 'on the same charge as the grandsons of Jude', i. e. of relationship to David.

[2] Above, p. 52.

[3] *H. E.* iii. 17. See Appendix IV b.

demands, by way of introduction, some notice of Vespasian; for it indicates a contrast between the policy of the two Emperors. If the passages about Vespasian and Domitian are both from the pen of Hegesippus they must have been in close proximity in his book.

IV

There remain no more than three or four short passages of the *Memoirs* of Hegesippus expressly quoted or alluded to by Eusebius in his *History*. The discussion of them will be fitly introduced by pointing out the probable bearing on Hegesippus's argument against his heretical opponents of the page of history contained in the fragments with which we have till now been concerned.

Amongst those with whom he contended, as Eusebius implies,[1] were the Saturnilians, Basilidians, and Carpocratians, with possibly the Simonians and Menandrianists. All these were the offspring, according to Hegesippus, of the seven Jewish sects.[2] Accordingly he shows, in the passages quoted above, the evil deeds of their progenitors. From them sprang false christs, false prophets, false apostles, who destroyed the unity of the Church at Jerusalem;[3] they were the informers at whose instance the trial of the two grandsons of Jude was held;[4] they brought about the death of Symeon.[5] And he is careful also to record the retribution which came upon them when their own weapons were turned against themselves. The accusers of Symeon were put to death on the very charge which they preferred against him.[6]

Again, a stock argument with controversial writers on

---

[1] *H. E.* iv. 7. 15; 8. 1.   [2] *H. E.* iv. 22 5.
[3] Appendix III l.   [4] Appendix IV f.
[5] Appendix III m, IV l.   [6] Appendix IV m.

the orthodox side was the recent origin of heresy, as contrasted with the deposit handed down from the apostles by the regular episcopal succession. This argument is applied by Hegesippus to the case of the Church of Jerusalem. He tells us that heresy first sprang into avowed existence there under the leadership of Thebuthis, in the time of Symeon.[1] On the other hand, James the Just was the first bishop and a colleague of the apostles; Symeon succeeded him after a regular election with apostolic sanction. But here there comes into view a feature of the argument which is not found in other writers. We have seen that kinship with the Lord is prominent in the second group of fragments as rendering persons who could claim it liable to persecution. In both groups stress is laid upon it from another point of view. Relatives of Christ had special honour in the Church. They with the apostles were recognized as in a unique sense guardians of the deposit of truth. James the Just was the Lord's brother.[2] Symeon was His cousin; and he was chosen as bishop on this account.[3] Those who elected him were the surviving apostles and disciples of Christ, together with His kinsmen according to the flesh.[4] The grandsons of Jude 'presided over every church as martyrs and of the Lord's kindred'.[5] Thus James and Symeon seem to have been custodians of orthodox doctrine not more as bishops of Jerusalem than in virtue of their close relationship to Christ.[6] Accordingly it

---

[1] Appendix III l.   [2] Appendix III c.   [3] Appendix III i.
[4] Appendix III h, i.   [5] Appendix IV k.
[6] In common with the other relatives of the Lord they had an additional claim to be authoritative exponents of orthodoxy. They were 'martyrs'. Such also were St. John, Zocer, and James, in the large sense in which Hegesippus used the word. That Hegesippus laid stress on this fact in the connexion which has been indicated is

was in the reign of Trajan—when the grandsons of Jude, possibly the last surviving near relatives of Christ, had passed away,[1] when Symeon was crucified,[2] when St. John was in extreme old age living at Ephesus,[3] or already dead[4]—that heresy gained a firm foothold in the Christian community.

It must be observed that just at this point, when he has indicated the moment of the introduction of heterodox teaching, Hegesippus's sketch of the history of the Church of Jerusalem, and consequently the argument founded upon it, seems to have come to an end. For though Eusebius gives a list of the bishops up to the reign of Hadrian, and tells us that they were short-lived,[5] and later on adds a list of their successors,[6] he tells us nothing else about the fortunes of the Church from the reign of Trajan to the end of the second century, except the fact that after the siege under Hadrian it became a Gentile community. For the siege itself he seems to depend on Aristo of Pella.[7] It is scarcely conceivable that if Hegesippus had carried his history beyond the death of Symeon Eusebius would not have used the material thus afforded.

If I have with any measure of correctness interpreted the argument of Hegesippus based on the history of the Church of Jerusalem, we shall gain from it some help towards surmounting the difficulties which encompass the group of passages which must next claim our attention. It relates to a journey of the writer to Rome, in the course of which he made a stay of some length at Corinth. This

---

obvious from the remark about the last two quoted in the text. He was but following the tendency of his age.

[1] Appendix IV k.   [2] Appendix III m, IV l.   [3] Appendix IV c.
[4] Irenaeus ap. *H. E.* iii. 23. 3.
[5] *H. E.* iv. 5.   [6] *H. E.* iv. 6. 4; v. 12.   [7] *H. E.* iv. 6. 3.

THE *HYPOMNEMATA* OF HEGESIPPUS 65

journey would not have been recorded in the *Memoirs* if it had not supplied material for his polemic. And if Hegesippus used the knowledge acquired during his tour about the Church of Corinth or those of Rome and other cities as a basis of argument, we might expect that the argument founded upon it would be of much the same kind as that which he founded upon his fuller knowledge of the Church of Jerusalem.

The group with which we are now concerned is not a large one. Eusebius's contributions to our knowledge of it are almost confined to a single chapter of his *History* —Bk. iv, chap. 22. In that chapter we have a direct quotation from the *Memoirs* containing a succinct account of the journey. Eusebius tells us that it was preceded by some information about the Epistle of Clement to the Corinthians. Now from an earlier part of his work we learn that Hegesippus had written about the schism which was the occasion of the Epistle.[1] Since the narrative of the schism would naturally precede the account of the letter which it called forth, we may count it as the first passage of the group. Of the second passage, containing 'some things' about the Epistle, we have information independent of Eusebius. It included at least one quotation which, as we have seen,[2] Epiphanius reproduces.

Passing now to Eusebius's direct quotation from that section of the *Memoirs* which immediately followed the notice of Clement's letter, we find indications that it is not a single fragment, but a collection of two or more. Eusebius here, as in other extracts from Hegesippus,[3] omits passages which do not suit his purpose, without directing attention to the fact that he has done so. He

[1] *H. E.* iii. 16. See Appendix V a.
[2] Above, p. 9 f. See Appendix V b.　　　[3] Above, pp. 20 ff.

begins this quotation with a sentence to the effect that the Church of Corinth remained orthodox to the time of Bishop Primus. And then he proceeds, 'with whom (οἷς) I made acquaintance (συνέμιξα) on my voyage to Rome.'[1] The relative 'with whom' has no antecedent. Thus we have reason to suspect a lacuna between the first and second clauses of the transcript. Our suspicion is confirmed when we turn to the paraphrase of the passage given earlier in the chapter.[2] In it Eusebius says that Hegesippus made the acquaintance (συνεμίξειεν) of very many (πλείστοις) bishops on his way to Rome, and found all of them orthodox. This would be a gross exaggeration if only Primus of Corinth had been visited by Hegesippus; scarcely less so if Eusebius intended to include the three bishops of Rome subsequently mentioned. Before the relative clause there must therefore have been a passage in which appeared the names of many bishops. It probably contained much more, but how much, or of what kind, it is vain to speculate.

Having stated that he stayed with the Corinthians for a good while, and was refreshed by their orthodoxy,[3] the quotation goes on to relate that he reached Rome and 'made a succession-list' (or, as some will have it, 'remained there') up to the episcopate of Anicetus, 'whose deacon was Eleutherus. And after Anicetus', proceeds Hegesippus, 'Soter succeeds, and after him Eleutherus.'[4] Then comes the remark, 'In every succession and in every city (the doctrine) is such as the law and the prophets and the Lord proclaim.'[5] Here several reflections suggest themselves. The extreme brevity of the notice of the Roman as compared with that of the Corinthian Church is surprising. For the latter included much to which Eusebius barely

[1] Appendix V c, d. [2] Appendix V d.
[3] Appendix V e. [4] Appendix V f. [5] Appendix V k.

alludes, and apparently some things to which he does not even allude. Then the character of the notice is peculiar. In the single sentence quoted by Eusebius an act of Hegesippus after his arrival at Rome is mentioned, and the names of three successive bishops are given; but there is nothing more. There is not a word which could have contributed anything to his contention against the heretics. Most remarkable of all is the absence of any special commendation of the Church of Rome for orthodoxy, such as that which had been bestowed on the Church of Corinth. For the next sentence does not relate specially to Rome. It is a summing up of the experience of Hegesippus throughout the entire period of his travels. It speaks of every city and every succession as being sound in the faith. It is impossible to believe that it could have followed without break on the bald statement that Eleutherus succeeded Soter as bishop of Rome. It seems manifest, therefore, that there is here another lacuna in Eusebius's transcript. He has omitted almost all that Hegesippus himself would have regarded as of special importance in his account of his stay at Rome.

Whether the two lacunae which have been pointed out are the only ones in this quotation it is impossible to determine. I am content to say that we are not entitled to assume so much. Not only, however, does Eusebius omit portions, and apparently large portions of the section which he transcribes; it is clear that he also leaves unnoticed much of the preceding context. Only the scantiest allusion is made to Hegesippus's remarks about Clement's Epistle. The historian has no interest in them; they are referred to, not for their own sake, but merely for the purpose of indicating the place in the *Memoirs* of the passages on which he desires to fix attention. He says nothing at all about the schism at

68 THE ΥΠΟΜΝΗΜΑΤΑ OF HEGESIPPUS

Corinth. And he gives us no information about the purpose of the journey, though there must have been some formal intimation of these things in the *Memoirs*.[1]

Now why did Eusebius omit so much and quote so little? What was his principle of selection? We may infer it, I believe, from the summary with which he introduces his quotation. His main interest, it appears, was the testimony of Hegesippus to the universal agreement of the bishops in doctrine. To mark its significance it was essential to mention the voyage to Rome which gave Hegesippus the means of knowing the opinions of the bishops of Western Christendom, and to give a general indication of his route. It is evident that there was much more than this in the passage which lay open before him. But with the exception of part of one sentence Eusebius actually quotes nothing which is not included within the limits thus defined. The exception is easily explained. He had evidently little material for fixing the chronology of Hegesippus's life.[2] But this section of the *Memoirs* supplied an indication of date in the reference to Bishops Anicetus, Soter, and Eleutherus. Accordingly the sentence in which they are mentioned is given in full. And elsewhere Eusebius seems to use it for the purpose of determining the duration of Hegesippus's sojourn at Rome.[3]

Now pruning carried out on so drastic a method is certain to result, not in the clearing away of useless branches, but in the loss of some parts of the main stem.

---

[1] As Zahn remarks (p. 246), such expressions as πλέων εἰς ʽΡώμην, γενόμενος ἐν ʽΡώμῃ cannot have been the earliest references to the journey.

[2] Note the very unsatisfactory evidence made use of in *H. E.* iv. 8. 2.

[3] *H. E.* iv. 11. 7. See Appendix V f.

THE *HYPOMNEMATA* OF HEGESIPPUS 69

Eusebius no doubt retained all of Hegesippus's travel narrative that mattered from what happened to be his point of view at the moment. But it is probable that what he omitted was not only of greater bulk, but also, from the point of view of the modern historian or the ancient theologian, of greater value than what he preserved.

This may be made clearer by an examination of the portion of our document relating to Corinth. It has been suggested that Hegesippus's treatment of this Church probably resembled his treatment of the Church of Jerusalem. And what we know of the facts answers to this expectation. Hegesippus gave some account of the history of the Jerusalem community from the Apostolic age onwards. There was a similar narrative of the history of the Church of Corinth, which certainly included the schism in the time of Domitian, and may have begun much further back. In regard to Jerusalem, again, he mainly concerned himself with the qualifications, the appointment, and the death of the successive bishops. It may have been so in regard to Corinth also; for it is significant that the Epistle of Clement is treated of in connexion with that Church, and not in connexion with Rome. It may be (who can say?) that the outcome of the schism, and the letter which followed it, was the appointment of the first monarchical bishop in that city, and that in that fact lay the interest of both for Hegesippus. If so, we are much the poorer for the loss of the part of the *Memoirs* which had to do with the Corinthian divisions and their consequences. But again, the remark that the Church of Corinth was orthodox till the time of Primus recalls the parallel statement that the Church of Jerusalem was a virgin, untainted by false teaching, up to the time of Symeon. The parallel may extend further. It is commonly assumed that Primus was bishop of Corinth when Hegesippus journeyed to Rome, and that he was one of the bishops (he is sometimes spoken of as if he were the only one) whose acquaintance Hegesippus made on the voyage. But there is no warrant for the hypothesis in the extant fragments of the travel narrative. We cannot be sure that he was still bishop when Hegesippus touched at Corinth, but even if he was, it is quite possible that he was mentioned, and that the survey of the history of the Corinthian Church ended with him, because in his episcopate heresy got a foothold in the Christian community there, just as the history of the Church of Jerusalem ended with Symeon because in his days Thebuthis introduced false doctrine. And lastly, at Jerusalem the bishops and relatives of the Lord were the guardians of the faith. In like manner these fragments show that in Corinth and other western cities, according to the view of Hegesippus, the bishops—for here obviously kinship with the Lord was out of the question—were invested with the same trust. And thus his intercourse with many bishops in the West provided him with a fresh argument against heresy. Wherever he went he found the rulers of the churches professing a doctrine identical with his own. Orthodoxy was maintained, to use the language of a later age, not only *semper* but *ubique et ab omnibus*.

Before leaving the fragments preserved by Eusebius it may be well to say a word about a reading which has given rise to much discussion—the words διαδοχὴν ἐποιησάμην.[1] With the single exception of the version of Rufinus, who renders 'permansi inibi', all the diplomatic evidence is in favour of the genuineness of these words. It has been supposed that Rufinus read διατριβὴν ἐποιησάμην. But this is far from certain: he may have

---
[1] § 3. See Appendix V f.

THE *HYPOMNEMATA* OF HEGESIPPUS 71

resorted to conjectural emendation, or, as Harnack suggests,[1] he may simply have borrowed 'permansi' from *H.E.* iv. 11.7. The fact is that Rufinus deserted his Greek on very slight provocation. A few lines higher up it can scarcely be doubted that he had before him the words οἷς συνέμιξα πλέων εἰς ʽΡώμην, καὶ συνδιέτριψα τοῖς Κορινθίοις, and he translated them 'quem Romam navigans vidi et resedi cum eo apud Corinthum'. But even if Rufinus could be shown to have used a copy in which the reading differed from that of the printed texts, its testimony could not stand against the consent of all other authorities, including the Syriac version, which is of a date only a few years later than the autograph.

But it is said that the words are meaningless and therefore must be emended. Without subscribing to the dictum that the phrase is absolutely without sense, one may admit that it is difficult. The Syriac translator, Nicephorus, and Rufinus (if he read as we do) could make nothing of it.[2] But is not that very fact an argument in favour of its genuineness? Eusebius's *History* was a much read, much copied, and early translated book. If Eusebius wrote the word διαδοχήν in error, why did no one correct it? Had none of the scholars into whose hands the *History* came a copy of Hegesippus with the true reading? The wonder is that with or without such authority words of so great difficulty remained without alteration. But Harnack[3] argues that we have an authoritative pronouncement on the question from Eusebius himself. He appeals to the statement,[4] 'Hegesippus relates that under Anicetus he took up his abode at Rome and remained there (παραμεῖναί τε αὐτόθι) until the episcopate of Eleutherus.' This, it is urged, proves that Eusebius either

[1] *Chronologie*, i. 182 f. [2] Ibid. ; cp. Zahn, p. 244.
[3] l. c. [4] *H. E.* iv. 11. 7. See Appendix V f.

read in our passage διατριβὴν (τὰς διατριβὰς) ἐποιησάμην or else understood διαδοχὴν ἐποιησάμην as meaning 'I remained'. I cannot but think that this criticism is somewhat hasty. It seems to take for granted that a single sentence quoted by Eusebius is all that Hegesippus wrote about his visit to Rome. Otherwise, why is it impossible that Eusebius should have learned the date of his arrival there from some other sentence? But whether based on our fragment or not Eusebius's statement really makes the reading διατριβὴν ἐποιησάμην impossible. How, after reading Hegesippus's own words that he 'remained in Rome up to Anicetus', could any one suppose that he arrived under Anicetus and remained until the time of Eleutherus?[1] On the other hand, if Eusebius took the words διαδοχὴν ἐποιησάμην, as they have been generally understood, to mean 'I made a succession-list', the inference that Anicetus was bishop when Hegesippus reached Rome and made the list was just as logical as the inference that he was still in Rome when he ascertained that 'Eleutherus succeeded Soter'.

Since it seems now to be a commonly held opinion that Hegesippus wrote διατριβὴν ἐποιησάμην or some similar phrase, it may be well to point out that in two other places he expresses the sense which such a phrase is supposed to convey, and that in neither does he use a periphrasis. He remained with the Corinthians many days, and in telling us so he writes συνδιέτριψα.[2] In an earlier passage he tells us that after taking up their abode at Pella the Christians of Jerusalem 'remained there'. And again he

---

[1] Harnack goes near to giving up his case when he writes, 'Er (Eusebius) erinnert sich der Stelle als laute sie, γενόμενος δὲ ἐν 'Ρώμῃ κατ' 'Ανίκητον τὰς διατριβὰς ἐποιησάμην αὐτόθι μέχρις 'Ελευθέρου.' So after all H. E. iv. 11. 7 witnesses to a text absolutely different from any that has ever been maintained to be genuine!

[2] H. E. iv. 22. 2. See Appendix V e.

seems to have used the verb διατρίβειν.¹ It may also be remarked that in the two examples cited as parallel to διατριβὴν ἐποιησάμην in the sense 'I tarried', the phrase actually used is τὰς διατριβὰς ἐποιεῖτο.² The article, the plural instead of the singular, and the imperfect tense instead of the aorist are all worthy of note. And we must not fail to observe that if in our passage we read διατριβὴν ἐποιησάμην and translate 'I tarried', some such adverb as αὐτόθι is necessary to complete the sense. The derivation of διαδοχήν from διατριβήν by mere clerical error is not probable; its derivation from τὰς διατριβάς is less so: that it should have been deliberately substituted for either is scarcely possible.

One may well be reluctant to abandon a reading so strongly supported by external evidence and transcriptional probability until it is clearly shown that no meaning can be attached to it consistent with its probable context, due allowance being made for the possibility of a solecism in such a writer as Hegesippus. But to this question we shall return hereafter.

Meanwhile, an attempt must be made to recover some passages of the *Memoirs* to which Eusebius makes no reference. We again invoke the aid of Epiphanius. We have already seen that he quotes from them a few words of the Epistle of Clement to the Corinthians.³ This quotation is made in *Haer.* 27. 6. Let us see whether there is any indication in the context that he made further use of the book which is thus proved to have been open before him while he wrote.

At the beginning of the same paragraph Epiphanius

---

[1] Epiph. *Haer.* 29. 7; 30. 2. See Appendix III f., and above, p. 33.

[2] *H. E.* iv. 11. 11; vi. 19. 16. And so also Epiph. *Haer.* 24. 1 (p. 68 c); *Chron. Paschal.* s. a. 303 (Dindorf, p. 515).

[3] Above, p. 9. Appendix V b.

speaks of one Marcellina, a follower of Carpocrates, who taught in Rome under Anicetus. In doing so he evidently uses the very words of his authority; for what he says is this:

'A certain Marcellina who had been led into error by them (the Carpocratians) paid *us* a visit some time ago. She was the ruin of a great number of persons in the time of Anicetus, bishop of Rome, who succeeded Pius and his predecessors.'[1]

The words 'paid us a visit' ($\mathring{\eta}\lambda\theta\epsilon\nu$ $\epsilon\mathring{\iota}s$ $\mathring{\eta}\mu\hat{a}s$) are evidently taken over from a contemporary document, the phraseology of which Epiphanius, with a carelessness of which we find other examples in the *Panarion*,[2] has forgotten to alter so as to make it suit its new environment. Further, if the next sentence is from the same document it would seem that it was written after, though not very long after,[3] the episcopate of Anicetus. And the expression 'bishop of Rome' may perhaps indicate that the writer was not himself a Roman. That Epiphanius believed that he was in Rome when he was visited by Marcellina, and that the visit was paid under Anicetus, becomes plain when we glance at the next page, where he repeats the information in a somewhat different form: 'In the times, as we have said, of Anicetus, the above-named Marcellina having come to Rome,' &c.[4] The record which Epiphanius uses in this place seems, therefore, to have come from the pen of some stranger who was in Rome in the time of Anicetus, and

---

[1] Appendix V h, i. The translation is that of Lightfoot (*Clem.* i. 329). I am not sure that the last words, τῶν ἀνωτέρω, should not be rendered 'those mentioned above'. If so, the predecessors of Pius must have been mentioned in an earlier passage of the writing from which Epiphanius is quoting. Cp. below, p. 84.

[2] See below, p. 127.

[3] Cp. ἤδη πως, 'some time ago,' which implies that the visit was recent.   [4] Both passages will be found in Appendix V h.

THE *HYPOMNEMATA* OF HEGESIPPUS 75

to have been written not long after the death of that bishop. Now if we are to believe Eusebius[1] Hegesippus came to Rome under Anicetus, and there is evidence that he wrote his *Memoirs* under Eleutherus,[2] who became bishop nine years after Anicetus's death. Is Epiphanius then quoting from the *Memoirs*? The suggestion is at least plausible.

But there is other evidence in favour of it. The statement about Marcellina is found also in the chapter about the Carpocratians in Irenaeus's work *Against Heresies*.[3] Now the whole of that chapter has obviously a close connexion with the passage of Epiphanius in which the notice of Marcellina occurs. In both we are told (1) that the Carpocratians 'sealed' members of their sect by branding them on the right ear, (2) that Marcellina made many converts under Anicetus, (3) that the Carpocratians were called Gnostics, (4) that they had images of Christ painted or formed of 'other material', which were said to have been made by Pilate while Christ was on earth, (5) that these images were placed beside images of philosophers such as Pythagoras, Plato, and Aristotle, and (6) that they were venerated with Gentile rites.[4] But Epiphanius certainly did not here borrow from Irenaeus. Irenaeus says that Marcellina came 'to Rome', Epiphanius that she came 'to us'. A late writer copying Irenaeus could not have substituted the latter for the former. And Epiphanius adds some particulars which are not in Irenaeus and which he can scarcely have invented. He mentions the instruments with which the branding was performed, he

---

[1] *H. E.* iv. 11. 7.   [2] Appendix V f.
[3] *Adv. Haer.* i. 25. 6. See Appendix V h.
[4] The first statement in Epiphanius precedes the first, the last four follow the second notice of Marcellina, where he returns, after a digression, to his original authority.

expands the 'other material' of Irenaeus into 'gold and silver and other material', and he refers at the end of the passage to the doctrine of the Carpocratians that salvation was of the soul only and not of the body. Thus it remains that Irenaeus and Epiphanius based their statements on a common document. No work, except the *Memoirs* of Hegesippus, can be suggested which fulfils the necessary conditions of time and place.[1]

Attention may be called to another point of contact between this passage of Epiphanius and the *Memoirs*. Hegesippus,[2] like the author of Epiphanius's source, classed the Carpocratians among the Gnostics, and it seems to be implied by Eusebius that they were one of the heretical sects against which he contended.[3] But we may go further. In the same context, and shortly before he comes to name Hegesippus as one of the champions of the faith against heretics, Eusebius makes reference to the chapter of Irenaeus on the Carpocratians: 'Irenaeus also writes that contemporary with these (Saturninus and Basilides) was Carpocrates, the father of another heresy called that of the Gnostics.'[4] Whence did he borrow this description of Carpocrates? Not, certainly, from Irenaeus; for he says no more than that the followers of Carpocrates called themselves Gnostics. But in the parallel passage Epiphanius tells us that 'thence—i.e. from the teaching of Marcellina at Rome, or perhaps from the Carpocratians generally—has come the origin (ἀρχή) of those who are called Gnostics'.[5] In tracing the origin of Gnosticism to the teaching of Carpocrates did Epiphanius

---

[1] Towards the end of the section Epiphanius uses the phrase Μαρκελλῖνα ἐν Ῥώμῃ γενομένη ... ἠφάνισε. Cp. Hegesippus (Appendix V f), γενόμενος δὲ ἐν Ῥώμῃ ... ἐποιησάμην.

[2] *H. E.* iv. 22. 5. See Appendix III 1.   [3] *H. E.* iv. 7 f.

[4] *H. E.* iv. 7. 9, referring to Iren. *Adv. Haer.* i. 25.

[5] *Haer.* 27. 6 (p. 108). See Appendix V j.

THE *HYPOMNEMATA* OF HEGESIPPUS 77

follow the source more exactly than Irenaeus? And in dubbing him 'the father of the heresy called that of the Gnostics' does Eusebius echo the same phrase?[1] If so, we have an indication that the source was known to Eusebius and was in fact the *Memoirs*. That ἀρχή (or a cognate) was actually the word used by Hegesippus may appear likely if we recall the words in which he speaks of the first entrance of heresy into the Church of Jerusalem, οὔπω γὰρ ἔφθαρτο ἀκοαῖς ματαίαις· ἄρχεται δὲ ὁ Θέβουθις ... ὑποφθείρειν ἀπὸ τῶν ἑπτὰ αἱρέσεων.[2] In the present passage all that is meant may perhaps be that the arrival of Marcellina marked the beginning of Gnostic teaching *in Rome*, just as the conduct of Thebuthis marked the beginning of 'vain doctrine' in Jerusalem, though Eusebius in both cases has given the words a wider significance.

Immediately after his first notice of Marcellina Epiphanius proceeds to give a list of the bishops of Rome, beginning with the 'apostles and bishops, Peter and Paul', and ending with Clement. Then comes a long digression about Clement, which has nothing to do with his main subject, the Carpocratian heresy. Near the end of the digression he mentions incidentally that the two bishops who followed next after the apostles, Linus and Cletus, ruled each for twelve years. Then he once more sets out the order of succession of the bishops, this time carrying it on to Anicetus, and resumes his account of the

[1] The phrase in each case is remarkable: Eus. αἱρέσεως τῆς τῶν γνωστικῶν ἐπικληθείσης. Epiph. γνωστικῶν τῶν καλουμένων, Iren. 'Gnosticos se vocant' (the Greek is unfortunately wanting). It seems as though in the original document the assumption of the name 'Gnostics' by heretics was described as a new thing.

[2] *H. E.* iv. 22. 4 f. See Appendix III 1. To the extract containing these words Eusebius prefixes the remark, Ὁ δ' αὐτὸς καὶ τῶν κατ' αὐτὸν αἱρέσεων τὰς ἀρχὰς ὑποτίθεται.

Carpocratians with a repetition in different words of what he had already said about Marcellina. Thus he returns to the document of which he had made use at the beginning of the paragraph.

The list of Roman bishops, part of which Epiphanius writes down twice, is taken from a document, and was not compiled by Epiphanius himself. This fact is betrayed, once more, by the carelessness of Epiphanius. The list, on repetition, ends with the name of Anicetus, on which follows, 'who has been already mentioned above in the catalogue' (ὁ ἄνω ἐν τῷ καταλόγῳ προδεδηλωμένος). Now there is in the *Panarion* no catalogue of bishops which can be referred to here. The obvious inference is that Epiphanius took his list from a writing in which its position was considerably earlier than the note, and that he has transcribed the latter, not observing that the omission of the κατάλογος from its proper place rendered it unmeaning.[1]

Further, most readers of this passage will probably

---

[1] Zahn (p. 260 f.) suggests that, like the following ἡ προδεδηλωμένη Μαρκελλίνα, the words glance back to the beginning of the paragraph. His attempt, however, to show that there Anicetus is named *in a catalogue* is not very successful. But his reasoning is open to further criticism. He argues, if I understand him, that because the remark quoted above is made of Anicetus alone, and not of the other bishops just named, the reference must be to an incomplete catalogue in which all the other names were not given. But, if this be so, would not the remark be somewhat pointless if *any* of the other names were included in the earlier list? On his own showing five out of the ten are there. And what could be the purpose of saying that one name in a complete list had been mentioned in an imperfect list now superseded? Once more, it is somewhat surprising to find that imperfect list called *the* catalogue, as if there were no other, immediately after a full *series episcoporum* had been written down. For that is what Epiphanius calls it, if he really refers to it here, and not 'the above catalogue' (*den obigen Katalog*) as Zahn translates his words.

agree with Harnack when he says [1] that the list of bishops and the episode of Marcellina are inseparably connected. They must have been taken from the same document. Hence, if the foregoing argument is sound the former as well as the latter comes from the *Memoirs* of Hegesippus. Thus we may account for the presence of such irrelevant matter as a list of the bishops of Rome in a passage whose subject is the heresy of Carpocrates. The account of the Carpocratians, including the sentences about Marcellina, was in the *Memoirs* inserted in the κατάλογος after the mention of Anicetus, in whose episcopate the heresy came into prominence at Rome through the influence of that lady. And Epiphanius when making use of it could not refrain from adding some information from its context which was little to his purpose. And so we discover that the κατάλογος was not the mere list of names which the word might seem to import.[2] The name of each bishop was associated with some account of his period of office. This inference is supported by the fact that Epiphanius tells us, no doubt relying on his κατάλογος, that Linus and Cletus each ruled the Church for twelve years. It is supported also by the digression about Clement. This is really a digression within a digression. Epiphanius breaks off his discourse about the Carpocratians to give the list of bishops, and he breaks off the list when he reaches Clement to explain the difficulty about his place in the succession. It is natural to suppose that something in the catalogue itself suggested this fresh interruption. This can have been nothing else than an assertion that he

---

[1] p. 184, following Lightfoot.

[2] A different explanation, however, may be suggested. If each historical note was headed by the name of a bishop as a sort of title or rubric, the word κατάλογος might be regarded as applying to the list of names as distinct from the notes.

was a contemporary of the apostles and was appointed bishop by St. Peter. The repetition of the former statement in successive clauses [1] leaves the impression that it was, as it were, the text of the discourse, and the use of a Hegesippean phrase [2] in the latter is significant.

If all this is true the κατάλογος which Epiphanius had in his hands must have been a kind of history of the early Roman Church not at all unlike the history of the early Church of Jerusalem which Hegesippus incorporated in his *Memoirs*. Two special features of resemblance between the two may be pointed out. As in the *Memoirs* the manner of the appointment to the episcopate of James and Symeon is dwelt upon, so here the appointment of Clement by St. Peter while he and St. Paul were still alive is recorded. And as there the introduction of heresy into Jerusalem by Thebuthis under Symeon is recounted, so here the introduction of Gnosticism into Rome by Marcellina under Anicetus is duly noted, and apparently dealt with at some length.

The conclusion to which we seem to be irresistibly led by all these circumstances is that the whole of this paragraph of the *Panarion* of Epiphanius, excepting only the argument about Clement, is directly based on a passage of Hegesippus's *Memoirs*. This conclusion is supported by the high authority of Lightfoot, who, indeed, was the first to suggest it. But distinguished scholars do not accept Lightfoot's results in their entirety. Zahn [3] admits

---

[1] Σύγχρονος ὢν Πέτρου καὶ Παύλου ... ὄντος τούτου συγχρόνου Πέτρου καὶ Παύλου. καὶ οὗτος γὰρ σύγχρονος γίνεται τῶν ἀποστόλων.

[2] Ἔτι περιόντων αὐτῶν. Cp. *H. E.* iii. 20. 1 (Appendix IV f) ἔτι δὲ περιῆσαν οἱ ἀπὸ γένους τοῦ κυρίου: *H. E.* iii. 11 (Appendix III h) πλείους γὰρ καὶ τούτων περιῆσαν εἰς ἔτι τότε τῷ βίῳ.

The same phrase may lie behind τοὺς εἰς ἔτι τῷ βίῳ λειπομένους a few lines higher up in *H. E.* iii. 11 and ἔτι τῷ βίῳ ἐνδιατρίβοντι in *H. E.* iii. 18. 1 (Appendix IV d).

[3] pp. 258 ff.

THE *HYPOMNEMATA* OF HEGESIPPUS

the passage about Marcellina to a place in the *Memoirs*, but rejects the hypothesis that that work contained a list of the Roman bishops. Harnack,[1] holding that the two are inseparable, thinks it impossible that either can have been in the *Memoirs*, though he admits the remote possibility that they may have appeared in some other treatise of Hegesippus. This possibility is, in truth, very remote, since there is not a particle of evidence that Hegesippus composed any work but the *Memoirs*. What then are the arguments which are urged to prove that Lightfoot's hypothesis is untenable?

It is said, in the first place, that Eusebius, one of the purposes of whose *History* was to record episcopal successions,[2] if he had known such a list drawn up by Hegesippus, would have been certain to quote, or at least to mention it. Does he not transcribe the later and very meagre list compiled by Irenaeus?[3] Now the argument *e silentio*, though it cannot be altogether avoided, is always treacherous. And it is not at its best when it is applied to an unsystematic writer like Eusebius. It would be no matter of surprise if for some reason not apparent he preferred the list of Irenaeus to one whose claim to precedence was a somewhat higher antiquity. But if we might hazard a guess, we should say that it was precisely the meagreness of Irenaeus's list that secured for it the honour of direct quotation almost in full. The catalogue, or history of the Roman bishops, fragments of which are incorporated in the *Panarion*, may well have been so long as to preclude such treatment. And it is quite possible that Eusebius did not consider its compiler a first-rate authority on Roman affairs, though he set much store by what he related about the history of the Christian com-

---

[1] *Chronologie*, i. 180 ff.   [2] *H. E.* i. 1. 1.
[3] *H. E.* v. 6.

munity at Jerusalem. That he wholly abstained from using his κατάλογος is, however, by no means certain. Where else did he get the information that Linus and Cletus each held office for a period of twelve years?[1]

Harnack[2] makes an ingenious attempt to turn one of Lightfoot's arguments against himself which must not be passed over. He accepts the theory that when Epiphanius says he found his quotation from Clement's Epistle in certain ὑπομνηματισμοί he means that he took it from the *Memoirs* of Hegesippus. But he thinks that by referring to the *Memoirs* for this one extract he implies that the facts recorded in the context were not taken from that work. This argument will scarcely carry conviction. If Epiphanius had given his references after the manner of a modern critic it might have been valid, but that is far from being the case.[3] It is no doubt curious that one who habitually gives no authority for statements taken from Hegesippus does so just here. But a reason may be suggested. Epiphanius was here not stating a mere fact of history: he was quoting in support of a disputable theory of his own a passage from a writing of which elsewhere he betrays no knowledge, and of which he probably expected his readers to be ignorant. He may have thought it well to assure them that he had sufficient ground for ascribing the saying to Clement. Moreover, it will be observed that to copy this saying he was obliged to turn to a different part of the *Memoirs* from

---

[1] *H. E.* iii. 13, 15. It will be remembered that Hegesippus is used as an authority in chapters 11, 12, 16–20.

[2] p. 185.

[3] See e.g. *Haer.* 29. 4 (Appendix III c, d), and especially *Haer.* 78. 7 (Appendix III j), where it might have been argued, on Harnack's principle, that the *only* information guaranteed by Jewish tradition was exactly that which in fact came from a wholly different source. See above, p. 35.

that which, *ex hypothesi*, he used in the preceding and following context. For the Epistle of Clement was noticed by Hegesippus in the section about Corinth, to which neither the story of Marcellina nor the appointment of Clement as bishop could have belonged. This in itself might have provided a motive for giving the reference.

Finally Zahn[1] tells us that Epiphanius's list of bishops cannot have been derived from the *Memoirs* because it gives to the successor of Linus the name of Cletus, while Eusebius and Irenaeus, who had read the *Memoirs*, always call him Anencletus. But why was Irenaeus bound to follow Hegesippus in this matter rather than the authority in which he found Anencletus? And Eusebius had read Irenaeus as well as Hegesippus. If he found Anencletus in one and Cletus in the other, was it to be expected that he would use both forms, or else of necessity prefer Hegesippus to Irenaeus?

I am not moved by such arguments to reject the view that the authority for all the historical facts mentioned in this paragraph is Hegesippus, and that all of them were drawn from his *Memoirs*. And if this theory be accepted there can be little question about the order in which the several statements followed one another in the passage from which Epiphanius took them. From this point of view, however, one clause merits further discussion. We have seen reason to regard the phrase ὁ ἄνω ἐν τῷ καταλόγῳ προδεδηλωμένος as a direct quotation. But if so it has wandered from its moorings. Where did it originally stand? It may be assumed that it followed a mention of Anicetus subsequent to the first occasion on which he was named. Now if we suppose that it occurred in the Marcellina section[2] in the genitive case this condition is fulfilled. Hegesippus may have written ἐν χρόνοις Ἀνικήτου ἐπι-

[1] p. 260.   [2] Appendix V h, j.

σκόπου 'Ρώμης τοῦ ἄνω ἐν τῷ καταλόγῳ προδεδηλωμένου. Since the notice of Marcellina occurs in the middle of the account of Carpocrates it may have been so long subsequent to the introductory mention of Anicetus as to make this cross-reference desirable. That Epiphanius should have divorced it from its context and written it a few lines higher up is not surprising. He performed a similar feat elsewhere.[1] And in the place to which we have assigned it we find in Epiphanius what may be counted a paraphrase of it: 'who succeeded Pius καὶ τῶν ἀνωτέρω.' The latter words have been rendered 'and his predecessors'. But they may mean 'and those mentioned above'. In that case we have an explicit reference to the κατάλογος as preceding the story of Marcellina.

It remains to inquire what was the position of the whole passage in the *Memoirs*. It is plain that it must have belonged to that part of the record of Hegesippus's travels which he devoted to the Church of Rome. It is equally clear that it cannot have preceded the sentence in which he records his arrival at the city.[2] And it is highly improbable that it followed the notice of the orthodoxy of all the cities about which Hegesippus had acquired information in the course of his voyage.[3] Between those two passages, therefore, in spite of the fact that they are successive sentences in Eusebius, we must insert it. And we see at once that there it is in perfect harmony with its surroundings. It enables us in the first place partially to fill the gap left at this place in Eusebius's extract from Hegesippus's account of his voyage.[4] And thus it saves us from the necessity of thinking that Hegesippus treated of the Roman Church in such scanty fashion as might have been inferred from Eusebius. Moreover, it gives some

[1] See above, p. 35.
[2] Appendix V f.
[3] Appendix V k.
[4] See above, p. 66 f.

sort of consistency to Hegesippus's method of argument. We find that, just as in the case of Jerusalem and Corinth, so in that of Rome, what he wrote was mainly a *résumé* of the history of the Christian community, special attention being paid to the circumstances under which each bishop succeeded to his charge and to the cause and time of the rise of heretical teaching. This we have already had occasion to observe. A further point may be noticed now. The balance of probability seems to be in favour of the supposition that the historical disquisition ended with the episcopate of Anicetus,[1] though there was material for carrying it on to that of Eleutherus. Why was this? Because, we may answer, it was under Anicetus that heresiarchs began to congregate at Rome, to proclaim their doctrines openly, and to win large numbers of disciples. Such at least seems to have been the opinion of the compiler; and it is supported by the statements of Irenaeus. It is true that from him we learn that the influx of heretics to Rome began earlier. Valentinus and Cerdon arrived during the short episcopate of Hyginus.[2] But if Valentinus attained the zenith of his influence under Pius, he was still in Rome in the earlier part of the rule of Anicetus. On the other hand, Cerdon does not appear to have been a formidable opponent of orthodoxy. When he was excommunicated we do not know, but before that

---

[1] That is all that can be said at the present stage of our argument, for it is certainly possible that, as Harnack suggests (p. 185), Epiphanius interrupted his transcription of the list of bishops in order to introduce the notice of the Carpocratians and had no further occasion to refer to it. But on the other hand, if the κατάλογος was the list of names as distinct from the historical notes appended to them (see above, p. 79), the phrase ὁ ἄνω ἐν τῷ καταλόγῳ προδεδηλωμένος seems to indicate that it was already completed when the note about Marcellina was written. If so, it did not extend beyond Anicetus.

[2] Iren. *Adv. Haer.* i. 27. 1; iii. 4. 3.

event he vacillated between avowal of orthodoxy and furtive teaching of heresy.¹ Of such secret propagation of error Hegesippus took no account.² Cerdon's successor Marcion attained a position of influence under Anicetus,³ and it was probably at that time that he had his famous interview with Polycarp.⁴ The very fact that Polycarp in the time of Anicetus succeeded in recovering to the Church many followers of Valentinus and Marcion⁵ is eloquent testimony to the success of their propaganda. And in the same episcopate Marcellina was no less successful in spreading the doctrine of Carpocrates.⁶ Heresy was in fact rampant at Rome under Anicetus as it had never been before. If with him Hegesippus brought his sketch of the history of the Roman Church to a close, the correspondence between his treatment of Jerusalem and Rome is complete.

Up to the present I have refrained from referring to the statement of Hegesippus that on his arrival at Rome he made a διαδοχή. I have contented myself with giving reasons for the belief that the words διαδοχὴν ἐποιησάμην are genuine. What then do they mean? Mr. McGiffert remarks that 'if these words be accepted as authentic, the only possible rendering seems to be the one which has been adopted by many scholars, "Being in [rather, 'when I arrived at'] Rome I composed a catalogue of bishops"'.⁷ But Harnack and Zahn agree that the words cannot possibly have this meaning. No example, it is said, of the use of διαδοχή in the sense of a list of bishops can be produced. In *H. E.* v. 5. 9, to which Lightfoot appealed,⁸ as in other passages, the διαδοχή is not a list, it is the matter of fact which in the κατάλογος is expressed in writing.⁹ Never-

---

¹ Iren. iii. 4. 3.   ² *H. E.* iii. 32. 7.   See Appendix III k.
³ Iren. iii. 4. 3.   ⁴ Ibid. iii. 3. 4.   ⁵ Ibid.   ⁶ Ibid. i. 25. 6.
⁷ Note 3 on *H. E.* iv. 22.   ⁸ *Clement*, i. 328.   ⁹ Zahn, p. 245.

theless the two words approach one another very closely in their meaning. If διαδοχή was sometimes used as equivalent to κατάλογος it would be no more surprising than the fact that λόγος means not only *ratio* but *verbum*. It is hard to see in what other sense Irenaeus uses the word διαδοχή when he says that Hyginus occupied the ninth place in the episcopal *succession* from the apostles.[1] Zahn admits that in one passage the word is used of a written list of successive bishops;[2] but he maintains that this passage is not to our purpose inasmuch as it is there in the plural.[3] But why it should be assumed that αἱ διαδοχαί means a single list, and not several, I do not know. If the choice must be made between altering the text and giving to the word διαδοχή a meaning which is unusual, though not without support, the latter is the alternative to be preferred.

But we are told that, whatever may be the meaning of διαδοχή elsewhere, here it cannot possibly indicate a list of successive bishops of Rome. 'Hegesippus, who in the preceding context had not spoken either of Roman bishops or of the succession of bishops in other churches, but of the Epistle of Clement, of his stay in Corinth, and of his arrival at Rome, must in that case have written something like τὴν τῶν αὐτόθι ἐπισκόπων διαδοχὴν ἐποιησάμην.'[4] The answer is simply that we do not know what Hegesippus spoke about in the preceding context, inasmuch as Eusebius has not quoted it fully. The only thing that is certain is that he mentioned many bishops. And with a similar answer we may meet Harnack's argument, that since in the case of Corinth Hegesippus recorded the

[1] Iren. i. 27. 1.
[2] *H. E.* v. 12. 2 μεθ' ὃν ἐπισκοπεῦσαι Καυσιανὸν αἱ τῶν αὐτόθι διαδοχαὶ περιέχουσι.
[3] It will be remembered nevertheless that τὰς διατριβὰς ἐποιεῖτο is cited as parallel to διατριβὴν ἐποιησάμην.
[4] Zahn, p. 244.

time of his visit and the orthodoxy of the Church, we might expect him to adopt a similar procedure in the case of Rome, and that therefore $διαδοχὴν ἐποιησάμην$ or the phrase which it displaced must express a date.[1] Such expectations, indeed, are liable to disappointment; but who knows whether the date appeared in one of the passages which Eusebius has omitted? There, at any rate, must have been the commendation of the orthodoxy of Rome if it was anywhere, since it is not in the present text. Zahn[2] makes merry over the notion that Hegesippus had no more important business to attend to when he got to Rome than to draw up a list of the Roman bishops, 'that his whole journey by land and water had actually no other purpose than the construction of a catalogue of bishops'. Certainly we find no hint of such a seeming absurdity in the words 'when I reached Rome I made a succession-list'. But what if the $διαδοχή$ was not a mere list of names, but such a document as lay before Epiphanius? If the purpose of the voyage of Hegesippus was to investigate the history of the churches of Corinth and other cities—above all Rome—and so to provide himself with material for his refutation of heresy, is there anything surprising in his announcement that he had no sooner reached Rome than he set about the work which had brought him there?

Now if Hegesippus wrote that on coming to Rome he at once engaged in historical research, this assertion has an important bearing on our inquiry. For in the first place it is improbable that the remark was wholly gratuitous. It is a very natural inference that his investigation had some connexion with the work in which the observation occurs. In other words, we might expect that the $διαδοχή$ which he made would in some form be incorporated in

[1] *Chronologie*, p. 181.   [2] p. 244.

the *Memoirs*, and, in all probability, it would follow this reference to it after no long interval. Thus we are confirmed in our belief that the history of the early Church of Rome which Epiphanius used was from the pen of Hegesippus, and that we have restored it to its true place in the *Memoirs*.

Again, on the same supposition, it is certain that the terminus of Hegesippus's investigation was the episcopate of Anicetus, a conclusion which on other grounds has already appeared probable. Thus we have additional reason for believing that the scope of his dissertation on the Roman Church was similar to that of his dissertation on the Church of Jerusalem.

And finally, whatever may have been the ground on which Eusebius made the statement that Hegesippus went to Rome when Anicetus was bishop,[1] we are now able to justify it. If immediately after his arrival at that city he drew up an account of the succession as far as Anicetus, it is plain that he cannot have made his visit to it before Anicetus succeeded to the bishopric. And he cannot have arrived under any later bishop, for under Anicetus he had his interview there with Marcellina. Hence it follows that it was during the rule of Anicetus that he took up his residence at Rome.

We have now to ask the same question about this whole section of the *Memoirs* which has been already asked about the portion of it which has been recovered from the *Panarion* of Epiphanius. What was its position in the treatise of Hegesippus? In this case the question must be answered with some degree of hesitation. But we may observe, in the first place, that, if we are correct in supposing that its argument was similar to that of the long section beginning with the account of James the

[1] *H. E.* iv. 11. 7.

Just, that fact gives us some ground for holding that it belonged to the same part of Hegesippus's work, or in other words that it was part of the fifth *Memoir*. And we may go further. The natural course of his argument would be to begin with that which he knew best, the history of the church of which he himself was a member, and to pass on from it to that with which he was less familiar, the knowledge of other churches which he acquired during his travels. It may be reasonably concluded that the notice of western churches, of which our third group is a part, had its place in the fifth *Memoir* after the notice of Jerusalem in the first and second groups.

V

Three isolated passages remain to be considered. The first is one in which a doctrine obviously based on 1 Cor. ii. 9 is denied on the ground that Christ taught the contrary in St. Matt. xiii. 16.[1] The persons whom Hegesippus was refuting were probably Gnostics of some kind who founded part of their teaching on St. Paul's words.[2] If we may trust Photius, to whom we are indebted for our knowledge of the passage, it was in the fifth *Memoir*, but it seems impossible to fix its position more accurately.

Another fragment consists of the end of one sentence, and the opening words of a second, in which Antinous is mentioned.[3] It seems to be taken from a polemic against paganism. It is therefore probably alien to the subject of the fifth *Memoir*, and in consequence I regard it as belonging to one of the first four.

---

[1] Photius, *Bibl.*, 232. See Appendix VI.

[2] Cp. Hippol. *Philos.* v. 24, 27. And see Milligan in *Dict. of Christ. Biog.* ii. 877; Burkitt, *Early Christianity outside the Roman Empire*, 1899, p. 80 f.

[3] *H. E.* iv. 8. 2. See Appendix I.

The third fragment relates to the seven sects of the Jews. About them Hegesippus tells us in his account of James the Just he had already written in his *Memoirs*.[1] The passage to which he refers therefore certainly preceded the first of our extracts from the fifth *Memoir*, and probably belonged to one of the first four.[2] A portion of it is no doubt preserved in the list of the sects quoted by Eusebius, by way of comment on a reference to them in connexion with Thebuthis.[3] It is impossible to determine whether the position of this fragment in the *Memoirs* was before or after that concerning Antinous.

VI

It will not be supposed that the passages to which attention has been given in this Essay, and which are collected in the Appendix, are regarded by the present writer as the only ones in which Eusebius has made use of the *Memoirs* of Hegesippus. In some of them we have no direct statement of the historian as to the authority on which he relied, and it would not be surprising if proof were found hereafter that in other parts of his *History* he in like manner quoted or paraphrased the same work without express acknowledgement of his indebtedness to it.

One passage may be mentioned here which is reasonably suspected to have been in part based on the *Memoirs*, though the evidence is not strong enough to warrant its

---

[1] *H. E.* ii. 23. 8. See Appendix III e τινὲς οὖν τῶν ἑπτὰ αἱρέσεων τῶν ἐν τῷ λαῷ, τῶν προγεγραμμένων μοι [ἐν τοῖς ὑπομνήμασιν] κτλ. The bracketed words are regarded by Schwartz as an addition of Eusebius, and Rufinus omits them. The question whether they are from the pen of Hegesippus is for our purpose immaterial.

[2] So Zahn, p. 232.

[3] *H. E.* iv. 22. 7. See Appendix II.

inclusion in the Appendix. I refer to the chapter in which he gives a list of the early bishops of Jerusalem.[1] It is true that there is no probability that the list itself comes from Hegesippus. Eusebius in fact tells us that he found it in the succession-lists preserved on the spot.[2] And Mr. C. H. Turner, after a careful examination of the evidence, has come to the conclusion that if it was not manufactured for his benefit, it was at least not long in existence when he wrote his *History*.[3] But it is not unlikely that Hegesippus mentioned some bishops of Jerusalem later than Symeon, just as he mentioned two bishops of Rome later than Anicetus, and if he did the names given by him would certainly be included in the apocryphal list. That list, as it came into Eusebius's hands, had no chronological notes. But after telling us this he adds, 'To be sure a record informs us that they were very short-lived.'[4] Now, as regards the thirteen bishops who followed Symeon, this might have been inferred from the list itself. Symeon was put to death, according to Hegesippus, in the reign of Trajan; Jerusalem was taken by Hadrian in A.D. 135. That is to say, thirteen bishops succeeded one another in thirty-five years. If from this we may not conclude that they died young, it is at any rate a permissible surmise that none of them ruled the Church for a long period. But the form of Eusebius's expression does not favour the supposition that his statement was a mere corollary from the number of names in his list. The remark would appear to have been explicitly made in the record to

---

[1] *H. E.* iv. 5.

[2] *H. E.* v. 12. 2. This applies only to the list of bishops succeeding Hadrian. But cp. *Dem. Ev.* iii. 5 (p. 124 C); *Theoph.* v. 45.

[3] *Journal of Theological Studies*, i. (1900) 552.

[4] *H. E.* iv. 5. 1 κομιδῇ γὰρ οὖν βραχυβίους αὐτοὺς λόγος κατέχει γενέσθαι.

THE *HYPOMNEMATA* OF HEGESIPPUS 93

which he appeals. And it is not likely to have been made in a bare list of names. It is also to be observed that, though this remark is by Eusebius made to apply to the whole series of bishops, it does not hold good of the first two. For both James and Symeon were aged men when they suffered martyrdom, and, according to Hegesippus, the episcopate of each of them lasted some thirty years or more.[1] This encourages us to think that Eusebius, borrowing it from a document in which it referred to the thirteen successors of Symeon, carelessly extended its scope. And it is at least a coincidence that in introducing it he makes use of the very phrase which in many other places served to indicate the *Memoirs* of Hegesippus.[2] A little lower down, too, he makes another observation, which, as Zahn notes,[3] has a Hegesippean ring. Just as Hegesippus did in the case of the western sees with which he became acquainted on his voyage, so here Eusebius commends the orthodoxy of the bishops of Jerusalem, and that in words which recall his paraphrase of Hegesippus's account of the election of Symeon:

'They say that being all Hebrews by descent they accepted the knowledge of Christ in sincerity, so that in fact by those who were able to judge of such matters they were also approved as worthy of the office of bishops.'[4]

---

[1] Compare Turner in *Journal of Theological Studies*, i. (1900) 535.

[2] See above, pp. 23, 50 f. I cannot think that Mr. Turner (l. c. 537) is right when he says that λόγος κατέχει here means 'no more than the local tradition of the Church at Jerusalem as it existed in Eusebius's day'.

[3] p. 287.

[4] § 2 οὓς πάντας Ἑβραίους φασὶν ὄντας ἀνέκαθεν τὴν γνῶσιν τοῦ Χριστοῦ γνησίως καταδέξασθαι, ὥστ' ἤδη πρὸς τῶν τὰ τοιάδε ἐπικρίνειν δυνατῶν καὶ τῆς τῶν ἐπισκόπων λειτουργίας ἀξίους δοκιμασθῆναι.

Compare *H. E.* iii. 11 (Appendix III h, i) βουλήν τε ὁμοῦ τοὺς πάντας περὶ τοῦ τίνα χρὴ τῆς Ἰακώβου διαδοχῆς ἐπικρῖναι ἄξιον ποιήσασθαι, καὶ . . . τοὺς πάντας Συμεῶνα . . . τοῦ τῆς αὐτόθι παροικίας θρόνου ἄξιον εἶναι

94 THE *HYPOMNEMATA* OF HEGESIPPUS

On the whole there is some ground for thinking that parts of this chapter come from Hegesippus, though we cannot attempt to determine how much may be referred to him, and how much to other sources.

It is hardly necessary to point out that whatever fragments of Hegesippus may lie buried in this chapter, they must all have come from that part of the *Memoirs* which intervened between our second and third groups of passages.

VII

Before bringing this Essay to a close it may be well to direct attention to some of the results to which our investigation has led us.

In the first place, the thesis which I undertook to maintain has, I believe, been fully established. We have rescued from the pages of Eusebius and Epiphanius a large number of fragments of the *Memoirs*, which fall into three groups, and are the remnants of two long passages. We have shown that the first of these passages [1] belonged to the fifth *Memoir*, and that the second [2] probably followed it in the same division of Hegesippus's treatise. They embrace all the known fragments from his pen dealing with the history of the Church. This goes far to prove that there were few, if any, references to Christian history in the earlier *Memoirs*, and to refute the charge often made that Hegesippus arranged his material at haphazard.

But in one or two other matters our researches have incidentally increased our knowledge. Some of the fragments included in the Appendix to this Essay are not

δοκιμάσαι. It is no doubt true that if in our passage Eusebius is quoting Hegesippus he uses φασί in a sense which is unusual with him, though not altogether without example. See above, p. 36.

[1] Appendix III, IV.   [2] Appendix V.

THE *HYPOMNEMATA* OF HEGESIPPUS

expressly cited by Eusebius or Epiphanius as from Hegesippus, and a few of them have not been generally recognized as his by modern scholars. The most important of these are perhaps the two which relate to the banishment of St. John.[1] Now evidence from the second century in regard to the date and authorship of the canonical Apocalypse is both scanty and, in some respects, difficult to interpret. But if the two passages referred to are really from Hegesippus we have his testimony that St. John the Apostle was banished to Patmos under Domitian, and resided at Ephesus under Nerva. That is to say, he must be added to the small band of early witnesses to the late date and apostolic authorship of the Apocalypse. And this is full of significance. It is not only that Hegesippus is the earliest writer who can be quoted in favour of that view. That, indeed, we may well claim for him. Clement of Alexandria, who speaks of the exile in Patmos, died no earlier than between 212 and 217;[2] Irenaeus, who affirms that ' John the disciple of the Lord '[3] resided in his later years at Ephesus, first comes into prominence in 177 when he became bishop of Lyons,[4] and was little more than a boy in 155.[5] But Hegesippus would seem to have already held a prominent position in the Church about 155, when he made his journey to Rome. He may have been only a few years younger than Papias of Hierapolis.[6] But the importance of the evidence

---

[1] Appendix IV d, e.

[2] Harnack, *Chronologie*, ii. 6.

[3] That by this phrase Irenaeus indicates the apostle is shown by J. H. Bernard in the *Irish Church Quarterly*, i. 52.

[4] *H. E.* v. 4 f.

[5] *H. E.* v. 20. 5; cp. Gwatkin, *Early Church History*, ii. 107 f.

[6] Harnack, op. cit. i. 357, dates the ἐξηγήσεις of Papias c. 145–160. Others however put his *floruit* much earlier, e. g. Sanday, *Criticism of Fourth Gospel*, p. 250 f.

supplied by Hegesippus seems to lie in another direction. A fragment attributed to Papias, which is extant in two manuscripts, contains the assertion that St. John the Apostle was put to death by Jews.[1] If this be true it disposes of the apostolic authorship of the Apocalypse.[2] And the testimony of Papias has great weight. If the apostle was martyred by Jews, he cannot have spent the closing years of his life at Ephesus. And if he lived at Ephesus, the bishop of Hierapolis cannot have been ignorant of the fact. But, on the other hand, Hegesippus, if he was not, as Eusebius supposed, a convert from Judaism,[3] was yet obviously in close touch with Palestinian Christianity. It is very difficult to believe that if St. John had suffered martyrdom in Palestine he would not have been aware of it. And if he had heard the story and gave credence to it, he could not have said that the apostle was sent to Patmos by Domitian, and lived at Ephesus under Nerva.

But of more importance for the student of Eusebius than fresh evidence on this disputed question is the light thrown by our investigation on the historian's method of quoting his authorities. Of the passages of his *History* with which we have been occupied five are of considerable length and claim to have been transcribed from the *Memoirs* of Hegesippus.[4] In no less than four of them it has been proved that the historian in copying omitted some parts of the text. It is true that in one case the omission is of

---

[1] On the question whether this statement was really made by Papias see Lightfoot, *Essays on Supernatural Religion*, p. 212 ; Harnack, op. cit. i. 665 ; Bernard, u. s., pp. 55 ff.

[2] H. B. Swete, *Apocalypse*², p. clxxx.

[3] *H. E.* iv. 22. 8.

[4] *H. E.* ii. 23. 4–18, Appendix III c–e ; *H. E.* iv. 22. 4–6, Appendix III g, h, i, 1 ; *H. E.* iii. 20. 1 f., Appendix IV f, h ; *H. E.* iii. 32. 6, Appendix IV k, l ; *H. E.* iv. 22. 2, 3, Appendix V c–f, k.

inconsiderable extent;[1] but in others the omitted portions were apparently nearly as long as those which have been preserved,[2] or even much longer;[3] and in none can we count them as of no importance. These are phenomena which cannot be confined to passages in which the direct quotation can be checked by comparison with a paraphrase in another part of the *History*, or in another writer such as Epiphanius; nor can they be limited to excerpts from a single source. It is clear that the direct quotations of Eusebius ought to be subjected to a closer scrutiny than they have yet received, with the special purpose of detecting signs of omission.

[1] Appendix IV f–h.   [2] Appendix III g–l.
[3] Appendix V c–k.

APPENDIX

THE REMAINING FRAGMENTS OF THE *HYPOMNEMATA*

Passages quoted by our authorities in the *ipsissima verba* of the texts of Hegesippus which lay before them are printed in larger type. Paraphrases of Hegesippus's language are in smaller type. Words which it has been found convenient to include, though they are not based on phrases of Hegesippus, are enclosed in square brackets. Words in columns other than the first, enclosed in angular brackets, are such as are probably derived from the genuine text of the *Memoirs*, notwithstanding the fact that they do not occur in the first column. Occasionally words are conjecturally inserted in the first column enclosed in angular brackets.

MEMOIRS I–IV

I

H. E. iv. 8. ². . οἷς κενοτάφια καὶ ναοὺς ἐποίησαν ὡς μέχρι νῦν· ὧν ἐστιν καὶ Ἀντίνοος, δοῦλος Ἀδριανοῦ Καίσαρος, οὗ καὶ ἀγὼν ἄγεται Ἀντινόειος, ὁ ἐφ' ἡμῶν γενόμενος. καὶ γὰρ πόλιν ἔκτισεν ἐπώνυμον Ἀντινόου καὶ προφήτας . . .

II

H. E. iv. 22. ⁷Ἦσαν δὲ γνῶμαι διάφοροι ἐν τῇ περιτομῇ ἐν υἱοῖς Ἰσραηλιτῶν κατὰ τῆς φυλῆς Ἰούδα καὶ τοῦ Χριστοῦ αὗται· Ἐσσαῖοι, Γαλιλαῖοι, Ἡμεροβαπτισταί, Μασβώθεοι, Σαμαρεῖται, Σαδδουκαῖοι, Φαρισαῖοι.

MEMOIR V

III

Epiph. *Haer.* 78. 7 (p. 1039 B). a. Ἔσχε δὲ οὗτος ὁ Ἰωσὴφ τὴν μὲν πρώτην αὐτοῦ γυναῖκα ἐκ τῆς φυλῆς Ἰούδα, καὶ κυίσκει αὐτῷ αὕτη παῖδας τὸν ἀριθμὸν ἕξ, τέσσαρας μὲν ἄρρενας θηλείας δὲ δύο, καθάπερ τὸ εὐαγγέλιον τὸ κατὰ Μάρκον καὶ κατὰ Ἰωάννην ἐσαφήνισαν.

Epiph. *Haer.* 78. 8 (p. 1040 A). b. Τίκτει μὲν τοῦτον τὸν Ἰάκωβον ἐγγύς που περὶ ἔτη γεγονὼς τεσσαράκοντα πλείω ἐλάσσω. μετ' αὐτὸν δὲ γίνεται παῖς Ἰωσῆ καλούμενος. εἶτα μετ' αὐτὸν Συμεών, ἔπειτα Ἰούδας, καὶ δύο θυγατέρες, ἡ Μαρία καὶ ἡ Σαλώμη καλουμένη, καὶ τέθνηκεν αὐτοῦ ἡ γυνή. καὶ μετὰ ἔτη πολλὰ λαμβάνει τὴν Μαρίαν χῆρος, κατάγων ἡλικίαν περί που ὀγδοήκοντα ἐτῶν εἰ καὶ πρώσω δὲ ἀνήρ.

| *H. E.* ii. 23. c. 'Διαδέχεται τὴν ἐκκλησίαν μετὰ τῶν ἀποστόλων ὁ ἀδελφὸς τοῦ κυρίου Ἰάκωβος, ὁ ὀνομασθεὶς ὑπὸ πάντων δίκαιος ἀπὸ τῶν τοῦ κυρίου χρόνων μέχρι καὶ ἡμῶν, ἐπεὶ πολλοὶ Ἰάκωβοι ἐκαλοῦντο, ⁵οὗτος δὲ ἐκ κοιλίας μητρὸς αὐτοῦ ἅγιος ἦν, οἶνον καὶ σίκερα οὐκ ἔπιεν, οὐδὲ | Epiph. *Haer.* 78. 7 (p. 1039 B) c. Ἔσχε μὲν οὖν (πρωτότοκον) τὸν Ἰάκωβον e. τὸν ἐπικληθέντα ὠβλίαν, ἑρμηνευόμενον τεῖχος, καὶ δίκαιον ἐπικληθέντα, c. ναζωραῖον δὲ ὄντα, ὅπερ ἑρμηνεύεται ἅγιος. καὶ πρῶτος οὗτος εἴληφε τὴν καθέδραν τῆς ἐπισκοπῆς, (ᾧ πεπί- | Epiph. 29. 4 (p. 119 B). c. ⁷Ἦν γὰρ (πρωτότοκος) τῷ Ἰωσὴφ καὶ ἡγιασμένος | Epiph. *Haer.* 78. 13 (p. 1045 B). c. Ὁ Ἰάκωβος ὁ ἀδελφὸς τοῦ κυρίου, ὃς 15' ὢν ἐτῶν τελευτᾷ, παρθένος γεγονώς· ἐφ' οὗ κεφαλῆς σίδηρος οὐκ ἀνῆλθεν, ὃς οὐκ ἐκέχρητο βαλανείῳ, ὃς ἐμψύχου οὐ μετέσχεν, ὃς χι- |

ἔμψυχον ἔφαγεν, ξυρὸν ἐπὶ τὴν κεφαλὴν αὐτοῦ οὐκ ἀνέβη, ἔλαιον οὐκ ἠλείψατο, καὶ βαλανείῳ οὐκ ἐχρήσατο . . .	στευκε κύριος τὸν θρόνον αὐτοῦ ἐπὶ τῆς γῆς πρώτῳ·) ὃς καὶ ἐκαλεῖτο ὁ ἀδελφὸς τοῦ κυρίου.		Epiph. Haer. 78. 14 p. 1046 A). c. (See below)	τάνιον δεύτερον οὐκ ἐνεδύσατο, ὡς τριβωνίῳ ἐκέχρητο λινῷ μονωτάτῳ, καθάπερ κτλ.
d. . . . ῾Τούτῳ μόνῳ ἐξῆν εἰς τὰ ἅγια ⟨τῶν ἁγίων⟩ εἰσιέναι·		d. Ἔτι δὲ καὶ (ἱερατεύσαντα) αὐτὸν κατὰ τὴν παλαιὰν ἱερωσύνην εὕρομεν. διὸ καὶ ἐφίετο αὐτῷ ἅπαξ τοῦ ἐνιαυτοῦ εἰς τὰ ἅγια ⟨τῶν ἁγίων⟩ εἰσιέναι, ὡς τοῖς ἀρχιερεῦσιν ἐκέλευσεν ὁ νόμος, κατὰ τὸ γεγραμμένον. [οὕτως γὰρ ἱστόρησαν πολλοὶ πρὸ ἡμῶν περὶ αὐτοῦ, Εὐσέβιός τε καὶ Κλήμης καὶ ἄλλοι.] ἀλλὰ ⟨καὶ τὸ πέταλον ἐπὶ τῆς κεφαλῆς ἐξῆν αὐτῷ φορεῖν.⟩[καθὼς οἱ προειρημένοι ἀξιόπιστοι ἄνδρες ἐν τοῖς αὐτοῖς ὑπομνηματισμοῖς ἐμαρτύρησαν].		d. μόνον τούτῳ τῷ Ἰακώβῳ ἐξῆν ἅπαξ εἰσιέναι τοῦ ἔτους εἰς τὰ ἅγια ⟨τῶν ἁγίων⟩, διὰ τὸ ναζωραῖον αὐτὸν εἶναι καὶ ⟨μεμίχθαι τῇ ἱερωσύνῃ.⟩
			d. Οὗτος ὁ Ἰάκωβος ⟨καὶ πέταλον ἐπὶ τῆς κεφαλῆς ἐφόρεσε·⟩	
οὐδὲ γὰρ ἐρεοῦν ἐφόρει, ἀλλὰ σινδόνας. καὶ μόνος εἰσήρχετο εἰς τὸν ναὸν ηὑρίσκετό τε κείμενος ἐπὶ τοῖς γόνασιν καὶ αἰτούμενος ὑπὲρ τοῦ λαοῦ ἄφεσιν, ὡς ἀπεσκληκέναι τὰ γόνατα αὐτοῦ δίκην καμήλου, διὰ τὸ ἀεὶ κάμπτειν ἐπὶ γόνυ προσκυνοῦντα τῷ θεῷ καὶ αἰτεῖσθαι ἄφεσιν τῷ λαῷ. . . .			⟨καὶ ποτὲ ἀβροχίας γενομένης ἐπῆρε τὰς χεῖρας εἰς οὐρανὸν καὶ προσηύξατο, καὶ εὐθὺς ὁ οὐρανὸς ἔδωκεν ὑετόν.⟩ ἐρεοῦν δὲ ἱμάτιον οὐδέποτε ἐνεδύσατο. τὰ δὲ γόνατα αὐτοῦ ἐσκληκίασαν δίκην καμήλων, ἀπὸ τοῦ πάντοτε κάμπτειν αὐτὰ ἐνώπιον κυρίου e. δι' ὑπερβολὴν ⟨εὐλαβείας.⟩ c. τοῦτον οὖν ὀνόματι οὐκέτι ἐκάλουν, ἀλλ' ὁ δίκαιος ἦν αὐτῷ ὄνομα. οὗτος οὐδέποτε ἐν βαλανείῳ ἐλούσατο· οὗτος ἐμψύχου οὐ μετέσχε, [καθὼς ἄνω μοι προδεδήλωται]· ⟨οὗτος σανδάλιον οὐχ ὑπεδήσατο⟩.	

Θ. ⁷Διά γέ τοι τὴν ὑπερβολὴν τῆς δικαιοσύνης αὐτοῦ ἐκαλεῖτο ὁ δίκαιος καὶ ὠβλίας, ὅ ἐστιν ἑλληνιστὶ περιοχὴ τοῦ λαοῦ, καὶ δικαιοσύνη, ὡς οἱ προφῆται δηλοῦσιν περὶ αὐτοῦ.[a] ⁸ τινὲς οὖν τῶν ἑπτὰ αἱρέσεων τῶν ἐν τῷ λαῷ, τῶν προγεγραμμένων μοι ἐν τοῖς ὑπομνήμασιν, ἐπυνθάνοντο αὐτοῦ τίς ἡ θύρα τοῦ Ἰησοῦ, καὶ ἔλεγεν τοῦτον εἶναι τὸν σωτῆρα· ⁹ ἐξ ὧν τινες ἐπίστευσαν ὅτι Ἰησοῦς ἐστιν ὁ Χριστός. αἱ δὲ αἱρέσεις αἱ προειρημέναι οὐκ ἐπίστευον οὔτε ἀνάστασιν οὔτε ἐρχόμενον ἀποδοῦναι ἑκάστῳ κατὰ τὰ ἔργα αὐτοῦ· ὅσοι δὲ καὶ ἐπίστευσαν, διὰ Ἰάκωβον. ¹⁰ πολλῶν οὖν καὶ τῶν ἀρχόντων πιστευόντων, ἦν θόρυβος τῶν Ἰουδαίων καὶ γραμματέων καὶ Φαρισαίων λεγόντων ὅτι κινδυνεύει πᾶς ὁ λαὸς Ἰησοῦν τὸν Χριστὸν προσδοκᾶν. ἔλεγον οὖν συνελθόντες τῷ Ἰακώβῳ· Παρακαλοῦμέν σε, ἐπίσχες τὸν λαόν, ἐπεὶ ἐπλανήθη εἰς Ἰησοῦν, ὡς αὐτοῦ ὄντος τοῦ Χριστοῦ. παρακαλοῦμέν σε πεῖσαι πάντας τοὺς ἐλθόντας εἰς τὴν ἡμέραν τοῦ πάσχα περὶ Ἰησοῦ· σοὶ γὰρ πάντες πειθόμεθα· ἡμεῖς γὰρ μαρτυροῦμέν σοι καὶ πᾶς ὁ λαὸς ὅτι δίκαιος εἶ καὶ ὅτι πρόσωπον οὐ λαμβάνεις. ¹¹ πεῖσον οὖν σὺ τὸν ὄχλον περὶ Ἰησοῦ μὴ πλανᾶσθαι· καὶ γὰρ πᾶς ὁ λαὸς καὶ πάντες πειθόμεθά σοι. στῆθι οὖν ἐπὶ τὸ πτερύγιον τοῦ ἱεροῦ, ἵνα ἄνωθεν ᾖς ἐπιφανὴς καὶ ᾖ εὐάκουστά σου τὰ ῥήματα παντὶ τῷ λαῷ. διὰ γὰρ τὸ πάσχα συνεληλύθασι πᾶσαι αἱ φυλαὶ μετὰ καὶ τῶν ἐθνῶν. ¹² ἔστησαν οὖν οἱ προειρημένοι γραμματεῖς καὶ Φαρισαῖοι τὸν Ἰάκωβον ἐπὶ τὸ πτερύγιον τοῦ ναοῦ, καὶ ἔκραξαν αὐτῷ καὶ εἶπαν, Δίκαιε, ᾧ πάντες πείθεσθαι ὀφείλομεν, ἐπεὶ ὁ λαὸς πλανᾶται ὀπίσω Ἰησοῦ τοῦ σταυρωθέντος, ἀπάγγειλον ἡμῖν τίς ἡ θύρα τοῦ Ἰησοῦ. ¹³ καὶ ἀπεκρίνατο φωνῇ μεγάλῃ, Τί με ἐπερωτᾶτε περὶ τοῦ υἱοῦ τοῦ ἀνθρώπου, καὶ αὐτὸς κάθηται ἐν τῷ οὐρανῷ ἐκ δεξιῶν τῆς μεγάλης δυνάμεως, καὶ μέλλει ἔρχεσθαι ἐπὶ τῶν νεφελῶν τοῦ οὐρανοῦ; ¹⁴ καὶ πολλῶν πληροφορηθέντων καὶ δοξαζόντων ἐπὶ τῇ μαρτυρίᾳ τοῦ Ἰακώβου καὶ λεγόντων Ὡσαννὰ τῷ υἱῷ Δαυίδ, τότε πάλιν οἱ αὐτοὶ γραμματεῖς καὶ Φαρισαῖοι πρὸς ἀλλήλους ἔλεγον, Κακῶς ἐποιήσαμεν τοιαύτην μαρτυρίαν παρασχόντες τῷ Ἰησοῦ· ἀλλὰ ἀναβάντες καταβάλωμεν αὐτόν, ἵνα φοβηθέντες μὴ πιστεύσωσιν αὐτῷ. ¹⁵ καὶ ἔκραξαν λέγοντες, Ὢ ὤ, καὶ ὁ δίκαιος ἐπλανήθη, καὶ ἐπλήρωσαν τὴν γραφὴν τὴν ἐν τῷ Ἡσαΐᾳ γεγραμμένην, Ἄρωμεν τὸν δίκαιον, ὅτι δύσχρηστος ἡμῖν ἐστιν· τοίνυν τὰ γενήματα τῶν ἔργων αὐτῶν φάγονται. ¹⁶ ἀναβάντες οὖν κατέβαλον τὸν δίκαιον. καὶ ἔλεγον ἀλλήλοις, Λιθάσωμεν Ἰάκωβον τὸν δίκαιον, καὶ ἤρξαντο λιθάζειν αὐτόν, ἐπεὶ καταβληθεὶς οὐκ ἀπέθανεν· ἀλλὰ στραφεὶς ἔθηκε τὰ γόνατα λέγων, Παρακαλῶ, Κύριε Θεὲ Πάτερ, ἄφες αὐτοῖς· οὐ γὰρ οἴδασιν τί ποιοῦσιν· ¹⁷ οὕτως δὲ καταλιθοβολούντων αὐτόν, εἷς τῶν ἱερέων τῶν υἱῶν Ῥηχὰβ υἱοῦ Ῥαχαβείμ, τῶν μαρτυρουμένων ὑπὸ

Epiph. Haer. 78. 14 (p. 1046 D). Θ. Τελευτᾷ δὲ οὗτος ὁ Ἰάκωβος ὁ ἀδελφὸς τοῦ κυρίου καὶ υἱὸς Ἰωσὴφ ἐν Ἱεροσολύμοις, βιώσας μετὰ τὴν τοῦ σωτῆρος ἀνάληψιν ἔτεσιν εἰκοσιτέσσαρσι, πλείω ἐλάσσω, ὢν ἐτῶν ϛς´, ὑπὸ τοῦ γναφέως τῷ ξύλῳ παισθεὶς τὴν κεφαλήν, ῥιφεὶς ἀπὸ τοῦ πτερυγίου τοῦ ἱεροῦ, καὶ κατελθὼν καὶ μηδὲν

---

[a] The text of this fragment seems to be corrupt. For an attempt to reconstruct it see above, p. 7.

THE ΗΥΡΟΜΝΕΜΑΤΑ OF HEGESIPPUS 101

Ἰερεμίου τοῦ προφήτου, ἔκραζεν λέγων, Παύσασθε· τί ποιεῖτε; εὔχεται ὑπὲρ ὑμῶν ὁ δίκαιος. ¹ˣκαὶ λαβών τις ἀπ᾽ αὐτῶν, εἷς τῶν γναφέων, τὸ ξύλον ἐν ᾧ ἀποπιέζει τὰ ἱμάτια, ἤνεγκεν κατὰ τῆς κεφαλῆς τοῦ δικαίου, καὶ οὕτως ἐμαρτύρησεν. καὶ ἔθαψαν αὐτὸν ἐπὶ τῷ τόπῳ παρὰ τῷ ναῷ, καὶ ἔτι αὐτοῦ ἡ στήλη μένει παρὰ τῷ ναῷ. μάρτυς οὗτος ἀληθὴς Ἰουδαίοις τε καὶ Ἕλλησιν γεγένηται ὅτι Ἰησοῦς ὁ Χριστός ἐστιν. καὶ εὐθὺς Οὐεσπασιανὸς πολιορκεῖ αὐτούς.

ἀδικηθείς, κλίνας δὲ τὰ γόνατα καὶ προσευξάμενος ὑπὲρ τῶν αὐτὸν ῥιψάντων, καὶ φάσκων Συγχώρησον αὐτοῖς· οὐ γὰρ οἴδασι τί ποιοῦσιν, ὡς καὶ Συμεὼν πόρρω ἑστώς, ὁ τούτου ἀνεψιός, υἱὸς δὲ τοῦ Κλωπᾶ, ἔλεγε, Παύσασθε, τί λιθάζετε τὸν δίκαιον; καὶ ἰδού, εὔχεται ὑπὲρ ὑμῶν τὰ κάλλιστα. καὶ οὕτως γέγονε τὸ αὐτοῦ μαρτύριον.

H. E. iii. 5. f. ²Μετά γε μὴν τὴν τοῦ σωτῆρος ἡμῶν ἀνάληψιν Ἰουδαίων πρὸς τῷ κατ᾽ αὐτοῦ τολμήματι ἤδη καὶ κατὰ τῶν ἀποστόλων αὐτοῦ πλείστας ὅσας ἐπιβουλὰς μεμηχανημένων, πρώτου τε Στεφάνου λίθοις ὑπ᾽ αὐτῶν ἀνῃρημένου, εἶτα δὲ μετ᾽ αὐτὸν Ἰακώβου, ὃς ἦν Ζεβεδαίου μὲν παῖς, ἀδελφὸς δὲ Ἰωάννου, τὴν κεφαλὴν ἀποτμηθέντος, ἐπὶ πᾶσί τε Ἰακώβου, τοῦ τὸν αὐτόθι τῆς ἐπισκοπῆς θρόνον πρῶτον μετὰ τὴν τοῦ σωτῆρος ἡμῶν ἀνάληψιν κεκληρωμένου, τὸν προδηλωθέντα τρόπον μεταλλάξαντος, τῶν τε λοιπῶν ἀποστόλων μυρία εἰς θάνατον ἐπιβεβουλευμένων καὶ τῆς μὲν Ἰουδαίας γῆς ἀπεληλαμένων, ἐπὶ δὲ τῇ τοῦ κηρύγματος διδασκαλίᾳ τὴν εἰς σύμπαντα τὰ ἔθνη στειλαμένων πορείαν σὺν δυνάμει τοῦ Χριστοῦ φήσαντος αὐτοῖς, Πορευθέντες μαθητεύσατε πάντα τὰ ἔθνη ἐν τῷ ὀνόματί μου, ³οὐ μὴν ἀλλὰ καὶ τοῦ λαοῦ τῆς ἐν Ἱεροσολύμοις ἐκκλησίας κατά τινα χρησμὸν τοῖς αὐτόθι δοκίμοις δι᾽ ἀποκαλύψεως ἐκδοθέντα πρὸ τοῦ πολέμου μεταναστῆναι τῆς πόλεως καί τινα τῆς Περαίας πόλιν οἰκεῖν κεκελευσμένον, Πέλλαν αὐτὴν ὀνομάζουσιν, ἐν ᾗ ᵃ τῶν εἰς Χριστὸν πεπιστευ-

Epiph. *Haer.* 29. 7 (p. 123 B). f. Ἐκεῖθεν γὰρ ἡ ἀρχὴ γέγονε μετὰ τὴν ἀπὸ τῶν Ἱεροσολύμων μετάστασιν, (πάντων) τῶν ἀποστόλων ᵇ τῶν ἐν Πέλλῃ ᾠκηκότων, Χριστοῦ φήσαντος

Epiph. *Haer.* 30. 2 (p. 126 C). f. Γέγονε δὲ ἡ ἀρχὴ τούτου ⟨μετὰ τὴν τῶν Ἱεροσολύμων ἅλωσιν⟩. ἐπειδὴ γὰρ ⟨πάντες⟩ οἱ εἰς Χριστὸν πεπιστευκότες τὴν Περαίαν κατ᾽ ἐκεῖνο καιροῦ κατῴ-

Epiph. *De Mens.* 15. (P. de Lagarde, *Symmicta*, ii. 167) f. ¹[Ὁ τοίνυν Ἀκύλας διάγων ἐν τῇ Ἱερουσαλὴμ καὶ ὁρῶν τοὺς μαθητὰς τῶν μαθητῶν τῶν ἀποστόλων κτλ.]—²ἦσαν γὰρ ὑποστρέψαντες ἀπὸ Πέλλης τῆς πόλεως εἰς Ἱερουσαλὴμ καὶ ἐν αὐτῇ διαιτώμενοι καὶ διδάσκοντες. ³ἡνίκα γὰρ ⟨ἔμελλεν⟩ ἡ πόλις ἁλίσκεσθαι ὑπὸ τῶν Ῥωμαίων καὶ ἐρημοῦσθαι, προεχρηματίσθησαν ὑπὸ ἀγγέλου ⟨πάντες

ᵃ The words ἐν ᾗ are bracketed by Schwartz.
ᵇ The reading μαθητῶν is perhaps to be preferred. See above, p. 28, note ⁴.

κύτων ἀπὸ τῆς Ἱερουσαλὴμ μετῳκισμένων, ὡς ἂν παντελῶς ἐπιλελοιπότων ἁγίων ἀνδρῶν αὐτήν τε τὴν Ἰουδαίων βασιλικὴν μητρόπολιν καὶ σύμπασαν τὴν Ἰουδαίαν γῆν, ἡ ἐκ Θεοῦ δίκη λοιπὸν αὐτοὺς ἅτε τοσαῦτα εἴς τε τὸν Χριστὸν καὶ τοὺς ἀποστόλους αὐτοῦ παρηνομηκότας μετῄει, τῶν ἀσεβῶν ἄρδην τὴν γενεὰν αὐτὴν ἐκείνην ἐξ ἀνθρώπων ἀφανίζουσα.

καταλεῖψαι τὰ Ἱεροσόλυμα καὶ ἀναχωρῆσαι δι' ἣν ⟨ἤμελλε⟩ πάσχειν πολιορκίαν. καὶ ἐκ τῆς τοιαύτης ὑποθέσεως τὴν Περαίαν οἰκήσαντες ἐκεῖσε, ὡς ἔφην, ⟨διέτριβον⟩.

κησαν τὸ πλεῖστον, ἐν Πέλλῃ τινὶ πόλει καλουμένῃ ⟨τῆς Δεκαπόλεως⟩ τῆς ἐν τῷ εὐαγγελίῳ γεγραμμένης, πλησίον τῆς Βαταναίας καὶ Βασανίτιδος χώρας, τὸ τηνικαῦτα ἐκεῖ μεταναστάντων καὶ ἐκεῖσε ⟨διατριβόντων⟩ αὐτῶν, γέγονεν ἐκ τούτου πρόφασις τῷ Ἐβίωνι.

οἱ μαθηταὶ⟩ μεταστῆναι ἀπὸ τῆς πόλεως, ⟨μελλούσης⟩ ἄρδην ἀπόλλυσθαι. οἵτινες μετανάσται γενόμενοι ᾤκησαν ἐν Πέλλῃ τῇ προγεγραμμένῃ πόλει πέραν τοῦ Ἰορδάνου. [4] ἡ δὲ πόλις (ἐκ Δεκαπόλεως) λέγεται εἶναι. [5] μετὰ δὲ τὴν ἐρήμωσιν Ἱερουσαλὴμ ἐπαναστρέψαντες (ὡς ἔφην) σημεῖα μεγάλα ἐπετέλουν— [6] [ὁ οὖν Ἀκύλας κτλ.]

H. E. iv. 22. g. [4] Καὶ μετὰ τὸ μαρτυρῆσαι Ἰάκωβον τὸν δίκαιον, ὡς καὶ ὁ κύριος, ἐπὶ τῷ αὐτῷ λόγῳ ... h. πάλιν. ...

i. ὁ ἐκ θείου αὐτοῦ Συμεὼν ὁ τοῦ Κλωπᾶ καθίσταται ἐπίσκοπος, ὃν προέθεντο πάντες, ὄντα ἀνεψιὸν τοῦ κυρίου, δεύτερον.
Epiph. *Haer.* 78. 7 (p. 1039 A).
j. Κατὰ δὲ τὴν ἀκολουθίαν ἐκ τῆς τῶν Ἰουδαίων παραδόσεως [δείκνυται ὡς οὐχ ἕνεκεν τοῦ ζευχθῆναι αὐτῷ (sc. τῷ Ἰωσὴφ) παρεδίδοτο αὐτῷ ἡ παρθένος (sc. Μαρία), κτλ. πῶς γὰρ ἠδύνατο ὁ τοσοῦτος γέρων παρθένον ἕξειν γυναῖκα, ὧν ἀπὸ πρώτης γυναικὸς χῆρος τοσαῦτα ἔτη]; οὗτος μὲν γὰρ ὁ Ἰωσὴφ ἀδελφὸς γίνεται τοῦ Κλωπᾶ, ἦν δὲ υἱὸς τοῦ Ἰακώβ, ἐπίκλην δὲ Πάνθηρ καλουμένου. ἀμφότεροι οὗτοι ἀπὸ τοῦ Πάνθηρος ἐπίκλην γεννῶνται.

H. E. iii. 11. g. Μετὰ τὴν Ἰακώβου μαρτυρίαν ⟨καὶ τὴν αὐτίκα γενομένην ἅλωσιν τῆς Ἱερουσαλὴμ⟩ [λόγος κατέχει] h. ⟨τῶν ἀποστόλων καὶ τῶν τοῦ κυρίου μαθητῶν τοὺς εἰσέτι τῷ βίῳ λειπομένους ἐπὶ ταὐτὸν πανταχόθεν συνελθεῖν ἅμα τοῖς πρὸς γένους κατὰ σάρκα τοῦ κυρίου (πλείοις γὰρ καὶ τούτων περιῆσαν εἰσέτι τότε τῷ βίῳ), βουλήν τε ὁμοῦ τοὺς πάντας περὶ τοῦ τίνα χρὴ τῆς Ἰακώβου διαδοχῆς ἐπικρῖναι ἄξιον, ποιήσασθαι,⟩ i. καὶ δὴ ἀπὸ μιᾶς γνώμης τοὺς πάντας Συμεῶνα τὸν τοῦ Κλωπᾶ, οὗ καὶ ἡ τοῦ εὐαγγελίου μνημονεύει γραφή, τοῦ τῆς αὐτόθι παροικίας θρόνου ἄξιον εἶναι δοκιμάσαι, ἀνεψιόν, ὥς γέ φασι, γεγονότα τοῦ σωτῆρος.

j. τὸν γὰρ οὖν Κλωπᾶν ἀδελφὸν τοῦ Ἰωσὴφ ὑπάρχειν [Ἡγήσιππος ἱστορεῖ].

H. E. iii. 32. k. [¹[Ἐπὶ τούτοις ὁ αὐτὸς ἀνὴρ διηγούμενος τὰ κατὰ τοὺς δηλουμένους (sc. Τραϊανὸν κτλ.) ἐπιλέγει ὡς ἄρα] μέχρι τῶν τότε χρόνων παρθένος καθαρὰ καὶ ἀδιάφθορος ἔμεινεν ἡ ἐκκλησία, ἐν ἀδήλῳ που σκότει ὡς εἰ φωλευόντων εἰσέτι τότε τῶν, εἰ καί τινες ὑπῆρχον, παραφθείρειν ἐπιχειρούντων τὸν ὑγιῆ κανόνα τοῦ σωτηρίου κηρύγματος.

H. E. iv. 22. 1. 'Διὰ τοῦτο ἐκάλουν τὴν ἐκκλησίαν παρθένον, οὔπω γὰρ ἔφθαρτο ἀκοαῖς ματαίαις· ³ἄρχεται δὲ ὁ Θέβουθις διὰ τὸ μὴ γενέσθαι αὐτὸν ἐπίσκοπον ὑποφθείρειν ἀπὸ τῶν ἑπτὰ αἱρέσεων, ὧν καὶ αὐτὸς ἦν, ἐν τῷ λαῷ, ἀφ' ὧν Σίμων, ὅθεν Σιμωνιανοί, καὶ Κλεόβιος, ὅθεν Κλεοβιηνοί, καὶ Δοσίθεος, ὅθεν Δοσιθιανοί, καὶ Γορθαῖος, ὅθεν Γοραθηνοί, καὶ Μασβώθεοι. ἀπὸ τούτων Μενανδριανισταὶ καὶ Μαρκιανισταὶ καὶ Καρποκρατιανοὶ καὶ Οὐαλεντινιανοὶ καὶ Βασιλειδιανοὶ καὶ Σατορνιλιανοὶ ἕκαστος ἰδίως καὶ ἑτεροίως ἰδίαν δόξαν παρεισηγάγοσαν. ⁶ ἀπὸ τούτων ψευδόχριστοι, ψευδοπροφῆται, ψευδαπόστολοι, οἵτινες ἐμέρισαν τὴν ἕνωσιν τῆς ἐκκλησίας φθοριμαίοις λόγοις κατὰ τοῦ Θεοῦ καὶ κατὰ τοῦ Χριστοῦ αὐτοῦ.

H. E. iii. 32. 1. ²[Καὶ τούτου μάρτυς αὐτὸς ἐκεῖνος, οὗ διαφόροις ἤδη πρότερον ἐχρησάμεθα φωναῖς, ‘Ηγήσιππος· ὃς δὴ] περί τινων αἱρετικῶν ἱστορῶν,

H. E. iii. 32. m. ³ἀπὸ τούτων [δηλαδὴ τῶν αἱρετικῶν] κατηγοροῦσί τινες Σίμωνος τοῦ Κλωπᾶ ὡς ὄντος ἀπὸ Δαυὶδ καὶ Χριστιανοῦ, καὶ οὕτως μαρτυρεῖ ἐτῶν ὢν ἑκατὸν εἴκοσιν ἐπὶ Τραϊανοῦ Καίσαρος καὶ ὑπατικοῦ Ἀττικοῦ.

m. [ἐπιφέρει δηλῶν ὡς ἄρα] ὑπὸ τούτων κατὰ τόνδε τὸν χρόνον ὑπομείνας κατηγορίαν, πολυτρόπως ὁ δηλούμενος ὡς ἂν Χριστιανὸς κτλ.

IV

H. E. iii. 12. a. [Καὶ ἐπὶ τούτοις (sc. Ἡγήσιππος ἱστορεῖ] Οὐεσπασιανὸν μετὰ τὴν τῶν Ἱεροσολύμων ἅλωσιν πάντας τοὺς ἀπὸ γένους Δαυίδ, ὡς μὴ περιλειφθείη τις παρὰ Ἰουδαίοις τῶν ἀπὸ τῆς βασιλικῆς φυλῆς, ἀναζητεῖσθαι προστάξαι, μέγιστόν τε Ἰουδαίοις αὖθις ἐκ ταύτης διωγμὸν ἐπαρτηθῆναι τῆς αἰτίας.

H. E. iii. 17. b. Πολλήν γε μὴν εἰς πολλοὺς ἐπιδειξάμενος ὁ Δομετιανὸς ὠμότητα οὐκ ὀλίγον τε τῶν ἐπὶ Ῥώμης εὐπατριδῶν τε καὶ ἐπισήμων ἀνδρῶν πλῆθος οὐ μετ' εὐλόγου κρίσεως κτείνας μυρίους τε ἄλλους ἐπιφανεῖς ἄνδρας ταῖς ὑπὲρ τὴν ἐνορίαν ζημιώσας φυγαῖς καὶ ταῖς τῶν οὐσιῶν ἀποβολαῖς ἀναιτίους, τελευτῶν τῆς Νέρωνος θεοεχθρίας τε καὶ θεομαχίας διάδοχον ἑαυτὸν κατεστήσατο. δεύτερος δῆτα τὸν καθ' ἡμῶν ἀνεκίνει διωγμόν, καίπερ τοῦ πατρὸς αὐτῷ Οὐεσπασιανοῦ μηδὲν καθ' ἡμῶν ἄτοπον ἐπινοήσαντος.

Cramer and de Boor, *u. s.* b. Δομετιανὸς υἱὸς Οὐεσπασιανοῦ πολλὰ κακὰ εἰς τοὺς ἐν τέλει Ῥωμαίων ἐνδειξάμενος

τὴν Νέρωνος νικήσας ὠμότητα δεύτερος κατὰ Χριστιανῶν διωγμὸν ἐποίησεν.

104 THE ΥΠΟΜΝΗΜΑΤΑ OF HEGESIPPUS

H. E. iii. 19. c. Τοῦ δ' αὐτοῦ Δομετιανοῦ τοὺς ἀπὸ γένους Δαυὶδ ἀναιρεῖσθαι προστάξαντος, [παλαιὸς κατέχει λόγος] κτλ.

H. E. iii. 18. d. [1] Ἐν τούτῳ [κατέχει λόγος] τὸν ἀπόστολον ἅμα καὶ εὐαγγελιστὴν Ἰωάννην ἔτι τῷ βίῳ ἐνδιατρίβοντα, τῆς εἰς τὸν θεῖον λόγον ἕνεκεν μαρτυρίας Πάτμον οἰκεῖν καταδικασθῆναι τὴν νῆσον.

Cramer and de Boor, u. s. d. Καθ' ὃν καὶ τὸν ἀπόστολον καὶ εὐαγγελιστὴν Ἰωάννην ἐν Πάτμῳ περιώρισεν.

H. E. iii. 20. e. [9] Τότε (sc. Νερούα τὴν ἀρχὴν διαδεξαμένου) δὴ οὖν καὶ τὸν ἀπόστολον Ἰωάννην ἀπὸ τῆς κατὰ τὴν νῆσον φυγῆς τὴν ἐπὶ τῆς Ἐφέσου διατριβὴν ἀπειληφέναι [ὁ τῶν παρ' ἡμῖν ἀρχαίων παραδίδωσι λόγος].

H. E. iii. 20. f. [1] Ἔτι δὲ περιῆσαν οἱ ἀπὸ γένους τοῦ κυρίου υἱωνοὶ Ἰούδα τοῦ κατὰ σάρκα λεγομένου αὐτοῦ ἀδελφοῦ· οὓς ⟨τῶν αἱρέσεών τινες⟩[a] ἐδηλατόρευσαν ὡς ἐκ γένους ὄντας Δαυίδ.

H. E. iii. 19. f. [Παλαιὸς κατέχει λόγος] ⟨τῶν αἱρετικῶν τινας⟩ κατηγορῆσαι τῶν ἀπογόνων Ἰούδα ⟨τοῦτον δ' εἶναι ἀδελφὸν κατὰ σάρκα τοῦ σωτῆρος⟩ ὡς ἀπὸ γένους τυγχανόντων Δαυὶδ καὶ ὡς αὐτοῦ συγγένειαν τοῦ Χριστοῦ φερόντων. [ταῦτα δὲ δηλοῖ κατὰ λέξιν ὧδέ πως λέγων ὁ Ἡγήσιππος.]

Cramer and de Boor, u. s. g. Ὁ μὲν ἐκαλεῖτο Ζωκήρ, ὁ δὲ Ἰάκωβος.

H. E. iii. 20. h. [1] τούτους ὁ ἠουοκᾶτος ἤγαγε πρὸς Δομετιανὸν Καίσαρα. ἐφοβεῖτο γὰρ τὴν παρουσίαν τοῦ Χριστοῦ ὡς καὶ Ἡρώδης. [2] καὶ ἐπηρώτησεν αὐτοὺς εἰ ἐκ Δαυίδ εἰσιν, καὶ ὡμολόγησαν. τότε ἠρώτησεν αὐτοὺς πόσας κτήσεις ἔχουσιν ἢ πόσων χρημάτων κυριεύουσιν. οἱ δὲ εἶπαν ἀμφότεροις ἐννακισχίλια δηνάρια ὑπάρχειν αὐτοῖς μόνα, ἑκάστῳ αὐτῶν ἀνήκοντος τοῦ ἡμίσεος, καὶ ταῦτα οὐκ ἐν ἀργυρίοις ἔφασκον ἔχειν, ἀλλ' ἐν διατιμήσει γῆς πλέθρων τριάκοντα ἐννέα μόνων, ἐξ ὧν καὶ τοὺς φόρους ἀναφέρειν καὶ αὐτοὺς αὐτουργοῦντας διατρέφεσθαι.

Cramer and de Boor, u. s. h. συντυχὼν δὲ Δομετιανὸς τοῖς υἱοῖς Ἰούδα τοῦ ἀδελφοῦ τοῦ κυρίου,

i. [3] Εἶτα δὲ καὶ τὰς χεῖρας τὰς ἑαυτῶν ἐπιδεικνύναι, μαρτύριον τῆς αὐτουργίας τὴν τοῦ σώματος σκληρίαν καὶ τοὺς ἀπὸ τῆς συνεχοῦς ἐργασίας ἐναποτυπωθέντας ἐπὶ τῶν ἰδίων χειρῶν τύλους παριστάντας. [4] ἐρωτηθέντας δὲ περὶ τοῦ Χριστοῦ καὶ τῆς βασιλείας αὐτοῦ,

i. καὶ γνοὺς ⟨τὴν ἀρετὴν⟩ τῶν ἀνδρῶν

[a] That some such words as these are to be supplied is suggested by the paraphrase in *H. E.* iii. 19. For the form see above, III e, § 8.

ὁποία τις εἴη καὶ ποῖ καὶ πότε φανησομένη, λόγον δοῦναι ὡς οὐ κοσμικὴ μὲν οὐδ' ἐπίγειος, ἐπουράνιος δὲ καὶ ἀγγελικὴ τυγχάνοι, ἐπὶ συντελείᾳ τοῦ αἰῶνος γενησομένη, ὁπηνίκα ἐλθὼν ἐν δόξῃ κρινεῖ ζῶντας καὶ νεκροὺς καὶ ἀποδώσει ἑκάστῳ κατὰ τὰ ἐπιτηδεύματα αὐτοῦ· [b] ἐφ' οἷς μηδὲν αὐτῶν κατεγνωκότα τὸν Δομετιανόν, ἀλλὰ καὶ ὡς εὐτελῶν καταφρονήσαντα, ἐλευθέρους μὲν αὐτοὺς ἀνεῖναι, καταπαῦσαι δὲ διὰ προστάγματος τὸν κατὰ τῆς ἐκκλησίας διωγμόν.

τοῦ καθ' ἡμῶν ἐπαύσατο διωγμοῦ.

H. E. iii. 32. k. [c] Ἔρχονται οὖν καὶ προηγοῦνται πάσης ἐκκλησίας ὡς μάρτυρες καὶ ἀπὸ γένους τοῦ κυρίου, καὶ γενομένης εἰρήνης βαθείας ἐν πάσῃ ἐκκλησίᾳ, μένουσι μέχρι Τραϊανοῦ Καίσαρος, l. μέχρις οὗ ὁ ἐκ θείου τοῦ κυρίου, ὁ προειρημένος Σίμων υἱὸς Κλωπᾶ, συκοφαντηθεὶς ὑπὸ τῶν αἱρέσεων, ὡσαύτως κατηγορήθη καὶ αὐτὸς ἐπὶ τῷ αὐτῷ λόγῳ ἐπὶ Ἀττικοῦ τοῦ ὑπατικοῦ. καὶ ἐπὶ πολλαῖς ἡμέραις αἰκιζόμενος ἐμαρτύρησεν, ὡς πάντας ὑπερθαυμάζειν καὶ τὸν ὑπατικὸν πῶς ἑκατὸν εἴκοσι τυγχάνων ἐτῶν ὑπέμεινεν, καὶ ἐκελεύσθη σταυρωθῆναι.

H. E. iii. 20. k. [c] Τοὺς δὲ ἀπολυθέντας ἡγήσασθαι τῶν ἐκκλησιῶν, ὡς ἂν δὴ μάρτυρας ὁμοῦ καὶ ἀπὸ γένους ὄντας τοῦ κυρίου, γενομένης τε εἰρήνης μέχρι Τραϊανοῦ παραμεῖναι αὐτοὺς τῷ βίῳ. [7] [Ταῦτα μὲν ὁ Ἡγήσιππος.]

H. E. iii. 32. 1. [2] Ἐπὶ πλείσταις αἰκισθεὶς ἡμέραις αὐτόν τε τὸν δικαστὴν καὶ τοὺς ἀμφ' αὐτὸν εἰς τὰ μέγιστα καταπλήξας, τῷ τοῦ κυρίου πάθει παραπλήσιον τέλος ἀπηνέγκατο.

H. E. iii. 32. m. [4] [Φησὶν δὲ ὁ αὐτὸς ὡς ἄρα] καὶ τοὺς κατηγόρους αὐτοῦ, ζητουμένων τότε τῶν ἀπὸ τῆς βασιλικῆς Ἰουδαίων φυλῆς, ὡς ἂν ἐξ αὐτῶν ὄντας ἁλῶναι συνέβη.

V

H. E. iii. 16. a. Ὅτι γε κατὰ τὸν δηλούμενον (sc. Δομετιανὸν) τὰ τῆς Κορινθίων κεκίνητο στάσεως, [ἀξιόχρεως μάρτυς ὁ Ἡγήσιππος].

H. E. iv. 22. b. [1] [Ἀκοῦσαί γέ τοι πάρεστιν μετά] τινα περὶ τῆς Κλήμεντος πρὸς Κορινθίους ἐπιστολῆς [αὐτῷ εἰρημένα ἐπιλέγοντος ταῦτα].

Epiph. Haer. 27. 6 (p. 107 B). b. Λέγει γὰρ ἐν μιᾷ τῶν ἐπιστολῶν αὐτοῦ,

⟨Ἀναχωρῶ, ἄπειμι, εὐσταθείτω ὁ λαὸς τοῦ θεοῦ,⟩ τισὶ τοῦτο συμβουλεύων· [ηὕρομεν γὰρ ἔν τισιν ὑπομνηματισμοῖς τοῦτο ἐγκείμενον].

H. E. iv. 22. c. [2] Καὶ ἐπέμενεν ἡ ἐκκλησία ἡ Κορινθίων ἐν τῷ ὀρθῷ λόγῳ μέχρι Πρίμου ἐπισκοπεύοντος ἐν Κορίνθῳ.

THE ΥΠΟΜΝΕΜΑΤΑ OF HEGESIPPUS

II. E. iv. 22. d. ... ² οἷς συνέμιξα πλέων εἰς Ῥώμην.

H. E. iv. 22. d. ¹ [Ὁ μὲν οὖν Ἡγήσιππος ἐν πέντε τοῖς εἰς ἡμᾶς ἐλθοῦσιν ὑπομνήμασιν τῆς ἰδίας γνώμης πληρεστάτην μνήμην καταλέλοιπεν· ἐν οἷς δηλοῖ ὡς] πλείστοις ἐπισκόποις συμμίξειεν ἀποδημίαν στειλάμενος μέχρι Ῥώμης.

H. E. iv. 22. e. ² Καὶ συνδιέτριψα τοῖς Κορινθίοις ἡμέρας ἱκανάς, ἐν αἷς συνανεπάημεν τῷ ὀρθῷ λόγῳ.

H. E. iv. 22. f. ³ Γενόμενος δὲ ἐν Ῥώμῃ, διαδοχὴν ἐποιησάμην μέχρις Ἀνικήτου· οὗ διάκονος ἦν Ἐλεύθερος, καὶ παρὰ Ἀνικήτου διαδέχεται Σωτήρ, μεθ' ὃν Ἐλεύθερος.

H. E. iv. 11. f. ⁷ Καθ' ὃν (sc. Ἀνίκητον) [Ἡγήσιππος ἱστορεῖ] ἑαυτὸν ἐπιδημῆσαι τῇ Ῥώμῃ παραμεῖναί τε αὐτόθι μέχρι τῆς ἐπισκοπῆς Ἐλευθέρου.

Epiph. *Haer.* 27. 6 (p. 107 A). g. Ἐν Ῥώμῃ γὰρ γεγόνασι πρῶτοι Πέτρος καὶ Παῦλος ἀπόστολοι καὶ ἐπίσκοποι, εἶτα Λίνος, εἶτα Κλῆτος,

Epiph. *Haer.* 27. 6 (p. 107 C). g. Μετὰ τὸ τετελευτηκέναι Λίνον καὶ Κλῆτον ⟨ἐπισκοπεύσαντας πρὸς δεκαδύο ἔτη ἕκαστον⟩ μετὰ τὴν τοῦ ἁγίου Πέτρου καὶ Παύλου τελευτήν, τὴν ἐπὶ τῷ δωδεκάτῳ ἔτει Νέρωνος γενομένην κτλ.

Epiph. *Haer.* 27. 6 (p. 107 D). g. Ὅμως ἡ τῶν ἐν Ῥώμῃ ἐπισκόπων διαδοχὴ ταύτην ἔχει τὴν ἀκολουθίαν· Πέτρος καὶ Παῦλος, Λῖνος καὶ Κλῆτος,

εἶτα Κλήμης, σύγχρονος ὢν Πέτρου καὶ Παύλου, οὗ ἐπιμνημονεύει Παῦλος ἐν τῇ πρὸς Ῥωμαίους ἐπιστολῇ. [Καὶ μηδεὶς θαυμαζέτω ὅτι πρὸ αὐτοῦ ἄλλοι τὴν ἐπισκοπὴν διεδέξαντο ἀπὸ τῶν ἀποστόλων, ὄντος τούτου συγχρόνου Πέτρου καὶ Παύλου.] καὶ οὗτος γὰρ σύγχρονος γίνεται τῶν ἀποστόλων. εἶτ' οὖν ἔτι περιόντων αὐτῶν ὑπὸ Πέτρου λαμβάνει τὴν χειροθεσίαν τῆς ἐπισκοπῆς [καὶ παραιτησάμενος κτλ.].

Κλήμης,

⟨Εὐάρεστος, Ἀλέξανδρος, Ξύστος, Τελεσφόρος, Ὑγῖνος, Πίος, Ἀνίκητος.⟩

Epiph. *Haer.* 27. 5, 6 (p. 106 D). h. Σφραγῖδα δὲ ἐν καυτῆρι, ἢ δι' ἐπιτηδεύσεως ξυρίου, ἢ ῥαφίδος ἐπιτιθέασιν οὗτοι οἱ ἀπὸ Καρποκρᾶ ἐπὶ τὸν δεξιὸν λοβὸν τοῦ ὠτὸς τοῖς ὑπ' αὐτῶν ἀπατωμένοις.

Iren. *Adv. Haer.* i. 25. h. ⁸ Τούτων (sc. τῶν ἀπὸ Καρποκράτου) τινὲς καὶ σφραγίζουσι καυτηριάζοντες[a] τοὺς ἰδίους μαθητὰς ἐν τοῖς ὀπίσω μέρεσι τοῦ λοβοῦ τοῦ δεξιοῦ ὠτός.

[a] So the Latin, 'signant cauteriantes'. The Greek has simply καυτηριάζουσι.

Ἦλθεν δὲ εἰς ἡμᾶς ἤδη πως Μαρκελλίνα τις ὑπ' αὐτῶν ἀπατηθεῖσα, ἣ πολλοὺς ἐλυμήνατο ἐν χρόνοις Ἀνικήτου ἐπισκόπου Ῥώμης,

Epiph. *Haer.* 27. 6 (p. 107 D). h. Ἐν χρόνοις τοίνυν, [ὡς ἔφημεν,] Ἀνικήτου [ἡ προδεδηλωμένη] Μαρκελλίνα ἐν Ῥώμῃ γενομένη τὴν λύμην τῆς Καρποκρᾶ διδασκαλίας ἐξεμέσασα πολλοὺς τῶν ἐκεῖσε λυμηναμένη ἠφάνισε.

Unde et Marcellina, quae Romam sub Aniceto venit, cum esset huius doctrinae, multos exterminavit.

i. τοῦ μετὰ τὴν διαδοχὴν Πίου καὶ τῶν ἀνωτέρω.

i. Epiph. *Haer.* 27. 6 (p. 107 D). ὁ ἄνω ἐν τῷ καταλόγῳ προδεδηλωμένος.

Epiph. *Haer.* 27. 6 (p. 108 A). j. Καὶ ἔνθεν γέγονεν ἀρχὴ γνωστικῶν τῶν καλουμένων. ἔχουσι δὲ εἰκόνας ἐνζωγράφους διὰ χρωμάτων, ἀλλὰ καὶ οἱ μὲν ἐκ χρυσοῦ καὶ ἀργύρου καὶ λοιπῆς ὕλης, ἅτινα ἐκτυπώματά φασιν εἶναι τοῦ Ἰησοῦ, καὶ ταῦτα ὑπὸ Ποντίου Πιλάτου γεγενῆσθαι, τουτέστιν τὰ ἐκτυπώματα τοῦ αὐτοῦ Ἰησοῦ, ὅτε ἐνεδήμει τῷ τῶν ἀνθρώπων γένει. κρύβδην δὲ τὰς τοιαύτας ἔχουσιν εἰκόνας, ἀλλὰ καὶ φιλοσόφων τινῶν, Πυθαγόρου καὶ Πλάτωνος καὶ Ἀριστοτέλους καὶ λοιπῶν, μεθ' ὧν φιλοσόφων ἕτερα ἐκτυπώματα τοῦ Ἰησοῦ τιθέασιν, ἱδρύσαντές τε προσκυνοῦσι καὶ τὰ τῶν ἐθνῶν ἐπιτελοῦσι μυστήρια. στήσαντες γὰρ τούτας τὰς εἰκόνας τὰ τῶν ἐθνῶν ἔθη λοιπὸν ποιοῦσι. [τίνα δέ ἐστιν ἐθνῶν ἔθη ἀλλ' ἢ θυσίαι καὶ τὰ ἄλλα;] ψυχῆς δὲ εἶναι μόνης σωτηρίαν φασὶ καὶ οὐχὶ σωμάτων.

Iren. *Adv. Haer.* i. 25. j. [5] Gnosticos se autem vocant: etiam imagines [a] quasdam quidem depictas quasdam autem et de reliqua materia fabricatas habent, dicentes formam Christi factam a Pilato illo in tempore [b] quo fuit Iesus cum hominibus.

Et has coronant, et proponunt eas cum imaginibus mundi philosophorum, videlicet cum imagine Pythagorae, et Platonis et Aristotelis, et reliquorum;

et reliquam observationem circa eas similiter ut gentes faciunt.

H. E. iv. 22. k. ⁸ Ἐν ἑκάστῃ δὲ διαδοχῇ καὶ ἐν ἑκάστῃ πόλει οὕτως ἔχει ὡς ὁ νόμος κηρύσσει καὶ οἱ προφῆται καὶ ὁ κύριος.

H. E. iv. 22. k. ¹ Καὶ [ὡς ὅτι] τὴν αὐτὴν παρὰ πάντων παρείληφεν διδασκαλίαν.

VI

Stephanus Gobarus ap. Photium *Bibl.* 232 (ed. Bekker, p. 288). Ὅτι τὰ ἡτοιμασμένα τοῖς δικαίοις ἀγαθὰ οὔτε ὀφθαλμὸς εἶδεν, οὔτε οὖς ἤκουσεν, οὔτε ἐπὶ καρδίαν ἀνθρώπου ἀνέβη. [Ἡγήσιππος μέν τοι, ἀρχαῖός τε ἀνὴρ καὶ ἀποστολικός, ἐν τῷ πέμπτῳ τῶν ὑπομνημάτων, οὐκ οἶδ' ὅτι καὶ παθών,] μάτην μὲν εἰρῆσθαι ταῦτα [λέγει,] καὶ καταψεύδεσθαι τοὺς ταῦτα φαμένους τῶν τε θείων γραφῶν καὶ τοῦ κυρίου λέγοντος, Μακάριοι οἱ ὀφθαλμοὶ ὑμῶν οἱ βλέποντες, καὶ τὰ ὦτα ὑμῶν τὰ ἀκούοντα, καὶ ἑξῆς.

[a] Greek, καὶ εἰκόνας δέ.
[b] Greek, κατασκευάζουσι τοῦ Χριστοῦ, λέγοντες ὑπὸ Πιλάτου τῷ καιρῷ ἐκείνῳ γενέσθαι.

THE HERESY OF THE PHRYGIANS

It may be well at the outset to make clear the purpose with which this Essay has been written. For some time the suspicion has forced itself upon me that a good deal that has been published on the subject of Montanism has been based on investigations which proceeded on a faulty method. I propose to set forth the reasons which have led me to entertain this suspicion. My hope is that, if my argument is not accepted, it may elicit criticism which shall suggest a truer interpretation of the evidence which is here presented.

The most illustrious adherent of the Montanist movement was undoubtedly Tertullian of Carthage. And for the purpose of the inquirer into the inner meaning of Montanism Tertullian has the advantage of being a voluminous writer, of whose treatises moreover many have survived. The later writings of Tertullian are in fact—if we except a few oracles of the Phrygian prophets not quoted by him—the only source from which we can acquire a first-hand knowledge of Montanist principles and practice. Historians can scarcely be blamed if they have given them a very high place among the materials now available for ascertaining the character of the Phrygian heresy. And the procedure usually adopted by investigators has, if I am not mistaken, been suggested by an unquestioning assumption of their primary authority for the purpose in hand. It has been assumed that what Tertullian reckons as Montanist doctrine and custom is really such. The evidence supplied by him has been accepted as indisputably reliable: the statements of

Catholic writers which appear to conflict with it have either been tortured into agreement with his *dicta*, or have been rejected as calumnies. It has thus come to pass that what passes current as Montanism is in the main identical with the later theology of Tertullian. We seek a description of a system which penetrated from its first home in Phrygia into many regions; and we have been content to accept instead an account which we have no assurance for believing to be more than the picture of a local development of the movement, or even of its embodiment in a single individual.

The hypothesis which is the ground of this method is the homogeneity of Montanism. Phrygian Montanism and African Montanism are assumed to be, in great measure, the same thing. But is this assumption justified? Was Montanism really homogeneous?

It seems to me that *a priori* we should scarcely expect this to be the case.

The movement began, as we learn from early documents preserved by Eusebius and Epiphanius, at an obscure village called Ardabau in Mysia, not far from the border of Phrygia. There, probably in the fifties of the second century, Montanus, a new convert to Christianity, who had been a priest of Cybele, began to prophesy. And his prophesyings were accompanied by strange phenomena closely resembling those associated with demoniacal possession. He spoke in an ecstasy, as his followers would have expressed it.

Montanus was soon joined by two women, Maximilla and Priscilla or Prisca, who also claimed to possess the prophetic charisma, and whose utterances were similar in matter and in manner to those of their leader. Before long the movement acquired a local centre at Pepuza and Tymion, villages of Phrygia, to which the name of Jerusalem was given by Montanus himself. Its adherents were by and by excommunicated by many synods, and Montanism became a sect with a definite organization. The prophecies of Montanus, Maximilla, and Priscilla were committed to writing,[1] were widely circulated, and were regarded by friends and foes as authoritative statements of all that distinguished the Montanistic teaching from current Christianity. By the Montanists themselves the prophetic oracles were placed at least on a level with the Gospels and the Apostolic Scriptures.

Now it is evident that the moment the oracles of the original exponents of the New Prophecy were written down, and read without the explanations of the prophets, they became, as truly as the Scriptures which they in part superseded, 'a nose of wax.' All depended on their interpretation. And as Montanism spread into different countries, and was accepted by men of different environment and mental training, the interpretations put upon them were certain to be diverse. From this we have ample warrant for the expectation that Montanism would, in some degree, display a divergent type in each country to which it gained admission.

It may, perhaps, make the meaning of what I have said clearer, and at the same time justify the conclusion which I have reached on *a priori* grounds, if I proceed to give what may be termed an example of the forces of disintegration at work.

Didymus of Alexandria,[2] or rather the early and valuable document[3] on which he bases his account of the sect

---

[1] This has been denied. See De Soyres, *Montanism and the Primitive Church*, p. 81. But the argument is unaffected if it be admitted that the *ipsissima verba* of the prophecies, or what were believed to be such, were preserved by oral tradition.   [2] *De Trin.* iii. 41.

[3] But see G. Ficker, in *Zeitsch. f. Kirchengesch.* xxvi. 447 ff.; G. Bardy. *Didyme l'Aveugle*, Paris, 1910, p. 237 f.

charges the Montanists with three errors. The first of them is, that on the plea of a prophetic revelation, supported by certain passages from the latter chapters of the fourth Gospel, they affirmed (ἀπομαντεύονται) that there is one πρόσωπον of the three divine ὑποστάσεις. That is to say, they taught what later came to be known as Sabellianism. The oracle on which they relied for this teaching, according to Didymus, was a saying of Montanus, 'I am the Father and the Son and the Holy Ghost.' This certainly sounds like Monarchian heresy. So also does a saying of Maximilla recorded by Asterius Urbanus,[1] 'I am Word and Spirit and Power'—for the words ῥῆμα, πνεῦμα, and δύναμις must be taken as equivalent to Montanus's Son, Spirit, and Father. And in support of the inference drawn from these, appeal might have been also made to some other oracles among the few that remain.[2] If we had only the statement of Didymus and the oracles to which I have referred we might have confidently classed the Montanists with the Sabellians. But we turn to Tertullian. There is no need to say that he, whether as Catholic or as Montanist, did not deviate from orthodoxy. He was an ardent opponent of the Monarchian Praxeas. And he declares that it was exactly his Montanism which specially fitted him to be the champion of the true faith.[3] For the Paraclete had made use of expressions which, without any such ambiguity as was found in the phrases of Scripture, denounced the teaching of Praxeas as false. It is true that the only oracle which he quotes in this connexion rather tells against his contention ;[4] but he

[1] Ap. Eus. *H. E.* v. 16. 17.
[2] e. g. the oracle quoted in Epiph. *Haer.* 48. 11.
[3] *Adv. Prax.* 2, 13, *De Carn. Res.* 63.
[4] *Adv. Prax.* 8. 'Protulit enim Deus sermonem, quemadmodum etiam Paracletus docet, sicut radix fruticem et fons fluvium sol radium.'

refers to another, which, if his paraphrase of it is reliable, must have been emphatically orthodox.¹ Moreover, he vouches for the orthodoxy of the entire body of the Montanists. No one, he assures us, had ever accused them of heresy.² Their rules of discipline—such is his argument—cannot be corrupt, for error in doctrine always precedes error in discipline.³

The fact is that, in spite of the vehemence of Tertullian, the Montanists were as much divided as their opponents on the question of the Divine Monarchy. Besides the orthodox party among them, to which Tertullian himself belonged, known as the Cataproclans, there was a heterodox party, which he was ignorant of, or, more probably, chose to ignore—the Cataeschinites. This we may gather from the *Philosophumena* of Hippolytus, and from the treatise *Against Heresies* of Pseudo-Tertullian, who, no doubt, here as elsewhere, derives his information from Hippolytus's *Syntagma*.⁴ It is unnecessary to cite other authorities in confirmation of the statements of Hippolytus. The remarkable fact is that both the orthodox and the heterodox parties among the Montanists sheltered themselves behind the oracles of the prophets.

But it was not only the difficulty of interpreting the oracles, and applying them to controversies which did not belong to the place and period of the original prophets, which tended to divide the Montanists. There were at least three other influences, all closely related to each other, which might well lead to this result.

The first of these was the oracles of later prophets. For the charismata were by no means confined to the first three. Theodotus, 'the first steward of the New Prophecy,' was a fellow worker of Montanus, and he was almost

---

¹ *Adv. Prax.* 30.   ² *De Ieiun.* 1.   ³ *De Monog.* 2.
⁴ Hippol. *Philos.* viii. 19, Ps.-Tert. *Haer.* 7.

THE HERESY OF THE PHRYGIANS

certainly a prophet.[1] Apollonius, about the year 200, mentions both a prophet and a prophetess;[2] and, notwithstanding the opinion of so eminent a historian as Harnack,[3] one can hardly suppose that they are to be identified with Montanus and Maximilla or Priscilla. In any case Apollonius implies that Maximilla and Priscilla had successors by his remark that they were the *first* prophetesses to abandon their husbands.[4] Firmilian, in his letter to Cyprian, speaks of a prophetess (probably a Montanist) who appeared in Cappadocia about 236 A.D.[5] And finally Epiphanius tells of a prophetess named Quintilla.[6] Whether she was one of those already mentioned we cannot determine.[7] She was certainly not a member of the original group. There is no evidence that the inspired utterances of these later prophets were circulated in writing. Certainly none of them is quoted in writings now extant. They probably had no more than a local celebrity. The same remark may be made about Themiso, whose Catholic epistle, written ' in imitation of the apostle',[8] claimed, we cannot doubt, to have been inspired. But that they furthered the development of Montanism in the districts where they were known it is impossible not to believe. And the narrower the sphere of their influence so much the more

[1] Anon. ap. Eus. *H. E.* v. 16. 14.
[2] Ap. Eus. *H. E.* v. 18. 4, 6, 7, 10.   [3] *Chronologie*, i. 370.
[4] Eus. *H. E.* v. 18. 3 δείκνυμεν οὖν αὐτὰς πρώτας τὰς προφήτιδας ταύτας ... τοὺς ἄνδρας καταλιπούσας.
[5] Cyp. *Ep.* 75. 10 (Hartel, p. 817). For the date see De Soyres, op. cit., p. 54; Ramsay, *The Church in the Roman Empire*, 1893, p. 464.
[6] *Haer.* 49.
[7] Bonwetsch (*Die Geschichte des Montanismus*, Erlangen, 1881, p. 171) suggests that she may have been the prophetess mentioned by Firmilian; Salmon (*Dict. of Christ. Biog.* iii. 939), that she was the prophetess referred to by Apollonius.
[8] Apollonius ap. Eus. *H. E.* v. 18. 5.

their sayings tended to generate purely local forms of the system.

In the West, so far as I know, there is no mention of later prophets. But Tertullian several times refers to the visions of sisters,[1] and he appeals on one occasion to the vision of Saturus, which we can still read in the Acts of Perpetua.[2] In each case the vision is used as giving authority to a disciplinary custom or a doctrine advocated by the writer. Thus in the West, as in the East, the means were at hand of explaining or adding to the original deposit of the New Prophecy by an authority which was held to be divine.

A second agent of development which must be taken into account is the weight of influence exerted by prominent members of the sect, who were not themselves prophets, or possessed of charismata which involved the capacity for receiving revelations by visions or otherwise.

Tertullian, in his own person, notably illustrates the power of this influence. He nowhere claims to have had revelations. He was simply, in his own view, an adherent of the Paraclete. Yet his influence in determining the form of Montanism in Africa must have been immense. Dr. Rendel Harris and Professor Gifford, in the introduction to their edition of the *Acts of the Martyrdom of Perpetua and Felicitas*,[3] direct attention to 'the difficulty with which any of his writings, except a very few tracts, can satisfactorily be labelled non-Montanist'. They have themselves transferred that which previous writers had regarded as 'probably Tertullian's earliest existing writing'[4] to the Montanistic period of his life. The fact

---

[1] e. g. *De. An.* 9, *De Virg. Vel.* 17.
[2] *De An.* 55. See also *De Spect.* 26, *De Idol.* 15.
[3] Cambridge, 1890, pp. 28 ff.   [4] *Dict. of Christ. Biog.* iv. 822.

is that the unquestionably Montanistic treatises are recognized merely by more or less explicit allusions to the revelations of the Paraclete. The doctrines and practices advocated in his latest works are, for the most part, essentially the same as those upheld in the earliest now extant.[1] If there is any difference between them it is amply accounted for by the development of opinion which would inevitably take place in a man of Tertullian's character. They are presented from new points of view and under new sanctions, but in their main substance they are unchanged. Of this fact it is superfluous to give proof, and the inference from it is irresistible. Tertullian brought far more to Montanism than he found in it. It is an inference which might have been drawn if we knew nothing more of the man than what his writings reveal of his masterful personality. But if African Montanism was largely made by Tertullian, it must have differed widely from the Montanism which in his day, or at any other time, existed in Phrygia.[2]

We have from Tertullian himself a story which well illustrates how the influence of later revelations and the influence of personality helped each other in producing the local development of Montanism. In his treatise *De Anima* 9 he speaks of a certain sister, who had the charisma of revelations. The material for visions was often supplied by the lessons, psalms, discourses, &c., of the

[1] Compare Gwatkin, *Early Church History*, ii. 238: 'He was a Montanist at heart long before he accepted the oracles of the New Prophecy.'

[2] Mr. De Soyres, speaking of the teaching set forth in Tertullian's treatises *De Virginibus Velandis*, *De Spectaculis*, and *De Corona Militis*, remarks (p. 96), 'It is significant that not even an Epiphanius found any capital in this department.' This fact Mr. De Soyres explains in his own way. But the true explanation may very well be that the opinions of Tertullian expressed in those tracts had no counterpart in Eastern Montanism, with which alone Epiphanius was concerned.

church service. During service, on one occasion, when Tertullian was discoursing on the soul, the sister fell into an ecstasy and saw a vision. Subsequently, when service was over, and the congregation dismissed, she was invited to describe her vision. Among other things she declared that she had seen a soul which displayed all the signs of a corporeal nature. Thus was established a favourite doctrine of the preacher, on which he had no doubt been insisting in his sermon. I shall have occasion to refer to this story again. For the present it is sufficient to observe that the preacher obviously, though he was unconscious that he had done so, produced the vision, while the vision in its turn was adduced to impart divine sanction to the preacher's doctrine. A new tenet was thus added to the official teaching of African Montanism, nominally by a revelation, really by the personality of Tertullian.

The third power which co-operated with revelations and personal force in the moulding of Montanism need only be mentioned—the power of local environment. This always exercises its subtle influence on a transplanted faith. It has in no small degree affected Christianity itself. And wherever its influence is effective it produces a change of form.

The conclusion to which these considerations compel us is, I believe, that any large measure of homogeneity in Montanism is a thing which could not be looked for beforehand. Any method of investigation which assumes it must therefore be radically wrong. The only way to arrive at a true conception of Montanism is to begin by examining Phrygian Montanism and African Montanism apart. It may be urged that the only Montanism of which we can learn anything is a developed or a decadent Montanism. That may be in part true. But we can reach a knowledge of its inner principle in no other way than by a preliminary study of the later forms, each by itself, and by tracing them back to their common root. By merely combining them we can attain no sure result. And for this purpose an inquiry into Phrygian Montanism—the heresy of the Phrygians in its original home, shaped only by its original environment—scanty and unsatisfying as the materials for such an inquiry are, is immeasurably more important than an inquiry into the exotic Montanism of Tertullian.

It remains to point out one or two very striking instances of dissimilarity between Phrygian Montanism and the current conception of Montanism, mainly drawn from Tertullian, which such a study seems to me to reveal.

Let us note, in the first place, what we may learn from the earliest documents as to the conception which was held in Phrygia of the nature of the New Prophecy. It is well known that Montanus and his companions prophesied in ecstasy, and that their utterances were accompanied by strange ravings.[1] The Catholics laid hold of this fact as demonstrating that they were inspired by an evil spirit; and the defenders of Montanism replied that being in a state of ecstasy was a condition of the exercise of the prophetic gift. But all this seems to me to have been an afterthought. The Catholics made much of the frenzy of the prophets merely as a way of evading an argument of the Montanists which, without bringing in this other issue, was not easily disposed of. This earlier argument is revealed by the anonymous writer quoted by Eusebius.[2] The Montanists, he says, evidently quoting

---

[1] Eus. *H. E.* v. 16. 7, 9.

[2] Lightfoot (*Ignatius*, i. 482 f.) and Harnack (*Chronologie*, i. 364 f.) agree in dating the anonymous treatise A.D. 192-193. It was undertaken at the request of Avircius Marcellus of Hieropolis in the

from one of their books, boasted of Agabus, Judas, Silas, the daughters of Philip, Ammia of Philadelphia, and Quadratus; and from the last two they claimed to have received the prophetic gift *by way of succession* (διεδέξαντο).[1] That is to say, they received their charismata as successors in the line of New Testament prophets, which all believed would remain until the end, just as the bishops had received their office from a line of predecessors which went back to apostolic days. They were the last prophets, no doubt; they had the gifts in a pre-eminent degree; in them was fulfilled the promise of the Paraclete. All Montanist writers maintained that position. But still, they were the last and the greatest *in a line of succession*.

It is hazardous to assert a negative. But I cannot recall any trace of this notion of a prophetic succession in the West. Tertullian seems consistently to ignore all prophecy between the Baptist, or at any rate the apostles, and Montanus.[2]

And I may here observe that the impression left by a perusal of the extant passages of Tertullian [3] in which he refers to ecstasy as a condition of prophecy is that the ecstasy which he contemplated was something very different from the violent and uncontrolled ravings of Phrygian Pentapolis (Eus. v. 16. 3), and the writer speaks of Avircius and Zoticus of Otrous, a neighbouring town, as his fellow presbyters (§ 5 τοῦ συμπρεσβυτέρου ἡμῶν Ζωτικοῦ). It is probable therefore that all three were bishops of the Pentapolis, and that Miltiades, against whose followers the treatise was directed, was a Montanist leader of the same district.

[1] Eus. *H. E.* v. 17. 3, 4.
[2] *De An.* 9; cp. *De Virg. Vel.* 1, *De Monog.* 3, *De Ieiun.* 12.
[3] See especially *De Anima* 45, where he makes use of the favourite Montanist text, Gen. ii. 21. The whole chapter should be compared with Epiph. *Haer.* 48. 3, 4. In several respects Tertullian appears to be more in harmony with the Catholic writer used by Epiphanius than with the Montanist opinions which that writer combats. See also *De Anima* 11, 21, *De Ieiun.* 3.

THE HERESY OF THE PHRYGIANS 119

the Phrygian prophets as reported (possibly not without exaggeration) by the Anonymous.[1] Epiphanius says truly that the word ἔκστασις has different meanings,[2] and I am inclined to think that western Montanists used it in one sense, and their Phrygian brethren in another. The account of the sister whose ecstasy was kept so well in hand that she could wait patiently till service was over before relating her vision stands in curious contrast to the narrative of the proceedings at Ardabau.

A comparison of these two stories recalls also another marked difference between the Montanism of Phrygia and that of Africa. In Phrygia women were given a high position in the native cults. And among the Montanists they retained it. Montanus evidently prophesied in the midst of a congregation. There were large numbers present (ὄχλοι), some of whom would have silenced him, while others opposed their efforts. And it seems to be suggested that Maximilla and Priscilla likewise addressed a Christian assembly.[3] But however that may be Firmilian, as we have seen, makes mention of a third-century prophetess, probably a Montanist, of whom he states that she baptized and celebrated the Eucharist.[4] Epiphanius describes a curious service of the Quintillians (who were obviously the Montanists under another name) at Pepuza, in which the officiants were seven virgins, who

[1] Ap. Eus. *H. E.* v. 16. 7, 8; 17. 2. It will be observed that the Anonymous substitutes for ἔκστασις the stronger word παρέκστασις.

[2] *Haer.* 48. 4.

[3] They spoke in the same way as Montanus (*H. E.* v. 16. 9). And it is added, by way of explanation, that they did so ἐκφρόνως καὶ ἀκαίρως καὶ ἀλλοτριοτρόπως. There is nothing corresponding to the second adverb in the description of Montanus's utterances. It may perhaps indicate that they spoke during a church service; which would be an improper occasion for speech for women, though not for a man.

[4] Cyprian, *Ep.* 75. 10 (Hartel, p. 818).

prophesied to the people; and he declares that they had female bishops and priests.[1] We are not surprised to find Catholics indignantly quoting St. Paul's injunction about women keeping silence in the Church.

This peculiarity of Montanism certainly never found its way into the West. It is not a Catholic, but Tertullian, in one of his most distinctly Montanist writings, who says, 'It is not permitted to a woman to speak in Church, nor yet to teach, nor to baptize, nor to offer, nor to assume any office which belongs to a man, least of all the priesthood.'[2]

Another feature of the Phrygian heresy deserves attention at this point. I have already mentioned the importance of Pepuza as the local centre of the sect in its earliest days. To this 'Jerusalem' Montanus would have gathered men from all quarters,[3] doubtless that they might await the Parousia of the Lord which it was believed would take place there.[4] Pepuza was in fact the Holy City of the Phrygian Montanists. And so it came to pass that by some they were called Pepuzians. But there is not a trace of any acknowledgement on the part of Tertullian of the sanctity of Pepuza. One must not, indeed, lay too much stress upon the fact that he never mentions it in his extant writings. But there is one piece of evidence of a more positive kind which is not to be overlooked. In a well-known passage of his Montanist treatise against Marcion [5] he avows his belief that a kingdom would be established on earth after the resurrection, 'in Jerusalem, the city prepared by God, let down from heaven.' And he speaks of an oracle of the New Prophecy

---

[1] *Haer.* 49. 2, 3.   [2] *De Virg. Vel.* 9.
[3] *H. E.* v. 18. 2. Maximilla prophesied there. Ib. § 13. And so did at least one other early prophetess.   Epiph. *Haer.* 49. 1.
[4] Epiph. 48. 4; 49. 1.   [5] iii. 24.

THE HERESY OF THE PHRYGIANS 121

which announced that an image of this city would be seen before its actual establishment on earth. The prediction, he declares, had been fulfilled not long before he wrote by a vision, which heathen as well as Christian witnesses beheld *in Judaea*, in the morning of forty successive days, of a city suspended from heaven. This passage is an unmistakable indication that Tertullian did not look for the reign of the saints at Pepuza or anywhere else in Phrygia; but that he clung to the belief held by Justin Martyr and other Christians of the second century that after the resurrection the faithful would be gathered together for a thousand years *in Jerusalem*, 'builded and adorned and enlarged.'[1] But if so, he was ignorant of, or repudiated, a belief which was of the essence of Phrygian Montanism. He was a Millenarian, but not a Millenarian of the Montanist type.

It is worth while to inquire how so startling a departure from Phrygian teaching can be accounted for. It is obvious, indeed, that belief in the sanctity of Pepuza would tend to become less vivid the further Montanism spread beyond the region of its birth. It would be difficult to persuade an Italian or an African that a little village in Asia, the very name of which he had never before heard, was the most sacred spot in the world, chosen by Christ as the scene of His second Advent. Montanist missionaries in Europe would perhaps not insist upon the doctrine too strongly; and so in time it would disappear from the minds of their converts. But how about Tertullian? He was familiar with the oracles of the prophets, and he would certainly not refuse to accept a doctrine which he found in them. Was there then no reference in the oracles to Pepuza or the Parousia to be expected there? This is scarcely conceivable.

[1] Justin, *Dial.* 80.

I may venture to make two suggestions, either of which, if well founded, will suffice to remove the difficulty. It may have been that wherever Pepuza was referred to in the oracles it was spoken of, not by its proper name, but by the new name of Jerusalem which Montanus had given it. In that case Tertullian may have misunderstood the meaning of the statements about the Parousia, taking 'Jerusalem' in its literal sense. Or, again, it may have been that his collection of the oracles was incomplete, and that in those to which he had access Pepuza was not referred to as a place of special sanctity.[1] If the latter supposition is correct it is easy to understand that Tertullian may have but imperfectly understood the character of the earlier Montanistic teaching, not only in this matter but in much else.

Not much is known of the penitential discipline of the eastern Montanists. But there is ground for believing that in this matter also they differed from the Africans. Apollonius [2] discusses the case of one Alexander, whom

---

[1] There is of course no difficulty in supposing that several collections of the sayings of the prophets were in circulation, the contents of which varied considerably. If it be true that they were not committed to writing, but transmitted orally, the oracles known to one Montanist congregation might differ widely from those known to another; and this would be specially likely in the case of communities outside Phrygia. It seems to me almost certain that Tertullian was ignorant of the oracle reported in Epiph. *Haer.* 49. 1. But possibly it is not genuine. Speaking generally, it is remarkable how little there is in common between the oracles quoted by Tertullian and those quoted by Greek writers.

[2] Apollonius says that he wrote forty years after the beginning of Montanism (Eus. *H. E.* v. 18. 12). Hence Harnack (*Chronologie*, i. 370-375) dates his treatise A.D. 196-197. But, though it is probable that Montanus prophesied for the first time in 156, we cannot be sure that Apollonius was accurately informed on that point, neither are we certain that he did not use round numbers when he spoke of the forty years that had elapsed since the New Prophecy began. The

the sectaries regarded as a martyr, but whom he affirmed to have been tried not for the Name but for robbery.[1] After his release he spent some years with a prophet. Apollonius sneers after his accustomed fashion : 'Which of them forgives the sins of the other? Does the prophet forgive the robberies of the martyr, or the martyr the extortions of the prophet?' This implies that prophets were supposed by the Montanists to have the power of absolution. And in this insinuation Apollonius is confirmed, not only by Tertullian, but also (which is more to the purpose) by an oracle which Tertullian quotes.[2] We have therefore no reason to doubt the further insinuation that martyrs were regarded as possessed of the same power.[3] But the African Montanists allowed no such prerogative to the martyrs. In Carthage it was only the Catholics who admitted the validity of their absolutions, and Tertullian heaps much scorn upon them for so doing.[4]

But we must now proceed to discuss two questions which will be recognized as of fundamental importance. Did Montanism inculcate asceticism? No one can doubt that, as expounded by Tertullian, it did. But we are concerned with Phrygian Montanism. What evidence have we as to asceticism among the adherents of the New Prophecy in Phrygia?

The writer who gives us most help in answering this question is Apollonius. In the passages quoted from him

---

recrudescence of prophecy to which he bears witness seems to indicate a longer period than four years between the Anonymous and him. Possibly therefore he wrote as late as A.D. 200. He was certainly an Asian, and possibly, as Praedestinatus says, bishop of Ephesus.

[1] Ap. Eus. *H. E.* v. 18. 6-9.

[2] *De Pud.* 21. Tertullian himself held that certain sins were unpardonable (§ 19), an opinion which he has some difficulty in reconciling with the oracle.

[3] Cp. Bonwetsch, p. 112.   [4] *De Pud.* 22.

by Eusebius he insists that the lives of the Montanist martyrs and prophets do not conform to the requirements of the Gospel. He roundly charges them with covetousness. Montanus himself, he tells us, appointed πρακτῆρας χρημάτων, agents for the collection of money,[1] and out of the fund raised by them he actually paid salaries to the teachers who propagated his doctrine. Moreover, he devised a system of receiving gifts under the name of 'offerings'. Accordingly the prophets took gifts,[2] and both prophets and martyrs made gain not only from the rich, but from the poor and orphans and widows. Prophets and prophetesses and martyrs, unmindful of the saying of our Lord, 'Ye shall not take gold or silver or two coats,' accepted offerings not only of gold and silver, but also of costly garments.[3] Themiso, a leader of the sect, who claimed to be a 'martyr', or as we should say, a 'confessor', was rich enough to purchase his liberation from prison with a large sum of money (πλήθει χρημάτων). Themiso was, in fact, clothed with covetousness as with a garment.[4] Another, who was counted as a prophet, was a moneylender. And, finally, Apollonius asks the scornful questions, 'Does a prophet dye his hair? Does a prophet paint himself? Does a prophet delight in self-adornment? Does a prophet play with tables and dice? Does a prophet lend money at interest?'; and he offers to prove that all these things were done by the Montanist prophets.[5]

In some of these statements and insinuations—those, namely, which relate to the financial organization of the sect—Apollonius is confirmed by the Anonymous. For when he calls Theodotus the 'first steward' of the new prophecy (τὸν πρῶτον τῆς ... προφητείας οἷον ἐπίτροπόν τινα[6]) I do not see why we may not take his words in

---

[1] Eus. *H. E.* v. 18. 2.   [2] Ib. § 11.   [3] §§ 4, 7.   [4] § 5.
[5] § 11.   [6] Ap. Eus. *H. E.* v. 16. 14.

their literal sense. And indeed the very innocency of some of the things laid to the charge of Montanus is a strong guarantee that the accusations are true. For who nowadays would find fault with a man who provided preachers with salaries, or who organized the collection of money for the purpose? And we shall not greatly blame prophets and confessors for taking the gifts which were offered to them, nor be greatly surprised if the more eminent and popular leaders became rich. There is really no need for Bonwetsch's suggestion that what Montanus aimed at was the establishment of a community of goods.[1] The statements about salaries and the wealth of certain individuals are quite inconsistent with such a supposition.

What scandalized Apollonius was perhaps the fact that Montanus was making the clerical and even the prophetic office into a profession.[2] His preachers no longer worked at secular trades, as, in all probability, most bishops and priests at that period did: they derived their income solely from the payment made to them for the exercise of spiritual functions. One who is not a member of an established Church may perhaps be allowed to express sympathy with him if he also felt that absorption in financial organization is not conducive to the highest spiritual interests of Church or sect.

We may take it, at any rate, that Montanus desired that

[1] p. 165.
[2] We are reminded of the indignation of a western writer contemporary with Apollonius—the author of the *Little Labyrinth*—called forth by the conduct of one Natalius, who, at the instance of Asclepiodotus and a banker named Theodotus, permitted himself 'to be called bishop of this heresy [*sc.* the Theodotians] at a salary, so that he received 150 denarii a month'. He remarks, quite after the manner of Apollonius, that Natalius was ensnared by the desire of filthy lucre ($αἰσχροκερδίᾳ$). *H. E.* v. 28. 8 ff.

the officials of his sect should live, not indeed in luxury, but in ordinary comfort.

The remainder of Apollonius's charges Bonwetsch [1] asks us to disbelieve, on the ground that Socrates (iv. 28) bears testimony to lack of zeal among the Paphlagonians and Phrygians of his day for the hippodrome and the theatre. The argument is scarcely convincing. He further reminds us, indeed, of Jerome's statement that in the lost work *De Ecstasi* Tertullian exposed the falsity of all Apollonius's assertions.[2] But even if we are bound to interpret rigorously the words of Jerome, we must still remark that an Asian writer is more likely to have known the facts than one who lived in Africa, and that if the probable prejudice of Apollonius is to be taken into account, the prejudice of Tertullian must not be left out of consideration. The explanation devised by Bonwetsch, for the benefit of those who are not disposed utterly to reject the witness of Apollonius—that the Montanists, in order to express their spiritual joy as Christians, indulged in an 'apparent worldliness' which as the symbol of mere earthly merriment would not have been permitted; and that the gay clothing of the prophetess served only to enhance her dignity, and to enforce the festive character of her utterances—need not detain us.

I am willing to grant that the statements of Apollonius are exaggerated. But is it possible that such charges could have been publicly made in Asia, and have been accompanied by an express challenge to the Montanists to disprove them, if they had not considerable foundation in fact? Could they have been made at all by him against the leaders of a numerous Asian community, of which

[1] p. 100.
[2] *De Vir. Ill.* 40 'septimum [volumen] proprie adversum Apollonium elaboravit in quo omnia quae ille arguit conatur defendere.'

THE HERESY OF THE PHRYGIANS

asceticism was one of the most prominent characteristics? And would Tertullian have answered them if they were so contrary to the truth that no one could have believed them?

But Apollonius makes two statements about Montanus which may seem to imply that he inculcated an asceticism which exceeded that of the Catholic Church. 'This,' he says, 'is he who taught dissolutions of marriages, and made laws of fasting' (ὁ διδάξας λύσεις γάμων, ὁ νηστείας νομοθετήσας).[1] It is scarcely probable, indeed, considering the context in which this sentence occurs, that it was intended to convey the idea of special austerity on the part of Montanus. For it is immediately followed by accusations of extortion and gluttony. But let us examine the statements in their order.

1. Montanus taught 'dissolutions of marriages'. It is quite certain that in the East as in the West, Montanism was so far ascetic as absolutely to reject second marriages (Epiph. *Haer.* 48. 8, 9;[2] Tert. *De Monog.* 3, &c.). But this can hardly be referred to here. The words λύσεις γάμων have sometimes been rendered 'dissolution of marriage', a phrase which suggests that Montanus was so

---

[1] Eus. *H. E.* v. 18. 2.

[2] Epiphanius evidently bases this part of his account of Montanism on a very early document. Bonwetsch (p. 36) argues, not altogether convincingly, that it was a treatise of Hippolytus. Its date seems to be earlier than the work of Apollonius, for the writer still asserts (§ 2) that there have been no prophets since the death of Maximilla, a statement which in the time of Apollonius would have been untrue. To connect it with Phrygia we have the statement (§ 11): 'Immediately after Montanus had said this '—viz. an oracle which he had quoted —['God] gave us a suggestion to remember the words of the Lord', &c. (ὅτε γὰρ εὐθὺς τοῦτο εἶπε Μοντανὸς ὑπόνοιαν ἡμῖν δέδωκεν ἀναμνησθῆναι κτλ.). This seems to imply that the writer had actually heard Montanus. Moreover, several of his arguments resemble those of the Anonymous.

strenuous an advocate of virginity as to lay it down that married couples on their acceptance of the new prophecy were bound to separate for the purpose of living in strict continence. And it is true that there is an oracle of Priscilla, which Tertullian quotes and understands as a commendation of chastity.[1] We only know it in Tertullian's Latin rendering, which is not free from ambiguity. But it certainly does not enjoin the annulling of marriages already contracted. And if Apollonius had wished to indicate the sanction by Montanus of such an annulling in all cases, would he not have used the singular, λύσιν? At any rate his language is easily explained as a rhetorical allusion to the fact, for which a somewhat later passage in his treatise[2] is our sole authority, that Maximilla and Priscilla (and probably other women also) deserted their husbands when they became prophetesses. Montanus must of course have sanctioned their conduct: he could not well have done otherwise, if it was his wish that prophetesses as well as preachers should give undivided attention to their spiritual work. But abandonment of married life under such circumstances does not necessarily imply an ascetic view of the relation between the sexes. It is true that it seems to be implied by Apollonius that the Montanists recognized an order of virgins. For after asserting that the prophetesses had left their husbands to join Montanus, he adds, 'How then did they speak falsehood, calling Priscilla a virgin?' But the existence of such an order did not strike the anti-Montanist writer as unfitting: what he counted outrageous was not the ascetic tendency of his opponents, but their laxity in giving one the rank of a virgin who had been married. So far as these indications go it would seem that the Montanists were

---

[1] *De Exhort. Cast.* 10.   [2] Eus. *H. E.* v. 18. 3.

less ascetic in their opinions about marriage than the Catholics.

2. But then Montanus 'made laws for fasting'. Does not this imply an unusually rigorous asceticism? Tertullian in his *De Ieiuniis* contrasts the Montanist fasts with those of the Catholics, and actually accuses the latter of gluttony because their fasts were less frequent and less severe. But how much meaning there is likely to be in such rhetoric may be judged when we find Apollonius making the same accusation against the Montanists because they had salaried preachers. The truth is that when we fix our thoughts on the facts which Tertullian mentions and not on the rhetoric beneath which they are buried, we perceive that the difference between him and the Catholics concerned far less the frequency and duration of fasts[1] than the principle on which they rested. The Catholics held that, with certain exceptions, they were 'ex arbitrio'; Tertullian held that they were 'ex imperio novae disciplinae'.[2] And similarly in Epiph. *Haer.* 48.8, where apparently Montanists and Gnostics are classed together, there is no allusion to difference in the amount of fasting, but only to difference in the principle which lies behind it.[3] And nothing more is implied in the words ὁ νηστείας νομοθετήσας. In Phrygia as in Africa

---

[1] Bonwetsch (p. 96) scarcely succeeds in proving that in these respects the Montanists (in Africa) differed to any considerable extent from the Catholics. He shows (p. 95) that Jerome exaggerated the number of fasts peculiar to the Montanists.

[2] *De Ieiun.* 2, 13. Cp. Gwatkin, *Early Church History*, ii. 81.

[3] Παῦλος ... προφητεύων ἔλεγε ... ὅτι ἀποστήσονταί τινες τῆς ὑγιαινούσης διδασκαλίας, προσέχοντες πλάνοις καὶ διδασκαλίαις δαιμόνων, κωλυόντων γαμεῖν, ἀπέχεσθαι βρωμάτων' ... ὡς σαφῶς ἐφ' ὑμῖν καὶ τοῖς ὁμοίοις ὑμῖν πεπλήρωται ἐξ αὐτῶν τῶν προκειμένων. αἱ γὰρ πλείους τῶν αἱρέσεων τούτων τὸ γαμεῖν κωλύουσιν, ἀπέχεσθαι βρωμάτων παραγγέλλουσιν, οὐχ ἕνεκεν πολιτείας προτρεπόμενοι, οὐχ ἕνεκεν ἀρετῆς μείζονος καὶ βραβείων καὶ στεφάνων, ἀλλὰ βδελυκτὰ ταῦτα ὑπὸ Χριστοῦ γεγενημένα ἡγούμενοι.

fasting was reduced to rule, no doubt by command of the Paraclete. But we have no proof that the rules enforced in the two regions were identical. And even if they were it does not follow that in either the fasts were increased in number or in severity. That would depend on the frequency and rigour of fasting in the already existing usage of Catholic Christians. The Montanist rule in Phrygia may even, in this matter, have fallen below the standard of Phrygian Catholic custom. It is at least remarkable that when Sozomen enumerates the local differences as to the duration of Lent, the shortest Lent which he mentions is that of those who 'minded the things of Montanus', and who kept but two weeks.[1]

The remark about marriage and fasting therefore leaves unimpaired the impression produced by the charges of greed and worldliness brought by Apollonius against the Montanists. We cannot regard those whom he had in view as an ascetic community.

Not unconnected, in the mind of Tertullian, with the question of asceticism, was the eagerness for martyrdom to which as a Montanist he urged his readers. It is necessary therefore to inquire what we can learn as to the attitude towards martyrdom of the Phrygian Montanists.

Tertullian quotes oracles of the prophets in favour of his view that Christians should seek rather than evade martyrdom;[2] but they are not appreciably stronger than words spoken by our Lord, upon which at least one of them is plainly founded. Both alike are patient of different interpretations by different men. What then was the actual practice of the Montanists of Phrygia? Did they court martyrdom or did they avoid it? The answer must be, I think, if we are to be guided by the available

[1] Soz. *H. E.* vii. 19.
[2] *De Fuga*, 9; cp. c. 11; *De Cor.* 1; *De An.* 55.

evidence, that they behaved much in the same way as Catholic Christians did under similar circumstances.

A passage of the Anonymous has been interpreted to mean that the Montanists had no martyrs. 'Is there any,' he asks,[1] 'of those who began to speak, from Montanus and the women on, who was persecuted by Jews or slain by lawless men?' And he answers, 'Not one.' It is instructive to observe the use which has been made of these words, and some others like them which follow. Mr. M°Giffert, in the notes to his English translation of Eusebius,[2] affirms that 'there is a flat contradiction' between them and a subsequent passage of the same writer, in which he admits that the Montanists had many martyrs; and he infers that the Anonymous had 'no regard whatever for the truth'. He adds that 'we know that the Montanists had many martyrs, and that their principles were such as to lead them to martyrdom even when the Catholics avoided it', referring to Tertullian's *De Fuga*. In the latter remark he assumes that African and Phrygian Montanism were identical in principle. And all that precedes it is based on a misinterpretation of the Anonymous.

For that writer is answering the argument—based on Matt. xxiii. 34, 'I send unto you prophets and wise men and scribes; some of them ye shall kill and crucify'—that because the Catholics had not received Montanus and his companions they were slayers of the prophets. Any one who reads the whole passage with attention will perceive that his answer amounts to this: The text must be taken literally; and in its literal sense it has not been fulfilled in the Montanist prophets. None of them has been put to death by any one, still less by the Jews, to whom Christ was speaking. Montanus and Maximilla and Theodotus were all dead, but not one of them had died as a

[1] *Ap.* Eus. *H. E.* v. 16. 12.   [2] p. 232 f.

martyr. The Anonymous makes no reference to the general body of Montanists. He neither denies nor affirms that they had martyrs. Hence his words cannot contradict the later passage in which he allows that the sect had numerous martyrs.

But it is not without significance that, if we may believe him—and I see no reason why we should not—none of the early Phrygian prophets had suffered for the faith. Is it likely, if they preached, with the vigour of a Tertullian, that the glory of martyrdom should be eagerly sought, that all of them should have passed through the persecution of Marcus Aurelius unscathed?

But let us proceed to consider the second passage of the Anonymous to which Mr. McGiffert refers. In it he tells us that when all other argument failed them the Montanists fell back on their martyrs. And he admits the truth of their contention that their martyrs were many in number.[1]

What was the argument based on this fact? The Anonymous only says that they regarded it as 'a proof of the power of the prophetic Spirit that was among them'. We may perhaps guess that what they meant was something of this kind. The Anonymous plainly refers to the persecution of Marcus Aurelius; for after it, according to him, the Church had enjoyed continuous peace up to the time when he wrote.[2] Now the martyrs of Lyons had during that persecution testified by their letters in favour of the Catholic party in Phrygia.[3] Their judgement would have had great weight with all Christendom. Just in the same way we cannot doubt that the arguments of Praxeas against the Montanists were the more readily listened to by the bishop of Rome

---

[1] *Ap.* Eus. *H. E.* v. 16. 20 f. [2] Ib. § 19.
[3] Eus. *H. E.* v. 3. 4.

THE HERESY OF THE PHRYGIANS

because of his 'martyrdom' of which he made such proud boasting, and the reality of which Tertullian so eagerly disputed.[1] By way of reply the Montanists may have appealed to their own martyrs: 'We too had then many martyrs who testified on our behalf.'

But, however that may be, the Anonymous gives us no reason to suppose that there was any balancing of one set of martyrs against another in regard either to their number or their eagerness and steadfastness. As yet we have nothing to guide us to a sure judgement about the attitude of the Phrygian Montanists towards martyrdom.

We turn to the treatise of Apollonius. Here at length we find a hint. Apollonius tells us that Themiso purchased his liberation from bonds with a large sum of money, and thereafter boasted as a martyr.[2] This statement may of course be false; but it is not proved to be false because Tertullian in his *De Fuga* denounced the practice of purchasing release.[3] And it is worthy of remark that in this case it is not a Montanist but a Catholic who says that Themiso's act of cowardice ought to have humbled him. Moreover, the statement (whether true or false) would hardly have been made if it had admitted of an easy retort. So far as it goes it indicates that in Phrygia the Montanists were more inclined to avoid martyrdom than the Catholics.

This is confirmed by a document of later date. Under Decius one Achatius, apparently a bishop, whose see, however, is unknown,[4] was examined by a governor named Martianus. The record of the examination was printed by Ruinart,[5] and has many marks of genuine-

[1] *Adv. Prax.* 1.   [2] *Ap.* Eus. *H. E.* v. 18. 5.
[3] Bonwetsch, p. 163.
[4] See B. Aubé, *Les Chrétiens dans l'Empire Romain*, iv. 181 f.
[5] *Acta sincera*, ed. Amsterdam, 1713, p. 152. See also Gebhardt, *Acta Martyrum Selecta*, 1902, p. 115.

ness. In it the governor is represented as urging Achatius to sacrifice by an appeal to the example of the Cataphrygians, 'homines religionis antiquae,' who had in a body abandoned Christianity and made their offerings to the gods. This address cannot have been put into the mouth of Martianus by an orthodox writer. For such a one would not have made him speak of the Montanists as men of an ancient religion; and still less would he have made him immediately afterwards contrast their faith with the 'nouum genus religionis' of their Catholic rivals. The governor is struck by the difference between the faint-heartedness of the Montanists and the courage of the Catholics.

Another indication of the position taken by the eastern Montanists in the matter of martyrdom remains to be noticed. The sect which was commonly known as 'the heresy of the Phrygians' must have included among its members a large number—perhaps the majority—of the Christians of Phrygia. And we have direct testimony that this was so even as late as the fifth century.[1] But Sir William Ramsay[2] points out that in Phrygia as a whole martyrdoms in the latter part of the second century, and throughout the third, were rare. From a study of the inscriptions he is able to suggest a reason for this fact. The Christians lived on good terms with their heathen fellow-countrymen, and did not obtrude their Christianity unnecessarily; and, speaking generally, a spirit of compromise and accommodation in matters religious prevailed. If this description is at all near the truth the attitude of the Phrygian Christians towards paganism and towards persecution must have been as different as

[1] Soz. *H. E.* ii. 32.
[2] *Cities and Bishoprics of Phrygia*, ii (1897), chaps. xii, xvii, esp. p. 501.

possible from that which is enforced in Tertullian's Montanist treatises, and, for that matter, in many other writings which have never been suspected of Montanist leanings. So far from courting persecution the Phrygian Christians sought to avoid it, and succeeded. If the Montanists had not been in this point in agreement with the Catholics such a result would have been impossible.

But this paper must be brought to a close. Professor Harnack, following many other writers, has said that 'what is called Montanism was a reaction against secularism in the Church'.[1] The considerations which I have now adduced seem to me to prove that, if this be true, Montanism, in the place of its birth, must have departed from its original standpoint far more rapidly than the Montanism which, in the last years of the second century, established itself at Carthage, and is represented, for us, by Tertullian.

[1] *Encycl. Brit.*[9] xvi. 777. The statement has been modified in the eleventh edition, 1911, xviii. 759.

ON THE USE BY EUSEBIUS OF VOLUMES OF TRACTS

AN important section of Eusebius's *Ecclesiastical History* is based upon documents which he had himself gathered—the letters of Origen, of which he possessed over a hundred. These, he tells us, he procured from various quarters and bound in volumes.[1] The volumes of Origen's letters in Eusebius's library remind us of the countless volumes of pamphlets, so interesting to the historian, which find a home in our great modern collections. It may very well be that they were but specimens of many similar volumes of the minor writings of early authors, stored in the two libraries which supplied him with materials for his work, those of Pamphilus at Caesarea,[2] and of Alexander at Jerusalem.[3] It may not be without instruction to search through his *History* for evidence of the use of such volumes of tracts.

1. *H. E.* iv. 15. We may begin with an instance which will scarcely be disputed. It was a volume of *Acts of Martyrs*, and contained the following: (1) *The Epistle of the Smyrnaeans on the Martyrdom of Polycarp*; (2) *The Acts of Metrodorus and Pionius*; (3) *The Acts of Carpus, Papylus, and Agathonice*. That these were all bound in a single volume (γραφή), and that Eusebius refers to them in the order in which they occurred in it, is evident from

---

[1] *H. E.* vi. 36. 3 ὧν ὁπόσας σποράδην παρὰ διαφόροις σωθείσας συναγαγεῖν δεδυνήμεθα, ἐν ἰδίαις τόμων περιγραφαῖς, ὡς ἂν μηκέτι διαρρίπτοιντο, κατελέξαμεν, τὸν ἑκατὸν ἀριθμὸν ὑπερβαινούσας.

[2] *H. E.* vi. 32. 3.   [3] *H. E.* vi. 20. 1.

his own words. After paraphrasing the first seven chapters of the Letter of the Smyrnaeans and quoting nearly the whole of the remainder, he proceeds:[1] 'In the same volume about him other martyrdoms also were attached ... with whom also Metrodorus... was delivered up to death by fire. Among those who lived at that time a famous martyr, one Pionius, flourished, whose ... confessions ... the writing about him contains in very full detail ... And after [this] there are extant also memoirs of others ... who were martyred, Carpus and Papylus and the woman Agathonice.' Here then we recognize one volume which lay before the historian as he wrote; and it is important to observe his method of dealing with it. In the course of his narrative he has touched upon most of the prominent ecclesiastics who flourished under Antoninus Pius. Before passing on to the times of Marcus Aurelius he extracts a passage from Irenaeus giving an account of Polycarp.[2] Then, having recorded the accession of Aurelius,[3] he goes on to describe Polycarp's martyrdom, which, according to his chronology, took place in this reign. For an account of this event he has recourse to the volume which we are now considering. Its first treatise suffices for his immediate purpose; but having opened the book he does not again close it till he has given a list of the remaining tracts included in it. The *Acts of Pionius* had for him a special interest,[4] and he is therefore not content with merely mentioning it, but adds a summary of its contents.

---

[1] §§ 46-48 Ἐν τῇ αὐτῇ δὲ περὶ αὐτοῦ γραφῇ καὶ ἄλλα μαρτύρια συνῆπτο ... μεθ' ὧν καὶ Μητρόδωρος ... πυρὶ παραδοθεὶς ἀνῄρηται. τῶν γε μὴν τότε περιβόητος μάρτυς εἷς τις ἐγνωρίζετο Πιόνιος ... ἑξῆς δὲ καὶ ἄλλων ... ὑπομνήματα μεμαρτυρηκότων φέρεται, Κάρπου καὶ Παπύλου, καὶ γυναικὸς Ἀγαθονίκης.

[2] *H. E.* iv. 14.

[3] Ib. § 10.

[4] He included them in his Book of Martyrdoms, *H. E.* iv. 15. 47.

This order of proceeding is similar, as we shall see, to that which he adopts in other cases.

The other volumes of tracts, as we suspect them to be, used by Eusebius, may be noticed in the order in which they are alluded to in the *History*.

2-6. *H.E.* ii. 18. *Writings of Philo*. In this chapter Eusebius gives a list, which is probably complete, of the works of Philo Judaeus which were known to him. He first mentions [1] his two great treatises on the Pentateuch, the *Legum Allegoriae* and the *Quaestiones et Solutiones*, or, to speak more accurately, of those parts of them which still bore these titles and related to the books of Genesis and Exodus. With the volumes which contained the greater part of these we have no concern. We have to consider the catalogue of shorter tracts which follows.

It begins [2] with the remark, 'There are besides these separate dissertations by him on certain questions,' after which thirteen treatises are named, and this section of the catalogue closes with the words, 'These are such of his works on Genesis as have come down to us.' [3] Now of the thirteen treatises, if we may accept the conclusions of modern scholars,[4] no less than eleven really belonged to the *Legum Allegoriae* from which Eusebius distinguishes them. Their connexion with that work had already been forgotten. That in giving their titles Eusebius is in fact merely transcribing them in the order in which they occurred in a volume or volumes into which they had been brought together is made tolerably

---

[1] § 1. In this discussion I have made much use of Schürer, *A History of the Jewish People in the Time of Christ*, Div. ii, vol. iii, § 34. 1, E. T. 1894, pp. 321-361.

[2] § 2 ἔστι δ' αὐτῷ παρὰ ταῦτα προβλημάτων τινῶν ἰδίως πεπονημένα σπουδάσματα.

[3] § 4 καὶ ταῦτα μὲν τὰ εἰς ἡμᾶς ἐλθόντα τῶν εἰς τὴν γένεσιν.

[4] Schürer, pp. 331, 334.

plain when we consider the following facts. Their true order, as parts of the *Allegoriae*, would have been that of the sections of the Book of Genesis with which they severally deal. But that is not at all the order in which Eusebius names them. The first four, indeed, *De agricultura, De ebrietate, De sobrietate,* and *De confusione linguarum*,[1] treat in succession of Gen. ix. 20, 21, 24, xi. 1 ff. ; but then come seven in an order entirely arbitrary, *De profugis*[2] on Gen. xvi. 6 ff., *De congressu quaerendae eruditionis causa*[3] on Gen. xvi. 1 ff., *Quis rerum divinarum haeres sit*[4] on Gen. xv. 1 ff., *De mutatione nominum*[5] on Gen. xvii. 1 ff., *De migratione Abrahami*[6] on Gen. xii. 1 ff., *De gigantibus*[7] on Gen. vi. 1 ff., and *De somniis*[8] on Gen. (xx. 3), xxviii. 12 ff., xxxi. 11 ff., xxxvii, xl. 41, &c. Again, among these are inserted two tracts from an entirely different group of Philo's writings,[9] *De fortitudine*, &c.,[10] and *De Abrahamo*.[11] The former of these has indeed no claim to be included in this list. It is not a dissertation on the Book of Genesis, and it is part of an appendix to the work *De specialibus legibus*[12] mentioned lower down in the chapter.[13] It is not the only tract whose right to stand here may be called in question. For though the two extant books (apparently the second and third)[14] of the *De somniis* discuss dreams recorded in Genesis, the fourth and fifth, which were in Eusebius's copy, must have travelled beyond its limits. And finally, though Eusebius gives us to understand that this list includes all the works of Philo on Genesis that he knew, he subsequently

---

[1] Mangey, i. 300–435. [2] Ib. 546–577.
[3] Ib. 519–545.   [4] Ib. 473–518.   [5] Ib. 578–619.
[6] Ib. 436–472.   [7] Ib. 262–299.   [8] Ib. 620–699.
[9] Schürer, pp. 338 ff.   [10] Mangey, ii. 375–407.   [11] Ib. 1–40.
[12] Ib. 210 358. See Schürer, pp. 343 ff.   [13] § 5.
[14] Schürer, p. 337.

mentions another which is based on passages of that book, his *De Iosepho*.[1]

It is obvious to suggest, as an explanation of all this confusion, that the list which we have been considering is merely an enumeration of the tracts contained in one or more volumes which bore some such title as 'Treatises of Philo on Genesis', while the tracts mentioned later on were preserved in volumes whose titles did not indicate that they treated of that book. Now it is manifestly improbable that so many tracts should have been included in a single manuscript volume. If printed, those which have been mentioned would fill about 650 pages of Mangey's edition. We are led, therefore, to inquire whether there is any evidence for their division among several volumes. And a scrutiny of the text of our list proves that such evidence is at hand. Eusebius divides the tracts into groups: 'Apart from these belong to him separate dissertations on certain questions, such as the two books *De agricultura* ... and yet again the tract *Concerning the three virtues* which, with others, Moses described. In addition to these the *De mutatione nominum* ... and yet again *De gigantibus*,' &c.[2] Does each of the four groups marked out by these phrases 'apart from these', 'and yet again', 'in addition to these', 'and yet again', correspond to a distinct volume? This is not likely, for in that case the volumes would have been of very unequal size. Indeed, the second of them would have had only one tract of somewhat less than the average length, that on *The three virtues*. But let us suppose that the words 'and yet again' do not imply a passing from one volume to another. The list is then broken up into two groups, and it turns out that they would

---

[1] § 6. See Schürer, p. 342.
[2] §§ 2-4 ἔστι δ' αὐτῷ παρὰ ταῦτα ... καὶ ἔτι ... πρὸς τούτοις ... καὶ ἔτι.

OF VOLUMES OF TRACTS 141

represent volumes of very nearly the same bulk. The first eight treatises occupy 274 pages of Mangey's edition, to which we must add about 35 pages for the first book of the *De ebrietate*, now lost.[1] The next five, introduced by the words 'in addition to these', take up 237 pages of Mangey, to which 105 pages are to be added for the three missing books of the *De somniis*. Thus our total is in one case 310, in the other 340, pages of Mangey —volumes, it is true, of large, but not of impossible size.

We pass to the next section,[2] which gives a list of the writings on Exodus. This includes five books of the *Quaestiones et Solutiones*, and some other tracts which seem to be identical with part of the *Vita Mosis*,[3] the *De specialibus legibus*[4] and the *De praemiis et poenis*.[5] There is considerable difficulty in determining the size of the treatises which compose this group because only two of the five books of the *Quaestiones et Solutiones* are now extant,[6] because we cannot be sure how much of the *Vita Mosis* is included, because Eusebius reckons as a distinct treatise in this group the *De victimis*,[7] which in extant manuscripts is reckoned as part of the *De specialibus legibus*, and because the latter work as we have it is imperfect.[8] However, the group seems to have contained about as much as 300 or 400 of Mangey's pages. Thus it would have filled a volume of about the same size as one of those which contained the works on Genesis.

After enumerating the treatises on Exodus Eusebius

[1] Schürer, p. 335. [2] § 5.
[3] Mangey, ii. 80-179. Eusebius calls it περὶ τῆς σκηνῆς : see Schürer, p. 348.
[4] Mangey, ii. 210-358. See Schürer, pp. 343 ff.
[5] Mangey, ii. 408-437.
[6] Schürer, p. 328.
[7] Mangey, ii. 237-250. See Schürer, p. 344, n. 46.
[8] Schürer, p. 343.

proceeds to describe another group.[1] 'In addition to all these,' he says, 'there are also extant works of his, each containing but one book'; and he names four, *De providentia, De Iudaeis*,[2] *De Iosepho*,[3] and *De Alexandro*.[4] The opening words 'in addition to all these' seem as before to indicate a fresh volume. And indeed it is difficult to understand why Eusebius treated these tracts as a separate group unless it was because they were bound together. Their subjects are various, and one of them, as we have seen, might have been included in the Genesis list. Their only bond of union is their size; and in that they are not exceptional, for in this chapter many other treatises are included which consisted of a single book.

We are next introduced to a group, consisting of what Eusebius reckons as four tracts, of which three seem beyond doubt to have stood together in a volume.[5]

'Besides these the tract *On every evil man being in bondage*, following which is the *Quod omnis probus liber*.[6] And after these have been set (or composed) by him the *De Vita contemplativa* or *Concerning Suppliants*,[7] ... and the *Interpretations of the Hebrew names in the Law and the Prophets* are said to be his work.'

The words 'following which' (ᾧ ἑξῆς) of themselves suggest that the second of these tracts succeeded the first in a volume; and that this was the case is made certain when we add that they are known to have been actually

---

[1] § 6 πρὸς τούτοις ἅπασι καὶ μονόβιβλα αὐτοῦ φέρεται.
[2] Schürer, pp. 354, 356.
[3] Mangey, ii. 41-79.   [4] Schürer, p. 355.
[5] § 6 ἐπὶ τούτοις ὁ περὶ τοῦ δοῦλον εἶναι πάντα φαῦλον, ᾧ ἑξῆς ἐστιν ὁ περὶ τοῦ πάντα σπουδαῖον ἐλεύθερον εἶναι· 7. μεθ' οὓς συντέτακται αὐτῷ ὁ περὶ βίου θεωρητικοῦ ἢ ἱκετῶν, ἐξ οὗ τὰ περὶ τοῦ βίου τῶν ἀποστολικῶν ἀνδρῶν διεληλύθαμεν, καὶ τῶν ἐν νόμῳ δὲ καὶ προφήταις Ἑβραϊκῶν ὀνομάτων αἱ ἑρμηνεῖαι τοῦ αὐτοῦ σπουδῇ εἶναι λέγονται.
[6] Mangey, ii. 445-470.   [7] Mangey, ii. 471-486.

the first and second parts of a single work.[1] The statement about the *De vita comtemplativa* might have been taken to mean that it was written by Philo after the others, were it possible to conceive that Eusebius had any evidence of such a fact. There is certainly none in the second and third tracts themselves if in their present form they are complete.[2] If the words are understood as conveying the information that the third followed the second according to their author's arrangement, they give us good reason for thinking that they were so placed in Eusebius's manuscript. But it may appear later on that Eusebius would have had little hesitation in concluding that one treatise was later than another from the mere fact that it came after it in a volume which included both.

There is no direct intimation in the text that the treatise which is next referred to, the *Interpretatio Hebraicorum nominum*, was found by Eusebius in the same volume as the other three. But the assumption is very natural. By themselves the three would have made a very small volume; and the *Interpretatio* is mentioned in close connexion with them. Moreover, we seem to have no choice between supposing that it was bound with them and holding that it was in a volume by itself. For the only work mentioned after it, that which Eusebius here calls περὶ ἀρετῶν, occupies in its present form over eighty pages of Mangey's edition,[3] and originally it must have been more than twice as long.[4] So large a work would scarcely have been bound with another which had no relation to it. Moreover, the hypothesis that the Onomasticon was contained in a volume with one or more

---

[1] Schürer, p. 349. It should be added, however, that the word ἑξῆς does not necessarily indicate *immediate* sequence. See *H. E.* i. 2. 25; 3. 6; ii. 7. 6; 17. 9; 21. 1; iii. 36. 14; v. 1. 4, 62, &c.
[2] The first is lost.   [3] ii. 517-600.   [4] Schürer, pp. 350 ff.

works of Philo serves to explain certain facts which are somewhat difficult to understand otherwise. In Eusebius's copy the work was plainly anonymous. Jerome had seen several copies of it, and apparently none of them gave the name of the author. Origen also seems to refer to it as anonymous.[1] Yet both Eusebius and Jerome ascribe it to Philo, and the latter does so on the authority of Origen. How is this to be accounted for? If the treatise was bound up with other works which bore the name of Philo in the manuscript which Eusebius used, the inference would have been natural enough that it came from Philo's pen. And Eusebius may have been guided to it by a marginal note in the manuscript.[2] Now it is quite probable that the copies of Philo known to Eusebius were in Origen's library at Caesarea. If Jerome had seen the volume he might have drawn from it the same inference as Eusebius, and, with less caution, he might have supposed that it had the sanction of the famous scholar who had made the collection.

I conclude then that the Hebrew Onomasticon was the last tract in a volume. But did the three which precede it in Eusebius's list constitute with it a separate volume? If they did, it would seem to have been much smaller than some of the others which are referred to in this chapter. And the same remark applies to the group of four short treatises previously discussed. For this reason I am inclined to suppose that the two sets of tracts were bound together. The words 'besides these' (ἐπὶ τούτοις)[3] which introduce the description of the group favour the

[1] The passages of Origen and Jerome are quoted by Schürer, p. 360 f.

[2] Compare for a somewhat similar case, Photius, *Bibl.* 48, discussed by Lightfoot, *Clement*, ii. 378 ff.

[3] Not πρὸς τούτοις, a phrase which elsewhere in the chapter indicates the beginning of a volume. Cp. above, p. 26.

hypothesis. But the evidence is far from being decisive; and I therefore count the two groups as corresponding to two volumes.

If the obscure hints of Eusebius have been rightly interpreted we find, then, that for his knowledge of the minor writings of Philo he depended on these five volumes, probably preserved in Origen's library:

(1) A volume of eight tracts described as being on the Book of Genesis.

(2) A volume of five tracts with a similar title.

(3) A volume containing five books of the *Quaestiones et Solutiones*, together with four tracts on Exodus.

(4) A small volume containing four short tracts.

(5) A small volume containing the two parts of a treatise by Philo, with separate titles, and two others of which the second was anonymous.

7. *H. E.* iv. 11-13; 16-18. *Works of Justin Martyr.* This volume contained the following: (1) The treatise (or treatises) *Adv. Graecos*; (2) *Apol.* i; (3) The Epistle of Marcus Aurelius addressed to the Commune Asiae; (4) *Apol.* ii. Let it first be remarked that if we are right in supposing that these tracts were collected in one volume the procedure of Eusebius with regard to Justin is similar to that which he followed in the case of Polycarp. He mentions two prominent writers of the time of Pope Anicetus, Hegesippus and Justin, and cites a passage from each which fixes his date.[1] For the latter writer the passage is taken from the first Apology. The volume containing it is open, and therefore, having made his extract, Eusebius proceeds to give an account of its contents. He names (1) and (2), from the latter of which he makes a further extract; he transcribes (3), which he ascribes to Antoninus Pius. Having got so far, his

[1] *H. E.* iv. 11. 7-9.

description is interrupted, for (4) does not (as he supposes) belong to the reign of Pius, of which he is at the moment treating, but to that of his successor. Hence the account of Polycarp is inserted, as it were parenthetically. This finished, he returns to Justin in ch. 16, mentioning (4), and making from it a lengthy quotation. The parallelism of all this to his treatment of Polycarp and the others mentioned along with him lends a certain probability to our hypothesis. But it is supported by other considerations. In the first place, why is Justin's work against the Greeks mentioned in iv. 11? It has no obvious relevance to the context; it is not a book which had any special attraction for Eusebius, since he makes no extract from it, and gives no account of its argument; and it is named again in its proper place in ch. 18, where a formal list is given of the writings of its author. Our answer is simple. It stood first in the volume which Eusebius was using at the time, and therefore, according to his habit, he named it in connexion with the other more important treatises with which it was bound. Again, if Eusebius found (2), (3), (4) succeeding one another in this order, his manuscript of these writings resembled the only known extant manuscripts which contain them. The two complete copies of the Apologies of Justin insert after the first the letter of Marcus Aurelius (followed by another spurious imperial epistle).[1] And lastly, our hypothesis partially removes a difficulty which has perplexed critics. Eusebius is so apparently contradictory in his references to Justin's Apologies that some writers have contended that what he names the *Second Apology* is a lost work, and

[1] Otto, *Corpus Apologetarum*, vol. i, pp. xxi ff. The MSS. referred to are not independent of one another. The order in them is (4), (2), (3); and there is evidence that in other manuscripts the two Apologies were transposed. Ib., p. xxviii f.

that our first and second Apologies were by him regarded as a single treatise and called the *First Apology*. This indeed appears, on any showing, very unlikely, since in *H.E.* iv. 16 he quotes from our *Second Apology*, and expressly tells us that his extract is from 'the second book on behalf of our doctrines'.[1] But what are the arguments on the other side? They are two in number. In iv. 8. 5, after quoting from the *First Apology*, he introduces an extract from the second with the words ἐν ταὐτῷ ... ταῦτα γράφει, which have been rendered, 'In the same work,' &c. But there seems to be no need to translate the phrase in this way. May we not understand some such word as βιβλίῳ[2] after ταὐτῷ, and translate, 'In the same *volume*'? There remains only iv. 17. 1, where ἐν τῇ προτέρᾳ ἀπολογίᾳ is certainly intended to refer to (our) *Second Apology*. We cannot safely build a theory on such a slender foundation. We may suppose that προτέρᾳ is a slip either of Eusebius or of a scribe, or that it is to be taken in an unusual sense as equivalent to δεδηλωμένῃ.

8. *H. E.* iv. 23. The Epistles of Dionysius of Corinth. Seven 'Catholic' Epistles are mentioned, and a letter addressed to a lady named Chrysophora. It has been remarked[3] that, in a note appended (as it seems) to the letter to the Romans, Dionysius complains that his epistles had been tampered with by heretics; and that two of them are addressed to churches in Crete, and that these are not named consecutively; from which facts the inference is drawn, 'that the letters had already been collected into a volume, and that they are enumerated by Eusebius in the order in which he found them there.' I

---

[1] This is explained away, not very satisfactorily, by making the words ἐν τῇ δεδηλωμένῃ ἀπολογίᾳ in § 2 refer, not to the work mentioned in § 1, but to the *First Apology*, quoted in ch. 13.

[2] Cp. *H. E.* v. 20. 2, and below, p. 177, note [1].

[3] *Dict. Christ. Biog.* i. 849.

confess that, while admiring the acuteness of the argument, I was not at first convinced by it. But the scale is turned when we find it confirmed by the words of Eusebius himself. After describing five of the letters he introduces the sixth with the words ταύταις ἄλλη ἐγκατείλεκται ... ἐπιστολή.[1] The verb seems naturally to imply a volume. Indeed a cognate word is used by Eusebius of the volumes in which he had arranged the letters of Origen.[2] And it is applied elsewhere to a treatise which Eusebius included in his lost book of Acts of Martyrdom.[3] If the Epistles of Dionysius were already gathered into a volume in the lifetime of their writer, it would appear that additions had been made to the collection before it fell into the hands of Eusebius. In the volume which he used the sixth Catholic Epistle seems to have been followed by the reply to it, addressed to Dionysius by Pinytus, bishop of the Cnossians, a paraphrased extract from which is given by Eusebius,[4] and at the end, after the note of Dionysius already referred to, came the letter to Chrysophora.

9-12. *H. E.* iv. 26. *Works of Melito of Sardis.* Of the works of Melito which were known to him Eusebius gives a long list. As in the case of the writings of Philo, discussed above, he seems to divide them into groups, which may very possibly represent separate volumes. The several groups are indicated, as before, by the connecting particles. 'Of these writers [Melito and Apollinarius] there have come to our knowledge those that are set out below. Of Melito: (1) The two books *On the Pascha*, and that *On the [Christian] mode of life and the prophets*, and [the treatise] *On the Church* and that *On the Lord's Day*;

---

[1] § 7.   [2] See above, p. 136.
[3] *H. E.* v. 4. 3 ὁ (*sc.* σύγγραμμα) καὶ αὐτὸ τῇ τῶν μαρτύρων συναγωγῇ πρὸς ἡμῶν, ὡς γοῦν ἔφην, κατείλεκται. Compare iii. 24. 2; 38. 1.
[4] § 8.

and yet again (2) that *On the faith of man*, and that *On Creation*, and that *On obedience of the senses to faith*; and in addition to these (3) that *On soul and body or mind*, and that *On the Laver*, and *On Truth*, and *On faith and the generation of Christ*; and (4) his discourse *On prophecy* and *On soul and body*, and that *On hospitality* and *The Key*, and the [books] *On the Devil and the Apocalypse of John*, and that *On the Incarnate God*. After all [these] also the booklet addressed to Antoninus.'[1] The first and third groups apparently contain four treatises each, the second group three, and the last six.[2] After giving this list as a complete enumeration, Eusebius proceeds to quote from the first and last of the series, and then makes an extract from Melito's *Selections*,[3] *a work not included in his list*. The explanation which may be suggested of this discrepancy is of this kind. By the writings of Melito which had come to his knowledge, Eusebius meant those which lay in one of the libraries to which he had constant access. The extract from the *Selections* may have been made from a copy borrowed from a friend, or may have been taken at second hand from an earlier writer.

13. *H. E.* iv. 27. *Works of Apollinarius.* This chapter is a continuation of the preceding, in which Eusebius undertook to give a catalogue of some of the works of

[1] § 2. τούτων εἰς ἡμετέραν γνῶσιν ἀφῖκται τὰ ὑποτεταγμένα· Μελίτωνος, τὰ περὶ τοῦ πάσχα δύο καὶ τὸ περὶ πολιτείας καὶ προφητῶν καὶ ὁ περὶ ἐκκλησίας καὶ ὁ περὶ κυριακῆς λόγος, ἔτι δὲ ὁ περὶ πίστεως ἀνθρώπου καὶ ὁ περὶ πλάσεως, καὶ ὁ περὶ ὑπακοῆς πίστεως αἰσθητηρίων καὶ πρὸς τούτοις ὁ περὶ ψυχῆς καὶ σώματος ἢ νοὸς καὶ ὁ περὶ λουτροῦ καὶ περὶ ἀληθείας καὶ περὶ πίστεως καὶ γενέσεως Χριστοῦ καὶ λόγος αὐτοῦ [περὶ] προφητείας καὶ περὶ ψυχῆς καὶ σώματος καὶ ὁ περὶ φιλοξενίας καὶ ἡ κλεὶς καὶ τὰ περὶ τοῦ διαβόλου καὶ τῆς ἀποκαλύψεως Ἰωάννου καὶ ὁ περὶ ἐνσωμάτου θεοῦ, ἐπὶ πᾶσι καὶ τὰ πρὸς Ἀντωνῖνον βιβλίδιον.

[2] But Schwartz regards περὶ λουτροῦ and the four following titles as mere chapter headings of a single work.

[3] ἐκλογαί.

Melito and Apollinarius, but actually spoke only of those of the former. It might be expected, then, that if the list of Melito's works, with the exception of the *Selections*, was simply a transcript of the titles of tracts bound in volumes which lay under his hand, the catalogue of the writings of Apollinarius would be compiled by the same easy method. And it will be observed that Eusebius is conscious that his enumeration is far from complete. Out of many books he names only a few which he himself had seen. He writes:

'Many books by Apollinarius are preserved in the possession of many persons, but those which have come into our hands are these: The discourse to the before-mentioned Emperor [Antoninus], and *To the Greeks* five books, and *On Truth* a first and second, and *To the Jews* a first and second, and those things which he wrote after these against the heresy of the Phrygians, which had recently come into existence, since it was then beginning as it were to shoot forth and Montanus with his false prophetesses was still in the act of introducing his error.'[1]

There is no indication here, such as we found elsewhere, that Eusebius, as he wrote down the titles of the books, was passing from one volume to another. But that the polemical work was in the same volume with those previously named, and followed them in it, is very probable. Eusebius says that Apollinarius wrote it 'after them'. How did he know this? He may have had evidence in the book itself sufficient to enable him to form an opinion as to its date. Indeed he implies as much. But it is hardly likely that the other treatises gave similar indications such as

[1] Τοῦ δὲ Ἀπολιναρίου πολλῶν παρὰ πολλοῖς σωζομένων τὰ εἰς ἡμᾶς ἐλθόντα ἐστὶν τάδε· λόγος ὁ πρὸς τὸν προειρημένον βασιλέα καὶ πρὸς Ἕλληνας συγγράμματα πέντε καὶ περὶ ἀληθείας α' β' καὶ πρὸς Ἰουδαίους α' β' καὶ ἃ μετὰ ταῦτα συνέγραψε κατὰ τῆς τῶν Φρυγῶν αἱρέσεως, μετ' οὐ πολὺν καινοτομηθείσης χρόνον, τότε γε μὴν ὥσπερ ἐκφύειν ἀρχομένης, ἔτι τοῦ Μοντανοῦ ἅμα ταῖς αὐτοῦ ψευδοπροφήτισιν ἀρχὰς τῆς παρεκτροπῆς ποιουμένου.

would warrant the assertion that they were all of earlier date. But let us suppose that they were included in a single volume in the order in which he mentions them. It is at least possible that he believed them to have been arranged chronologically, and therefore concluded that the last in place was also the latest in time. That Eusebius had at any rate no better ground for his assertion than this becomes probable when we observe that his inference is almost certainly incorrect. For he tells us that Apollinarius related the story of the *Legio Fulminata*.[1] It cannot be doubted that he found it in one of the treatises mentioned in this chapter, and most likely in the *Apology*. But the book in which the story was told must have been published after the year 174. And a work the appearance of which coincided with the beginning of the Montanist movement cannot have been written so late. For we know that by 177 Montanism had spread to Rome.[2] Eusebius himself dates its rise in 172,[3] and it probably originated much earlier. Hence it is scarcely possible that the statement that the treatise against the Phrygians was written after the rest of Apollinarius's works is true, or that Eusebius made it as the result of a critical investigation.

14. *H. E.* vi. 22. *Works of Hippolytus.* Of the writings of this famous person, Eusebius confesses that he had but little knowledge. He enumerates seven as having come into his hands, but adds that a very large number of others were preserved by various owners. The seven which he mentions are these: (1) *On the Hexaemeron*, (2) *On the things following the Hexaemeron*, (3) *Against Marcion*, (4) *On the Song of Solomon*, (5) *On parts of Ezekiel*, (6) *Concerning the Pascha*, (7) *Against all Heresies*. All these are lost or imperfectly known, but the last was a

---

[1] *H. E.* v. 5. 4.   [2] *H. E.* v. 3. 4.   [3] *Chron.*, Schoene, ii. 173.

short work,[1] and there seems no reason why all should not have been included in one volume. Before giving the list Eusebius mentions the Paschal Cycle of Hippolytus, professing to derive his information about it from the book *Concerning the Pascha*. It was, in fact, the circumstance that this work could be assigned to the reign of Alexander Severus that led Eusebius to mention it in this place. Having named it, he proceeds, *more suo*, to give the contents of the volume in which he found it. It is not without significance that he introduces his list with the words, 'But of his *other* treatises those which have come into our hands are the following,'[2] and then, among the rest, mentions the treatise *Concerning the Pascha* again.

15. *H. E.* vi. 43. *Letters on the Schism of Novatian.* These seem to have been four in number—(1) A letter[3] from Cornelius of Rome to Fabius of Antioch, telling of the proceedings at a Roman synod, and throughout Italy and Africa, against Novatian; (2) A letter[4] from Cyprian, in the Latin language, urging mild treatment of the lapsed and the excommunication of Novatian; (3) A letter[5] from Cornelius, giving the acts of the synod; (4) A letter[6] from the same to Fabius, recounting the doings of Novatian and others, from which copious extracts are given. But were these contained in a single volume? This seems to be clearly implied by the words used with reference to the third and fourth epistles: ταύταις ἄλλη τις ἐπιστολὴ συνῆπτο ... καὶ πάλιν ἑτέρα. We have already noticed the similar use of συνῆπτο in a like connexion.[7] And other indications point to the same conclusion. Only the first

---

[1] βιβλιδάριον, Photius, *Bibl.* 121.
[2] τῶν δὲ λοιπῶν αὐτοῦ συγγραμμάτων τὰ εἰς ἡμᾶς ἐλθόντα ἐστὶν τάδε.
[3] § 3 ἐπιστολαί, which may mean one letter. See Lightfoot, *Ignat.*, vol. ii, pp. 911, 932. Apparently Jerome so understood it, *De Vir. Ill.* 66.   [4] ἄλλαι.   [5] ἄλλη τις ἐπιστολή.
[6] ἑτέρα.   [7] Above, p. 137. See also *H. E.* i. 13. 11.

and fourth epistles are directly stated to have been addressed to Fabius, and he can hardly have been the recipient of the third, which must have covered much the same ground as the first. Eusebius, if he had been arranging the letters for himself, would naturally have brought the first and fourth together. No less natural would it have been to name together the three written by Cornelius, but, in fact, between two of them intervenes the letter of Cyprian. We infer, as we did in a former case,[1] that the historian follows the order of the volume which lay before him.

It is not easy to reconcile this passage of Eusebius with the list of the letters of Cornelius given by Jerome,[2] with which, nevertheless, it has an obvious connexion. Jerome states that Cornelius wrote four letters:

(1) To Fabius: De synodo Romana et Italica et Africana.
(2) De Novatiano et de his qui lapsi sunt.
(3) De gestis synodi.
(4) A very prolix letter to Fabius 'et Novatianae haereseos causas et anathema continentem'.

The third and fourth of these are plainly our third and fourth; and it might appear equally plain that the first is our first. But Benson takes a different view.[3] He contends that the ἐπιστολαί about the Roman Synod and the decisions of the Italians and Africans are not a single letter, but two or more;[4] and he concludes that they correspond to Jerome's first and second. But if so, Jerome manifestly could not have learned the subject of the second epistle from the text of Eusebius. He must have had independent knowledge of the letters of Cornelius. And yet he names them in Eusebius's order. This is a

---

[1] Above, p. 147. [2] *De Vir. Ill.* 66.
[3] *Cyprian, his life, his times, his work*, 1897, p. 168.
[4] An unnecessary assumption. See above, p. 152, note [3].

coincidence which can scarcely be explained otherwise than by supposing that both writers found them collected together in a volume. Thus from Jerome, on Benson's hypothesis, we gain additional reason for believing that Eusebius had access to a volume of letters on the schism.

But I confess that I find it easier to think that Jerome was entirely dependent on Eusebius for his knowledge of Cornelius's writings. His description of the contents of his second letter applies to the letter which stands second in Eusebius. We need only suppose that he carelessly overlooked the statement that it was written by Cyprian. It would be strange, if he had first-hand knowledge of the correspondence of Cornelius, that he should follow Eusebius so closely as he actually does. With the exception of this supposed addition to the list of the letters he tells absolutely nothing which is not in Eusebius's text. Like Eusebius he allows us to doubt whether the third letter was addressed to Fabius or another. He leaves us in similar ignorance, it will be observed, as to the destination of his second letter, though on Benson's theory the *History* actually states that it was addressed to Fabius. This omission confirms our conjecture, for Eusebius does not give the name of the person to whom Cyprian wrote on the same subject. In short, I have little doubt that Jerome's paragraph on Pope Cornelius is nothing more than a careless and meagre epitome of *H. E.* vi. 43.

16. *H. E.* vi. 44–46. *Letters of Dionysius of Alexandria on the same subject.* In chapter 44 a letter from Dionysius to Fabius is mentioned and quoted, from which extracts had already been made in chapters 41, 42. Then follows, in chapter 45, a short letter to Novatian, seemingly given in full. Immediately connected with this is chapter 46, beginning 'And he writes *also* to the Egyptians [1] a letter

---

[1] By a similar formula the letter to Novatus is connected with that

concerning Repentance', which letter to the Egyptians is the first of a list of thirteen or fourteen epistles occupying the entire chapter.[1] The list professes to be a complete one, for the heading of the chapter is 'Concerning the other letters of Dionysius'. It is therefore with no little surprise that we read the words with which the chapter closes: 'And in the communication which he held in writing *with many others* he has bequeathed manifold profit to those who still at this present time diligently study his compositions.' And it is with equal surprise that

to Fabius in cap. 45: 'Let us see how he *also* wrote to Novatus'; 'these things *also* to (*or* against) Novatus.'

[1] xliv. Τῷ δ' αὐτῷ τούτῳ Φαβίῳ, ὑποκατακλινομένῳ πως τῷ σχίσματι, καὶ Διονύσιος ὁ κατ' Ἀλεξάνδρειαν ἐπιστείλας πολλά τε καὶ ἄλλα περὶ μετανοίας ἐν τοῖς πρὸς αὐτὸν γράμμασι διελθὼν τῶν τε κατ' Ἀλεξάνδρειαν ἔναγχος τότε μαρτυρησάντων τοὺς ἀγῶνας διιών, μετὰ τῆς ἄλλης ἱστορίας πρᾶγμά τι μεστὸν θαύματος διηγεῖται, ὃ καὶ αὐτὸ ἀναγκαῖον τῇδε παραδοῦναι τῇ γραφῇ, οὕτως ἔχον . . . xlv. Ἴδωμεν δ' ὁ αὐτὸς ὁποῖα καὶ τῷ Νοουάτῳ διεχάραξεν, ταράττοντι τηνικάδε τὴν Ῥωμαίων ἀδελφότητα . . . xlvi. ταῦτα καὶ πρὸς τὸν Νοουάτον· Γράφει δὲ καὶ τοῖς κατ' Αἴγυπτον ἐπιστολὴν περὶ μετανοίας, ἐν ᾗ τὰ δόξαντα αὐτῷ περὶ τῶν ὑποπεπτωκότων παρατέθειται, τάξεις παραπτωμάτων διαγράψας. 2. καὶ πρὸς Κόλωνα (τῆς Ἑρμουπολιτῶν δὲ παροικίας ἐπίσκοπος ἦν οὗτος) ἰδία τις περὶ μετανοίας αὐτοῦ φέρεται γραφὴ καὶ ἄλλη ἐπιστρεπτικὴ πρὸς τὸ κατ' Ἀλεξάνδρειαν αὐτοῦ ποίμνιον. ἐν τούτοις ἐστὶν καὶ ἡ περὶ μαρτυρίου πρὸς τὸν Ὠριγένην γραφεῖσα· καὶ τοῖς κατὰ Λαοδίκειαν ἀδελφοῖς, ὧν προΐστατο Θηλυμίδρης ἐπίσκοπος, καὶ τοῖς κατὰ Ἀρμενίαν ὡσαύτως περὶ μετανοίας ἐπιστέλλει, ὧν ἐπεσκόπευεν Μερουζάνης. 3. πρὸς ἅπασι τούτοις καὶ Κορνηλίῳ τῷ κατὰ Ῥώμην γράφει, δεξάμενος αὐτοῦ τὴν κατὰ τοῦ Νοουάτου ἐπιστολήν, ᾧ καὶ σημαίνει δηλῶν ἑαυτὸν παρακεκλῆσθαι . . . ὡς ἂν ἐπὶ τὴν σύνοδον ἀπαντήσοι τὴν κατὰ Ἀντιόχειαν, ἔνθα τοῦ Νοουάτου κρατύνειν τινὲς ἐνεχείρουν τὸ σχίσμα. 4. πρὸς τούτοις ἐπιστέλλει μηνυθῆναι αὐτῷ Φάβιον μὲν κεκοιμῆσθαι . . . γράφει δὲ καὶ περὶ τοῦ ἐν Ἱεροσολύμοις αὐτοῖς ῥήμασιν φάσκων . . . 5. ἑξῆς ταύτῃ καὶ ἑτέρα τις ἐπιστολὴ τοῖς ἐν Ῥώμῃ τοῦ Διονυσίου φέρεται διακονικὴ διὰ Ἱππολύτου· τοῖς αὐτοῖς δὲ ἄλλην περὶ εἰρήνης διατυποῦται, καὶ ὡσαύτως περὶ μετανοίας, καὶ αὖ πάλιν ἄλλην τοῖς ἐκεῖσε ὁμολογηταῖς, ἔτι τῇ τοῦ Νοουάτου συμφερομένοις γνώμῃ· τοῖς δὲ αὐτοῖς τούτοις ἑτέρας δύο, μεταθεμένοις ἐπὶ τὴν ἐκκλησίαν, ἐπιστέλλει. Καὶ ἄλλοις δὲ πλείοσιν ὁμοίως διὰ γραμμάτων ὁμιλήσας ποικίλας τοῖς ἔτι νῦν σπουδὴν περὶ τοὺς λόγους αὐτοῦ ποιουμένοις καταλέλοιπεν ὠφελείας.

we find numerous allusions, in the next book of the *History*, to letters of Dionysius not mentioned here, and even from time to time formal lists of them. How is the inconsistency to be explained? Easily enough. The list in *H. E.* vi. 46 is a complete enumeration of the letters *in a single volume*. Those alluded to at the end of the chapter, and catalogued elsewhere, belonged to other volumes. With this conclusion agree the words used of the sixth and seventh letters, 'Among these there is also the letter on Martyrdom written to Origen, and [a letter] to the brethren in Laodicea.'[1] The phrase 'among these' implies a definite collection of documents, which would probably be bound in a volume. And our hypothesis receives further support from the words with which the mention of the tenth letter is prefaced, 'After this there is also another letter.' What else can this statement mean than that the tenth letter followed the ninth in a book which Eusebius was looking through as he wrote?

Of the letters which we may suppose to have been brought together in this volume the following is a list:

(1) To Fabius, bishop of Antioch, when he leaned towards the schism. Contained many things concerning Repentance, an account of the sufferings of the Christians of Alexandria in the persecution, and arguments against harsh treatment of the lapsed founded thereon.

(2) To Novatus (i. e. Novatian). Quoted, apparently in full.

(3) To the Egyptians concerning Repentance, in which he sets forth his views in regard to the treatment of the lapsed.

(4) To Colon,[2] bishop of Hermopolis, on Repentance. An

---

[1] § 2.

[2] So Schwartz reads the name. Earlier editors (with Jerome, *De Vir. Ill.* 69) have 'Conon'.

extant fragment [1] shows that it dealt with various classes of persons who should receive absolution on repentance, especially those who are apparently *in articulo mortis*. It has some remarkable points of contact with no. 3.

(5) Admonitory letter to the Alexandrians.
(6) To Origen on Martyrdom.
(7) To the Laodiceans.
(8) To the Armenians concerning Repentance.[2]
(9) To Cornelius, bishop of Rome, when he had received his letter against Novatus. Gives information about the Synod at Antioch convened when an attempt was being made to establish the schism there.[3]
(10) To the Romans by Hippolytus: a 'diaconic' letter.
(11) To the same on Peace.
(12) To the same on Repentance.[4]
(13) To the Confessors at Rome while they still adhered to the opinions of Novatus.
(14) To the same when they had come over to the Church.
(15) To the same.

Now of the contents of four of these letters (1, 2, 3, 9) we have sufficient knowledge to affirm with complete certainty that they dealt directly with the Novatianist schism; and the same may be said with almost as much confidence of three others (13–15). Of these seven two (1, 3) treat also of the cognate topic of repentance. We may conclude that the remaining letters 'concerning

---

[1] C. L. Feltoe, *Letters of Dionysius of Alexandria*, 1904, p. 60.

[2] Jerome (*De Vir. Ill.* 69) adds 'et de ordine delictorum'. But if he depended on Eusebius he may have attached to this epistle the description of no. 3, which he apparently does not mention—γράφει δὲ καὶ τοῖς κατ' Αἴγυπτον ἐπιστολὴν περὶ μετανοίας, ἐν ᾗ τὰ δόξαντα αὐτῷ περὶ τῶν ὑποπεπτωκότων παρατέθειται, τάξεις παραπτωμάτων διαγράψας.

[3] Possibly Eusebius refers here to more than one letter.

[4] It is not clear that 11 and 12 are distinct letters. Eusebius may mean that both subjects were dealt with in a single epistle.

Repentance' (4, 8, 12) regarded the subject from the same point of view. In other words, they discussed the question whether, and under what conditions, those who had fallen away in persecution could be received back into communion with the Church. If so, they also were letters on the schism of Novatian. We need not doubt that the discussion on Peace, whether or no it filled an entire letter (11), was a protest against the schism. The short letter to Novatian (2) itself might fitly have been entitled 'Concerning Peace', ending as it does with the prayer that he might 'fare well clinging to peace'. There is no difficulty in believing that a letter on Martyrdom (6) written, let us say, about the year 251, if it was not wholly taken up with the great controversy of the day, at least touched upon it in many passages.[1] There remain three letters (5, 7, 10), about the subject of which Eusebius gives us no hint.[2] But the assumption is not rash that they as well as the others had some connexion with the Novatianist movement. Thus it is easy to guess the reason which may have led to the binding of this

---

[1] This indeed is not true of the fragments printed by Feltoe (p. 231), some parts of which have been regarded by eminent scholars as belonging to this letter. But in them martyrdom is only twice referred to (p. 243), and never in the portions which have been accepted as coming from the letter to Origen. And, as Dr. Feltoe says (p. 230), 'The Dionysian authorship of any of these extracts must be considered very doubtful.'

[2] Dom Morin, indeed (*Rev. Bénéd.* 1900, pp. 241 ff.), thinks that the word διακονική implies that the tenth letter was a tract on ministerial functions, and identifies it with the *Canons of Hippolytus*. But the Canons are not cast in epistolary form, and the mention of them would be as much out of place among the other letters enumerated by Eusebius as would their association with them in the same volume. On the meaning of διακονική cp. Benson, *Cyprian*, p. 171 f. If we may believe Jerome (*De Vir. Ill.* 69) the letter to the Laodiceans (7) was 'de paenitentia'.

OF VOLUMES OF TRACTS 159

collection of letters in one volume. They were all concerned, in the main, with a single topic.

17. *H. E.* vii. 2-9. *Letters of Dionysius of Alexandria on Baptism.* Five of the seven letters mentioned in these chapters are numbered:

'To him (i. e. Pope Stephen) Dionysius composes the *first* of the letters about Baptism . . . . [*Extract*].[1] And when Stephen had fulfilled his ministry for two years Xystus succeeds him. In writing to the latter a *second* letter about Baptism Dionysius declares both the opinion and the judgement of Stephen and the other bishops, speaking thus about Stephen: [*Extracts*]. And also in the *third* of the [letters] about Baptism, which the same Dionysius writes to Philemon, the presbyter at Rome, he sets out these facts: [*Extracts*]. The *fourth* of his letters about Baptism was written to Dionysius of Rome, who then held office as a presbyter, but not long afterwards obtained the bishopric of the people of that place. . . . And in his letter to him after other things he mentions the followers of Novatus in these words: [*Extract*]. And the *fifth* also was written by him to Xystus, bishop of the Romans, in which . . . he relates a certain event of his time, saying: [*Extract*]. In addition to those already mentioned there is extant also *another* letter of his about Baptism, from him and the community over which he ruled to Xystus and the Church at Rome. . . . And there is also extant *another* after these to Dionysius of Rome, the letter about Lucian.'[2]

[1] Eusebius (*H. E.* vii. 4) expressly states that his quotation is from the end of the letter. Fragments from the earlier part of it are printed in a Syriac version by Feltoe, pp. 45 ff.

[2] ii. Τούτῳ τὴν πρώτην ὁ Διονύσιος τῶν περὶ βαπτίσματος ἐπιστολῶν διατυποῦται . . . v. 3. Στέφανον δ' ἐπὶ δυσὶν ἀποπλήσαντα τὴν λειτουργίαν ἔτεσι Ξύστος διαδέχεται. τούτῳ δευτέραν ὁ Διονύσιος περὶ βαπτίσματος χαράξας ἐπιστολήν, ὁμοῦ τὴν Στεφάνου καὶ τῶν λοιπῶν ἐπισκόπων γνώμην τε καὶ κρίσιν δηλοῖ, περὶ τοῦ Στεφάνου λέγων ταῦτα . . . vii. Καὶ ἐν τῇ τρίτῃ δὲ τῶν περὶ βαπτίσματος, ἣν Φιλήμονι τῷ κατὰ 'Ρώμην πρεσβυτέρῳ ὁ αὐτὸς γράφει Διονύσιος, ταῦτα παρατίθεται . . . 6. ἡ τετάρτη αὐτοῦ τῶν περὶ βαπτίσματος ἐπιστολῶν πρὸς τὸν κατὰ 'Ρώμην ἐγράφη Διονύσιον, τότε μὲν πρεσβείου ἠξιωμένον, οὐκ εἰς μακρὸν δὲ καὶ τὴν ἐπισκοπὴν τῶν ἐκεῖσε παρειληφότα· ἐξ ἧς γνῶναι πάρεστιν ὅπως καὶ αὐτὸς οὗτος

No explanation of these numbers is so plausible as that which regards them as indicating the order of succession of the letters in a volume. It might have been thought, indeed, that a chronological arrangement was intended. But this appears to be negatived by the fact that the third and fourth letters of the series are alluded to in the second.[1] It may also be remarked that Eusebius seems to abandon his rule of the chronological treatment of history, in order to bring these letters together. For he places the whole series under Gallus. In his reign Stephen succeeded to the episcopate, and according to Eusebius survived his appointment only two years.[2] Thus the first letter might be dated before the death of Gallus. But the fifth and sixth belong to the episcopate of Xystus and therefore to the reign of Valerian, whose accession is not recorded till chapter 10.

18. *H. E.* vii. 20–23. *Festal Epistles of Dionysius of Alexandria.* Under this head a catalogue of letters is given, but Eusebius intimates that his list is not complete. It will conduce to clearness if it is reproduced with some omissions.

λόγιός τε καὶ θαυμάσιος πρὸς τοῦ κατ' Ἀλεξάνδρειαν Διονυσίου μεμαρτύρηται. γράφει δὲ αὐτῷ μεθ' ἕτερα τῶν κατὰ Νοουάτον μνημονείων ἐν τούτοις. ... ix. Καὶ ἡ πέμπτη δὲ αὐτῷ πρὸς τὸν Ῥωμαίων ἐπίσκοπον Ξύστον γέγραπτο· ἐν ᾗ πολλὰ κατὰ τῶν αἱρετικῶν εἰπών, τοιοῦτόν τι γεγονὸς κατ' αὐτὸν ἐκτίθεται λέγων ... 6. ἐπὶ ταῖς προειρημέναις φέρεταί τις καὶ ἄλλη τοῦ αὐτοῦ περὶ βαπτίσματος ἐπιστολή, ἐξ αὐτοῦ καὶ ἧς ἡγεῖτο παροικίας Ξύστῳ καὶ τῇ κατὰ Ῥώμην ἐκκλησίᾳ προσπεφωνημένη, ἐν ᾗ διὰ μακρᾶς ἀποδείξεως τὸν περὶ τοῦ ὑποκειμένου ζητήματος παρατείνει λόγον. καὶ ἄλλη δέ τις αὐτοῦ μετὰ ταύτας φέρεται πρὸς τὸν κατὰ Ῥώμην Διονύσιον, ἡ περὶ Λουκιανοῦ.

[1] *H. E.* vii. 5. 6 καὶ τοῖς ἀγαπητοῖς δὲ ἡμῶν καὶ συμπρεσβυτέροις Διονυσίῳ καὶ Φιλήμονι, συμψήφοις πρότερον Στεφάνῳ γενομένοις καὶ περὶ τῶν αὐτῶν μοι γράφουσιν, πρότερον μὲν ὀλίγα, καὶ νῦν δὲ διὰ πλειόνων ἐπέστειλα. At least two of the four letters here mentioned seem to have been written during the pontificate of Stephen.

[2] *Chronica,* A. Abr. 2270 (Schoene, ii. 182 f.); *H. E.* vii. 2 ; 5. 3.

'Dionysius, in addition to the letters of his which were mentioned, composed at that time also the festal epistles which are still extant. ... Of these he addresses one to Flavius, and another to Domitius and Didymus (in which he sets out a canon based on a cycle of eight years . . .). In addition to these he pens another letter to his fellow presbyters at Alexandria, and to others likewise in different places. And these [he writes] while the persecution is still proceeding. But peace is no sooner come than he returns to Alexandria. Again, however, sedition and war broke out there, so that it was not possible for him to exercise oversight over all the brethren throughout the city, since they were divided into various parts by the sedition, and once more at the Paschal festival, as though he were some exile, from Alexandria itself he held communication with them by letter. And also after these things, in the course of another festal epistle to Hierax, a bishop of the people in Egypt, he mentions the sedition of the Alexandrians, which took place under him, in these words: [*Extract*]. After these things, when a pestilential sickness had succeeded the war, and the feast was drawing near, once more he holds communication with the brethren in writing, describing the sufferings due to this misfortune in these words: [*Extracts*]. And after this epistle also, when the dwellers in the city had attained peace, he once more sends a festal letter to the brethren in Egypt, and besides this again he writes others. And there is a certain letter of his extant about the sabbath and another about discipline. And again when communicating with Hermammon and the brethren in Egypt by letter, and after passing in review many things about the evil deeds of Decius and his successors, he mentions the peace under Gallienus.' [1]

---

[1] xx. Ὁ γε μὴν Διονύσιος πρὸς ταῖς δηλωθείσαις ἐπιστολαῖς αὐτοῦ ἔτι καὶ τὰς φερομένας ἑορταστικὰς τὸ τηνικαῦτα συντάττει ... τούτων τὴν μὲν Φλαυίῳ προσφωνεῖ, τὴν δὲ Δομετίῳ καὶ Διδύμῳ (ἐν ᾗ καὶ κανόνα ἐκτίθεται ὀκταετηρίδος, . . .). πρὸς ταύταις καὶ ἄλλην τοῖς κατ' Ἀλεξάνδρειαν συμπρεσβυτέροις ἐπιστολὴν διαχαράττει, ἑτέροις τε ὁμοῦ διαφόρως, καὶ ταύτας ἔτι τοῦ διωγμοῦ συνεστῶτος. xxi. Ἐπιλαβούσης δὲ ὅσον οὔπω τῆς εἰρήνης, ἐπάνεισι μὲν εἰς τὴν Ἀλεξάνδρειαν, πάλιν δ' ἐνταῦθα στάσεως καὶ πολέμου συστάντος, ὡς οὐχ οἷόν τε ἦν αὐτῷ τοὺς κατὰ τὴν πόλιν ἅπαντας ἀδελφούς, εἰς ἑκάτερον τῆς στάσεως μέρος διῃρημένους, ἐπισκοπεῖν, αὖθις ἐν τῇ τοῦ πάσχα ἑορτῇ, ὥσπερ τις ὑπερόριος, ἐξ αὐτῆς τῆς Ἀλεξανδρείας διὰ γραμμάτων αὐτοῖς ὡμίλει. 2. κα

From this long passage we learn that the following ten festal letters of Dionysius were known to Eusebius:

(1) The letter to Flavius.
(2) The letter to Domitius and Didymus.
(3) A letter to his fellow presbyters at Alexandria and others.[1]
(4) A letter to the brethren in Alexandria.
(5) A letter to Hierax.
(6) A second letter to the brethren.[2]
(7) A letter to the brethren in Egypt.
(8) A letter on the Sabbath.
(9) A letter on 'Discipline'.
(10) A letter to Hermammon and the brethren in Egypt.

Ἱέρακι δὲ μετὰ ταῦτα τῶν κατ' Αἴγυπτον ἐπισκόπῳ ἑτέραν ἑορταστικὴν ἐπιστολὴν γράφων, τῆς κατ' αὐτὸν τῶν Ἀλεξανδρέων στάσεως μνημονεύει διὰ τούτων ... xxii. Μετὰ ταῦτα λοιμικῆς τὸν πόλεμον διαλαβούσης νόσου τῆς τε ἑορτῆς πλησιαζούσης, αὖθις διὰ γραφῆς τοῖς ἀδελφοῖς ὁμιλεῖ, τὰ τῆς συμφορᾶς ἐπισημαινόμενος πάθη διὰ τούτων ... 11. μετὰ δὲ καὶ ταύτην τὴν ἐπιστολήν, εἰρηνευσάντων τῶν κατὰ τὴν πόλιν, τοῖς κατ' Αἴγυπτον ἀδελφοῖς ἑορταστικὴν αὖθις ἐπιστέλλει γραφήν, καὶ ἐπὶ ταύτῃ πάλιν ἄλλας διατυποῦται· φέρεται δέ τις αὐτοῦ καὶ περὶ σαββάτου καὶ ἄλλη περὶ γυμνασίου. 12. Ἑρμάμμωνι δὲ πάλιν καὶ τοῖς κατ' Αἴγυπτον ἀδελφοῖς δι' ἐπιστολῆς ὁμιλῶν πολλά τε ἄλλα περὶ τῆς Δεκίου καὶ τῶν μετ' αὐτὸν διεξελθὼν κακοτροπίας, τῆς κατὰ τὸν Γαλλιηνὸν εἰρήνης ἐπιμιμνήσκεται.

[1] Compare letter 10, 'To Hermammon *and the brethren in Egypt.*' In the present instance, however, Feltoe (pp. 65, 90) distinguishes the letter 'to others' from that to the presbyters, and he is possibly right. But in that case we should have expected some such word as ἄλλην before ἑτέροις.

[2] Feltoe (p. 79 note) regards no. 4 and no. 6 as identical. But this is scarcely possible. Eusebius says that no. 5 was written after no. 4, and no. 6 after no. 5. He tells us also that no. 4 was written at Easter, and no. 6 when Easter was approaching. And in describing no. 6 he says that Dionysius 'once more' (αὖθις) wrote to the brethren, apparently implying that he had mentioned another letter to the same persons. Moreover, as Feltoe himself points out, the account given of the circumstances under which no. 4 was written, gathered no doubt from the letter itself, is not confirmed by the extract given by Eusebius from no. 6.

The last of these epistles is not expressly stated by Eusebius to have been festal in character. But the closing words of his second extract from it put the matter almost beyond question: 'in which (viz. the ninth year of Gallienus) *let us keep festival*' (ἑορτάσωμεν).[1]

Very noteworthy is the phrase in the opening sentence of this list: 'in addition to the letters which were mentioned.' It might be supposed that the inference was to the numerous letters alluded to in earlier chapters, and especially in those more immediately preceding. Such, for example, are the letters to Hermammon, and to Domitius and Didymus, quoted in vii. 1, 10, 11, and that headed πρὸς Γερμανόν, from which extracts are given in vii. 11. But this is unlikely.[2] For two of these are actually named in the list itself, and we shall presently give reason for supposing the third to be also included. The 'fore-mentioned epistles' therefore are probably those formally enumerated in the lists already considered. This appears to be indicated further by the tense, δηλωθείσαις for the more usual δεδηλωμέναις. We have in this phrase, therefore, a confirmation of the conclusion already reached, that those lists are exhaustive enumerations of definite collections of letters, and an encouragement to think that the list now before us may be another of the same kind.

Another indication which points in the same direction is found in two fragments of letters of Dionysius printed by Dr. Feltoe.[3] The first of these is headed, 'From the second Epistle,' and deals with the state of mind which befits those who keep festival. The second is headed, 'From the fourth Festal Epistle.' Thus both are extracts from festal letters of Dionysius, and the title in each case

---

[1] *H. E.* vii. 23. 4. So Dittrich, *Dionysius d. Grosse*, 1897, p. 119.
[2] Not, however, impossible. See above, p. 152.   [3] p. 90.

implies a recognized order of the letters which would naturally have its origin in some early collection of them in a single volume. It cannot be proved that they came from the same collection, or that either of them is from a letter included in Eusebius's list. But the assumption is not improbable in itself, and there is no evidence on the other side. It is true that the first has no point of contact with the quotations which Eusebius makes from his second letter—that which was addressed to Domitius and Didymus.[1] But neither has the Paschal Canon which it certainly included.[2] As to the second, there is nothing to hinder us from believing that it is part of the epistle which stands fourth in Eusebius's catalogue. For though his extract from the letter to Hierax[3] is wholly taken up with a description of the horrors that followed in the wake of bloodshed and pestilence, the letter may also have contained some reference to the loving deeds of the Christians which such times of calamity always called forth,[4] in the context of which this little piece on the devices by which love wins its way in seeking to help others might well find place.

It has been hinted that the epistle πρὸς Γερμανόν is probably one of those indicated in our list. The title is ambiguous, but the tenor of one of the extracts from it,[5] in which Germanus is spoken of contemptuously in the third person, makes it difficult to believe that the epistle was addressed to him. We may therefore render its heading '*Against* Germanus'. To whom then was it sent? The concluding clause of the same passage seems to give a hint as to the answer to this question. After alluding to his sufferings under Valerian, Dionysius adds, 'I forbear

[1] *H. E.* vii. 11. 20-25. [2] *H. E.* vii. 20. [3] *H. E.* vii. 21. 2-10.
[4] See the letters to Domitius and Didymus (*H. E.* vii. 11. 24) and the brethren in Alexandria (ib. 22. 7 ff.).
[5] *H. E.* vii. 11. 18 f.; cp. § 2.

to give to the brethren who know them a detailed narrative of the things that happened.'[1] The letter would appear to have been written to certain brethren who had knowledge, or easy means of gaining knowledge, of what he had endured in the recent troubles. They must have been Egyptians. They probably lived in Alexandria, or its neighbourhood. The letter may therefore be identical with (3), (4), or (7) in the list.

If this guess be correct—and only less so if it be not— and if the Festal Epistles formed a separate volume, it clearly appears that Eusebius deals with this volume just as he dealt with that containing the Martyrdom of Polycarp. In recording the incidents of the persecution of Valerian he has occasion to use three of these letters. Extracts from them are accordingly given in chaps. 10, 11. Then, after some further remarks of a desultory kind, he proceeds to give a list of the contents of the volume, making extracts from, or remarks upon, several of the letters which it contains as he goes along. But perhaps the most convincing indication that we have here a *volume* of letters is the fact that, in dealing with these epistles, Eusebius makes mistakes which we might expect him to make if they were bound together, but which are almost inexplicable otherwise. Of these mistakes some account will be rendered below.

19. *H. E.* vii. 26. *Epistles of Dionysius of Alexandria on the Sabellian Heresy.* The twenty-fourth and twenty-fifth chapters of the seventh book of the *History* are devoted to a consideration of the controversy between Dionysius and the Egyptian bishop Nepos on the subject of Chiliasm. The outcome of the discussion was a treatise in two books, en-

---

[1] Or perhaps 'I leave to the brethren who know them the task of giving a detailed narrative'. τὴν καθ' ἕκαστον τῶν γενομένων διήγησιν παρίημι τοῖς εἰδόσιν ἀδελφοῖς λέγειν.

titled *Concerning Promises*, from the pen of Dionysius, several fragments of which have been preserved by Eusebius. It appears to have been a long and elaborate work, and may well have been bound in a volume apart. But in the twenty-sixth chapter we come upon another group of minor writings. About these Eusebius is reticent; perhaps because they were connected with a passage in Dionysius's life upon which he did not wish to dwell. The group consists of four letters on Sabellianism to different persons (probably all Egyptian bishops), and four letters to Dionysius of Rome on the same topic. These eight may have made a volume. With the mention of them and three other works which he knew, and a general reference to many other epistles, the catalogue of the works of Dionysius ends.

We have now found traces of some nineteen volumes of tracts of which Eusebius appears to have made use. The existence of some of them, no doubt, may be disputed; but it must be remembered that our argument has been in some sense cumulative. If the *a priori* likelihood that such volumes were in his hands is admitted, evidence of their use in particular cases is worth considering which might otherwise have been ruled out, and the better attested instances increase the probability of our conclusion where positive evidence is scanty.

But it is now time to show in what way these volumes influenced the chronology of our historian. The principle on which the documents were grouped, in the cases which we have examined, seems to be mainly an arrangement according to subjects, no attention having been paid to chronology. But certainly in one instance, probably in others, if not in all, Eusebius assumed that the principle was the exact contrary, and hence he was led into error as regards dates.

This is manifest upon a consideration of his use of the volume containing the Martyrdom of Polycarp.[1] He quite unmistakably makes Pionius and Metrodorus contemporaries of Polycarp. But the *Acts* of their martyrdoms are in our hands,[2] and we learn from them that they suffered a century after Polycarp, under Decius. The conclusion is forced upon us that Eusebius regarded the martyrdoms as synchronous merely because the records of them were bound together. Lightfoot, indeed, suggests that the *Acts* themselves may have been partly responsible for his error. He uses the phrase ὑπὸ τὴν αὐτὴν περίοδον τοῦ χρόνου, which he may have taken from them. Capable as it is of two meanings, either 'at the same time', or 'at the same season of the year', Eusebius may have taken it in the former sense, while the martyrologist used it in the latter. He may also have been misled by the opening statement, that Pionius was celebrating the birthday of Polycarp. This explanation might serve if we had only Pionius and Metrodorus to deal with. But what shall we say about Carpus and the rest? Here, again, we can consult the genuine *Acts*. From a careful examination of the slight indications of date which they supply, Lightfoot gathers that Carpus and Papylus probably suffered either under Marcus Aurelius, or under Septimius Severus. So that in this case Eusebius's date may be correct. But the chronological data of the *Acts* are very meagre. If Eusebius had noticed them at all, which does not seem likely, he could scarcely have made use of them. They would reveal nothing to one who was not pretty familiar with the history of the Antonine Emperors. His mistakes in regard to them are portentous, as we shall just now see in one striking instance. Here at least, then, it seems

[1] See Lightfoot, *Ign.* i. 624 ff., 696 ff., and Valois, ad loc.
[2] Gebhardt, *Acta Mart. Sel.*, p. 96. For the *Acts of Carpus, &c.*, see p. 13.

impossible to suppose that his chronology had any better foundation than the whim of the librarian who arranged his volume of tracts.

Let us turn now to another case, in which Eusebius has admittedly gone astray in a date. He places the *Second Apology* of Justin Martyr, and consequently his martyrdom, which he believed to have occurred shortly after it was written, in the reign of Marcus Aurelius. But internal evidence marks the *Second Apology* as very little later in date than the first, and as presented to the same Emperors,[1] while the *Acta Iustini*, even if they be not admitted to be genuine, give us good reason for believing that he suffered after the end of the reign of Antoninus Pius.[2] How, then, did the error of the historian arise? It can be explained without difficulty if we suppose that Eusebius used the volume which we have marked 7 above, and assumed that the documents which it contains were arranged in chronological order. He had before him the *First Apology*, which he put under Antoninus Pius. It was followed by the spurious letter to the Commune Asiae. To whom was it to be referred? To be sure it had the name of Marcus Aurelius in its first line. But this had evidently no weight with Eusebius, and naturally so, for readers of the *History* are well aware that he did not know the imperial name of this Emperor. He had to decide the matter on other grounds. Suppose then he gave it to Marcus Aurelius, he is at once in difficulties. Marcus Aurelius was a persecutor. He could not have penned such a letter. But if he did, how could the *Second Apology* have followed it, with its tale

---

[1] *Dict. of Christ. Biog.* iii. 563 ff.

[2] Ib. pp. 562, 564. It is hardly possible to suppose that the name of the prefect Rusticus is an invention, and if it be true that Justin suffered under him, the date of the martyrdom is brought down to A.D. 163 at the earliest.

of the sufferings of the Christians quoted in *H.E.* iv. 17?
And how could Justin himself have been shortly afterwards put to death? So the epistle to the Commune must be assigned to the reign of Pius. It is there in its right place, for *Pius did not persecute*.[1] And for the same reason the subsequent *Apology* and martyrdom must be thrown forward into the following reign. If Eusebius reasoned in this way as to the dates of the letter to the Commune Asiae and the *Second Apology*, the further step was easy of connecting the *First Apology* with the letter in the way of cause and effect. And this step he seems to have taken; for, after quoting the first sentence of the *Apology*, ending with the words τὴν προσφώνησιν καὶ ἔντευξιν πεποίημαι, he proceeds, ἐντευχθεὶς δὲ καὶ ὑφ' ἑτέρων ὁ αὐτὸς βασιλεὺς ἐπὶ τῆς Ἀσίας ἀδελφῶν ... τοιαύτης ἠξίωσε τὸ κοινὸν τῆς Ἀσίας διατάξεως.[2] That there had been several ἐντεύξεις besides that of Justin he may have gathered from the letter itself: καὶ ἐμοὶ δὲ περὶ τῶν τοιούτων πολλοὶ ἐσήμαναν.[3]

It is well known that Eusebius is guilty of an extraordinary blunder with reference to the persecution of Valerian. He quotes, as giving a narrative of the sufferings of Dionysius during that persecution, two passages from the letter to Domitius and Didymus.[4] We have only to compare the passages quoted with others which he extracts from the Epistle against Germanus[5] to be convinced that Dionysius is speaking, not of what happened to him under Valerian's persecution, but of the events of the earlier persecution of Decius.[6] Possibly a consideration of

---

[1] The only martyrdom under Pius recorded by Eusebius is that of Pope Telesphorus, which he assigns to the first year of his reign (*H. E.* iv. 10). This martyrdom is not mentioned in the *Chronica*.

[2] *H. E.* iv. 12.   [3] *H. E.* iv. 13. 6.
[4] *H. E.* vii. 11. 20 ff.   [5] *H. E.* vi. 40.
[6] It was written apparently at a late period of the persecution. Only two of his five original companions now remained with him.

the volume of Festal Epistles marked 18 above may help us to understand how so gross an error was perpetrated. It will be seen that Eusebius dates some of the epistles in that volume with very considerable (if misleading) precision. The first three—to Flavius, to Domitius and Didymus, and to the Alexandrian presbyters—were written while the persecution was proceeding, i.e. between A.D. 258 and 260. The next was written at Easter,[1] after Dionysius's return to Alexandria, when the persecution was scarcely over, i.e. Easter 261. The letter to Hierax was written 'after these things' ($\mu\epsilon\tau\grave{a}$ $\tau\alpha\hat{v}\tau\alpha$), and as it was a Festal Epistle we cannot put it earlier than the period preceding Easter in the following year, A.D. 262. The sixth letter is again 'after these things', which brings us down to A.D. 263. It was written 'when the feast was approaching'.[2] With the phrase 'and after this epistle' applied to the seventh letter, we advance to A.D. 264, the year before the date given in the *Chronica* for the death of Dionysius. After this the dates are prudently omitted, except in the case of the tenth epistle, to Hermammon, which is dated by Eusebius from internal evidence apparently in 262.

One seems to have returned to Alexandria, and another had, perhaps, died (*H. E.* vii. 11. 24). See also Feltoe, p. 66, notes on ll. 9, 10.

[1] Not, as in the case of an ordinary Festal Epistle, *before* Easter.

[2] It is of course possible that two letters (in addition to that to Hermammon) were written in view of the Paschal festival of 262, the fifth about the beginning of the year and the sixth a couple of months 'after these things', when the festival had almost come. This is Dr. Feltoe's view (p. 84). If it is correct the seventh letter must be dated before Easter 263. I cannot think, however, that these are the dates which Eusebius intended to indicate. If they were, it remains to be asked, How did Eusebius know which of the two came first? It is hardly likely that the text of the letters supplied him with information on this point. And if these letters truthfully describe the state of affairs at Alexandria in the period preceding Easter 262, it is not easy to find place in that period for the exultant words of the letter to Hermammon in *H. E.* vii. 23.

It is obvious to remark that, as our author is ten years out in the date of the letter to Domitius and Didymus, too much reliance need not be placed on his chronology of the others. And indeed it might be plausibly argued that the preposition μετά was not intended by him to indicate temporal sequence, but merely order in the volume in which the letters were bound, were it not that he definitely connects the letters with successive events. The fourth was penned while sedition and fighting were proceeding, as was the fifth likewise, the sixth during a pestilence which followed the sedition, the seventh when peace was restored. Let us now glance at the fourth and fifth letters. In the former, according to Eusebius (and he is doubtless paraphrasing correctly), the writer mentions that, on account of the sedition, he was obliged to communicate with his flock, not in person, but by letter. In the latter he ' mentions the sedition '. Here some critics find fault with our historian. 'He introduces,' says Dr. Bright,[1] 'as referring to an Alexandrian sedition, a letter of Dionysius which evidently refers to an Alexandrian pestilence.' But the letter does refer to the sedition more than once. The harbours, he writes, are an image of those through which the Israelites passed, ' for oftentimes from the murders committed in them they are as it were a Red Sea '. ' And always ', whether in flood or nearly dry, the river which runs by the city 'flows defiled with blood and murders and drownings', even as it did in the days of Pharaoh, ' when it changed into blood and stank.'[2] This is not a reference to slaughter which had ceased. For the dead bodies which lie unburied after war is over, though they may pollute the rivers, do not

---

[1] *Eusebius's Ecclesiastical History*, p. 1. And similarly Feltoe, pp. 79, 85, 86.
[2] *H. E.* vii. 21. 4, 6.

cause them to run with gore. And is not the following unmistakable?—

'Verily with my own loved ones (σπλάγχνα), brethren who dwell in my own house, who are of one soul with me, citizens of the same Church, I must needs communicate in writing. And that I should dispatch the letters seems impossible. For it is easier for a man to journey not merely into a neighbouring province, but even from the East into the West than from one part of Alexandria to another.'[1]

It was surely not pestilence but war that made the main street of the city 'impassable' for its devoted bishop. In fact these words so exactly describe the position to which Dionysius was reduced by the sedition when the fourth letter was penned, that it seems impossible to believe that the two epistles were separated by an interval of a year, or indeed by many weeks. Nevertheless it remains that the main concern of Dionysius is, in this letter, not the sedition, but the pestilence. The pestilence, however, Eusebius tells us, *followed* the sedition, and was the subject of the sixth letter, A.D. 263. The confusion of all this is manifest. It is now time to make the attempt to unravel it.

Here then is my suggestion. Eusebius took up the volume of Festal Epistles. In one of them he found a definite date. The epistle to Hermammon seems to connect itself with Easter 262. On the assumption that the arrangement is chronological this brings all the epistles in the volume into the epoch the central event of which was the edict of toleration of Gallienus. He turns then to the second epistle, that addressed to Domitius and Didymus. This was evidently written before the persecution to which it refers had concluded. 'And now', says its writer, 'I and Gaius and Peter are shut up in a

[1] *H. E.* vii. 21. 3.

desert and parched place in Libya.'[1] Eusebius accordingly dates it before the end of the persecution of Valerian. But the letters *ex hypothesi* succeeded one another in the order in which they appeared in the volume. Hence the fourth, written as it was from Alexandria, is put at the earliest possible moment after Dionysius's return from banishment. The fifth and sixth follow in successive years, and are attached, as well as might be, to the historical events by which Eusebius supposed that the persecution was followed.

But what were those events? They were easily discovered from the sixth letter. It was evidently written, as Eusebius states, during a pestilence,[2] and it refers to past sufferings. First there was a persecution (assumed of course to have been that which happened under Valerian). This was followed by war and famine. Then came a brief period of rest,[3] and finally the pestilence which was still raging.[4] Between the persecution and the pestilence the fourth and fifth letters must be placed. They are both therefore connected with the only outstanding events which Eusebius supposed to have marked the interval, the war and the famine which accompanied it.

If this suggestion be correct, it will follow that the dates given by Eusebius for the Festal Epistles have no independent value. And even if it be not well founded, it is difficult to see how, in view of the mistakes which he has certainly made, they can be relied upon, unless they are supported by the internal evidence of the fragments of these letters which still remain.[5]

[1] *H. E.* vii. 11. 23. [2] ἡ νόσος αὕτη, *H. E.* vii. 22. 6.
[3] βραχιτάτης ἀναπνοῆς. [4] *H. E.* vii. 22. 4-6.
[5] Apart from the portions preserved by Eusebius we have only the short extracts mentioned above, p. 163, and a sentence from the letter περὶ γυμνασίου (Feltoe, p. 256). None of these supply any chronological data.

Now of the ten Festal Letters no extracts are given by Eusebius from the first, seventh, eighth, and ninth. Their dates are therefore of no importance, and cannot be fixed. The second, to Domitius and Didymus, was written under Decius. Eusebius's date is therefore incorrect. The third, if we may identify it with the Epistle against Germanus, was written while the Valerian persecution was proceeding, for in it Valerian and Gallienus are mentioned[1] as the reigning Emperors, and Dionysius speaks of the sufferings which he still endures under Valerian's prefect Aemilianus.[2] Here, therefore, Eusebius is probably correct. We have already given reasons for believing that the fourth and fifth, written as Eusebius rightly says in time of war, were not separated by the interval of a year by which he assumes that they were parted. Whether they are rightly connected with the persecution of Valerian, or should not rather have been placed under Decius or Gallus, must be left an open question. As to the sixth, Eusebius is again right in supposing it to have been penned while Alexandria was suffering from pestilence. But it seems equally certain that the pestilence is not that which is alluded to in the previous epistles, for in them the pestilence and the war are synchronous, while the sixth letter states that the war was divided from the following pestilence by an interval of rest. If, therefore, the fourth and fifth letters belonged to the reign of Gallienus, the sixth must be put back to the time of Gallus.[3]

We may now turn to the letters on the Novatianist

---

[1] *H. E.* vii. 11. 8.   [2] Ib. § 18.
[3] I observe that Professor Gwatkin regards this as its true date (*Early Church History*, 1909, vol. ii, p. 263). The pestilence began under Decius (in the autumn of 250 ?) and continued to rage under Gallus. Since it came from Ethiopia Alexandria was probably the

schism (15). In connexion with this schism, two important Synods are mentioned both by Eusebius and by Cyprian— one in Rome, the other in Africa. Which came first? Eusebius seems to imply that the Roman Synod preceded the African when he speaks of 'a very great Synod having been gathered at Rome... and the bishops of the remaining provinces having considered independently in their several districts what was to be done'—the final phrase being explained lower down by the words touching 'the things that seemed good to those in Italy and *Africa* and the districts there'.[1] But, if so, he contradicts Cyprian, who appears to date the African Synod immediately after the close of the Decian persecution, a subsequent letter to Cornelius being followed by the Roman Synod.[2] Cyprian is, of course, the better authority, and accordingly Benson puts the African Synod in April, the Roman in June or July 251.[3] Probably Eusebius was misled by finding the letter of Cyprian and the African bishops after that of Cornelius containing the proceedings of the Synod held at Rome, in the volume which he used.

This suggestion leads to a further remark. If our argument has any force it is always unsafe to rely on the statements of Eusebius as to the relative dates of documents, if there is a reasonable suspicion that the documents

first city visited by it (Zonaras, xii. 21 ; Cedrenus, p. 257 f.). It reached Carthage in 252 (Benson, *Cyprian*, p. 241).

[1] vi. 43. 2, 3.

[2] *Ep.* 55. 6 (ed. Hartel, p. 627 f.): 'Persecutione sopita, cum data esset facultas in unum conueniendi, copiosus episcoporum numerus ... in unum conuenimus ... Ac si minus sufficiens episcoporum in Africa numerus uidebatur, etiam Romam super hac re scripsimus ad Cornelium collegam nostrum, qui et ipse cum plurimis coepiscopis habito concilio in eandem nobiscum sententiam ... consensit.'

[3] *Cyprian*, pp. 127f., 156, 163 f. Hefele, *Conciliengeschichte*, i. 2. § 5 (E. T. vol. i, p. 94 f.), dates the African Synod in May and the Roman in October.

in question were bound together in a single volume. Let us take some examples.

In *H. E.* vii. 9. 6 Eusebius seems to say that a letter of Dionysius of Alexandria to his namesake of Rome concerning one Lucian was subsequent to two written to Pope Xystus. This is, of course, certainly correct if Dionysius was bishop when he received the letter. But our certainty is not increased by the testimony of Eusebius, for two reasons: first, because the letter happens to have followed those addressed to Xystus in our seventeenth volume; and, secondly, because we cannot be sure that in such a case the words 'After these letters' (μετὰ ταύτας) have a temporal sense. They may simply indicate the fact to which we have just now called attention, the position of the letter about Lucian in the volume which Eusebius was using at the moment.[1]

Again, stress has been laid on the words in *H. E.* iv. 26. 2, ἐπὶ πᾶσι καὶ τὸ πρὸς Ἀντωνῖνον βιβλίδιον, as indicating that the *Apology* was Melito's last work.[2] But here again we seem to be dealing with a volume of tracts (12 above), and it is therefore possible that ἐπὶ πᾶσι may mean no more than last of all in the order of arrangement. But if it has a chronological sense it may only express Eusebius's inference from the phenomena of the volume itself.

In conclusion one or two other cases may be mentioned in which it may be well to bear in mind Eusebius's practice of quoting from volumes in which were bound together

---

[1] Is it possible that the Lucian about whom Dionysius wrote was the person of the same name at whose request Cyprian wrote a letter to Quintus on the baptism of heretics (*Ep.* 71, Hartel, p. 771)? If so, it is not difficult to understand why it was included in the volume of Epistles about Baptism, and it may be dated *c.* 257, to which period all the other letters in the volume are naturally referred.

[2] *Dict. of Christ. Biog.* iii. 894.

tracts which were possibly widely separated in date. The statement is sometimes made that the heretic Blastus was contemporary with Florinus, on the ground that Eusebius names them together in *H. E.* v. 20. But it is not improbable that the letter of Irenaeus to Blastus is here mentioned immediately before the two to Florinus merely because it stood first in the volume in which they occupied the second and third places. In that case the adjuration quoted by Eusebius may be regarded as a scribe's note applying to the entire volume.[1] It is some confirmation of this hypothesis, that Eusebius, after transcribing the note, proceeds to quote, not from the third, but from the second of the tracts referred to. It is of course admitted that the evidence for the existence of this volume is not strong, and for that reason it has not been included in the list given above. All that is contended is that the possibility of its existence diminishes the force of the argument in favour of Blastus and Florinus having taught at Rome at the same time.

An inference has been drawn as to the date of Quadratus, bishop of Athens, from the fact that he was mentioned in a letter of Dionysius of Corinth.[2] Eusebius in his *Chronica* gives A.D. 171 as the *floruit* of Dionysius. But this date appears to have been merely an inference from the only one of the epistles in the same volume (8 above) which furnished chronological data. It was certainly written during the episcopate of Pope Soter (166–174).[3] But we have no right to conclude that the other letters were penned about the same time, though Eusebius may have done so. There is no reason why the letter to the Athenians may not have been written twenty years before the accession of Soter. And it is not certain that Quadratus was alive when it was sent. On the contrary,

---

[1] βιβλίον, a papyrus roll.   [2] *H. E.* iv. 23. 3.   [3] § 9.

it seems to be implied that the Athenians had lapsed from the vigour of faith to which his zeal had roused them after the martyrdom of his predecessor Publius. But, however that may be, there is no difficulty in supposing that he was the Quadratus who presented an Apology to the Emperor Hadrian.[1]

As I have mentioned the Apology of Quadratus, I am tempted to make another suggestion. Dr. Rendel Harris[2] has drawn attention to the similarity between its title, gathered from various references to it by Eusebius, and that of the newly recovered Apology of Aristides. The former he supposes, with Harnack, to have run somewhat thus: λόγος ἀπολογίας ὑπὲρ τῆς τῶν Χριστιανῶν θεοσεβείας. And the latter: ἀπολογία ὑπὲρ τῆς θεοσεβείας. How is the resemblance to be explained? I venture to think it possible that Eusebius had in his hands a volume containing both with a general title, such as ἀπολογίαι ὑπὲρ τῆς θεοσεβείας. When they were copied separately each would be superscribed with this title, the singular being of course substituted for the plural.

---

[1] For the same reason the argument of Dr. Rendel Harris (*Texts and Studies*, vol. i, pt. 1, p. 11), that on the assumption that the Apologist and the bishop were the same person the Apology must have been presented to Antoninus Pius, seems to have little weight.

[2] Ib. p. 10.

THE CHRONOLOGY OF
EUSEBIUS'S *MARTYRS OF PALESTINE*

THE work of Eusebius of Caesarea which is known by the title *De Martyribus Palestinae* has come down to us in two forms. The better known of these is the Greek recension, which in most of the printed editions of the *Ecclesiastical History* of the same writer follows the eighth book. But it is now half a century since a Syriac version of another recension was made generally accessible by the labours of the late Dr. Cureton.[1] It is contained in the British Museum MS. Add. 12150, which bears the date A.D. 411. It is obviously a translation from a Greek original; but the manifest corruptions of the text suggest that it is considerably later than the Syriac exemplar from which it is ultimately derived, and certain erroneous readings of the underlying Greek which can still be detected point to the conclusion that the manuscript from which the rendering was made was in its turn separated by some decades from the autograph. Thus there can be little doubt that the original work was contemporary with Eusebius († 339).[2] And there is not wanting evidence, internal and external, that both it and the more familiar Greek recension are products of his pen.[3] Lightfoot's theory of the relation between the two forms of the work is probably correct. He held that the longer edition, now

[1] *History of the Martyrs in Palestine by Eusebius, Bishop of Caesarea, discovered in a very antient Syriac manuscript*: edited and translated into English by William Cureton. London, Edinburgh, and Paris, 1861.
[2] *Dictionary of Christian Biography*, ii. 318 f.   [3] Ib. 320.

represented by Cureton's Syriac, was the original form of the book, and that it was written mainly for the instruction of the Christians of Caesarea; while the shorter edition, on the other hand, was abridged from it, and was but a part of a larger work intended for a wider public.[1] But it is not necessary in this paper to assume the truth of Lightfoot's conclusion. We may rest content with the assurance that the Syriac and the Greek recensions are two editions of the same treatise, both of which received their final form from Eusebius of Caesarea.

Now both of them present a very striking contrast to the two books of the *Ecclesiastical History* which cover the same period. The ninth book of the *History* is absolutely devoid of explicit chronological data; the eighth has only a few, and those for the most part vague and difficult to interpret. The *De Martyribus*, on the contrary, bristles with dates. Of almost every event recorded in it we are told the year, the month, the day of the month, and even sometimes the day of the week. Quite apart, therefore, from certain incidents of the persecution of Diocletian, of which our knowledge is derived from it alone, this work ought, in virtue of the number and accuracy of its dates, to serve as a valuable supplement to the *History*. But there is an initial difficulty to be overcome. If we except one passage of the Greek recension, which seems to have been copied from the *History*,[2] and has no parallel in the Syriac, the chronology of the *Martyrs* is expressed, not in terms of the regnal years of the Emperors, but in terms of the years of the persecution. The customary formula in its most complete form is seen, for example, at the beginning of chap. 6: τετάρτῳ γε μῆν τοῦ

[1] *Dictionary of Christian Biography*, ii. 320 f. See also below, pp. 279-283.
[2] *M. P.* (Grk.) Pref. Cp. *H. E.* viii. 2. 4, 5.

καθ' ἡμῶν ἔτει διωγμοῦ, πρὸ δώδεκα καλανδῶν Δεκεμβρίων, ἢ γένοιτ' ἂν μηνὸς Δίου εἰκάδι, προσαββάτου ἡμέρᾳ, κτλ. ; for which we have in the Syriac,[1] 'It was in the fourth year of the persecution in our days, and on Friday the twentieth of the latter Teshri,' &c. What did Eusebius mean by a 'year of the persecution'? On what days of the year, according to our reckoning, did such a year begin and end? This is a question to which we must find an answer if we are to understand the chronology of the persecution.

It will be admitted that the most obvious assumption is that the first year covered a period of twelve months, counted from the actual outbreak of the persecution, and that each of the later years covered a like period, and began in the same month of our reckoning. This assumption, indeed, does not supply a full answer to our question, for the outbreak of the persecution is variously dated. According to Lactantius[2] the first edict of Diocletian against the Christians was issued February 24, 303, the persecution having actually begun on the previous day; Eusebius, in *H.E.* viii. 2, places the publication of the edict in March,[3] and in *M.P.* (Grk.) Pref., in April, of the same year. These dates may perhaps be reconciled. But a mere reconciliation of the dates cannot determine whether Eusebius's persecution-years began in February, in March, or in April.[4] But I hope to be able to show that discussion of that problem is superfluous.

The possibility of finding an answer different from this, and perhaps more satisfactory, was suggested to the present

[1] Cureton, p. 19.   [2] *De Mort. Pers.*, 12 f.
[3] So also in the *Chronica*, ed. Schoene, ii. 189.
[4] Mr. McGiffert holds that Eusebius dated the beginning of the persecution-years sometimes before, sometimes after, April 2, though always in April. But why not in March ? See his note on *M. P.* 7. 1, in *Nicene and Post-Nicene Fathers*, vol. i, p. 348.

writer by a short but illuminating discussion by Mr. C. H. Turner of the meaning of regnal years in Eusebius, which was printed in an early number of the *Journal of Theological Studies*.[1] The conclusion at which Mr. Turner arrives is, that the beginning of a regnal year was independent of the actual day of accession of the emperor, and that it was in all cases regarded by Eusebius as falling in the month of September. What if it should prove that the starting-point of the persecution-years was likewise independent of the actual date of the outbreak of the persecution? Once this hypothesis is admitted as possible, some of the arguments urged by Mr. Turner in favour of his theory, that all regnal years in Eusebius began in September, might be used to prove that persecution-years began in the same month. It will be found, however, if I am not mistaken, that the latter conclusion is inconsistent with the facts.

The validity of both these suggestions must be tested by an appeal to the text of the *Martyrs*. But a word may first be said as to the method of indicating dates in the two recensions. The Greek has a double notation. First the date is given in the ordinary Roman fashion, counting backwards from Kalends, Nones, and Ides, the Roman names of the months being used. Then it is given in the style to which we are accustomed, counting forwards from the first day of the month, the Roman names being replaced by the names of the Macedonian months which correspond to them. In the Syriac, only the second of these methods is used; and instead of the Macedonian names we find what the translator regarded as their Syriac equivalents. Thus the martyrdom of Procopius (June 7) is dated in the Greek (1. 2) vii. id. Jun.=Daesius

---

[1] Vol. i, pp. 188 ff.

7, while in the parallel passage of Syriac it is dated Khaziran 7.

Now the year which has the largest number of martyrdoms is the seventh. The Greek does not mark the point at which we pass from the sixth year to the seventh, though it indicates that, so far as the proceedings at Caesarea are concerned, the record of those two years extends from chap. 8 to chap. 11.[1] But in the Syriac two successive passions are headed respectively, 'The confession of Ares, and Primus, and Elias, in the sixth year of the persecution in our days at Ashkelon,' and 'The confession of Peter, who was surnamed Absalom, in the seventh year of the persecution in our days in the city of Caesarea'.[2] These two passions correspond to the two sections of the tenth chapter of the Greek. It may be assumed, therefore, that chapter 10, § 2, and chapter 11 of the Greek text contain the narrative of the seventh year at Caesarea. The martyrdom of Peter, then, is the first recorded as belonging to the seventh year. It is dated in the Greek Audinaeus 11 = 3 id. Jan. (i. e. January 11), and in the Syriac Conun 10 (i. e. January 10). The last martyrdom of the year is that of Peleus[3] and his companions. The Syriac dates it Elul 19; and as Elul included the greater part of September with a portion of October, we may interpret this to mean September 19. It is true that in the Greek this martyrdom is without date; but there is at any rate nothing in the context at variance with the date given in the Syriac.[4] Thus we see that the seventh year

---

[1] See 8. 1; 13. 1.   [2] Cureton, p. 34 f.

[3] *M. P.* (Grk.) 13. 1-3; Cureton, p. 46. This is the correct form of the name. See Eus. *H. E.* viii. 18. 5. The Syriac calls him Paulus.

[4] It is necessary to emphasize this, because the opening words of the chapter have sometimes been mistranslated 'The seventh year of our conflict was completed', the martyrdom of Peleus being thus

of the persecution began before January 11, and ended after September 19. This fact puts out of court the hypothesis that the persecution-years began on or near the anniversary of the promulgation of the first edict of Diocletian. We cannot regard any date in February, March, or April as the first day of such a year: it must have begun between September 19 and January 11. This, of course, still leaves open the possibility that it ran from September to September. Let us see then whether its beginning may be determined within narrower limits.

The first dated martyrdom in the sixth year—that of Khatha and Valentina—took place on July 25, according to both recensions[1]; the last—that of Ares and others—again according to both recensions, on December 14.[2] The beginning of the year cannot have been in September. It must have commenced between December 14 and January 11. If we conclude that the normal persecution-year of Eusebius was simply the ordinary Roman year, which began on January 1 and ended on December 31, we cannot be astray by more than a few days.

The conclusion being thus reached that the beginning of the persecution-years, according to Eusebius, was on or about January 1, and as a consequence that they approximately coincided with years of our A.D. reckoning, the solution of a further problem may be attempted: With what year of our era did each several persecution-year synchronize? A consideration of the account given

apparently thrown into the eighth year. They should rather be rendered 'was approaching completion' ($\dot{\eta}\nu\dot{\upsilon}\epsilon\tau o$), which suits one of the later months of the seventh year. It is not implied that the events narrated in the immediate sequel belonged to the eighth year.

[1] *M. P.* (Grk.) 8. 12; Cureton, p. 31.

[2] *M. P.* (Grk.) 10. 1; Cureton, p. 34. The Greek does not give the number of the year.

of the passion of Apphianus, or, as the Syriac calls him, Epiphanius,[1] and of the context which leads up to it,[2] supplies us with the answer to our question. After mentioning the abdication of Diocletian and Maximian, Eusebius proceeds to describe the renewal of the persecution after the accession of Maximin, and the consternation which as a result fell upon the Christians of Palestine. Apphianus appears to have been the first victim of his fury at Caesarea. After proceedings which must have occupied at least several days—more probably some weeks —Apphianus was seized, imprisoned, tortured, brought three times before the judge, and finally cast into the sea. The date is given in both recensions as April 2, in the third year of the persecution. Now we learn from Lactantius[3] that the abdication of Diocletian took place on May 1, 305. The earliest possible date for the martyrdom is therefore April 2, 306. It could not have been April 2, 307, for on no possible hypothesis could the year 307 have been reckoned as the third of the persecution. It follows therefore that A.D. 306 was the third persecution-year.

It may indeed be suggested that Eusebius was in error as to the date of the abdication, and supposed that it occurred before April 2, 305. It is in fact probable that he did not know the day on which it happened. For he dates it vaguely. 'At this time',[4] he writes, 'a change of

[1] Apphianus is correct, since another Syriac version of his passion has Appianus. See S. E. Assemani, *Acta SS. Martt. Orient. et Occident.*, Rome, 1748, vol. ii, p. 189. So also the Greek fragment of the longer recension printed in Schwartz, ii. 912.

[2] *M. P.* (Grk.) 3. 5–4. 15; Cureton, pp. 12 ff.

[3] *De Mort. Pers.* 19. Lactantius in the context exhibits minute knowledge of the movements of Diocletian at this period, and his dates cannot reasonably be doubted. See chaps. 12-14, 17.

[4] ἐν τούτῳ. See *H. E.* iii. 18. 1; 21; iv. 1; 15. 1; 30. 3; v. 13. 1; vi. 7; 8. 1, 7; 18. 1; 21. 2; 27; 31. 1; vii. 1; 14. 1; 27. 1; 28. 3

rulers took place.' This is the more remarkable inasmuch as in the *Martyrs* Eusebius seems to avoid indefinite notes of time.[1] Diocletian abdicated, and Maximin was invested with the purple, at Nicomedia.[2] Even if the latter had 'armed himself for persecution' the very next day, some time would be required for the preparation of his instructions to the provincial governors, and proceedings could not have begun at Caesarea till at least a few days after they were dispatched.[3] To this period must be added the interval between the appearance of Apphianus before Urban and his execution on April 2. If Eusebius took account of all this his error must have been very considerable. He must have put the abdication and the subsequent action of the governor at Caesarea six weeks or two months too early. Is it likely that he was so much astray about the date of an event which cannot but have impressed itself vividly on his memory? But that is not all. For there can be no doubt that the martyrdom in actual fact followed the accession of Maximin, and did not precede it. That is not only stated by the historian; it is implied throughout the entire narrative. If, to relieve ourselves of the necessity of placing the martyrdom of Apphianus in the year 306, we assume that Eusebius antedated the abdication, we must therefore also assume that he antedated the martyrdom: a second improbability which is not easy to be got over. Moreover, it is quite certain that in whatever month he supposed the abdication to have occurred he assigned it to the second year of the

31. 1 ; viii. 6. 6, &c. In all these places the phrase may be rendered ' at this period '.

[1] Those in Pref. *ad fin.* and 1. 3 occur in quotations from *H. E.* viii. Those in chap. 5 were apparently inevitable.

[2] Lactantius, *De Mort. Pers.* 17 ; Eus., *Chron.* ed. Schoene, ii. 189.

[3] The first edict of Diocletian against the Christians, of February 24, 303, did not reach Caesarea, as it seems, till April. *M. P.* (Grk.) Pref.

persecution,[1] and the martyrdom of Apphianus to the third. If therefore the former took place in 305 (and Eusebius cannot have put it in the wrong year) the latter must belong to 306. And finally there is some evidence that in the early months of the reign of Maximin his dominions were comparatively free from persecution. He himself tells us that when he 'first came into the East' he did not use severity towards the Christians.[2] And Lactantius uses language which seems to imply that at this period he forbade them to be put to death. For the peace which the Church enjoyed from May to October 311 reminds him of a similar period of rest earlier in Maximin's reign, to which he does not elsewhere allude.[3] All this harmonizes well with the long interval by which Eusebius, as we have interpreted him, separates his appointment as

[1] *H. E.* viii. 13. 10 ; App. 2 ; *Chron.* ed. Schoene, ii. 189.

[2] *H. E.* ix. 9. 15-17. Commenting on this passage Dr. Mason says (*Persecution of Diocletian*, 1876, p. 335) that 'no Turk ever lied more shamelessly'. But even Sultans do not utter falsehoods when there is no likelihood that their falsehoods will deceive any one. Maximin, no doubt, lied ; but his lies must have had such a semblance of truth as to encourage the hope that they would be believed by a good many of the Christians of Asia Minor and Syria. That would have been impossible if after his accession the fourth edict had not been allowed to fall into abeyance in those regions for a season. Compare below, pp. 232 ff.

[3] *De Mort. Pers.* 36. 6, speaking of the period following the death of Galerius (May 311), 'Facere autem parabat *quae iamdudum* in Orientis partibus fecerat. Nam *cum clementiam specie tenus profiteretur, occidi seruos Dei uetuit*, debilitari iussit.' On the other hand the Syriac recension of *M. P.* ignores the clemency, such as it was, shown to the Christians at the beginning of Maximin's reign. He is said to have gone forth, 'even from his very commencement, to fight, as it were, against God' (Cureton, p. 12). No facts, however, are alleged in support of this statement. It will be observed that Eusebius is quite explicit about the absolute immunity of the Christians from persecution for part of the year 311 (*H. E.* ix. 1. 7 ff.; 2. 1), while Lactantius will admit no more than that for a time Maximin abstained from open infliction of the death penalty.

Caesar from the first martyrdom which took place under his rule at Caesarea. We may conclude then that the third year of the persecution coincided with A.D. 306.

There are similar indications that the second year coincided with A.D. 305. It is sufficient for our purpose to repeat the remark already made, that Eusebius states in unambiguous language that the abdication, the approximate date of which he must have known, occurred in the second year of the persecution.

If we have argued correctly thus far, the third year of the persecution must have ended about December 31, 306, the second about December 31, 305, and the first about December 31, 304. This is certainly an unexpected result. For the actual beginning of the persecution at Nicomedia is dated by Lactantius February 23, 303, and Eusebius represents it to have commenced in other parts of the Empire in March or April of the same year.[1] The first 'year' must therefore have been a period, not of twelve, but of at least twenty months.[2] The tenth 'year', on the same computation, began January 1, 313; and as it

---

[1] Lact. *De Mort. Pers.* 12; Eus. *H. E.* viii. 2. 4; *M. P.* (Grk.) Pref.

[2] In other words, a considerable part of 303 is reckoned by Eusebius as belonging to 304. In like manner the period between the accession of an Emperor and the following September was regarded by him as belonging to the first regnal year, which in strictness began in the latter month. Dr. Carleton makes the interesting suggestion that Eusebius, in thus making a persecution-year or a regnal year include a period prior to its nominal beginning, may have been influenced by a rule of the Metonic Cycle, in the adaptation of which to ecclesiastical purposes he took a leading part. In that cycle a lunation was conceived as belonging to the year in which it ended. Thus the twelfth lunation of the tenth year of the cycle ended December 3. The following lunation, because it ended on January 2, was held to belong to the *eleventh* year. So a Julian year, nominally beginning on January 1, might include nearly a month prior to January 1. See S. Butcher, *The Ecclesiastical Calendar, its theory and construction*, Dublin, 1877, pp. 61 ff.

ended with the edict of Maximin, probably in September or October,[1] it included about ten months.

It may be well, however, at this point, to anticipate a possible objection. We have relied on the accuracy of the texts, Greek and Syriac, in regard to chronological data. But it may be urged that their dates are demonstrably inaccurate in some places. I do not think that much stress will be laid on a few passages in which the two recensions are inconsistent with each other. Of this we have several examples. Alphaeus and Zacchaeus were beheaded, and Romanus was burned at the stake, according to the Greek on November 17, according to the Syriac on November 7;[2] Domninus was given to the flames according to the Greek on November 5, according to the Syriac on November 1;[3] Peter, called Apselamus (Absalom), suffered according to the Greek on January 11, according to the Syriac on January 10.[4] But such slight discrepancies are not more serious or more numerous than might be expected in two independent texts, each of which has suffered to some extent at the hands of transcribers. In all cases one of the dates is almost certainly what Eusebius held to be correct; and whichever be accepted as his, our argument is unaffected.

Another class of passages demands more consideration. Four times in the Greek, and once in the Syriac, a date is defined not only by the year, the month, and the day of the month, but also by the day of the week. Let us examine the passages.

[1] Eus. *H. E.* ix. 10. For the date see below, p. 227.
[2] *M. P.* (Grk.) 1. 5; 2. 1; Cureton, p. 6. The Syriac version of this passion edited by S. E. Assemani, op. cit., vol. ii, p. 177, has November 17. The Greek is therefore in this case almost certainly correct.
[3] *M. P.* (Grk.) 7. 3 f.; Cureton, p. 24.
[4] *M.P.* (Grk.) 10. 2; Cureton, p. 35. With the latter agrees Assemani's Syriac version, op. cit., ii. 208.

The Greek text, after stating that the martyr Apphianus was drowned on April 2 of the third year of the persecution, adds that the day was Friday.[1] We have used this date to prove that 306 was the third year of the persecution; and it is therefore important for our theory. Now April 2 is Friday only in a year whose Sunday letter is C (or a leap year whose Sunday letters are DC). But the Sunday letter of 306 is F, and in it April 2 was Tuesday. Thus, if the date is correct, our theory cannot be maintained. It is true that the Syriac gives no support to the statement that Apphianus suffered on Friday; and so it may be that the note in the Greek is due, not to Eusebius, but to a scribe who desired to indicate a parallel between his passion and that of Christ. But there is no need for such a suggestion. The fact is, that the only years falling within the period of the persecution which have the Sunday letter C are 303 and 308; and on no scheme of the chronology could April 2 in either of those years be counted as belonging to the third persecution-year. We must, therefore, make our choice between rejecting the day of the week in the Greek text, and rejecting the day of the month in both Greek and Syriac. Here the Syriac comes to our aid. In it we read, 'Such was the termination of the history of Epiphanius, on the second of the month Nisan, *and his memory is observed on this day.*'[2] Thus contemporary tradition confirms the date April 2. This is decisive in

[1] ἡμέρᾳ παρασκευῆς. *M. P.* (Grk.) 4. 15.

[2] Cureton, p. 17. So also Assemani's Syriac (op. cit., ii. 189). The underlying Greek, as printed by Schwartz (ii. 918), which also omits the words ἡμέρᾳ παρασκευῆς, runs, τοιούτου μὲν δὴ τέλους τὸ κατὰ τὸν θαυμάσιον Ἀπφιανὸν ἔτυχε δρᾶμα· Ξανθικοῦ μηνὸς ⟨δευτέρᾳ⟩ πρὸ δ' νωνῶν Ἀπριλλίων ἡ τοῦδε μνήμη τελεῖται. It has been suggested by H. Browne in his *Ordo Saeclorum*, London, 1844, p. 535 f. (§ 479), that Eusebius 'has confounded the date of the martyr Apphianus's first hearing, Tuesday, April 2, with the date of his martyrdom on the third day following, i. e. Friday, April 5'.

favour of the supposition that the words ἡμέρᾳ παρασκευῆς are an incorrect gloss, whether of Eusebius or another.

But again, the Greek and the Syriac agree in dating the death of Agapius on November 20, the birthday of the Emperor Maximin, in the fourth year (307, according to the theory here advocated); and once more the Greek adds that the day was Friday.[1] This requires the Sunday letter D (or ED), while the Sunday letter of 307 is E. But the first year after 302 which has the Sunday letter D is 313;[2] and by November 20, 313, the persecution was over. Since there is no reasonable ground for doubting that November 20[3] was observed as Maximin's birthday, the phrase of the Greek, προσαββάτου ἡμέρᾳ, must once more be rejected as unhistorical.[4]

The next date to be considered is that of the martyrdom of Procopius, which both recensions assign to June 7 in the first year, the Greek adding that it was on 'the fourth

[1] *M. P.* (Grk.) 6. 1; Cureton, p. 19.

[2] Not counting 308, which has D in January and February only.

[3] We might have expected May 1, the day of Maximin's accession. But by substituting May 1 for November 20 we do not get rid of our difficulty, for the former falls on the same day of the week as the latter. Dodwell (*Dissertationes Cyprianicae*, Oxford, 1684, p. 322) plausibly suggests that Maximin observed Diocletian's day as his own.

[4] Browne (*ubi sup.*) writes: 'I understand it thus: November 20 (Wednesday) the martyr was thrown to the wild beast. Dreadfully mangled, he was taken back to his prison, and there lingered one whole day. On the day after that he was cast into the sea (i. e. Friday). Eusebius again throws together the month-date noted in the Roman Acta, and the week-date of the Passion.' Thus he concludes that Agapius was martyred in 306, in which November 22 was Friday. But both Greek and Syriac imply that he was cast into the sea the day following his contest in the arena, not two days after it. If Browne's suggestion as to the source of Eusebius's error is correct, the date of the martyrdom is November 21, which was Friday, not in 306. but in 307, the year to which by independent reasoning we have assigned it.

day of the week.'[1] On our theory this might mean either June 7, 303, or June 7, 304. But it can be proved that June 7, 303, is intended. For the martyrdoms of Alphaeus, Zacchaeus, and Romanus are said to have taken place on November 17 in the first year, and they are definitely connected with the vicennalia of Diocletian, which immediately followed them.[2] But the vicennalia were celebrated November 20, 303.[3] Now the martyrdom of Procopius must have been earlier than those just mentioned, not merely because it precedes them in our texts, but because Procopius is stated to have been the first of the Palestinian martyrs.[4] But in 303 the 7th June was not Wednesday, but Monday. Clearly, either June 7 or Wednesday is an error.[5]

[1] *M. P.* (Grk.) 1. 2 ; Cureton, p. 4.
[2] *M. P.* (Grk.) 1. 5 ; 2. 1, 4 ; Cureton, pp. 4 ff.
[3] Lactantius, *De Mort. Pers.* 17. Mason, following Hunziker, thinks that this date is due to a blunder of Lactantius or of a scribe, and that the true date is not 12 Kal. Dec., but 12 Kal. Jan. = 21 December. (A. J. Mason, *The Persecution of Diocletian*, Cambridge, 1876, p. 205.) But he relies mainly on two rescripts in the Codex of Justinian (II. iii. 28 ; IV. xix. 21) which seem to have been incorrectly dated. See Mommsen in the *Abhandlungen der königl. Akademie der Wissenschaften zu Berlin*, 1860, pp. 357, 372, 437 f. It is somewhat to our purpose, however, to observe that in an argument based on Eusebius's account of the sufferings of Romanus he appears to have misapprehended the facts. He says that Romanus had his tongue cut out on November 17, and contends that 'the three days that would elapse between Romanus's mutilation and the 20th of November could hardly be called πλεῖστος χρόνος' [see *M. P.* (Grk.) 2. 4]. This implies that he died on the day of the vicennalia. But what Eusebius says is that after his mutilation, for which no date is given, he suffered a long imprisonment, and died November 17, τῆς ἀρχικῆς εἰκοσαετηρίδος ἐπιστάσης. This, so far from furnishing an argument against the date given by Lactantius, actually confirms it. For the phrase just quoted is inconsistent with the supposition that five weeks intervened between the martyrdom and the vicennalia.
[4] *M. P.* (Grk.) 1. 1 ; Cureton, p. 3.
[5] The Latin version of the passion of Procopius, which, like the

Finally, both Greek and Syriac give April 2 in the fifth year as the day of the martyrdom of Theodosia.[1] The Syriac declares that it was Sunday; and the Greek addition may have the same meaning—ἐν αὐτῇ κυριακῇ ἡμέρᾳ τῆς τοῦ Σωτῆρος ἡμῶν ἀναστάσεως. But both recensions are certainly incorrect. Twice during the persecution did April 2 fall on a Sunday—in 304 and 310. But no part of either of these years can have coincided with the fifth persecution-year. This example is interesting, because the agreement of the Syriac and the Greek makes it highly probable that the error originated with Eusebius himself.[2]

Thus every one of these four dates is incorrect. And not only is each by itself proved to be erroneous, but they are also inconsistent with one another. It is impossible that a year in which April 2 fell on Friday could be followed by a year in which November 20 fell on Friday, or that it in turn should be followed by a year in which April 2 fell on Sunday.

Syriac, does not mention the day of the week, gives the date as 'Desii septima Julii mensis, quae nonas Julias dicitur apud Latinos'. (Cureton, p. 50; Ruinart, *Acta sinc.*, Amsterdam, 1713, p. 353.) And it so happens that July 7, 303, was Wednesday. But the text is evidently corrupt, for 'Desii' is transliterated from the Greek, and is the Macedonian equivalent of June. Thus the Latin is a fresh witness for the date June 7. On Browne's principle it might be conjectured that the arraignment was on Monday, June 7, and the martyrdom on Wednesday, June 9. But Greek, Syriac, and Latin all leave the impression that Procopius was brought before Flavian immediately after his arrival at Caesarea, and having declined to make a libation to the Emperors was on the same day (αὐτίκα) put to death.

[1] *M. P.* (Grk.) 7. 1; Cureton, p. 22 f.

[2] Browne (*ubi sup.*), in his attempt to account for the error in this date, asserts that April 2 fell on Friday in 307, and places the martyrdom in that year. In fact, April 2 was Friday in 308, the year to which we have assigned it. The Syriac seems to imply that the proceedings occupied more than one day; and the suggestion that Theodoric was arraigned on Friday, April 2, and executed on Sunday is possibly right.

Are we to conclude then that the dates in the *Martyrs* are too untrustworthy to be used for our purpose? That is not a necessary conclusion. For in two, if not three, cases out of the four which have been examined we have seen reason to believe that the month-day is correct and only the week-day at fault. And it is on the month-days alone that our argument rests. Now there are fourteen dates reported in both recensions. In every instance the Greek and the Syriac are in agreement as to the month; in only three cases they differ as to the day of the month, and that but slightly. This is a sufficient guarantee that the dates which Eusebius wrote have been preserved to us in both recensions where they agree, in one or other of them where they differ. And it must be remembered that our argument is based only on the belief which Eusebius held as to the dates of the several martyrdoms which he records, not on the actual facts. Its validity is in no way affected if some or all of Eusebius's dates should prove to be historically inaccurate.

Nevertheless, recognizing the possibility of textual error in some of the dates which we have used, we may notice some further considerations which tend to confirm our conclusion.

We take first two passages which have been used already. The date of the martyrdom of Peter Apselamus has been referred to as indicating that persecution-years began before January 11; but for placing it in the seventh year we were obliged to rely on the Syriac alone. It is therefore worth observing that the next series of events recorded is the trial and death of Pamphilus and those who suffered with him.[1] It cannot be doubted that Eusebius assigned this group of martyrdoms to the seventh year. Not only is this directly stated in the

---

[1] *M. P.* (Grk.) 11; Cureton, pp. 36 ff.

Syriac: both Greek and Syriac add that the martyrs had been imprisoned for 'two full years', or 'about two years' before their trial.[1] The latter assertion must be discussed later. For the present it may suffice to say that it is inexplicable if Pamphilus was imprisoned in the fifth,[2] and brought to trial in the sixth year of the persecution. Moreover, after a parenthetic chapter which follows the recital of the passion of Pamphilus, Eusebius makes the remarkable statement that 'the seventh year was approaching completion'.[3] But the arraignment of Pamphilus is dated in both recensions February 16. Hence that day is the latest on which this narrative allows us to place the beginning of a persecution-year.

Eusebius dates the martyrdom of Timolaus and others March 24 in the second year,[4] and, as we have seen, places the abdication of Diocletian in the same year. If he agreed with Lactantius that the date of the latter incident was May 1, the supposition that a persecution-year began between March 24 and May 1 is excluded. Again, if we suppose the first persecution-year to have begun earlier than March 25, 303, and each year to have consisted of twelve months, it is impossible that the martyrdom of Timolaus could have been in the second year, unless we place it in 304, which can hardly be done, due regard being had to the statements of Eusebius.[5] And one other remark must be made. It is implied both in the Syriac and in the Greek that Timothy

[1] *M. P.* (Grk.) 11. 5 ; Cureton, p. 40.
[2] *M. P.* (Grk.) 7. 6 ; Cureton, p. 25.   [3] *M. P.* (Grk.) 13. 1.
[4] *M. P.* (Grk.) 3. 3 f.; Cureton, pp. 10 ff. (where Timolaus is called Timothy).
[5] The narrative of Timolaus is followed by the assertion that 'at this time' the Emperors abdicated. This does not permit us to separate the martyrdom from the abdication by more than a year (March 24, 304-May 1, 305).

suffered in the second year, but before Timolaus and at Gaza.¹ And since the Syriac makes it plain that the praeses Urban was at Gaza when Timothy was executed, and both recensions represent him to have been at Caesarea during the festival at which Timolaus was condemned, there must have been a considerable interval between the two martyrdoms. The second year must therefore have been some way advanced by March 24, 305.

In the fourth year we find but one martyrdom, that of Agapius, put to death on November 20.² If this event belongs to the close rather than to the earlier months of the year, it proves that the year ended after November 20.

The record of the fifth year supplies two dates, April 2 for the martyrdom of Theodosia, and November 5 (or 1) for the exile of Silvanus.³ The former proves that the year began before April 2. After the latter date are placed many important events,⁴ all of which apparently belonged to the same year.⁵ Urban, the governor, adopted a fresh policy of greater cruelty towards the Christians, of which several examples are given;⁶ after an interval⁷ came the imprisonment of Pamphilus, and finally, a little later,⁸

---

¹ *M. P.* (Grk.) 3. 1; Cureton, p. 8 f.
² *M. P.* (Grk.) 6; Cureton, pp. 19 ff.
³ *M. P.* (Grk.) 7. 1, 3; Cureton, pp. 22, 24.
⁴ *M. P.* (Grk.) 7. 4–7; Cureton, p. 24 f.
⁵ See *M. P.* (Grk.) 7. 1; 8. 1; Cureton, pp. 24, 26. That the imprisonment of Pamphilus belonged to the fifth year is again implied in *M. P.* (Grk.) 11. 5; Cureton, p. 40.

⁶ The Greek prefixes to this statement the words μεθ' ὅν; but in the Syriac the order of events is different, and it is said that all these things and the banishment of Silvanus happened 'in the same day', and indeed 'in one hour'.

⁷ Syr., 'After all these things which I have described.' There is no note of time in the Greek.

⁸ Grk. εὐθὺς καὶ οὐκ εἰς μακρὸν τοῖς κατὰ τοῦ Παμφίλου τετολμημένοις. Syr., 'forthwith, and immediately, and without any long delay.' The

the deposition of Urban. It is not extravagant to demand at least a month for all this, and thus the end of the year is pushed forward to December.

It may now be pointed out that our scheme of the chronology throws light on some statements about the course of the persecution inaugurated by the Emperor Diocletian. We may turn first to a passage near the close of the Greek recension of the *Martyrs* which has no counterpart in the Syriac. In it we are told [1] that in Italy, and the West generally, the persecution lasted not two complete years. The context informs us that peace in the West was brought about by the division of the Empire. What is meant is more clearly stated in a somewhat similar passage, *H. E.* viii. 13. 10 f., where the division is said to have followed immediately upon the abdication of Diocletian and Maximian. But the persecution began in February 303, and the abdication did not take place till May 1, 305. How does this period come to be described 'as not two complete years'? Probably because Eusebius had in view his arbitrary persecution-years,[2] the first of which lasted, as we have seen, twenty months. He simply means that peace was established in the West before December 31, 305. And so in the passage of his *History* referred to above, he puts the matter differently: οὔπω δ' αὐτοῖς τῆς τοιᾶσδε κινήσεως δεύτερον ἔτος πεπλήρωτο κτλ.

In a somewhat similar way we may perhaps explain Eusebius's comment on the final edict of toleration issued by Maximin,[3] that it was put forth 'not a complete year purpose of the writer is obviously to minimize the interval between the tyranny and the degradation of Urban.

[1] *M. P.* (Grk.) 13. 12 τὰ γάρ τοι ἐπέκεινα τῶν δεδηλωμένων, Ἰταλία, κτλ., οὐδ' ὅλοις ἔτεσιν δυσὶ τοῖς πρώτοις τοῦ διωγμοῦ τὸν πόλεμον ὑπομείναντα.

[2] This indeed is implied by the words τοῖς πρώτοις.

[3] *H. E.* ix. 10. 12.

(οὐδ' ὅλον ἐνιαυτόν) after the ordinances against the Christians set up by him on pillars'. This note seems to be a bungling inference from the words of the edict, which obviously referred to something quite different—'Last year (τῷ παρελθόντι ἐνιαυτῷ) letters were sent to the governors of each province.'[1] There is nothing in the phrase to exclude the supposition that the letters referred to were sent more than twelve months previously. But the interval between them and the edict was 'not a complete year', because it was made up of parts of two successive years, and did not include an unbroken calendar year.

In general the phrase 'so many complete years' was used by Eusebius to indicate a series of unbroken years, together with parts of the years preceding and following the series. Thus, having inferred from one statement of Josephus[2] that Pilate was sent to Judaea in 12 Tiberius, and from another[3] that he was recalled immediately before the Emperor's death, i.e. in 23 Tiberius, he states that he was in Judaea 'ten complete years',[4] viz.: 13–22 Tiberius, and portions of 12 Tiberius and 23 Tiberius. In the same way he states that Demetrius was bishop of Alexandria forty-three full years, meaning that he was appointed in 10 Commodus, and died in 10 Severus,[5] and therefore held the bishopric for the 43 regnal years, 11 Commodus–9 Severus, and for a short time before and after. And similarly when he says that he knew Meletius as a fugitive in Palestine in the time of the persecution for seven complete years (ἐφ' ὅλοις ἔτεσιν ἑπτά)[6] he indicates that he knew him during the whole course of the persecution until he himself left Palestine for Egypt early in the eighth year.[7]

[1] *H. E.* ix. 10. 8.   [2] *Ant.* xviii. 2. 2.   [3] Ib. 4. 2.
[4] *H. E.* i. 9. 1 f.   [5] *H. E.* v. 22; vi. 26.   [6] *H. E.* vii. 32. 28.
[7] See *M. P.* (Grk.) 13. 8.

More difficult to explain is the remark that Pamphilus and his companions were in prison for 'two complete years' (ἐτῶν δυεῖν ὅλων χρόνον) before their final examination.[1] For Pamphilus was arrested under the praeses Urban not earlier than November 308;[2] and he was brought before Firmilian February 16, 310. This period of fifteen months included one unbroken persecution-year (309), and parts of two others. It might therefore, according to the usage of which examples have been given, be described as 'one complete year', or 'not two complete years', but not as 'two complete years'. The simplest hypothesis seems to be that the word 'complete' is a later insertion. It is absent from the Syriac ('about two years'),[3] and also from an extant Greek fragment of the longer recension.[4]

One further remark remains to be made. When the dates of the events recorded in the *Martyrs of Palestine* are noted and compared, we are at once struck with the intermittent character of the persecution—at least in Caesarea. It was very far from being, as it is sometimes pictured, a reign of terror which continued everywhere in the East without cessation for ten years or more. The first edict of Diocletian against the Christians was issued February 24, 303. It reached Palestine six weeks or two months later. But no record of proceedings at Caesarea under its provisions has come down to us. For it might plausibly be argued that the protomartyr, Procopius, who suffered in June 303, was arrested, not in consequence of this edict, but under the ordinary law:

---

[1] *M. P.* (Grk.) 11. 5.

[2] *M. P.* (Grk.) 7. 5 f.; Cureton, p. 25.

[3] Cureton, p. 40.

[4] Printed from four MSS. *Analecta Bolland.* xvi. 129 ff., and by Schwartz underneath his shorter Greek text. It reads here δυεῖν ἐτῶν χρόνον for ἐτ. δυ. ὅλων χρ.

certainly sentence of death was passed upon him on account of language which was regarded as insulting to the Emperors.[1] It appears, however, that in the latter part of the year active measures were taken against the Christian clergy under the second edict—provoked, it may be, by the somewhat extravagant conduct of Procopius. The result of these proceedings was a large number of imprisonments, the infliction of tortures in many cases, and two martyrdoms on November 17, 303.[2] But after this there appears to have been a lull for fifteen or sixteen months. We hear of no martyrdoms and no acts of violence till March 305. It seems clear that throughout the Empire the rigour of the persecution must have largely depended on the anti-Christian zeal of the local authorities, and that the praeses who held office at Caesarea up to the end of 304— Flavian by name—was not eager to exceed his duty in the enforcement of the imperial edicts.

But if slackness of administration on the part of Flavian accounts for the paucity of records of persecution in Palestine during the year 303, there was another

[1] *M. P.* (Grk.) 1. 1 ; Cureton, p. 4. The first edict ordered the destruction of churches. Yet, if we may believe the statements of the Syriac recension, churches were still standing in or near Caesarea in 310; for the bodies of Pamphilus and his companions, we are told, 'were burie with honourable burial, as they were worthy, and were deposited in shrines [*lit.* houses of shrines] : and into the temples [i. e. the naves as distinct from the sanctuaries of the churches] they were committed, for a memorial not to be forgotten, that they might be honoured of their brethren who are with God.' I owe the translation to the kindness of Dr. Gwynn. Cureton (p. 45) is inaccurate. The longer Greek runs thus : τῆς προσηκούσης τιμῆς καὶ κηδείας λάχοντα, τῇ συνήθει παρεδόθη ταφῇ, ναῶν οἴκοις περικαλλέσιν ἀποτεθέντα ἐν ἱεροῖς τε προσευκτηρίοις εἰς ἄληστον μνήμην τῷ τοῦ θεοῦ λαῷ τιμᾶσθαι παραδεδομένα.

[2] *M. P.* (Grk.) 1. 3–5; Cureton, pp. 4–6. Somewhat earlier than this date we may probably put the so-called 'Third Edict' (Eus. *H. E.* viii. 6. 10). See Mason, p. 206 f.

circumstance which in combination with it explains their complete absence in 304, and which affected a much wider area. After celebrating his vicennalia Diocletian left Rome on December 19, 303. Shortly afterwards he contracted a slight illness which developed into a serious disorder affecting both body and mind. For the greater part of his journey to Nicomedia he had to be carried in a litter, and so slowly did he travel that he did not reach that city till August.[1] Apparently for seven months after his arrival there he appeared in public only once, and then with grave consequences to his health. By the middle of December a rumour was current that he was dead, and this suspicion was only dispelled when in March 305 he ventured outside the palace, scarcely recognizable after nearly a year of sickness.[2] He was still afflicted with attacks of temporary insanity.[3]

During the greater part of that period Diocletian must have taken a very small share in the government of the Empire, and for at least the four months preceding March 305 he appears to have been wholly incapacitated. From beginning to end of his illness it is probable that not only Flavian, but all the other provincial governors in his dominions[4] were left to their own discretion as to the enforcement or relaxation of the laws against the Christians. If in 303 it was in the power of Flavian to be lenient towards them, in 304 and the early days of 305 there was no need for him to persecute at all.

---

[1] 'Aestate transacta', Lactantius. A rescript was issued in his name at Nicomedia, August 28, 304. *Cod. Iustin.* iii. 28. 26.

[2] 'Vix agnoscendus quippe qui anno fere toto aegritudine tabuisset.' The previous narrative implies that the illness had begun more than a year earlier. Probably therefore 'anno fere toto' refers to the period during which Diocletian was completely laid aside.

[3] Lact. *De Mort. Pers.* 17.

[4] Viz. the Diocese of Pontus and the East, including Egypt.

It is at any rate remarkable that the increased violence of the proceedings in March 305 is directly connected, both in the Greek and the Syriac,[1] with the advent of a new praeses, one Urban, and the issue of the fourth anti-Christian edict of Diocletian.

But the argument may be carried somewhat further. Dr. Mason is probably right in supposing that the fourth edict, which has just been mentioned, was put forth by Maximian on the occasion of the ludi saeculares at Rome, in consequence of a popular outcry, and with the approval of the Senate, at the end of April 304.[2] Professor Gwatkin follows Dr. Mason 'with some hesitation';[3] but he has difficulty in reconciling Diocletian's illness with the publication of the edict in Palestine. 'It was not all Maximian's doing,' he writes.[4] 'Diocletian may not have been quite laid aside by illness till later in the year; and if so Maximian's edict would not have been carried out in Palestine if Diocletian had not been at least willing to try the experiment.' The suggestion here apparently made, that Diocletian gave his consent to the edict some time between May and August, is not very easy to square with Lactantius's circumstantial account of the progress of his illness. But there is no need to make the attempt. As a matter of fact the fourth edict was not promulgated in Palestine till after Diocletian's partial recovery.[5] He made his public appear-

---

[1] *M. P.* (Grk.) 3. 1; Cureton, p. 8.

[2] *The Persecution of Diocletian*, 1876, pp. 212 ff.

[3] *Early Church History to A.D. 313*, vol. ii, p. 336. He strengthens Mason's argument by a reference to Zosimus, ii. 7, for the ludi saeculares of A.D. 304, and discusses a difficulty which Mason did not observe.

[4] Ibid. p. 337.

[5] In the second year of the persecution (305), and some time before March 24. *M. P.* (Grk.) 3. 1, 4; Cureton, pp. 8 ff.

ance on March 1. Within three weeks from that day the order went forth at Caesarea 'that all persons without exception in every city should offer sacrifice and make oblations to the idols'. What is the meaning of all this?

Perhaps we may interpret it thus. During Diocletian's illness it was impossible to carry the new persecuting edict into operation in his dominions. But there was nothing to hinder it from being acted upon in the dominions of Maximian and Galerius. It was not an edict to which Diocletian would have readily given his consent.[1] But by the time it was possible for him to dissociate himself from a law which had doubtless been issued by his colleagues in his name, it was in active operation throughout half the Empire. Resistance on his part, which at an earlier stage might have been effective, had now become futile. Diocletian therefore gave his unwilling sanction to an accomplished fact, the edict was published in Palestine, a praeses was sent there who was willing to execute its provisions, and so the persecution began again with added horrors.

Less than six weeks after the martyrdom of Timolaus and his seven companions Diocletian had ceased to be Emperor. His abdication is one of the enigmas of history. It was perhaps long contemplated, though there is little evidence to show that Diocletian's contemporaries drew from the magnificence of his buildings at Salona the inference which modern writers have based upon it.[2] When it came it took men by surprise. It is obvious that if the design had been some time in existence its

[1] Lact. *De Mort. Pers.* 11. 8.
[2] e.g. Duruy, *Roman Empire*, Eng. Tr., vi. 2, p. 629; Gwatkin, op. cit., ii. 337. It has been argued from Lact. *De Mort. Pers.* 20. 4; *Paneg. Vet.* vi. 9; vii. 15, that the simultaneous retirement of the Augusti in Diocletian's twentieth year was included in his original scheme. But the inference is very precarious.

accomplishment was achieved sooner than had been intended. Why was the momentous decision so suddenly made? The reason given to the general public at the time was Diocletian's ill health and his need of rest.[1] And accordingly this explanation of the proceedings of May 1, 305, found its way into the pages of many early writers.[2] But the explanation of important acts of statecraft vouchsafed to the multitude is not always the real one, and the allegations of Diocletian were not at the time accepted as the whole truth by men who had the best opportunities of judging. Lactantius[3] will have it that Galerius bullied his master into resigning the purple, taking advantage of the opportunity which his infirmity offered. Eusebius in one place professes himself ignorant of the reason.[4] Aurelius Victor[5] holds that Diocletian was moved to retire by the belief that the Empire was threatened with calamity.

Perhaps the facts now before us may suggest, if not the sole cause of the abdication, at least an element in the circumstances which must not be lost sight of as we try to understand it. Advantage had been taken of the incapacity of Diocletian to force the pace of the persecution. An edict had been issued which violated the principle on which he had insisted from the beginning, that in the effort to destroy the Church blood should not be shed. When therefore he was sufficiently recovered from his illness to take some part in public affairs he found himself in a pitiable position. If he continued to be Emperor he had to take his choice between insisting on the recall

---

[1] Lact. op. cit. 19. 3.
[2] Eus. *H.E.* viii. 13. 11 ; Const. *Orat.* 25 ; *Paneg. Vet.* vi. 9; Eutropius, *Breviarium Hist. Rom.* ix. 27.
[3] Op. cit. 18. 1–7.   [4] *V. C.* i. 18.
[5] *Caes.* 39. 48. Cp. Lact. op. cit. 18. 15.

of the fourth edict, or acquiescing in a policy of which he could not approve, and becoming a mere tool in the hands of his own Caesar and his fellow-Augustus. And what chance had a man, feeble in body and mind, of holding his own against a colleague like Galerius, who was ambitious and bloodthirsty, masterful and unscrupulous? As it was, Galerius compelled him to nominate as Caesars Maximin Daza and Severus, passing over Constantine whom, almost certainly, he had designated to the purple.[1] If he had power to do this, he had power to thwart Diocletian in other matters as well. It had in fact become impossible for Diocletian to continue to rule as first Augustus with honour to himself; and therefore he determined to resign his office with as little delay as might be. It is by no means impossible that he had already made up his mind to take this course when early in March he suffered the fourth edict to be put in force in the East. Aurelius Victor's notion that he foresaw disasters may not be altogether beside the mark. His own settled policy concerning the Christians had now been definitely abandoned; and he declined to be responsible for the result.

But to return. If Urban was more zealous than his predecessor, his activity was speedily checked. Eight martyrs were beheaded by his order on March 24, 305; but no act of persecution and no martyrdom is recorded after that day till the following year, when Maximin put forth an edict more severe than any that had preceded it,[2] and as a result Apphianus was put to death, April 2, 306. It is evident that there was a cessation of persecution for the greater part of a year. This agrees well, as has been

[1] Lact. op. cit. 18. 8 ff. See also Gwatkin, op. cit. ii. 338.
[2] *M. P.* (Grk.) 4. 8; Cureton, p. 13 f. This seems to have been a republication of the fourth edict in a more stringent form.

already pointed out, with the fact that Maximin became Emperor on May 1, 305, and that for some time after that date his policy was favourable to the Church. Afterwards, indeed, Maximin became a bitter persecutor, but the change in his attitude towards Christianity was probably gradual; and Caesarea may very well have been unaffected by it till the spring of 306.[1]

It is surprising to find that the execution of Apphianus was succeeded by another long respite of a year and a half.[2] The next event recorded as having taken place at Caesarea was the martyrdom of Agapius, November 20, 307.[3] On this occasion the revival of persecution was due to the presence of Maximin himself at Caesarea, and his desire to celebrate his birthday by a spectacle of an unusual kind. After the birthday games of Maximin the persecution seems to have been continued steadily, and with increasing violence, under Urban and his yet more ferocious successor Firmilian, until July 25, 309, the day of the martyrdom of the virgin Khatha, her companion Valentina, and Paul at Gaza.[4] Then there was another intermission which for several reasons demands special attention.

In the first place, it is the only cessation of persecution

[1] It is remarkable that in the *History* there is very little evidence that Maximin persecuted the Church before the death of Galerius in 311. In *H. E.* viii. 14. 9 his violence against the Christians is coupled with his efforts to restore paganism, by rebuilding the temples and establishing a hierarchy. The rebuilding of the temples seems to have begun in November 309 (see below, p. 208); the formation of the hierarchy belongs to the end of 311 or later (*H. E.* ix. 2–4).

[2] This is not an argument *e silentio*. See Cureton, p. 19: 'The next confessor after Epiphanius [Apphianus] who was called to the conflict of martyrdom in Palestine was Agapius.' Cp. the longer Greek recension, Schwartz, p. 920. The statement, it will be observed, is not limited to Caesarea.

[3] *M. P.* (Grk.) 6; Cureton, pp. 19 ff.

[4] *M. P.* (Grk.) 8. 4–13; Cureton, pp. 26 ff.

to which Eusebius explicitly directs attention. Hitherto the fact that there were periods of comparative rest to the Church has been brought to light only by careful attention to the chronology. The historian makes no mention of any of them. A hasty reader might easily suppose that the persecution was continuous from the day when the first edict of Diocletian reached Palestine in April 303 to the month of August in the sixth year. But the most careless student of the Greek recension of the *De Martyribus* cannot overlook the cessation of activity at which we have now arrived. Eusebius records it as follows:—

'After (or, as a result of) so many heroic acts [1] of the noble martyrs of Christ, the fire of the persecution having decreased, and being as it were in the course of being quenched by their holy blood, and release and liberty having been granted in the Thebaid to those who laboured for Christ's sake in the mines there, and we being about for a little while to breathe the pure air,' &c.[2]

And yet this interval of peace upon which stress is thus laid was much shorter than the others which Eusebius passes over in silence. For three martyrs were sentenced to death no later than November 13, 309.[3] Thus the pause cannot have lasted much more than three months. Why, then, did Eusebius think it worthy of remark? Probably because it was not limited to Caesarea or Palestine, but extended throughout the whole of Maximin's dominions. That this was the case seems to be implied by the mention of the convicts of the Thebaid. And the universality of this breathing-space leads us to another inference. The brief respite was not due to the carelessness or apathy of provincial officials. Rather the persecu-

---

[1] ἐπὶ δὴ τοῖς τοσούτοις . . . ἀνδραγαθήμασι.

[2] *M.P.* (Grk.) 9. 1. It is also mentioned, but much more briefly, in the Syriac. Cureton, p. 31.

[3] *M.P.* (Grk.) 9. 5; Cureton, p. 32.

tion ceased, as it was presently resumed, by the fiat of the Emperor himself.

Eusebius is at a loss to explain the fresh outbreak of the persecution; and the reason which he seems to suggest for its temporary abandonment will scarcely satisfy a historian. But perhaps a sufficient account can be given of both. The time of rest ended with the issue of the 'Fifth Edict'. The summary of it which is given by Eusebius[1] leads one to think that it was differentiated from its forerunners mainly by increased stringency and brutality. But one of its clauses arrests attention: the imperial officers are commanded to rebuild the fallen temples. This indicates a change of policy. The persecution was no longer to be a mere effort to destroy Christianity by brute force, though brute force was still to be used. It was to be accompanied by a revival of paganism. And with this revival of the ancient religion the remaining provisions of the edict were not improbably closely associated. We may believe that it was less with the purpose of embarrassing the Christians than to bring the heathen rites into closer relation with the daily lives of the mass of the people that such commands were given as Eusebius summarizes from his own standpoint: 'That all men, as well as women and household servants, and even children at the breast, should sacrifice and perform libations, and that they should be made to taste the abominable sacrifices, and that things exposed for sale in the market should be defiled with the libations of the sacrifices, and that those who were making use of the baths should be defiled with the execrable sacrifices.' It is evident, at any rate, that henceforth there was to be a contest, not merely of the State with the Church, regarded as a political danger, but of the old faith, aided by the State, with the new.

[1] *M. P.* (Grk.) 9. 2; Cureton, p. 31.

We are at once reminded of the later attempt of Maximin, elsewhere recorded—so like, and yet so unlike, that of Julian half a century afterwards—to organize a new pagan hierarchy.[1] No doubt these two movements, for the building of temples and for the establishment of a heathen priesthood, were parts of the same general policy.[2] The temporary cessation of persecution was due to the recognition by Maximin of the failure of the old policy; it gave the time and leisure which were needed for the evolution of the new.

After the issue of the Fifth Edict the persecution appears to have raged unceasingly at Caesarea for four months. It then ended as far as actual martyrdoms are concerned. For Eubulus, 'the last of the martyrs at Caesarea,' was thrown to the beasts March 7, 310.[3] It was prolonged for a year in other parts of Palestine, where the Bishop Silvanus and his companions—'the final seal of the whole contest in Palestine'—were beheaded May 4, 311.[4] This last martyrdom occurred four days after the publication of the 'palinodia' of Galerius,[5] with which, as the final proclamation of peace for Palestine, the Greek recension of the *De Martyribus* fitly closed.[6]

Glancing back through this brief survey, we see that at

[1] Eus. *H. E.* viii. 14. 9; ix. 4. 2; Lact. *De Mort. Pers.* 36. 4. Cp. Eus. *H. E.* ix. 7. 7, 12.

[2] They are mentioned together in *H. E.* viii. 14. 9.

[3] *M. P.* (Grk.) 11. 30; Cureton, p. 45.

[4] *M. P.* (Grk.) 13. 5; Cureton, p. 48. The exact date is given in the Syriac only.

[5] April 30, 311. See Lact. *De Mort. Pers.* 35; Eus. *H. E.* viii. 17.

[6] The Greek recension of the *De Martyribus* obviously implies that the palinodia brought the persecution to an end in Palestine. Our scheme of the chronology is therefore strongly confirmed by the fact that it makes the last martyrdom so nearly synchronize with it. The copy of the edict which originally followed *M. P.* (Grk.) 13 has disappeared from that place in the MSS.

Caesarea the persecution took the form of five spasmodic onslaughts[1] on the Church, of which four were ushered in by imperial edicts, and the fifth by a visit of Maximin himself to Caesarea for the celebration of his birthday, and each of which was followed by a period of inactivity. The first lasted about six months, June to November 303. The second and third seem to have been very brief, and may be dated respectively March 305 and March-April 306. The fourth was much the longest, continuing for about a year and eight months, November 307 to July 309. The last embraced some five months, November 309 to March 310. It ended about three years and a half before the final edict of toleration of Maximin. Even in the intervals which were free from martyrdoms, no doubt, there was persecution of a sort: the Christians were not allowed full liberty of worship,[2] and confessors who had been imprisoned were not released;[3] but it is improbable that fresh arrests were made, or that Christians, as such, were examined by the magistrates. Thus the time of actual, whole-hearted persecution was limited. At Caesarea, where the rigour of the government officials is not likely to have been less than in other places, all the periods of active persecution of the Faith taken together amounted to less than three years out of the ten years and a half which intervened between the first edict of Diocletian and the last edict of Maximin.

[1] ἐπαναστάσεις, as Eusebius would have called them. See *M. P.* (Grk.) 4. 8.

[2] Yet see *M. P.* (Grk.) 13. 8; Cureton, p. 46.

[3] Pamphilus and his companions were kept in prison even during the cessation which procured liberty for the exiles in the Thebaid. *M. P.* (Grk.) 11. 5; Cureton, p. 40.

THE CHRONOLOGY OF THE NINTH BOOK OF THE *ECCLESIASTICAL HISTORY*

THE ninth book of the *History* is destitute of exact chronological data. It is the aim, however, of this paper to show that careful attention to the vague hints given by Eusebius and the documents quoted by him, and to the much more explicit information supplied by Lactantius,[1] enables us to fix the dates of the principal events referred to with some degree of precision. The investigation may also provide material for a clearer account of the second persecution of Maximin than is given by either of our authorities.

A few preliminary remarks are necessary. Some of our calculations, as will appear presently, are based on assumptions as to the time which the Emperor Maximin and his victorious rival Licinius may have occupied in transporting their armies from one part of Asia Minor to another. Here two questions are involved. At what rate did a Roman army proceed on long marches? And what distance would have been traversed by an army, about A.D. 300, in a march from, let us say, Antioch in Syria to Nicomedia?

Neither of these questions is easy to answer. The rapidity of advance must have depended to a considerable extent on the character of the roads, the time of year and other circumstances. Hence it is not surprising to find that the scanty evidence on this subject collected by

[1] See Appendix II to this Essay.

Dr. L. C. Purser[1] is unsatisfactory and to some extent contradictory. But on the whole it seems to indicate an average speed on good roads (such as those of Asia Minor), and under normal conditions, of about eighteen Roman miles a day. Allowing for one day's rest in seven this would give us 108 Roman miles, or 100 English miles, a week. It may be remarked that Lactantius seems to imply that on one occasion Maximin actually did march eighteen miles in a day.[2] And the correctness of our hypothesis is confirmed by the fact that its use in the present Essay leads to consistent results.

The question as to the distance from Antioch to Nicomedia is also a difficult one. The Antonine Itinerary might indeed be supposed to give us all the information we require. It states that the distance between the two places was 682 miles. But unfortunately the Itinerary, at any rate for Asia Minor, is not to be relied on.[3] We must actually measure the distances for ourselves on the best maps available. And in doing this we are obliged to make some assumption as to the route followed. Both route and distances from Antioch to Tyana, by Tarsus and the Gates of Cilicia, are easily determined. But it is less clear what road an army would have used in proceeding from Tyana to Nicomedia. The course which I have actually followed is this. I have measured the distances, from point to point, along the Byzantine Military Road, as traced by Sir William Ramsay,[4] making use of his excellent maps. The 'organization' of this road is apparently of later date than our period,[5] and it is not the

---

[1] See Appendix I.
[2] From Perinthus-Heraclea to the next mansio. Lact. *De Mort. Pers.* 45. 6.
[3] See Ramsay, *Historical Geography of Asia Minor*, 1890, p. 66.
[4] Ibid. part ii, chap. G. p. 197 ff.   [5] Ibid. p. 200.

OF THE *ECCLESIASTICAL HISTORY* 213

shortest route from Tyana to Nicomedia.¹ But it probably followed, in the main, an older track; and the difference in length between it and the Pilgrims' Road, described in the Itineraries, is not sufficient to affect our argument.² Along the Military Road we get the following measurements:

	English miles
Nicomedia to Tyana	450
Tyana to the Gates of Cilicia	46
The Gates to Tarsus	27
Tarsus, by Aegaeae, to Antioch, about	140
Nicomedia to Antioch	660

It may be added that similar measurements give us as the distance from Nicomedia to Chalcedon, 55 English miles.³

The ninth book of the *Ecclesiastical History* begins with a reference to the publication of the palinode of Galerius 'in Asia and the neighbouring provinces',⁴ by which no doubt Eusebius means the Diocese of Asia, which with the Diocese of Pontus constituted the eastern dominions of Galerius. Since, according to Lactantius,⁵ the edict was issued at Nicomedia on April 30, 311, it may be assumed that it was promulgated in Asia in May and came into the hands of Maximin in the same month.⁶ Eusebius tells us that Maximin concealed the terms of the edict, but never-

---

¹ Ibid. p. 199.

² The distance by it from Nicomedia to Tyana, measured on Ramsay's maps, is about 440 miles, only some ten miles shorter than by the Military Road. For the whole distance from Nicomedia to Antioch the Itinerary gives 682 Roman miles, equivalent to about 630 English miles.

³ 60 Roman miles, which is the distance given in the Itinerary.

⁴ *H. E.* ix. 1. 1.   ⁵ *De Mort. Pers.* 35. 1.

⁶ The imperial post travelled at the rate of about 120 Roman miles a day (Friedländer, *Sittengeschichte Roms*, vol. ii, p. 17). Thus it would reach Antioch from Sardica (1,150 miles) in about ten days.

theless gave orders to the governors that the persecution of the Christians should cease.[1] The letter issued by Maximin's Praetorian Prefect, Sabinus, to the provincial governors is quoted, apparently in full.[2] It is evidently founded, so far as the preamble is concerned, on the edict of Galerius; but the operative clauses fall far short of the provisions of that document, merely directing, or permitting, a suspension of active measures against the Church.

The letter of Sabinus was misconstrued by the governors, who acted in excess of the powers conferred upon them, glad enough no doubt, in many cases, to be rid of an unpleasant duty. The imprisoned confessors were released, and Christians who were undergoing penal servitude at the mines were set at liberty. Those who had suffered for the faith returned to their homes, and assemblies were freely held as of old. It is obvious, if Eusebius may be trusted—and he is not likely to have overstated the case —that all believed that an era of peace had begun.[3] However, the expectation was doomed to disappointment. The Church had rest 'not six whole months'.[4] In accordance with Eusebius's usage this phrase may be taken to mean a period of five calendar months, with portions of the months immediately preceding and following it.[5] Thus the resumption of persecution which followed it probably took place in November 311. This we may take as a second fixed date.

It is not unimportant for our purpose to ask the question, why did Maximin allow the persecution to cease during

---

[1] *H. E.* ix. 1. 1.   [2] §§ 3-6.

[3] Ibid. 1. 7-11. Lactantius (36. 6 f.) does not paint the picture in such glowing colours; but he may include in his survey a later period when, according to Eusebius, the persecution had recommenced, though it had not reached its most violent stage.

[4] *H. E.* ix. 2. 1 οὐδ' ὅλους ἐπὶ μῆνας ἕξ.

[5] See above, p. 198.

the period of six months that followed the edict of Galerius?

Licinius was with Galerius when he died at Sardica a few days after the publication of the palinode, and he was evidently designated to succeed to that Emperor's dominions.[1] But in his effort to get possession of them he had to deal with a rival who was not only alert but, as it proved, for the moment successful. No sooner had tidings reached Maximin that Galerius was dead than he hurried up, as Lactantius tells us,[2] from the East—probably from Antioch—' that he might occupy the provinces and, while Licinius was otherwise engaged (*morante*), secure for himself the whole region up to the straits of Chalcedon.' His aim was to forestall Licinius by at once possessing himself of the Dioceses of Pontus and Asia. With designs like this in hand it was plainly expedient not too quickly to reveal his intentions in regard to persecution. If he had at once declared against the edict he would have brought Licinius to the East, and a surprise would have been impossible; and with Licinius would probably have come Constantine as his ally. He therefore issued a letter which, if not fully accepting the edict, was capable of being so understood. His object, in short, was to steal a march on Licinius, to conciliate his subjects, Christian as well as heathen, and to fight not two emperors but one. And he succeeded in attaining his end. 'There was discord,' says Lactantius, 'almost war,' between Licinius and Maximin. But Constantine took no part in the quarrel; and apparently Licinius did not feel strong enough to take the field against his opponent. The two concluded a treaty which left Maximin master of the whole of Asia Minor.

---

[1] Lact. 35. 3. For the fact that Galerius died at Sardica see Bury's Gibbon, vol. i, p. 411, n. 45.   [2] c. 36.

The next event of first-rate importance in the narrative of Eusebius is the sending of memorials from various cities to Maximin praying that the Christians should be expelled from their borders.[1] Lactantius connects them with the return of the Emperor from the Bosporus. Eusebius leaves the impression that the first of the memorials came from the city of Antioch; and both writers regard them as the starting-point of the later persecution. We might therefore be tempted to date the Antiochene memorial in November 311.

But this inference would be too hasty. In the first place it is probable that Maximin was near Antioch when the deputation waited on him from that city. Eusebius asserts that he had some hand in arranging that it should be sent,[2] and Lactantius confirms his statement.[3] If we can rely on Eusebius, the preliminaries must have occupied a considerable time.[4] But it is unlikely that Maximin should have left Bithynia immediately after it had come under his rule; and if he did he would scarcely have travelled so quickly as to be at Antioch within five months of his departure from it.[5] And again, if Eusebius declares in one place that as a result of the memorials the flame of persecution was again kindled,[6] in another he intimates that

---

[1] *H. E.* ix. 2-4.   [2] Ibid.
[3] 36. 3 'subornatis legationibus ciuitatum'.   [4] *H. E.* ix. 3; 4.
[5] The whole distance from Antioch to Chalcedon and back was 1,430 miles. On his outward journey Maximin was accompanied by an army, and he must have brought a portion of it back with him. But a march of 1,430 miles, under ordinary conditions, would have taken some fourteen weeks, or over three months, without allowing for delays. In this case there appears to have been at least one stoppage on the outgoing march, at Nicomedia (Lact. 36. 1.), and probably another at Chalcedon. The return journey was of the nature of an imperial progress through newly-won dominions, and would therefore almost certainly be very slow.
[6] *H. E.* ix. 4. 2.

it began with the prohibition of assemblies in the cemeteries.[1] This was obviously not due to the granting of petitions which demanded the expulsion of the Christians. It must therefore be placed at an earlier time. And finally we have evidence that Antioch was not the first city to present a memorial. Maximin himself gives a different account of the matter in a letter to Sabinus, the Prefect already mentioned, the text of which is preserved by Eusebius. 'When I went last year', he writes,[2] 'under auspicious circumstances to Nicomedia, and was tarrying there, the citizens of that city came to me with images of the gods, earnestly praying that such a nation [the Christians] should by no means be permitted to dwell in their country.' The petition from Nicomedia was for a while refused; but it is instructive to note it. The very fact that it was rejected marks it as earlier than the series of memorials of the same purport which began with that which emanated from Antioch. For they were all granted.

Let us consider the passage which I have quoted a little more in detail. In connecting the renewal of the persecution with memorials from the cities Maximin agrees with both Lactantius and Eusebius. I shall presently have occasion to suggest that his seeming contradiction of the latter writer in the matter of the priority of the Antiochene memorial is more apparent than real. Meanwhile we have sufficient reason to believe that the Nicomedian petition was presented before the persecution was resumed; that is, in or before November 311.

Its occasion was a somewhat prolonged visit of the Emperor to that city. Now Maximin must have gone to Nicomedia after his treaty with Licinius. And it is in

---

[1] *H. E.* ix. 2.   [2] *H. E.* ix. 9. 17 τῷ παρελθόντι ἐνιαυτῷ.

harmony with the probabilities of the case that he should have remained there some time resting his troops after their long march. But there were other matters of much importance to detain him. Nicomedia was the seat of the imperial government under Galerius, and under his predecessor Diocletian. It was the principal city of Asia Minor and the most natural place in which to make arrangements for the government of the extensive territories which had now come into Maximin's hands. It is hardly possible to find room for a second visit there between the treaty with Licinius and the end of the year 311;[1] and certainly no other visit which he paid to it could be so fitly described as made 'under auspicious circumstances'. We may assume, therefore, that the reference is to a sojourn there immediately after Licinius's cession of his Asiatic dominions. And the letter states that it began 'last year'.

Now the date of the letter to Sabinus can be fixed within narrow limits. In the first place it followed the receipt of the Edict of Milan by Maximin.[2] But, after the victory of the Milvian Bridge (October 27, 312),[3] Constantine and Licinius remained about two months in Rome.[4] They cannot therefore have reached Milan much before December 27. The composition of the edict, and the marriage of Licinius to Constantine's sister, Constantia,

[1] There was a visit later on—apparently late in 312—during which Lucian was martyred (*H. E.* viii. 13. 2 ; ix. 6. 3). But Eusebius seems to imply that the persecution was then at its height, and that the petitions had been already granted. This is confirmed by the *Apology* of Lucian preserved by Rufinus (*H. E.* ix. 6; see also Routh, *Rel. Sac.* iv. 5) in which reference is made to the forged *Acts of Pilate*.

[2] *H. E.* ix. 9. 12 f. That the edict was drawn up at Milan appears from the text of the letter of Licinius, *H. E.* x. 5. 4 ; Lact. 48. 2.

[3] Lact. 44. 4.

[4] *Paneg. Vet.* x. 33. 'Quicquid mali sexennio toto dominatio feralis inflixerat bimestris fere cura sanauit.' Cp. Lact. 45. 1.

OF THE *ECCLESIASTICAL HISTORY* 219

which took place on the same occasion, must therefore be placed in the last days of 312 or early in 313.[1] News of the two events cannot have reached Maximin, who at this time was in Syria,[2] presumably at or near Antioch, till well on in January 313, probably about the 20th.[3] That is therefore the earliest possible date for the letter to Sabinus.

Again, Lactantius informs us that when Maximin heard of the marriage of Licinius he marched from Syria to the Bosporus, and crossed over into Europe. He was in Europe three weeks before his defeat at Campus Serenus, April 30, 313.[4] Hence he must have reached the straits by April 9 at the latest. Let us suppose that he had got as far as Nicomedia by April 6. How much time was spent on the road from Antioch to that place? Maximin no doubt advanced with all possible speed.[5] But the way

---

[1] It is curious that a law of Constantine is dated at Rome January 18, 313 (*Cod. Iust.* xi. 58. 1). If this date is correct the earliest possible date for the letter is about February 10. [2] Lact. 45. 2.

[3] The Antonine Itinerary (Parthey and Pinder, p. 57 f.) gives the distance from Milan to Antioch as 2,167 miles. At the ordinary rate of the imperial post—120 miles a day (see above, p. 213)—this distance could be traversed in eighteen days.

[4] Lact. 45. 5 f.; 46. 8 f. He was eleven days at Byzantium, several days (apparently at least three) at Perinthus-Heraclea; and it would seem that the armies were encamped opposite one another for a day or two before battle was joined. To all this must be added the time required for the march from Byzantium to the mansio after Heraclea (Tzurulum)—a distance of over 80 Roman miles—which would occupy five days.

[5] Lact. 45. 2 'Mansionibus geminatis in Bithyniam concurrit'. I take this obscure phrase to mean that Maximin, on account of the difficulties of the march, could not go as quickly as he would, and therefore stopped for rest after comparatively short stages. It is not of course to be inferred that the stages were only half the usual length. I do not know why Mason says (p. 333) that 'he loitered on the march', or (p. 335) that when he reached Bithynia 'he was obliged to wait for some time to recruit'.

was long, and it led over the Taurus mountains, the passage of which could not, under any circumstances, have been quickly made.[1] And Maximin encountered fierce winter weather. His army marched through mud, in snow and rain and cold.[2] It is therefore unlikely that, in spite of his exertions, the average pace of the advance was greater than that of an ordinary march on a level road. We may fairly conclude that it was not above 100 miles a week, possibly much less. If Maximin reached Nicomedia seven weeks after his departure from Antioch, he must be regarded as having performed a considerable feat, considering the adverse conditions. Now counting back seven weeks from April 6 we reach February 16 as the latest date for the beginning of the expedition. It is also the later limit of date for the letter to Sabinus. For the purpose of that letter must have been either to conciliate his Christian subjects by way of preparation for his war against Licinius, or to conceal his hostile intent from his fellow emperors, if it was not designed to achieve both these ends. To be effective in either direction it was plainly desirable that it should be issued as soon as possible, and, at any rate, before the troops actually began to move. Thus we may with some confidence place it between January 20 and February 16, 313.

Yet this letter refers to a visit to Nicomedia not later than November 311 as having taken place 'last year'. This would obviously have been impossible if Maximin, in

[1] The road from Tarsus ascends in the course of 25 or 30 miles to a height of nearly 4,000 feet, through a very narrow and difficult pass. See Ainsworth in the *Journal of the London Geog. Society*, x. 499 ; cp. W. M. Ramsay, *Hist. Geog.*, p. 58. The road was mountainous the whole way from Tarsus to Tyana, a distance of over 70 miles. See Ramsay's map opposite p. 330.

[2] Lact. l. c.

OF THE *ECCLESIASTICAL HISTORY* 221

Roman fashion, had counted January as the first month of the year. But, this supposition being excluded, it is probable that in his reckoning the year began in September.[1] For this hypothesis we shall find confirmation as we proceed. If it is correct, Maximin writing early in 313 would naturally describe an event in, or shortly before, November 311 as belonging to the previous year. But he could not have so spoken of the visit to Nicomedia if it had been earlier than September. Maximin's arrival at Nicomedia after his compact with Licinius must therefore be set provisionally between September and November 311.

Before carrying the argument to a further stage we may pause here to inquire how far this date fits in with what we can infer from other considerations. Galerius died at Sardica early in May 311. The news may have reached Antioch before the end of the same month.[2] Now, as we have seen, a march from Antioch to Nicomedia would have been accomplished in a little under seven weeks.[3] Thus if the expedition set out on June 1 it would have reached Nicomedia about July 15. Here there was a delay the length of which cannot be determined. It was sufficient however to enable Maximin to purchase the allegiance of the Bithynians by removing an oppressive tax.[4] A further march of four days brought him to Chalcedon.[5] So we reach the last week of July. At

---

[1] Or perhaps October. See C. H. Turner in *Journal of Theological Studies*, i. 188.

[2] See above, p. 213. The death of Galerius seems to have been announced at Nicomedia May 15 (Lact. 35. 4). It might have been made known at Antioch a week later.

[3] Maximin does not seem to have been so anxious on this occasion as in the expedition of 313 to advance at high speed. But the time of year was more favourable.

[4] Lact. 36. 1.   [5] 60 Roman miles.

Chalcedon he was perhaps obliged to wait for his adversary,[1] and when he came some days would be occupied in stormy negotiations conducted by the two emperors from opposite sides of the straits. For all this a week may be allowed. To this we have to add four days for the return to Nicomedia. Thus we may take the first or second week in August as the earliest date for the commencement of his sojourn in that city. But obviously it is more likely than not to have been considerably later. He may, for all we know, have been far south of Antioch when the report of Galerius's death came. He may not have been able to mobilize a sufficiently strong army in a few days. There may have been delays on the way, or at Chalcedon, which we have not allowed for. There would be nothing to surprise us if Maximin did not arrive at his new capital till September was pretty far advanced.

I may now attempt the task of dating another important document, the reply to the memorials from the cities. For it is to be observed that it was a single document. Each several petition did not receive a separate answer, as we might perhaps have expected; but when all had come in, a rescript was issued which was sent to all the cities and other places concerned. This is implied by Eusebius more than once. Thus, after stating that the officials in other cities and the provincial governors followed the example of Theotecnus of Antioch in procuring petitions, he goes on to

---

[1] There is nothing improbable in this. If Licinius had been near Byzantium Maximin would not have stopped at Nicomedia and thus given him time to land troops at Chalcedon. The secrecy with which Maximin contrived to envelop his movements is very remarkable. It will be remembered that he was some weeks in Europe in 313 before Licinius met him. It seems as though Licinius knew nothing about his advance until he had actually landed (Lact. 45. 5).

say that the tyrant 'by a rescript' expressed approval of the memorials that had been voted.[1] And again, when he comes to insert in his *History* a translation of the Emperor's reply, as he found it inscribed on a pillar at Tyre, though at the beginning of the chapter he speaks of it as one of a number of imperial ordinances,[2] yet lower down he calls it 'this document which was set up on pillars'.[3] That Eusebius's hints may be relied on as accurate is proved by an inscription lately discovered at Arykanda in Lycia.[4] In it we have the text of the memorial of the citizens of that place in Greek, to which the reply of the Emperor, in the Latin language, was prefixed. Of the latter only a small portion remains; but it is clearly identical with the underlying Latin of the conclusion of the Tyrian inscription quoted by Eusebius.[5]

Now this rescript must have been sent out between November 311 and the date of the letter to Sabinus (January–February 313). The text preserved by Eusebius has an indication of the time of year at which it was written; for the Emperor appeals to the ripe corn in the broad plains, and the meads bright with flowers after the rain, as a mark of divine favour.[6] This points to the late summer. The rescript may therefore be assigned to August or September 312. This agrees with the state-

---

[1] *H. E.* ix. 4. 2 ὧν δὴ καὶ αὐτῶν τοῖς ψηφίσμασιν δι' ἀντιγραφῆς ἀσμενέστατα ἐπινεύσαντος τοῦ τυράννου.

[2] Ibid. 7. 1 διατάξεων ἀντιγραφαί. Cp. 10. 12.

[3] § 2 ἐνταῦθά μοι ἀναγκαῖον εἶναι φαίνεται αὐτὴν δὴ ταύτην τὴν ἐν στήλαις ἀνατεθεῖσαν τοῦ Μαξιμίνου γραφὴν ἐντάξαι. See also § 16; and compare the title of the Tyrian inscription Ἀντίγραφον ἑρμηνείας τῆς Μαξιμίνου πρὸς τὰ καθ' ἡμῶν ψηφίσματα ἀντιγραφῆς, ἀπὸ τῆς ἐν Τύρῳ στήλης μεταληφθείσης.

[4] See Gebhardt, *Acta martyrum selecta*, Berlin, 1902, p. 184 f.

[5] *H. E.* ix. 7. 13 f.   [6] § 10.

ment of Eusebius immediately following, that the boasts of Maximin were falsified, when in some places the messengers who carried the rescript to the governors had scarcely reached their journey's end, by the failure of the winter rains.[1] The setting up of the pillars must be put somewhat later in the year 312. They would hardly have been erected in the midst of the calamities which signalized the following winter,[2] nor after the letter to Sabinus.

The last document of this period quoted by Eusebius is Maximin's Edict of Toleration, published a short time before his death.[3] To it we must now turn. The course of events which led up to it is traced by Lactantius,[4] though the edict itself is not referred to by him. He tells us that after his defeat at Campus Serenus Maximin fled in disguise to Nicomedia, and thence to Cappadocia, where he resumed the purple, and collected an army. It was composed of fugitives from Campus Serenus and reinforcements from beyond the Taurus. His object, according to Lactantius, was to escape to the Diocese of the East, intending there, no doubt, to make a stand against Licinius. Licinius also proceeded eastwards, but with no great haste, for he was still at Nicomedia, when he published the Edict of Milan, on June 13, 313. Subsequently, but how long after we have no hint, he went in pursuit of Maximin. On receiving word of his approach Maximin resumed his retreat, and betook himself to the Taurus mountains, where he fortified the passes. Licinius had a march of 450 miles before he reached Tyana, on the lower slopes of the Taurus. This must have consumed a month. Then began the advance of forty-five miles through extremely narrow and dangerous passes to

[1] *H. E.* ix. 7. 16 ; 8. 1. [2] *H. E.* ix. 8.
[3] Ibid. 10. 7. [4] c. 47 ff.

the Gates of Cilicia.[1] Each mile of the road must have been contested, with every advantage on the side of the defending army. In the end, however, Maximin's forts were reduced, and he was driven out of the Taurus and retired on Tarsus.[2] Thus far we may follow Lactantius. But when he adds that Maximin, seeing that all hope was gone, took poison and died some days after in great agony, we may withhold our assent. Eusebius says nothing about poison; but he does tell us that Maximin issued an edict in favour of the Christians as ample as that of Milan. This seems to prove that Maximin did not regard himself as finally beaten. He was, indeed, dispossessed of Pontus and Asia, but he apparently hoped to retain his old dominions in Syria and Egypt.[3] He may have perceived that in order to accomplish this a frank and permanent abandonment of the policy of persecution had become necessary. Thus I would explain the issue of his last edict. But if that was his purpose it was frustrated almost immediately afterwards by his death. That this took place very soon after Licinius's victory in the Taurus

---

[1] 'It is said that the rocky walls which form the Gates approached so close that, until Ibrahim Pasha blasted a road for his artillery, a loaded camel could just pass between them.' Ramsay, op. cit., p. 58.

[2] Mason (p. 336) writes, 'He secured himself at Tarsus (to which he had retreated ...) by blockhouses in the passes of the Taurus'—implying that Maximin went to Tarsus before Licinius carried his forts. But I can find no support for this in Lactantius. Some such inference, indeed, might perhaps be drawn from *H. E.* ix. 10. 14 if Lactantius be ignored. But the two accounts are not irreconcilable. Maximin may have withdrawn at the last moment, when he found that the passes could no longer be held.

[3] The new army which Maximin got together in Cappadocia was composed of fugitives from Campus Serenus and reinforcements *from the East* (Lact. 47. 6). Obviously the legions in his original dominions were ready to fight for him.

is implied by the statement that he died 'in the second campaign of the war'.[1]

From all this we cannot fix the date of Maximin's death with any approach to accuracy. But if we allow no more than six weeks for Licinius's advance from Nicomedia and the capture of the Taurus passes, with a few days for Maximin's retreat to Tarsus, the issue of the edict, and his illness, and if we assume that Licinius left Nicomedia on June 14, we cannot put the final scene further back than the first week of August.[2] But if we suppose that Maximin died in that month we encounter some difficulties. They may be summed up in the question, Why did not Licinius follow up his successes? Why did he leave Maximin unharmed at Tarsus to make plans for successful resistance in the following year?

The dilatory tactics of Licinius are indeed puzzling. But we may account for the fact that he was still in Bithynia, allowing the enemy to gather a fresh army, in June. He had a small army when he reached Campus Serenus in April, and he was probably obliged to wait for reinforcements before undertaking a further expedition. That, however, will not explain the fact that when he had advanced to the Gates of Cilicia he did not descend to Tarsus and try conclusions with a demoralized foe. Some other reason must be suggested; and the most obvious one is that winter was already approaching. If he should chance to experience a reverse in Cilicia, and be obliged to recross the mountains late in the year harassed by an army more used to the severities of winter in high

---

[1] *H. E.* ix. 10. 13.

[2] I cannot follow those who put the edict in June—e. g. Mason, p. 336; Bright, *Ecclesiastical History of Eusebius*, p. 325 (with hesitation); Gwatkin, *Early Church History*, ii. 359. The last-named writer implies that it was issued before the letter of Licinius (June 13).

altitudes than his own, he might suffer irretrievable disaster. This consideration may lead us to suspect that the death of Maximin occurred not nearly so early as the beginning of August: more probably in September or October.

Let us examine the edict itself. In it Maximin declares that 'last year he had decreed by letters sent to the governors of every province that if any one wished to follow the custom [of the Christians] or the observance of that religion' he should be at liberty to do so, but that his commands had been misunderstood.[1] This undoubtedly refers to the letter to Sabinus of January or February 313. Since the writing of the letter, therefore, it appears that a new year, on Maximin's reckoning, had begun. Is the edict then to be dated in 314? It must belong to the early days of that year if Maximin's year began in January. This date does not seem to be absolutely impossible. But it is later than the arguments already advanced would lead us to expect. It seems, for example, to involve the supposition that Licinius postponed till mid-winter the attack on Maximin's fortifications in the passes of the Taurus, which is not likely. It is therefore desirable to date the edict a couple of months further back, if the facts permit us to do so. There is no obstacle in the way if we again assume that Maximin's year began in September. On that hypothesis the edict and the death of the Emperor may be assigned to September or October 313: but earlier than the September of that year they cannot be placed.

A note of time is given by Eusebius himself which might seem likely to help us here. But unfortunately it is ambiguous. After transcribing the Greek version of the edict, he remarks, 'These are the words of the tyrant,

[1] *H. E.* ix. 10. 8 f.

penned not a whole year after the ordinances against the Christians set up by him on pillars.'[1] Since, according to Eusebius's usage, the phrase 'not a whole year' is in this sentence practically equivalent to 'in the next year',[2] he seems to state that the rescript of August 312 and the edict of 313 belong to successive years. If his year began in January, that is in agreement with the conclusion that we have reached. But it is much more probable that his reckoning of years was the same as Maximin's and that he counted them as beginning in September.[3] In that case the rescript and the edict cannot have been issued in successive years, the former having been promulgated in the year before the letter to Sabinus and the latter in the year after it. Several solutions of this difficulty may be proposed. In the first place it may be urged, not unreasonably, that Eusebius may have fallen into error. It seems that the rescript was drafted only a few weeks before, and the edict perhaps only a few days after the beginning of a year. A very slight misplacement of either would account for his mistake. It is to be remembered that he was making a point of the shortness of the interval that separated them. But again, Eusebius may not have been referring to the date of the drafting of the rescript, but to that of the setting up of the pillars, which was of course later, and almost certainly at the beginning of the next year.[4] Or he may have had in mind the date of its arrival at some city in his own neighbourhood, as for instance Tyre;[5] for we know that in some places it was not received till the beginning of the winter.[6] If either of these suppositions

---

[1] *H. E.* ix. 10. 12. [2] See above, p. 198.
[3] See Turner, *u. s.* [4] See above, p. 224.
[5] So he dates the first edict of Diocletian April 303, in *M. P.* (Grk.) Pref., obviously intimating the time of its publication at Caesarea.
[6] *H. E.* ix. 7. 16.

is correct, Eusebius's words confirm our conclusion as to the date of the edict. It must have been issued in the year which began in September 313. But I confess that another solution seems to me quite as probable as any of these. The assertion may be merely a false inference from the text of the edict itself. Eusebius may have supposed that the letters stated therein to have been sent to the governors 'last year' were not the epistle to Sabinus but the rescript afterwards inscribed on pillars. If so, he is only expressing in his own language what he understood the edict to say, and we cannot use his words as evidence at all. A sentence which is so difficult to interpret can have no weight on either side.

Having determined with sufficient accuracy for our purpose the dates of the leading events recorded by Eusebius, we may now return to an earlier period, and endeavour to combine into a consistent narrative the various notices of the outbreak of Maximin's second persecution of the Christians.

We have seen that after his treaty with Licinius, Maximin entered Nicomedia about September 311. There he tells us he made some stay. Before he left—it may have been in November—some of the citizens, as he informs us,[1] urged him to prohibit the Christians from living in their territory. There can be no doubt that this statement is true. It is borne out by the text of his reply to the petitions from other cities, which proves that this was the request made by them all,[2] and by several passages in Eusebius.[3] And the very fact that Maximin does not pretend that the request was made by the citizens as a body increases its credibility.

It is easy to understand that the petition presented at

[1] *H. E.* ix. 9. 17. [2] Arykanda inscription; *H. E.* ix. 7. 12.
[3] *H. E.* ix. 2; 3; 4. 1.

Nicomedia placed Maximin in a difficult position. It was no doubt much to his liking. But his plans can hardly then have been matured, and it was perhaps too soon to show his hand and enter upon a serious war against the Church. Besides, it was the petition of a party, perhaps of a minority. So it was politely refused. Nevertheless it was politic to retain the loyalty of the Nicomedians, with whom he was just then in high favour. And so we may with some probability date at this time the prohibition of gatherings in the cemeteries of which Eusebius speaks.[1] This was not a very severe measure, as compared with others of which the Christians had had experience in the past. It might be justified on religious or political grounds. The Christians at such assemblies might worship the martyrs,[2] or they might hatch plots against the State. It would satisfy the less extreme of the persecuting party and it would not displease those who were tired of bloodshed. But by Eusebius it would certainly be counted an end of the peace.

Not long after the presentation of the petition we may suppose the Emperor began his long journey back to Syria. And possibly during that journey he devised the carefully thought out scheme on which he soon after proceeded to act. It included, on the one hand, a sharp persecution, and on the other, definite measures for the restoration of paganism. Some years before Maximin had ordered the rebuilding of the temples;[3] he now proposed to supplement this ordinance by the establishment of a heathen hierarchy in imitation of the Christian ministry, and by the direction that the forged *Acts of Pilate* should be used as a school manual.[4] The hierarchy was to be employed not only as a means of revivifying paganism,

---

[1] *H. E.* ix. 2. [2] See *H. E.* viii. 6. 7.
[3] *M. P.* (Grk.) 9. 2; Cureton, p. 31. [4] *H. E.* ix. 4; 5.

but as an instrument of persecution.¹ But none of these things were to be set on foot by the unsupported fiat of the Emperor. If he wished to persecute, as no doubt he did, it is not at all improbable that he also wished, as Lactantius affirms, to appear to be coerced into persecuting.² And the petition from Nicomedia may have given him a hint how this was to be accomplished. Through Theotecnus he got an oracle from Jupiter Philius, and as an almost necessary consequence, a petition from the pagan citizens of Antioch, praying him to fulfil the behests of the god.³ But there was no indecent haste in acceding to their request. Maximin merely indicated his gratification. That was sufficient to produce similar memorials from many other cities, and at length from country districts. When a large number had reached him he published the rescript, which banished the Christians, hinted that the gods should be more zealously worshipped, and rewarded the memorialists by inciting them to ask a further boon which he would certainly grant.⁴ The reply was dispatched to all the cities which had sent in memorials, not even Nicomedia being forgotten⁵ This rescript, as we have seen, was issued about August 312. If we suppose that the petition from Antioch was presented about April or May we leave ample time for a leisurely progress of Maximin through Asia Minor during the winter months, and also for the engineering of petitions far and wide.

It is evident that with the publication of this rescript the final persecution began in earnest.⁶ It probably came to an end some five months later, when Maximin issued

---

¹ *H. E.* ix. 4. 3 ; Lact. op. cit. 36. 4.
² *De Mort. Pers.* 36. 3.   ³ *H. E.* ix. 2 ; 3.
⁴ Ibid. 7. 4, 7, 12, 13 f.   ⁵ Ibid. 7. 1, 15 ; 9. 19.
⁶ Lact. 36. 3-7 ; *H. E.* ix. 5 ; 6.

his letter to Sabinus, and entered upon his disastrous conflict with Licinius.

It may be well before bringing this Essay to a close to say a few words in view of a possible objection. I have made considerable use of Maximin's letter to Sabinus as evidence for historical facts. But this letter has been stigmatized as unworthy of credit. Dr. Mason sums up his opinion of it in these words:

'In this curious letter Maximin contradicts himself often enough to make his Christian subjects dizzy. First he justifies bloody persecution, then plumes himself upon having stopped it, next apologizes for having set it again on foot, then denies that it was going on, and lastly orders it to cease. We cannot wonder at what Eusebius relates, that the people whose wrongs the letter applauded and forbade, neither built church nor held meeting in public on the strength of it; for they did not know where to have it.'[1]

I cannot think that this criticism is altogether fair. For what are the statements of the letter on which it is founded? Maximin certainly justifies the edicts of Diocletian and Maximian, just as Galerius had done before him; and, like Galerius, he does so in the very act of proclaiming a cessation of violence against the Christians. But he says nothing about any later edicts, and his words, taken strictly, do not defend the punishment of the Christians by death. He then asserts (why should he be said to 'plume himself'?) that on his accession he stopped the persecution. There is good ground to believe that this is true,[2] whatever may be thought of the reasons which he alleges to have moved him thereto. They are at any rate not unlike those which he gave at the time, and which were taken from the edict of Galerius.[3] Maximin next recounts the circumstances under which the persecution had lately

---

[1] Mason, p. 334. Quoted in part by Gwatkin (ii. 356), with approval.
[2] See above, p. 187.   [3] *H. E.* ix. 1. 5.

been renewed. That may in a sense be called an apology for his recent action. But it is not inconsistent with his previous assertions; and when he connects the fresh outbreak of violence with petitions from the cities he is in agreement with Eusebius and Lactantius. He could scarcely be expected to add, with them, that he had himself taken measures to procure the petitions. On what words of the letter Dr. Mason founds the statement that Maximin denies that persecution was going on, I do not know. He certainly ' orders it to cease '.

When Dr. Mason goes on to mention the distrust with which the letter was received, the incautious reader might suppose that this was due to its misstatements and contradictions. But Eusebius gives a very different reason for the fact that they 'neither built church nor held meeting in public'. It was because the letter contained no express permission to do these things.[1] They had had bitter experience in the past of the unwisdom of going beyond the letter of Maximin's concessions.[2] They were determined to be more cautious this time. There is nothing to suggest that they were in any way influenced by the inaccuracy of the Emperor's history.

In one matter, nevertheless, Maximin was certainly guilty of *suppressio veri*. If we had no other document in our hands than his letter we might have supposed that there was no persecution in his dominions from the middle of 305 to the end of 311. This is, of course, contrary to fact. There was peace apparently from May 305 to April 306, and from May to November 311; and there seem to have been considerable intervals of rest in the intervening period.[3] But from November 309 to May 311 there was fierce and continuous persecution. Maximin writes as though it had not been. And it is probably true that in

[1] Ibid. 9. 23 f.   [2] Ibid. 1. 7.   [3] See above, pp. 199 ff.

other parts of his letter 'no Turk ever lied more shamelessly', though Dr. Mason is not altogether happy in his selection of the particular statement to which this remark should be applied. The Emperor was naturally anxious to put the best face possible on his actions. But however discreetly Maximin may have avoided disagreeable subjects, it is really incredible that in a deliverance obviously designed to conciliate his Christian subjects he should make direct and positive statements which every one of them must have known to be absolutely untrue. The statements of the letter on which I have relied are either such as if they were not true must at the time have been notoriously false, or relate to matters about which there is no conceivable reason why Maximin should have lied. Of the former class is his testimony that the persecution was stayed on his appointment as Caesar, and that its recent renewal was the sequel of memorials from his subjects. Of the latter is the date which he gives for his visit to Nicomedia, and the implication that it was the first city from which a memorial against the Christians had come to him.

APPENDIX I

THE RATE OF MARCH OF A ROMAN ARMY

By L. C. PURSER, Litt.D.

IT is not very easy to fix definitely the normal day's march of a Roman army. A *iustum iter* was considered to be what was accomplished in about five hours, and varied according to circumstances from 15 to 20 Roman miles. Caesar marched from Corfinium to Brundisium, a distance stated to be 465 kilometers (=289 English, 315 Roman miles), in 17 days. If he marched every day, the rate would be 17 English miles a day : if he rested during two days, the rate would be almost $19\frac{1}{2}$. If this statement of the distance is correct, the rate assigned in Tyrrell's and my Cicero (vol. iv. p. xxix), viz. 15 Roman miles a day, is quite too low : for the march was a rapid one (cp. Cic. *Att.* viii. 14. 1 f.). But I am not quite sure that the distance is so great as 289 English miles. Recruits when practising marching were expected three times a month in five summer hours to do 20 Roman miles (75 Roman = 69 English miles) if they went at regulation rate (*militaris gradus*), 24 if at quick march (*plenus gradus*), see Vegetius i. 9 : but in a continuous series of days' marching I think that this rate could only be maintained under special circumstances ; especially if we remember that the Roman soldier had to carry 60 Roman pounds weight of pack (60 Roman = 45 English lb.). Asparagium is about 15 English miles from Dyrrhachium, and Caesar did that distance in a *iustum iter* (*Bell. Civ.* iii. 76). In *Bell. Gall.* v. 47. 1 we find Caesar marching 20 Roman miles in a day beginning at nine o'clock. A sudden excursion from Gergovia (*Bell. Gall.* vii. 40, 41) of 25 Roman miles forward and 25 backward appears to have been done within 30 hours, but that was a special effort. In *Bell. Gall.* vii. 10, 11, the distance (72 Roman miles) from Agedincum (Sens) to Cenabum (Orleans) seems to have been traversed in four days=18 miles a day. Mr Rice Holmes (*Caesar's Conquest of Gaul*, p. 627) tells us that experienced soldiers (e. g. the Duc d'Aumale) say that an army *could* march 28 kilometers (nearly 19 Roman miles) a day for ten days successively, but that, they say, is very hard work. He quotes Lord Wolseley (*Soldier's Pocket Book* (ed. 3), p. 226) as stating that the length of ordinary marches for a force not stronger than one division moving by one road should be from 12 to 15 English miles ($=13$ to $16\frac{1}{4}$ Roman miles) a day for 5 out of 6 days, or at most for 6 out of 7: but French military men say that ancient armies could march faster, as they had not to drag about so many impedimenta and had not so many necessities as modern soldiers.

APPENDIX II

THE AUTHORSHIP OF THE *DE MORTIBUS PERSECUTORUM*

THE question whether the tract *De Mortibus Persecutorum* is from the pen of Lactantius, as its discoverer, Baluze, supposed, and as has been assumed in the foregoing Essay, has often been debated. For the historical inquirer it is of minor importance, and I do not intend to discuss it fully here. The arguments have been set forth in recent years by Brandt, Bury,[1] and Pichon.[2] Something, however, may be said about what is generally regarded as the strongest part of the evidence against the Lactantian authorship.

Jerome tells us[3] that Lactantius, having taught rhetoric for some time at Nicomedia, was in his old age the tutor of the Caesar Crispus in Gaul. And it is probably to him that we owe the statement, which appears in the *Chronica* of Eusebius under the year 317[4]—the year of Crispus's appointment as Caesar—that he instructed him in Latin literature. Now Lactantius composed his *Institutiones* in Gaul before 310 and probably before 308. Therefore he must have left Nicomedia not later, at any rate, than 310. It is inferred that he cannot have been in Nicomedia between 311 and 313. But the author of the *De Mortibus* describes the events of those years at Nicomedia as an eyewitness. Hence he cannot have

[1] In his edition of Gibbon, vol. ii, p. 531, where references to the discussions of Brandt and others are given.
[2] R. Pichon, *Lactance, étude sur le mouvement philosophique et religieux sous le règne de Constantin*, Paris, 1901, p. 337.
[3] *De Vir. Ill.* 80. [4] Schoene, ii. 191.

been Lactantius. I have attempted to show elsewhere[1] that the fifth book of the *Institutiones*, or rather a tract *De Iustitia*, which is embedded in it, was composed in Gaul as early as 306. It may be suggested that Lactantius left Nicomedia early in that year with Constantine, when the latter fled from Galerius.[2] By that time Maximin had established himself in Bithynia, persecution had again broken out in his dominions, and there was every prospect that it would be of a more violent type than anything that Diocletian had sanctioned before the eve of the abdication. It was just the time when a Christian living at Nicodemia, if the opportunity offered, would seek refuge in the only part of the Empire where he would be secure from molestation.

How then can the Lactantian authorship of the *De Mortibus* be defended? There is much force in the contention that Lactantius did not become the tutor of Crispus at Trier till 317, and that there is nothing to hinder us from supposing that he returned for a time to Nicomedia, and was there from 311 until the *De Mortibus* was written (313 or 314). But I think we may go further. The evidence that the writer of the *De Mortibus* was at Nicomedia from 311 to 313 is not very strong. It is true that he knew the exact day on which the news of Galerius's death became known there.[3] He knew also the date of the letter of Licinius, published at Nicomedia, and the fact that he supported it with a speech.[4] But these are things of which he might have received information from his Nicomedian friends.

On the other hand, he makes a mistake about a matter of capital importance which gives us good reason to believe that he was not living at Nicomedia during the later persecution by Maximin. We have seen that the ostensible cause of the renewal of persecution was a series

---

[1] *Hermathena*, vol. xii, no. 29 (1903), pp. 452 ff.
[2] *De Mort. Pers.* 24.   [3] Ibid. 35. 4.   [4] Ibid. 48. 1, 13.

of memorials to the Emperor; and that, according to Eusebius and the authorities quoted by him, as well as the Arykanda inscription, the purport of all the memorials was the same, a prayer that the Christians should be banished. The evidence is specially strong that it was so in the case of the memorial from Nicomedia.[1] The author of the *De Mortibus* is alone in telling us that the memorials merely demanded that Christians should not be allowed to build churches within the cities. If he had been in Nicomedia when the memorial from that city was presented he could hardly have fallen into this error.

Further, there is no hint in the *De Mortibus* that in the later persecution Christians were put to death, as such, by public process of law. Indeed the contrary is implied.[2] But Eusebius gives the names of several prominent martyrs of this period—among them that of Lucian who suffered at Nicomedia.[3] The author of the *De Mortibus* could hardly have written as he did if he had been resident in Nicomedia at the time.

Now if Lactantius left Nicomedia in the company of Constantine and remained in Europe under his protection till 317 or later, he would have been an eyewitness of the persecution at Nicomedia for about three years; but of its later history, though he might have had accurate information, he could have had little first-hand knowledge. How does that agree with the supposition that he was the author of the *De Mortibus Persecutorum*? No one who reads the chapters of that work which narrate the beginning of the persecution and the events which followed it up to the abdication in May 305[4] can fail to carry away the impression that the man

---

[1] Above, p. 217.   [2] 36. 6 f.; 37. 1.

[3] *H. E.* ix. 6. 3. To him might be added Anthimus, bishop of Nicomedia, if he was beheaded at that time (*H. E.* viii. 13. 1). But Eusebius seems to be right in placing his martyrdom much earlier. See below, pp. 268 ff.

[4] cc. 10-20.

who wrote them was on the spot during that period. They are full of accurate dates and vivid detail. And if the author relates a conversation between Diocletian and Galerius, of which a private citizen would not be likely to have known,[1] it is to be remembered that his imagination may have been assisted by reports from Constantine, if he was already on friendly terms with him. The chapters which follow, giving detailed information concerning the administration of Galerius,[2] are such as may well have been written by one who was living at the seat of government. They contain particulars which could not easily have been ascertained in Gaul. But for our purpose it is as necessary to note what the writer omits as what he tells in this part of his work. He seems to have been ignorant of some not unimportant facts. Thus he has not much to say about Diocletian's visit to Rome.[3] He passes over in silence Maximian's important edict of April 304.[4] He implies that Maximian abdicated about the same time as Diocletian,[5] but he gives no particulars. That is to say, he evinces little knowledge of contemporary events in the West.

After the flight of Constantine there are sections of the book which suggest, if not first-hand knowledge, at least abundance of information. But they are not the sections which are concerned with Asia Minor. They may be divided into two groups. The first consists of those chapters which relate the course of events in the West, from the proclamation of Maxentius as Emperor at Rome up to his defeat at the Milvian Bridge.[6] It includes a very full account of the plots of Maximian, much of which is not recorded elsewhere. In the latter part of the narrative the earlier stages of Constantine's Italian campaign are omitted, perhaps with a view to brevity. But a reverse which he sustained, apparently not far from

[1] c. 18.   [2] cc. 21-23.   [3] 17. 1 f.
[4] Above, p. 202.   [5] 20. 1.   [6] cc. 26-30, 43, 44.

Rome, is noticed. It is obvious that a great deal of the information given in these chapters would be accessible to a hanger-on of the court of Constantine. It may be suggested, however, that while the writer was in Gaul up to the death of Maximian (apparently early in 310), he was in or near Rome when Constantine entered it (October 27, 312). It is at least remarkable not only that, as I have just observed, no mention is made of the battles of Susa, Turin, and Verona, but that the highly important proceedings at Milan after the final defeat of Maxentius are touched upon very slightly.[1]

Another group of passages, also concerned with the West, suggests a connexion of the writer rather with Licinius than with Constantine. Three chapters relate the story of the last illness and death of Galerius and give the text of his Edict of Toleration.[2] It will be remembered that Licinius, as the writer tells us, was with Galerius at Sardica when he died. Three chapters are also devoted to the defeat of Maximin at Campus Serenus.[3] Here remarkable knowledge of detail is displayed. Almost every day is accounted for from the time Maximin set foot in Europe; and dates and distances are carefully recorded. The narrator knows about the message sent from Byzantium to Licinius, and a careful calculation makes it probable that Licinius was at Sardica when it arrived.[4] The detailed account of the movements of

---

[1] 45. 1.   [2] 33–35.   [3] 45–47.

[4] While Maximin lay before Byzantium letters were sent to Licinius, informing him of the invasion of his territory. Supposing him to have been at Sardica the letters would have reached him in three or four days (400 Roman miles). A march, at the ordinary rate, from Sardica to Druzipara (16 miles from Tzurulum, 304 Roman or 280 English miles from Sardica) would have taken two weeks and five days. By a forced march Licinius might therefore have reached that place within three weeks from the time of the dispatch of the letters. (The rate would have been about the same as that of Caesar's march from Corfinium to Brundisium. See above, p. 235.) That is about the time,

Maximin's army in Europe is thrown into striking relief by the comparative meagreness of the particulars supplied of his previous march across Asia Minor, and of the movements of both emperors after the battle of Campus Serenus. One is tempted to conjecture that the writer may have resided for some time at Sardica in 311 and again in the early months of 313. He may have left Rome not long after the battle of the Milvian Bridge.

It is obvious that all this fits in with what we know independently of Lactantius. He seems to have left Nicomedia in 306. He was in Gaul till about 308. After that we lose sight of him till 317, when he was at Trier.

as we saw (p. 219), which intervened between Maximin's landing in Europe and his arrival at Tzurulum.

THE EARLIER FORMS OF
THE *ECCLESIASTICAL HISTORY*

IT is evident that the tenth book of the *Ecclesiastical History* was a supplement not included in the original design. Of this we are informed by the writer himself. 'Since it was in response to thy prayers', he writes,[1] 'that we added (ἐπιθέντες) at this time the tenth book (τόμον) to those which were already completed of the Ecclesiastical History, let us inscribe it to thee, my most holy Paulinus, proclaiming thee as it were the seal of the whole matter.' An edition of the *History* had therefore been in circulation which ended with the ninth book.

Dr. Schwartz,[2] however, has recently put forth the theory that two editions of the entire work in ten books were published by the author, the earlier before and the latter after the downfall of the Emperor Licinius in 323. This theory is based on the phenomena of the authorities for the text—the seven manuscripts which he indicates by the symbols A T E R M B D, the ancient Syriac version (Σ), and the Latin version of Rufinus (Λ). Schwartz observes that in the last three books the group A T E R has a number of words, phrases, and longer passages which are not found in M B D Σ Λ, and he claims that these belonged to the earlier text and were excised in the final edition, which according to him is represented by the second group.

[1] *H. E.* x. 1. 2.
[2] E. Schwartz and T. Mommsen, *Eusebius Werke*, Zweiter Band. *Die Kirchengeschichte. Die lateinische Übersetzung des Rufinus*, dritter Teil, Leipzig, 1909, pp. xlvii ff.

To make good this contention it is necessary to assign some probable motive for the supposed omissions, and to show that they were made by Eusebius himself.

Now, according to Schwartz six or seven of the omissions are obviously due to the desire to get rid of the mention of Licinius as the partner of Constantine in his efforts on behalf of the Church. If that is so the passages in question must have been struck out after the final defeat of Licinius. But since this motive would have been inoperative after the death of Constantine the edition in which the passages were omitted must have been published in his reign and therefore by the authority of Eusebius.

Some points of the argument as thus briefly stated invite criticism. In the first place, one may venture to doubt whether all alterations made in the text during the reign of Constantine must necessarily have had the authority of Eusebius. In the second century we have the complaint of Dionysius that his letters had been tampered with,[1] and the well-known adjuration appended to Irenaeus's lost work on the Ogdoad[2] indicates a fear that his writings might be similarly dealt with. It is worthy of note that Eusebius quoted this adjuration at the beginning of the second part of his *Chronicle*.[3] But, again, it is not clear that hatred of Licinius, the last of the persecuting emperors, would not have led to alteration of the text after the death of Constantine. Such changes may no longer have been necessary to make the book acceptable to the court; but many a Christian scribe would have been tempted to discredit Licinius without any such aim in view. And it must be observed that, apart

---

[1] *H. E.* iv. 23. 12.   [2] Ibid. v. 20. 2.
[3] Migne, *P. G.* xix. 325. It does not appear at the corresponding place in Schoene (ii. 10).

from the evidence adduced by Schwartz, there is little reason to believe that Eusebius made any attempt, by the omission or modification of his statements, to deprive Licinius of credit to which he was justly entitled. In several parts of the tenth book his eulogies of him remain in all the authorities for the text;[1] and if in the ninth book he has in a couple of places inserted ill-natured references to his later 'madness',[2] at least one of the passages to which they are added has been left otherwise unchanged, not a word of the praise accorded to Licinius being withdrawn.

The exemplar from which the manuscripts A T E R were derived was not a copy of the supposed earlier edition of the last three books of the *History*, since they give unanimous testimony to certain passages which must have been written after the fall of Licinius. It was therefore—so Schwartz would have us think—a transcript of the final edition interpolated with extracts from the edition that preceded it. But if interpolation in a manuscript is once admitted it cannot be assumed without proof that the added sentences were derived from a single source. If some of the additions in A T E R should turn out to be relics of an earlier edition of the *History*, it will not follow that the others came from it also.

And one further remark must be made. In the mind of the present writer there is no doubt that the eighth and ninth books of the *History* passed through two or more editions under the hand of their author, and that the later editions differed more or less widely from their predecessors. It is quite possible that traces of these successive editions may be found in the extant manuscripts and versions. The question in dispute is whether two editions of the *tenth* book were published by Eusebius,

[1] x. 2. 2; 4. 16, 60.   [2] ix. 9. 1, 12.

the later of which differed in its text from the earlier. If that cannot be proved Schwartz's theory is untenable.

Let us now examine as briefly as possible the examples of omission in the final edition which he produces. I take first those which are obviously the most important—omissions which he alleges to be clearly due to *damnatio memoriae Licinii*.

The first of them is at once granted. It is the omission of the name and titles of Licinius from the Toleration Edict of Galerius.[1] It will be necessary to return to it later.

The next example is perhaps less convincing. It is found in the introduction to the account of the defeat of Maxentius by Constantine.[2] It runs thus, the bracketed words being omitted in M B D Σ Λ:

'So then Constantine, whom we have already mentioned as an emperor born of an emperor, pious son of a father most pious and in all things most prudent, [and Licinius who was next to him in rank, men honoured for good sense and piety,] stirred up by the all-ruling God and Saviour of the universe, and making war [—two men beloved by God—] against [two][3] most impious tyrants,' &c.

Assuming that the longer form of this passage belonged to an earlier edition, its abbreviation might well be due to hatred of Licinius. But two questions may be asked. On this assumption, why was not the work of eliminating reference to him more thoroughly done? For in a later clause the victory over Maximin is ascribed to Licinius: and quite unnecessarily, since it lies altogether outside the scope of the chapter and there was no need to mention it at all. And the longer form represents the facts more

---

[1] *H. E.* viii. 17. 5.   [2] ix. 9. 1.
[3] M B D Σ have 'the'. In this recension the participles are of course in the singular number instead of the plural.

correctly, for it is not true that Constantine made war against Maximin as the shorter text implies. Is it not possible that the longer form was evolved from the shorter, in the interest of historical accuracy, while Licinius was still in power? But on the whole the balance of probability seems to be in favour of the priority of the text of A T E R.

If further on in the same chapter[1] the authors of the Edict of Milan are described as 'both Constantine himself and with him the Emperor Licinius', and the shorter text drops the title 'Emperor', the exhibition of malignity is not very striking. A sufficient motive for the omission lies in the fact that Constantine is given no title in either text. Lower down, after the text of Maximin's letter to Sabinus has been quoted, mention is made of a letter written by 'the advocates of peace and piety—Constantine and Licinius' to their eastern colleague.[2] That M B D Σ (the underlying Greek of Λ is uncertain) here omit the names Constantine and Licinius can scarcely be due to *damnatio memoriae Licinii*, for it would equally damn the memory of Constantine; and it would leave to Licinius his share of credit for the letter, and the title of 'advocate of peace and piety'. It is more natural to suppose that 'Constantine and Licinius' is a gloss—not altogether unneeded, since neither name has been mentioned in the narrative for a considerable time. And in like manner when in the next chapter[3] we read in A T E R that the victory over Maximin was given 'to Licinius, the ruler at that time',[4] we cannot find much trace of malice in the mere omission by M B D Σ (Λ paraphrases) of the name. The words 'the ruler at that time' would very naturally be glossed by the insertion of 'Licinius', and it is not at

---

[1] ix. 9. 12. [2] ix. 9. 25. [3] ix. 10. 3.
[4] τῷ τότε κρατοῦντι.

all necessary to assume that the glossator laboriously transcribed the name from another manuscript.

We have now considered five instances in which, according to Schwartz, Eusebius in his last edition omitted references to Licinius. It has perhaps been made sufficiently clear that at least three of them are doubtful. We now pass to another alleged case of omission, which is more important than any of these, both because the passage concerned is of much greater length, and because it is the only one in the tenth book.

The collection of imperial ordinances contained in chapters 5-7 of that book appear in A T E R M, but not in B D Σ. Whether they were in the Greek from which Λ was translated is uncertain, since Rufinus omitted not only these chapters but the greater part of the book. We note, in the first place, that here the grouping of the manuscripts is not the same as before. M has gone over to the side of A T E R. It is extremely difficult, on Schwartz's theory, to account for this eclecticism of M. Why, if it is really a manuscript of the supposed second edition of Books viii-x, did it draw upon the first edition only in this place and, as we shall see, in one other? It is at least possible that it is derived from a recension in which Books viii, ix appeared without the passages peculiar to A T E R, or the greater number of them, while Book x was substantially in the form in which it is printed in most modern editions, including the imperial ordinances. M, therefore, so far as it goes, is a witness against the theory that the passages peculiar to A T E R hitherto examined were struck out at the same time as chapters 5-7 of the tenth book.

That these chapters were, in any case, dropped out with the object of casting odium on Licinius is hardly credible. They contain six ordinances. Only in the first of the series—that which is often described with doubtful accuracy as the Edict of Milan—does the name of Licinius occur. The second, though the first person plural [1] is used throughout, is in the heading, and no doubt rightly, ascribed to Constantine.[2] His name stands in the next three, and the last, which is anonymous, certainly emanated from him. It is obvious that the supposed purpose of the omission of the edicts would have been achieved if the first of the six, or even the clause of it in which the name of Licinius appears, had been deleted. Is it conceivable that Eusebius should have struck out six ordinances, every one of which, from his point of view, redounded to the credit of Constantine, merely to blacken the character of Licinius?

But it is evident that in the fourth century a recension of the *History* was current in some quarters, from which these chapters were absent. We must then observe that there is much difficulty in believing that it was published by the authority of Eusebius. For we have in an earlier passage [3] a reference to them which could not escape the notice even of a cursory reader. After touching upon the building of churches which followed the conclusion of the persecution, Eusebius writes:

'Moreover the supreme Emperors, by successive ordinances on behalf of the Christians, confirmed to us further and more effectively (εἰς μακρὸν ἔτι καὶ μεῖζον) the blessings which had come from the Divine bounty, and letters, honours and gifts of money were sent by the Emperor to the several bishops. It will not be amiss if at a fitting point of the discourse I insert in this book, as on a sacred pillar, the text (φωνάς) of them, translated from the Latin into the Greek language, that they may be transmitted to all who come after us as a memorial.'

[1] x. 5. 16 f. βουλόμεθα, προηρήμεθα, &c.
[2] πεποίηται A T E M. R, followed by many modern editors, reads πεποίηνται.   [3] x. 2. 2.

These words are vouched for by all our authorities.[1] There can be no doubt that they stood in the final edition of the *History*. On Schwartz's theory we must suppose that Eusebius, while striking out the ordinances, allowed this passage to remain unchanged. This is not probable. Schwartz himself thinks that the deletion of the ordinances involved the deletion of another passage in which the allusion to them is certainly less definite, and which from its position in the work was more likely to be overlooked. To it we must now turn.

It is the closing sentence of Book ix according to the majority of the printed editions and the manuscripts A T E R M. It runs thus:

'So then, the impious ones having been purged out, the government, which was theirs by right, was preserved firm and undisputed for Constantine and Licinius; who having first of all purged out of the world hostility to God, recognizing the benefits conferred upon them by God, displayed their love of virtue and of God and their piety and gratitude to the Deity by their ordinance on behalf of the Christians.'

This is a passage which might well have been altered after the fall of Licinius. And accordingly in B D Σ Λ (here again, we note deserted by M) we have in its place the thanksgiving with which in all the printed editions, as in A T E R M, the tenth book opens. Apparently it stood in both places in the exemplar from which B D Σ Λ were derived. Why was this new ending substituted for the one that we have quoted? Not merely, according to Schwartz, because of the prominence which the latter

[1] Σ, naturally enough, and M, for some reason which is less obvious, omit the remark that the ordinances were translated from Latin into Greek. Λ, dealing with the whole passage very freely, also omits this clause, and in addition the statement that copies were to be inserted later on. Otherwise there is no substantial difference among the authorities.

THE *ECCLESIASTICAL HISTORY* 251

gives to Licinius, but because it refers to x. 5–7 and was therefore necessarily omitted along with those chapters. Schwartz holds, in fact, that the collection of ordinances originally had its place after this sentence at the end of Book ix—thus serving as the close of the entire work. The tenth book was subsequently added for the purpose of including the panegyric at Tyre ; and the ordinances were transferred from their old place, so that they might still be the conclusion of the *History*. Thus the first edition of Book x consisted of the first seven chapters of the book. After the fall of Licinius the eighth and ninth chapters were added, the collection of ordinances was struck out, and with it ix. 11. 8 b. Thus the discarding of the old ending of Book ix is definitely connected with the issue of a second edition of Book x.

But is it true that the received ending (as we may call it) of Book ix alludes to the six ordinances preserved in Book x ? It certainly reads like a preface to an imperial concession to the Christians, the text of which was placed, or was intended to be placed, at the close of the book, just as the Toleration Edict of Galerius stands at the close of Book viii. But the passage itself suggests that the concession was contained in a single ordinance, not in a series of letters. It is called a $\nu o\mu o\theta\epsilon\sigma i\alpha$: in x. 2. 2 the series preserved in the tenth book is spoken of as $\nu o\mu o\theta\epsilon\sigma i\alpha\iota$, in the plural. Further, the $\nu o\mu o\theta\epsilon\sigma i\alpha$ in question is said to have been issued by Constantine and Licinius acting in concert. That was true of the first of the ordinances of Book x— the letter of Licinius from Nicomedia—but it was not true of any of the others. And it is worthy of note that the word $\nu o\mu o\theta\epsilon\sigma i\alpha$ is actually twice applied to the letter of Licinius in the document itself, according to the translation which Eusebius gives.[1] Apart from this circum-

[1] x. 5. 14.

stance it may fairly be argued that the ordinance here mentioned was the law of which an account was given in an earlier chapter:

'After these things (*sc.* the defeat of Maxentius) both Constantine and with him the Emperor Licinius, ... praising God the author of all good things to them, both with one counsel and mind draw up in the fullest way a most perfect law on behalf of the Christians, and send an account of the wonderful things done for them by God and of the victory against the tyrant, and the law itself, to Maximin, who was still ruling over the nations in the East and feigning friendship towards them.'[1]

The law spoken of here was of course the Edict of Milan; and the inference seems inevitable that either it or the letter of Licinius founded upon it was the document the text of which was reserved for the end of the book.

But we may go a step further. Any one who compares the received ending of Book ix with the earlier passage just quoted will, I believe, come to the conclusion that the man who allowed the latter to stand would not feel compelled to suppress the former merely on account of the prominence which it gives to Licinius as a believer in God and a friend of the Church. This argument is not weakened but strengthened by the fact that Eusebius in his last revision added a clause to the earlier passage about the later 'madness' of that Emperor. If that clause had not been inserted we might have supposed that Eusebius let the passage remain through sheer carelessness. Its presence proves the contrary. The historian in the obtruded note remarked, as he might fairly do, that ultimately the relation of Licinius to the Church became one of hostility. To have withdrawn any of the statements which he had made when the final catastrophe was still future would have been a *suppressio veri*: and to that he did not

---

[1] ix. 9. 12.

stoop. He left Licinius in possession of all the credit which, in spite of his subsequent conduct, he deserved, from Eusebius's point of view, for his early friendship to the Christians. Nevertheless I deem it probable that the closing sentence of Book ix was deleted and that now found in B D Σ Λ put in its place by Eusebius himself. The cause of this alteration will be considered presently. It is sufficient to say now that the assimilation of the end of Book ix to the beginning of Book x was in Eusebius's manner.¹ The deleted passage was in fact not wholly suppressed but removed, with some necessary changes, to the end of Book x, where it now appears in all the manuscripts and the two versions. It is not probable that Eusebius closed two successive books of the *History*, in the same edition, with sentences so closely parallel.

It is not necessary to examine in detail the remaining four passages found in A T E R and wanting in the other authorities, because, supposing them to have been omitted in a later edition, they afford no indication that the date of that edition followed the death of Licinius, and they do not in any way connect themselves with the variations in the manuscripts of the tenth book. Two of them, according to Schwartz, were omitted because they described Galerius as the author of the persecution;² and one of these omissions attained the further end of getting rid of an allusion to the death of Diocletian.³ Two others

¹ See below, p. 289.

² viii. 16. 2 f.; App. He points to the silence of *Orat. Const.* 25 about Galerius. In one sense it was untrue that Galerius was the originator of the persecution, since Diocletian persecuted before the edict of 303. See *H. E.* viii. 4. 2; Lact. 10. This might account for the omissions in question.

³ viii. App. Cf. *V. C.* i. 23. The principle enunciated in the Life of Constantine, that no account should be given of the deaths of persecuting Emperors, is not very strictly adhered to in the last edition of the *History*. See e.g. ix. 10. 14 f. Moreover, the evidence that

are accounted for as an effort to save Constantine from the imputation of having accused the Christians of unreasoning obstinacy.[1] But these are motives which might have operated as powerfully before Constantine became sole Emperor as afterwards.

I conclude then that from the variations among the authorities for the text we have no sufficient reason for believing that Eusebius issued two editions of his tenth book. I believe, indeed, that stronger evidence for Schwartz's theory might have been discovered in those parts of the text of the book itself which have the support of all the authorities. The first chapter might have led us to expect that nothing would follow it save chapter 2, § 1 and chapters 3, 4. And even when we read the intimation of chapter 2, § 2, that a collection of ordinances was to be included, are we not prepared for the last two chapters on the war between Constantine and Licinius? But to recognize all this is no more than to admit that the book is badly constructed,[2] an admission which must be made in the case of other books of the same work. It does not give us a sure foundation on which to build a theory of successive editions.

And if it is difficult to believe that some of the passages of the Tyrian panegyric which laud the actions of

---

viii. App. was intended by Eusebius to form part of the *History* is weak, as will be seen presently.

[1] viii. 16. 7; ix. 1. 3–6. The omission in M B D in viii. 16. 7 does not appreciably soften the strictures on the Christians; and it is not likely that any one would have based a charge against Constantine on the letter of Sabinus in ix. 1. The letter may have been omitted because it has at least the appearance of contradicting the statement of the previous sections, that Maximin did not issue written commands to the provincials. Sabinus certainly wrote in his name.

[2] In spite of Schwartz's remark (p. liv) I do not see why x. 8. 1 a may not refer to cc. 5–7.

Licinius[1] were given to the public at the same time as the chapters which describe his subsequent wrongdoing,[2] it must be remarked that the same difficulty attends us when we maintain that those passages were left unaltered in a second edition of the book in which the closing chapters were added. In either case the only explanation that can be given is that Eusebius, in spite of all attempts to prove the contrary, was an honest historian who would not withdraw what he had written until he became convinced that it was false. The tenth book, whatever view we take of the manner of its composition, is a witness to his unswerving desire to be just, under strong temptation. Biased he no doubt was—his final chapters prove it—

ERRATA

Page 193 *note* 2 *for* Theodoric *read* Theodosia
Page 200 *note* 1 *for* burie *read* buried
Page 254 *line* 16 *for* are we not prepared . . . Licinius? *read* we are not prepared . . . Licinius.

Lawlor, *Eusebiana*   August, 1912
Face page 254

written Eusebius was not aware of the rupture of Licinius with Constantine which happened in 314;[4] and it appears

[1] x. 4. 16, 60.   [2] See e. g. x. 8. 3, 5 ff.
[3] See Lightfoot in *Dict. of Christ. Biog.* ii. 322 f. See also the excellent lecture on 'Eusebius, the Father of Church History' by Westcott, of which Lightfoot made use. It has been published in the volume entitled *The Two Empires, the Church and the World*, 1909. The difficulty about Paulinus (*Dict. of Christ. Biog.* iv. 232) does not invalidate Lightfoot's reasoning.
[4] No doubt Westcott wrote in ignorance of the fact that Constantine and Licinius were at peace again in 315. But his argument seems to

are accounted for as an effort to save Constantine from the imputation of having accused the Christians of unreasoning obstinacy.[1] But these are motives which might have operated as powerfully before Constantine became sole Emperor as afterwards.

I conclude then that from the variations among the authorities for the text we have no sufficient reason for believing that Eusebius issued two editions of his tenth book. I believe, indeed, that stronger evidence for Schwartz's theory might have been discovered in those parts of the text of the book itself which have the support of all the authorities. The first chapter might have led us to expect that nothing would follow it save chapter 2, & 1

---

viii. App. was intended by Eusebius to form part of the *History* is weak, as will be seen presently.

[1] viii. 16. 7; ix. 1. 3–6. The omission in M B D in viii. 16. 7 does not appreciably soften the strictures on the Christians; and it is not likely that any one would have based a charge against Constantine on the letter of Sabinus in ix. 1. The letter may have been omitted because it has at least the appearance of contradicting the statement of the previous sections, that Maximin did not issue written commands to the provincials. Sabinus certainly wrote in his name.

[2] In spite of Schwartz's remark (p. liv) I do not see why x. 8. 1 a may not refer to cc. 5–7.

Licinius [1] were given to the public at the same time as the chapters which describe his subsequent wrongdoing,[2] it must be remarked that the same difficulty attends us when we maintain that those passages were left unaltered in a second edition of the book in which the closing chapters were added. In either case the only explanation that can be given is that Eusebius, in spite of all attempts to prove the contrary, was an honest historian who would not withdraw what he had written until he became convinced that it was false. The tenth book, whatever view we take of the manner of its composition, is a witness to his unswerving desire to be just, under strong temptation. Biased he no doubt was—his final chapters prove it— but never a conscious tamperer with truth.

In the remainder of this Essay, then, I shall assume that Eusebius issued but one edition of the tenth book. And, as a necessary consequence, I shall regard it as having been published in its first and final form after the fall of Licinius in 324 or early in 325.[3]

It seems clear that the ninth book was composed ten years or more before this final supplement was added to the work. To quote the words of Westcott, which have been adopted in their entirety by Lightfoot:

'If we compare the closing sentences of the ninth and tenth books it is evident that when the ninth book was written Eusebius was not aware of the rupture of Licinius with Constantine which happened in 314;[4] and it appears

[1] x. 4. 16, 60.   [2] See e. g. x. 8. 3, 5 ff.
[3] See Lightfoot in *Dict. of Christ. Biog.* ii. 322 f. See also the excellent lecture on 'Eusebius, the Father of Church History' by Westcott, of which Lightfoot made use. It has been published in the volume entitled *The Two Empires, the Church and the World*, 1909. The difficulty about Paulinus (*Dict. of Christ. Biog.* iv. 232) does not invalidate Lightfoot's reasoning.
[4] No doubt Westcott wrote in ignorance of the fact that Constantine and Licinius were at peace again in 315. But his argument seems to

also that he was at the same time very imperfectly informed of the course of affairs in the West, which led to the decisive victory of Constantine over Maxentius in 312, though he was well acquainted with the eastern campaign, which ended with the death of Maximin in 313. We may therefore suppose that the nine books were composed [rather completed] not long after the Edict of Milan in 313.'[1]

It has been remarked that the ninth book in its original form appears to have concluded with the Edict of Milan, or rather with the letter of Licinius founded upon it.[2] This letter, issued at Nicomedia on June 13, 313,[3] cannot have been published south of the Taurus till after the East had been acquired by Licinius. Thus we may date the penultimate edition of the *History* about the end of 313 or in the earlier part of 314.

It probably contained the first nine books nearly in their present form. But not quite. For three sentences in Book ix show traces of revision. The words applied to Licinius in chapter 9, ' not yet at that time seized with madness,'[4] almost proclaim themselves intruders by their unsuitability to the context. They were certainly added after the final breach between Constantine and Licinius. At the same time must have been inserted the similar remark about him lower down in the same chapter, ' his understanding had not yet at that time been turned to that madness into which he later fell.'[5] So too when we find him described as one 'who then ruled'[6] we recognize

me to hold good. Schwartz dates the book in 315, on the ground that the letter of Constantine to Chrestus, bishop of Syracuse (x. 5. 21), originally belonged to it.

[1] Westcott, op. cit. p. 6. Perhaps it should rather have been said ' not long after the death of Maximin '. For as long as the East was in the hands of Maximin, and he at war with Licinius, Eusebius would have little opportunity of acquiring information of western affairs.

[2] See Gwatkin, *Early Church History*, ii. 357.

[3] Lactantius, *De Mort. Pers.* 48.

[4] *H. E.* ix. 9. 1.   [5] § 12.   [6] *H. E.* ix. 10. 3.

the hand of a reviser who wrote after he had ceased to be Emperor. How the original text may have run in this place we cannot tell. But the three readings which have been mentioned are attested by practically all the extant authorities. They certainly came from Eusebius himself.

A fourth passage must be mentioned, though we cannot speak of it with the same confidence. I have assumed that as first issued the book closed with the received ending, followed by the rescript of Licinius issued at Nicomedia. In place of that ending we find in B D Σ $\varLambda$ a sentence identical with the opening sentence of Book x, and reasons have been given for the belief that the original ending was in fact transferred to the close of the entire work when Book x was added. Why was this change made? Probably because Eusebius had decided to include in the new book a collection of imperial concessions to the Church. This collection would naturally begin with the most important of them all—that which hitherto stood at the end of Book ix. But when it was gone the sentence which had introduced it became unmeaning. Something else had to be put in place of it; and according to his common practice Eusebius made the same sentence serve both for the end of Book ix and the beginning of the book which was now made to follow it.[1]

We have called the edition containing nine books the penultimate rather than the first because the question whether it was preceded by another, or others, ought not to be prejudged. It has in fact been suggested that the ninth book, like the tenth, is a supplement to the original work.[2] We must now endeavour to appraise the likelihood of that suggestion being correct.

[1] See below, p. 289.
[2] McGiffert, *Eusebius* (*Nicene and Post-Nicene Fathers*), pp. 334,

In the long sentence with which Eusebius begins the first book of the *Ecclesiastical History* we find a full statement of the purpose of the whole work. He mentions, first of all, a number of subjects which obviously could not be dealt with in separate sections, such as 'the successions of the holy apostles', the rulers of the distinguished Christian communities, the founders of heretical systems, and so forth. The treatment of such subjects as these must evidently, in a work constructed on a chronological basis, proceed *pari passu*. But the historian intimates that, having followed all these different threads for some distance, he will in the end let most of them drop, and confine himself to a single topic. One of the many things which he proposes to set down in writing is an account of the occasions on which 'the divine word has been made war upon by the Gentiles' and of the men 'who as each occasion came endured the conflict which through blood and tortures was fought on its behalf'; and having announced this as one of the topics to be dealt with, he proceeds, 'And it is also my purpose to relate the martyrdoms which took place after these in our own time and the propitious and gracious succour afforded at the end of all by our Saviour.' This opening sentence, like most prefaces, must be taken, not as such a crude statement of his aim as might be possible for the author to make when he first took up his pen, but rather as his reflection on his work when it had reached the form in which it was offered to the public. It therefore conveys to us the information that the last section of the *History* recorded a contemporary persecution and closed with the return of rest to the Church,—rest which the writer clearly regarded as destined to be permanent. The point at

---

340. These passages suggested the present Essay. But Schwartz has now discussed the question with much fuller knowledge of the data.

which this last section begins is definitely marked. In the last sentence of the seventh book Eusebius tells us that having in it and the preceding books enlarged upon the subject of 'the succession of the apostles',[1] he is now about to relate ' the conflicts in our own time of those who contended valiantly for piety'.

The final section of the work therefore begins with the eighth book. Where did it originally end? There are three incidents in the story of the great persecution each of which in its turn must have seemed the beginning of the final peace; and each of them is related at the end of a book of the *History*. They are the defeat of Licinius, with which the work in its present form ends; the Edict of Milan at the close of Book ix, the last book, as we have seen, of an earlier edition; and the Toleration Edict of Galerius recited in the last chapter of Book viii. Any one of these might have been called 'the succour of the Saviour'. But had the last named, which is the earliest in point of date, any appearance of introducing permanent rest?

It seems to me that it must have been so regarded at the time. It was, to begin with—for I believe the evidence warrants the statement[2]—a renunciation, in the name of

[1] So viii. Pref., which is a re-statement of the substance of vii. 32. 32. In the latter the phrase is ' the matter of the successions'.

[2] On this point the evidence is very strong. Lactantius (36. 3) speaks of the edict as 'indulgentia Christianis *communi titulo* data', where his point seems to be that Maximin was so base as to repudiate a document in which his own name appeared along with those of his fellow emperors. Eusebius twice states that the palinode was issued by the very men who had made war on the Church (*H. E.* viii. 13. 8; 16. 1.) This implies that it ran in the name of more than one persecutor. But if, as has been sometimes asserted, Maximin had no hand in it this would not be the case, since neither Constantine nor Licinius had persecuted. And it may be asked, could an edict have been issued in the names of three out of the four emperors, that of the fourth being omitted? It is instructive to observe that the inscription found at Arykanda proves that the memorial of the citizens of that place,

all the four reigning emperors, of the policy which had till that moment been in theory common to all, and which had been carried into effect by two of them. That must have seemed likely to usher in a more peaceful era. As a matter of fact peace had been established over half the Empire for several years. Since the year of the abdication there had been no persecution in the West. And the new edict produced much effect elsewhere. It put an end to persecution everywhere except in the dominions of Maximin. And even there it was followed by a respite of six months. For that period there was no official persecution of Christians in any part of the Empire. Nothing can be plainer than that even the Christian subjects of Maximin believed that a lasting peace had come. One has only to read the first chapter of Eusebius's ninth book to be impressed with their absolute confidence that they were at the beginning of a new era.[1] What if Eusebius himself, in spite of comments with which later experience moved him to intersperse his facts in this very chapter, shared the confidence and the rejoicing of those six months? If he did he must for the time have regarded Galerius's edict as 'the succour of our Saviour' which had inaugurated lasting peace between Church and State—the goal of Church history. There is nothing to prevent us, if the direct evidence points that way, from supposing that an edition—probably the first—of the *Ecclesiastical History* was completed and published during the six months' peace between May and November 311, and that

though actually presented to Maximin, was addressed to all the reigning emperors, Maximin, Constantine and Licinius. The only evidence on the other side is the fact that Maximin's name does not occur in the copy of the palinode given by Eusebius. An opportunity will occur hereafter of discussing the question whether its absence can be accounted for.

[1] See above, p. 214.

it included only our first eight books. What then is the evidence?

Let us turn first to the Preface to the eighth book. There we have a formal statement which implies that the book to which it is prefixed was to be the last of the work:

'Having described in seven entire books[1] the succession of the apostles we regard it as a duty in this eighth fasciculus[2] to commend to the knowledge of those who shall come after us the events of our own time[3]—which are worthy of permanent record—some part, at least, of the most remarkable of them.'

It is clear that when he penned this sentence Eusebius intended to confine all that he had to say about contemporary happenings to a single book, and that it was to be the last book of the *History*. The inference, if the words are to be accepted in their natural meaning, is that Book ix was an afterthought—an appendix added after the original design had been completed. Possibly, however, some may prefer to adopt the alternative view, that as he went on Eusebius changed his mind, finding that the matter which he had accumulated for a single book could more conveniently be distributed between two. In that case the present Books viii and ix are really two divisions of the projected eighth book.

The latter of these two views is scarcely probable. That which we know as the ninth book seems to have been a separate book from the beginning. It was certainly such when the tenth book was added. For not only is the latter designated 'the tenth book'[4] in its opening sentences;

[1] βιβλίοις.

[2] συγγράμματι. I do not suppose that it will be contended that this word indicates Books viii, ix, or Books viii-x.

[3] That he means by this phrase the history of the persecution is evident from vii. 32. 32.

[4] τόμον.

Eusebius actually makes a point of the fact that it is the tenth: 'Fitly,' he writes, 'under[1] a perfect number we shall compose the perfect and panegyrical book[2] of the renewal of the Churches.' But we may go further back. A passage which will be quoted immediately proves that if the original plan of the eighth book was modified, the modification had already been made by the time the writer reached the thirteenth chapter. Now if in the course of writing, or shortly afterwards, Eusebius had made out of his intended eighth book an eighth and a ninth, it is scarcely likely that he would not have altered the opening sentence in such a way as to make it agree with the facts.

But there are two other passages in the book which support the construction I have put on the Preface. It is plain that when he wrote them Eusebius believed that the edict of Galerius had stayed the persecution, and that he was unaware that any renewal of it had taken place since its publication.

The first of these has been referred to just now. I must quote it, as I shall have occasion to make use of it again. The historian has made mention of a large number of martyrs, concluding with the remark that there were thousands more commemorated by the Christian communities in every country and place. He then proceeds:

'The task is not ours to chronicle the conflicts of those men who contended all over the world for piety towards the Divine Being, and to relate in detail all that happened to them; but let it be done by those who beheld their sufferings. Those with which I myself was conversant I will make known to posterity in another treatise. In the present book,[2] however, I will subjoin to the things already said the recantation of those who wrought against us and

---

[1] ἐν. [2] λόγον.

the things that happened from the beginning of the persecution—most profitable as they are for my readers.'[1]

First, by way of commentary on this passage let it be noted that Eusebius here sketches accurately the contents of the remainder of Book viii. He immediately afterwards takes up the thread of his story where he had let it fall in chapter 6, and proceeds, with one or two digressions which will be mentioned presently, to the end, concluding with the text of the 'recantation', the edict of Galerius. Thus, as already observed,[2] he had determined at least thus early that the eighth book should end as it now does.

But again, in the passage before us he exhibits no consciousness that the edict was not the end of the persecution or that the Christians had any further sufferings to endure after its issue. He intimates too that, in accordance with his plan, he omits many martyrdoms, especially a number which he himself had witnessed. The latter were to be related in a treatise not yet written. There can be little doubt that the treatise referred to is one of the recensions of the *Martyrs of Palestine*, which was thus intended to serve in some sort as a parallel to the *History* on which he was then engaged. It is surely then most significant that, as has already been pointed out,[3] the last martyrdom in that work, both in the Syriac and the Greek, took place only a few days later than the issue of the 'recantation'.

---

[1] *H. E.* viii. 13. 7 f. ὧν ἀνὰ τὴν πᾶσαν οἰκουμένην ὑπὲρ τῆς εἰς τὸ θεῖον εὐσεβείας ἠγωνισμένων γραφῇ παραδιδόναι τοὺς ἄθλους ἐπ' ἀκριβές τε ἕκαστα τῶν περὶ αὐτοὺς συμβεβηκότων ἱστορεῖν οὐχ ἡμέτερον, τῶν δ' ὄψει τὰ πράγματα παρειληφότων ἴδιον ἂν γένοιτο· οἷς γε μὴν αὐτὸς παρεγενόμην, τούτους καὶ τοῖς μεθ' ἡμᾶς γνωρίμους δι' ἑτέρας ποιήσομαι γραφῆς. κατά γε μὴν τὸν παρόντα λόγον τὴν παλινῳδίαν τῶν περὶ ἡμᾶς εἰργασμένων τοῖς εἰρημένοις ἐπισυνάψω τά τε ἐξ ἀρχῆς τοῦ διωγμοῦ συμβεβηκότα, χρησιμώτατα τυγχάνοντα τοῖς ἐντευξομένοις.

[2] Above, p. 262.   [3] Above, p. 209.

The other passage occurs somewhat later, at the point where he begins to speak at length of the edict of Galerius. Here he uses a phrase which clearly indicates that with it the persecution came to an end. He declares that the emperors—'the very persons by whom the warfare was in our time prosecuted—changing their minds, in a most wonderful way, issued a recantation,' thereby ' quenching the fire of persecution which had blazed forth to so great a height against us '.[1] This plain statement that the edict of Galerius ' quenched ' the flames of persecution is not in accordance with subsequent events. It directly contradicts Book ix, the subject of which is a recrudescence of persecution, which ' seemed far more terrible than the former '.[2] It could not have been made after the peace of the Church had again been disturbed by Maximin towards the end of 311.

But that is not all. After thus describing the effect of the edict Eusebius immediately proceeds to point out its true source.[3] It had no human origin. It was not to be attributed to the kindness of emperors who had raged more furiously as time went on ; it rather proceeded from Divine Providence. For on the one hand God was being reconciled to His people, and on the other He was punishing Galerius, the author of the troubles, by inflicting him with the foul disease which wrung from him the recantation. What is all this but an expansion of the phrase ' the succour of our Saviour ', by which Eusebius had already indicated the end of the persecution, and the last incident to be recorded in his *History* ? In a similar passage in the

---

[1] *H. E.* viii. 16. 1. τότε δῆτα καὶ οἱ καθ' ἡμᾶς ἄρχοντες, αὐτοὶ δὴ ἐκεῖνοι δι' ὧν πάλαι τὰ τῶν καθ' ἡμᾶς ἐνηργεῖτο πολέμων, παραδοξότατα μεταθέμενοι τὴν γνώμην, παλινῳδίαν ᾖδον χρηστοῖς περὶ ἡμῶν προγράμμασιν καὶ διατάγμασιν ἡμερωτάτοις τὴν ἐπὶ μέγα ἀφθεῖσαν τοῦ διωγμοῦ πυρκαϊὰν σβεννύντες.
[2] Ibid. ix. 6. 4.   [3] Ibid. viii. 16. 2.

Martyrs of Palestine[1] the same edict is spoken of as a manifestation of the Divine favour towards the Church. No language so direct and forcible connects either the final edict of Maximin or the Edict of Milan with the Divine intervention.

One other fact which seems to point to the existence of an early edition of the *History* containing only the first eight books may be mentioned here. It is the insertion at the end of Book viii, in some manuscripts, of the brief Appendix which appears in that place in all the printed editions. It is probably an excerpt from another work of Eusebius in which he dilated upon the miserable deaths of the persecuting emperors, contrasting them with the happy end of Constantius. That it should have come into its present place when the eighth book was immediately followed by the ninth is scarcely possible. Schwartz indeed supposes that it was added to the eighth book by Eusebius himself when he published the first edition of the tenth book, and therefore after the ninth book had been added. He holds that it was omitted in the final edition, some parts of it being at the same time inserted in the thirteenth chapter of Book viii. It appears to me that in itself the supposition that Eusebius thus destroyed the connexion between the eighth and ninth books is wholly improbable. One event recorded in the Appendix—the death of Diocletian—if not later than the last included in Book ix, cannot have preceded it by many months.[2] And when Schwartz attempts to work out the details of his theory[3] he finds difficulties which he does not surmount, and which are perhaps insurmountable. He is also forced to

[1] *M. P.* (Grk.) 13. 14. In both places the words ἐπισκοπὴν εὐμενῆ καὶ ἵλεω are reminiscent of i. 1. 2.

[2] The date 316 is strongly attested. But Lact. 43. 1 seems to imply that Diocletian died before Maximin. Cp. Aurelius Victor, *Epit.* 39.

[3] p. lii.

regard the sentence which now closes Book viii—'It is now time to review what happened after these things'— as having been introduced in the last edition, the edition, namely, in which the tenth book, as he thinks, was remodelled.[1] It could, indeed, hardly have stood as an introduction to the Appendix. But why it should have been written long after the ninth book had been published rather than when it was first added to the work is not easily understood. But the fact is that the evidence that the Appendix was intended by Eusebius to follow Book viii, or to form a part of the *History*, is not strong.[2] It is found only in the manuscripts A E R and their derivatives. In the exemplar from which the group A T E R was derived it had a heading[3] which stated that it was found in some manuscripts, ὡς λεῖπον: from which it may be inferred that in the manuscripts from which it was taken it did not follow Book viii without a break. A heading must have preceded it; and it possibly suggested a doubt as to whether it was really part of the book. Thus, perhaps, we may account for its omission from T. It is not unlikely that it is an extract from a lost work of Eusebius, added to some copies of the first edition of the *History* which remained in circulation after the second edition in nine books appeared.

But it now becomes necessary to ascertain, as far as possible, what passages in the earlier books of the *History* must, on our theory, have been added after the work in its original form had been completed. With this end in view I shall pass in review all the sentences known to

---

[1] p. 794.

[2] The fact that Zonaras (xii. 33) had it in his copy of Book viii counts for little.

[3] A: τὸ ὡς λεῖπον ἔν τισιν ἀντιγράφοις ἐν τῷ η΄ λόγῳ. That the word λεῖπον comes from the exemplar is confirmed by the remark in E that the Appendix was added in some manuscripts οὐχ ὡς λείποντα κτλ.

THE *ECCLESIASTICAL HISTORY* 267

me which rest under the suspicion of betraying knowledge of events which took place after November 311.

1. *H. E.* i. 9. 2 f. Here Eusebius exposes an anachronism in certain memoirs against our Saviour which had quite recently been put in circulation.[1] These are no doubt the forged 'memoirs of Pilate and our Saviour' which in 312 received the approval of Maximin, and were ordered by him to be publicly exhibited and taught in the schools.[2] But, though in 312 they were still recent forgeries, it is unreasonable to suppose that they had not for some time been in circulation before Maximin made use of them for his own purposes. There is nothing to compel us to believe that they had not come into Eusebius's hands by 311; and it is to be observed that there is no hint in the passage before us that they had received imperial recognition. It need not therefore be regarded as a later addition.

2. *H. E.* vii. 32. 31. Peter, bishop of Alexandria, is said to have been beheaded in the ninth year of the persecution (312) after an episcopate of twelve entire years.[3] This statement obviously could not have been made in 311. But if an account of his episcopate up to that year had place here in the original edition, it was inevitable that in 313 it should be completed by a notice of his martyrdom. Eusebius could not leave untouched a sentence which implied that he was still alive. And the passage seems to bear traces of the reviser's hand, for the chronological notes are verbally inconsistent. Peter is said to have been bishop for *less* than three [4] years before the persecution,

[1] οὐκοῦν σαφῶς ἀπελήλεγκται τὸ πλάσμα τῶν κατὰ τοῦ σωτῆρος ἡμῶν ὑπομνήματα χθὲς καὶ πρῴην διαδεδωκότων.

[2] *H. E.* ix. 5. 1.

[3] ἐφ' ὅλοις δυοκαίδεκα ἐνιαυτοῖς. A notice of his martyrdom appears also in ix. 6. 2.

[4] τρισὶν οὐδ' ὅλοις ἔτεσιν.

to have been martyred *in* the ninth year of the persecution, and yet to have ruled the Church for twelve entire years. So contradictory a remark could hardly have been made originally. The confusion may have arisen from the use in the revision of a different system of reckoning years. Peter's death may be dated November 312.[1] If he became bishop shortly before September 300, his rule would have been counted as twelve entire years, the years beginning in September. But from before September 300 to the beginning of the persecution would be 'not three entire years', the years beginning, as the persecution-years did, in January.

3. *H. E.* viii. 6. 6. The martyrdom of Anthimus is said to have taken place 'at this time', an expression which is lower down defined as meaning 'at the beginning of the persecution'. This section comes between the notices of the first and second edicts of Diocletian. But it is to be noticed that some of the events referred to in it seem to belong to a later period. The putting to death of whole families, the drowning of Christians, the digging up of bodies which had been buried and casting them into the sea, suggest rather the rule of Galerius than that of Diocletian. It is not probable that they were connected with the fires at the palace soon after the first edict, as the reader of Eusebius might suppose. It seems likely, therefore, that Eusebius has gone astray in his dates. And this may be accounted for if we observe that he appears at this point to have depended on a document for his information.[2] If the document, giving a confused account of the persecution at Nicomedia, mentioned the fires in

---

[1] November 24, 311, according to Schwartz: but the ninth year of the persecution was 312. See further below, p. 274.

[2] ὅ τε λόγος ἔχει. Was this document the letter of the martyr Lucian mentioned below?

connexion with the other things here recorded we can easily understand that it might have misled Eusebius. And so we need not lay too much stress on the date assigned by him to the martyrdom of Anthimus. But some writers hold that the martyrdom did not take place until late in 312. In that case Eusebius has made a mistake of over nine years. Considering the eminence which must have belonged to the bishop of Nicomedia, and the opportunities of obtaining information which Eusebius possessed, this is very improbable. We shall not accept this view unless the evidence for it is very strong.

We may take Hunziker[1] as its best exponent. He points out that Lactantius says nothing of this martyrdom in the chapter following that in which he gives the fires,[2] though he mentions the execution of *presbyteri ac ministri*. But in that chapter Lactantius gives no names of martyrs, and he obviously includes events not immediately connected with the fires, but belonging to a later time. It is absurd to suppose that bishops were wholly exempt from persecution during the whole period contemplated in the chapter. But again, Anthimus is mentioned along with Lucian, who certainly suffered in 312, in *H. E.* viii. 13. 1 f. The arrangement of that passage, however, is not chronological but topographical. The juxtaposition of the two martyrdoms is due to the fact that they both took place at Nicomedia.[3] A third argument is derived from a

---

[1] O. Hunziker, 'Zur Regierung u. Christenverfolgung des Kaisers Diocletianus u. seiner Nachfolger,' in Büdinger's *Untersuchungen zur römischen Kaisergeschichte*, vol. ii (1868), p. 281.

[2] *De Mort. Pers.* 15.

[3] If we suppose that Eusebius, when he wrote *H. E.* viii. 13, regarded Anthimus and Lucian as having suffered at the same period we must believe either that he dated the martyrdom of Anthimus in 312, which contradicts viii. 6, or that he dated that of Lucian in 303, which contradicts ix. 6.

letter of Lucian, announcing the martyrdom of Anthimus to the Church of Antioch.[1] But there is nothing in the fragment of the letter which remains to show that Lucian was a prisoner when he wrote, as Hunziker states, and nothing to imply that the time of his own martyrdom was drawing near. Hunziker also cites three Acts of Martyrs—including the late and unreliable Greek Acts of Anthimus himself—in which Maximian (i. e. either Galerius or Maximin) is named as the Emperor. But who will attach much weight to such evidence on such a point? Finally, if the Greek Acts of Anthimus date his martyrdom September 3, and if this suits well enough the assumption that he suffered in the autumn of 312 and Lucian somewhat later in the same year, there is nothing in the text of Eusebius to prohibit the belief that Anthimus was beheaded as late as September 303. We should be inclined to place even later some of the events referred to in the same section. On the whole the arguments for dating the martyrdom of Anthimus after 311 do not appear to be strong enough to stand against the express statement of Eusebius.

4. *H. E.* viii. 9. 1-5. This is a passage relating to the sufferings of confessors and martyrs in the Thebaid. Before examining it we must remark that it occurs in a section of the book in which we might expect additions to be made, if it was re-edited some years after its first publication. At the end of the sixth chapter, after mentioning the third edict, Eusebius for a considerable space[2] entirely abandons the chronological method of arranging his materials. He gives a list of martyrs, with

---

[1] The extant fragment of the letter, preserved in the Paschal Chronicle under the year 303 (Dindorf, p. 516), runs thus: Ἀσπάζεται ὑμᾶς χορὸς ἅπας ὁμοῦ μαρτύρων. εὐαγγελίζομαι δὲ ὑμᾶς, ὡς Ἄνθιμος ὁ πάπας τῷ τοῦ μαρτυρίου δρόμῳ ἐτελειώθη. It is printed in Routh, *Rell. Sacr.* iv. 5.
[2] *H. E.* viii. 7. 1-13. 7.

some details of their sufferings, disposed, not according to the order of time, but mainly according to the places where they suffered—the Egyptians who were martyred at Tyre, while he himself was there, those who suffered in Egypt, in the Thebaid, at Alexandria, in Phrygia, in Arabia, at Antioch, in Pontus—ending up with a list of episcopal martyrs. Clearly these examples are not taken from any one period of the persecution, but belong for the most part to the later stage which began with the issue of the fourth edict in April 304.[1] It is plain that in preparing a new edition an author, and more especially an unsystematic writer like Eusebius, would be tempted to complete such a section as this by adding in their proper places the names of illustrious martyrs who had been brought to his knowledge after the work, in its original form, had left his hands. We can recognize such insertions with certainty only when there is evidence that they belong to a later date than the edict of Galerius.

One of them must be at least a part of the account of the martyrs of the Thebaid. For Eusebius writes as an eyewitness of the evil work of one day: 'We ourselves saw, when we came to the places, many crowded together in the course of one day.'[2] But it appears that from the beginning of the persecution till the year 311 he was in Caesarea and its neighbourhood. He does not seem to have visited Egypt till after the edict of that year.[3] Thus we must count at least §§ 4, 5 as an insertion. We shall find reason just now to believe that the earlier sections of the same chapter, though in themselves they contain nothing to mark them as later than 311, were probably added at the same time.

But first an attempt must be made to show that the

[1] Above, p. 202. [2] § 4.
[3] See *Dict. of Christ. Biog.* ii. 311 f., and above, p. 198.

later sections and the whole of the following chapter, containing accounts of Philoromus and Phileas, and an epistle of the latter, belong to the earlier period. According to the *Acts of Phileas and Philoromus*[1] these two persons were beheaded on the same day after examination before Culcianus. Since Culcianus was a creature of Maximin[2] this fixes the date not earlier than the end of 305. The later limit is determined thus. A letter is extant, in a Latin version, which was written in the names of Phileas and three other Egyptian bishops, protesting against ordinations performed by Meletius within the jurisdiction of Peter, bishop of Alexandria. The bishops were at the time in prison. After their martyrdom Peter, from his exile, wrote a letter directing that communication should not be held with Meletius.[3] We may safely infer that the martyrdom of Phileas took place a considerable time before that of Peter, who probably suffered in November 312, immediately after the resumption of persecution by Maximin in Egypt. He seems, indeed, to have been the first martyr of that short season of violence. Thus we may place the death of Phileas before the edict of Galerius. It is in fact a plausible conjecture that Peter returned from his exile shortly after its publication.[4]

But further, Phileas and Philoromus seem to have been executed at Alexandria. This is apparently the statement of all the authorities which name the place of the martyrdom.[5] And it is supported by the passage quoted from Phileas by Eusebius, in which, writing in prison shortly before his death, he describes the persecution in that city.

---

[1] Ruinart, *Acta sincera*, 1713, p. 494. [2] *H. E.* ix. 11. 4.
[3] Routh, *Rell. Sacr.* iv. 91 ff., 94.
[4] *Dict. of Christ. Biog.* iv. 333. See also below, p. 274.
[5] See Valois on *H. E.* viii. 9.

THE *ECCLESIASTICAL HISTORY* 273

That, at any rate, Phileas did not suffer in the Thebaid [1] is pretty certain, since he was bishop of Thmuis in Lower Egypt.

These facts show that the account of Philoromus and Phileas, and the narrative of the persecution by the latter, cannot have been intended by Eusebius as an illustration of his general remarks about the martyrs of the Thebaid,[2] but must rather be read with what he says in the previous chapter about the Egyptians 'who suffered in their own land'. The intervening passage obscures the connexion, and so might have been suspected as a later addition, apart from any theory as to the date of the composition of the book in which it is found.

5. *H. E.* viii. 13. 1–7. Here we have a list of rulers of the Church who suffered martyrdom. The following are mentioned: Anthimus, bishop of Nicomedia; Lucian, a presbyter of Antioch; Tyrannion, bishop of Tyre; Zenobius, a presbyter of Sidon; Silvanus, bishop of the churches about Emesa; Silvanus, bishop of the churches about Gaza; Peleus and Nilus, Egyptian bishops; Pamphilus; Peter, bishop of Alexandria, and with him the presbyters Faustus, Dius and Ammonius; Phileas, Hesychius, Pachymius and Theodorus, Egyptian bishops. There are in all eleven bishops and six presbyters. Of these, eight certainly suffered before the short peace which followed the edict of Galerius, namely, Silvanus of Gaza,[3] Peleus, Nilus,[4] Pamphilus,[5] Phileas, Hesychius, Pachymius, and Theodorus,[6] to whom we may add

---

[1] Epiphanius, *Haer.* 68. 1, makes Culcianus praeses of the Thebaid, but he may have been misled by Eusebius.
[2] 9. 1–5.   [3] *M. P.* (Grk.) 7. 3; 13. 4 f.; Cureton, pp. 24, 47.
[4] Ibid. 13. 3; Cureton, p. 46.   [5] Ibid. 11; Cureton, p. 36.
[6] These are the authors of the letter against Meletius referred to above. McGiffert, after remarking that Silvanus of Emesa, Peter of Alexandria, and Lucian suffered 'in the year 312 or thereabouts',

Anthimus.[1] On the other hand, Lucian, Silvanus of
Emesa, Peter of Alexandria and his three companions
were all 'perfected' in the later persecution of Maximin.[2] Of Tyrannion and Zenobius nothing is known.
Thus six (perhaps eight) of the seventeen martyrdoms
mentioned were, on our theory, added when the book
was revised. The account of them occupies about half
the paragraph.

Such additions, as we have already remarked, are no
more than might be expected in this section of the book.
But it is worth while to note the way in which Peter of
Alexandria is spoken of. Eusebius's language is not free
from ambiguity. But he seems to call him 'first of those
who were perfected at Alexandria and throughout the
whole of Egypt and the Thebaid'.[3] This is not true to
fact, for Phileas and his fellow-bishops suffered before
him. But it is explained if we take the meaning to be
that he was the protomartyr of the persecution which
began in 312. That this was the case seems to be implied
by the unexpectedness of his execution.[4] It is not
difficult to understand that the epithet 'first' might be
applied to him inadvertently in this sense, if the words
relating to him are an addition; but not so easy if the
entire sentence, containing also the names of Phileas and
the rest, was penned at the same time.

It must be admitted as a difficulty in the way of the

adds, 'We may assume it as probable that all mentioned in this
chapter suffered about the same time': an observation which, if it
has any definite meaning, is contradicted by his subsequent notes.

[1] See above, pp. 268 ff.   [2] H. E. ix. 6.
[3] H. E. viii. 13. 7 τῶν δ' ἐπ' Ἀλεξανδρείας . . . τελειωθέντων πρῶτος
Πέτρος . . . ἀναγεγράφθω (cp. § 1). If the words are to be rendered
'Let Peter be first mentioned' it is hard to see why the Thebaid is
referred to. No examples of martyrdom from that region are given,
nor indeed, it seems, from any part of Egypt outside Alexandria.
[4] H. E. ix. 6. 2.

theory here proposed that it obliges us to assume that the mention of the martyrdoms of Peter of Alexandria, Lucian of Antioch, and Silvanus of Emesa in the seventh[1] and eighth books was inserted at the very time when the ninth book was added; for they are all related again in that book.[2] The difficulty is perhaps sufficiently met by observing the difference of the contexts in which they occur in the different books. The only way of removing it is by carrying forward the date of the composition of the eighth book to a period subsequent to the last of these martyrdoms. And this Schwartz does. He puts it between January 312 and the summer of 313. If, as I believe, Peter was put to death in November 312, he must bring it yet further down. But this lands us in the very much greater difficulty of supposing that Eusebius put forth the first edition of his *History* when the persecution of Maximin was at its height. In spite of the pleading of Schwartz[3] this seems to me impossible. But even if the book was written after the martyrdom of Peter, we still have his martyrdom mentioned both in the seventh and eighth books, and that of Anthimus mentioned twice in the eighth. Is that very much easier to believe than that three martyrdoms were inserted in earlier books at the same time that they were recounted in the ninth?

6. *H.E.* viii. 13. 15. Mention is made of the destruction of the public memorials of Maximian. If, as Lactantius tells us,[4] this contributed to the death of Diocletian, which seems to have taken place not earlier than the middle of 313,[5] this note is probably later than 311. But, on the other hand, the destruction of the memorials might be expected immediately to follow Maximian's death, which occurred in 310.

---

[1] See no. 2. [2] Cp. Schwartz, p. lvi. [3] p. lvii.
[4] *De Mort. Pers.* 42. [5] *Cod. Theod.* xiii. 10. 2. See above, p. 265.

7. *H. E.* viii. 14. 7–16 a. The sections relating to Maximin, and a few other passing references to him in the same chapter,[1] are probably insertions. The references to the secret alliance between Maxentius and Maximin,[2] which followed the betrothal of Licinius and Constantia (312),[3] to the establishment of Maximin's heathen hierarchy,[4] and to the victory of Licinius at Campus Serenus,[5] must all be dated after 311. It is true that these allusions might be deleted without altering the general drift of the passage. But the awkward construction of the chapter itself lends countenance to the hypothesis that the mention of Maximin in this place was an afterthought. All the preceding sections are devoted to Maxentius; and to him Eusebius suddenly returns at § 16 b, in a paragraph which would have had a more appropriate place in the earlier part of the chapter.

8. *H. E.* viii. 15. This chapter professes to give an account in general terms of the state of affairs throughout the Empire during the entire 'decade'[6] of the persecution. And the picture is faithful enough, though no doubt rhetorical and exaggerated, until we reach the last sentence. That sentence, however, merely from the point of view of grammar, reads like an addition, and, unlike the rest of the chapter, it contains a note of time which indicates that it did not apply to the period as a whole. It runs thus:—

'To these are added the famine and pestilence which came after these things; about which we shall relate what is fitting at the proper time.'

The allusion is apparently to the calamities which overtook Maximin in 312, recorded in *H. E.* ix. 8. According to that chapter they did not extend to the whole Empire,

---

[1] §§ 16 b, 18.   [2] § 7.   [3] Lact. 43; Zos. ii. 7.
[4] § 9.   [5] § 7.   [6] δεκαέτους. Cp. 16 1.

but were confined to Maximin's dominions. The sentence therefore proclaims itself to be an intruder. Probably when the book was revised ὀκταέτους in the first line was changed into δεκαέτους, and the tale of misery was completed by adding the awkward reference to the newly-written ninth book.

9. *H. E.* viii. 16. 1. The opening sentence of the sixteenth chapter runs thus :—

'Such were the events which continued throughout the entire persecution, which in the tenth year by the grace of God was completely stayed, but after the eighth year, however, began to decrease.'[1]

Comment on the grammatical clumsiness of this is almost needless. As originally conceived the sentence can hardly have contained two participial clauses co-ordinate with each other and agreeing with the same substantive. But, apart from this, certain questions suggest themselves. Why was the tenth year mentioned here at all? Why, being mentioned, was it referred to before instead of after the eighth? And why was so misleading a statement made as that the persecution began to be less after the eighth year? For, in one sense, it had begun to abate long before : there had been no persecution in the West since 305. In another part of the Empire— the European dominions of Galerius—it came absolutely to an end, not after but *in* the eighth year. Under the sway of Maximin, on the other hand, after the eighth year, according to Eusebius himself, it attained the height of its fury. And the sentence becomes even more suspicious when it is considered in connexion with the remainder of the book. In it, if we except the last line, there is no further reference to anything that happened

[1] Τοιαῦτ' ἦν τὰ διὰ παντὸς τοῦ διωγμοῦ παρατετακότα, δεκάτῳ μὲν ἔτει σὺν θεοῦ χάριτι παντελῶς πεπαυμένου, λωφᾶν γε μὴν μετ' ὄγδοον ἔτος ἐναρξαμένου.

after April 311. It is wholly taken up with the edict of Galerius, and we have seen that it leaves the impression that that edict ended the persecution. It would simplify matters if we might regard the sentence as an editorial revision of one which ran somewhat as follows: 'Such were the events which continued throughout the entire persecution, which in the eighth year, by the grace of God, was completely stayed.'[1] Such a remark would imperatively call for revision when the ninth book was added.

10. *H. E.* viii. 17. 3. Here begins the text of the edict of Galerius, in which all the authorities omit the names and titles of the Emperor Maximin. They must have been in the edict.[2] Their omission in Eusebius's translation might have been due to accident.[3] But the similar omission of the name and titles of Licinius in the manuscripts M B D and Σ Λ does not admit of this explanation, and must be regarded as a deliberate excision after the fall of that Emperor, by Eusebius or the scribe of the exemplar of this group. Hence it is probable that the name of Maximin was deleted when Book ix was added after his death.

11. *H. E.* viii. 17. 11. The remark 'It is now time to examine what happened after these things' must obviously have been penned when the ninth book was added. We may compare the very similar closing sentence of the *Theophania*, Book ii.

---

[1] Compare the last sentence of *M. P.* (Grk.) 11.

[2] See above, p. 259.

[3] From the Arykanda inscription compared with this edict we may infer that the four emperors would have been named in the order Galerius, Maximin, Constantine, Licinius. But the imperial names of the first two were identical—Imperator Caesar Galerius Valerius Maximianus (Maximinus). The dropping out of the second would be an instance of a very common form of clerical error. It might have occurred in the autograph of Eusebius, or in a very early copy.

We have now considered eleven passages, as to which there was some ground to suspect that if the *History* originally ended with the eighth book they must have been revised when the ninth book was added. In two—perhaps three—of them the suspicion proved to be not well founded.[1] There remain eight or nine passages which we must suppose to have been altered or inserted in the second edition,[2] three of them of considerable length.[3] If it seems difficult to believe that Eusebius revised his work in such drastic fashion, it must be borne in mind that some of the changes which we suppose to have been made in the text were on our hypothesis absolutely necessary emendations,[4] and others just such alterations as might have been expected if a revision was undertaken at all.[5] And it must further be remembered that six of the eight passages bear more or less obvious marks of the reviser's hand, quite apart from any theory as to the date of the completion of the first eight books.[6] These passages lend support to the theory, the main arguments for which have been drawn from considerations of a different kind.

Assuming then that the *Ecclesiastical History* in an early, if not the earliest edition, ended with Book viii, we may now consider the relation to it of the *Martyrs of Palestine*.

All conclusions on this question must be held with some reserve owing to the uncertainty which still remains as to the relation between the two recensions of the *Martyrs*. Is the longer recension, represented by the Syriac version and some fragments of its underlying Greek, an earlier edition of which the Greek recension usually printed with the *History* is an abridgement? or is the former an ex-

---

[1] Nos. 1, 3, and perhaps no. 6.
[2] Nos. 2, 4-11.
[3] Nos. 4, 5, 7.   [4] Nos. 2, 8, 9.
[5] Nos. 4, 5.   [6] Nos. 2, 4, 5, 7, 8, 9. Cp. no. 10.

pansion of the latter? Lightfoot held the former view, and I believe rightly.[1] His argument is apparently based on the assumption that the recension which is at once more diffuse, more didactic, and obviously intended mainly for readers who lived in Caesarea and its neighbourhood, has a prima facie claim to priority over a recension of reduced bulk from which local allusions and hortatory passages have been excised, and which bears marks throughout of being designed for a larger public. The argument is of course not conclusive. But it may be supplemented by a more minute comparison between the two recensions.

For example, there is a passage in which Eusebius, after giving a short account of the death of the praeses Urban, proceeds thus in the Greek:

'But let this be said by us by the way. But a fitting time may come when we shall relate at leisure the ends and the disgraceful deaths of those impious men who specially made war against us, [both of Maximin himself and of those associated with him].'[2]

The Syriac is more diffuse in the first clause; but in the remainder it is practically identical with the Greek, except that it omits the words which I have enclosed in brackets. Now these words are so alien to the context—which obviously refers not to the Emperor, but to Urban and his like—that they rest under grave suspicion of being a later addition. If, then, they are part of the original text of the shorter recension we can scarcely avoid the conclusion that it is later than the longer, which lacks them. But let us make the contrary assumption. Let us suppose that the clause about Maximin belonged to the original text and was omitted in a later edition. It follows

---

[1] See *Dict. of Christ. Biog.* ii. 320 f.
[2] *M. P.* (Grk.) 7. 8; Cureton, p. 26.

that the projected work of Eusebius which is referred to was at first intended to include Maximin, and that its scope was afterwards restricted to such underlings as Urban and Firmilian—a direction which the development of the plan is not very likely to have taken. It will presently appear indeed that I do not regard the words relating to Maximin as having had a place in the text of the shorter recension as first written. I am therefore obliged to concede that, so far as this passage is concerned, the longer recension of the *Martyrs* may have been later than the shorter. But I believe it most improbable that the passage as it stands in the Syriac text was written after the shorter text had assumed its present form, or, indeed, after the death of Maximin. No Palestinian writer would have planned a book which should recount the deaths of a few praesides of the province and omit that of their master the arch persecutor, if it had already taken place.[1]

The impression that the shorter recension of the *Martyrs* is later in date than the longer is left by two passages of the former which have no parallel in the latter. They relate to the Tyrian martyr Ulpian[2] and the Egyptian confessor John.[3] It is obvious that these sections are more in place in the edition of the work which was

[1] Schwartz (p. lxi) doubts whether Eusebius ever really intended to write such a book, in spite of his express statement. But he might well have thought of doing so, while Maximin still lived. As I understand Schwartz, he supposes that the shorter recension, with its reference to the death of Maximin, was written before the ninth book of the *History*, the longer a good many years afterwards, when the promise to relate the death of Maximin had already been fulfilled in that book. The clause referring to him was accordingly struck out, but the remainder of the sentence survives, though 'it may be doubted' whether Eusebius had any intention of carrying into effect the design of which it speaks. All this seems most unlikely.

[2] *M. P.* (Grk.) 5. 1.   [3] Ibid. 13. 6-8.

intended for wider circulation than in that which was addressed to Palestinian readers. But the fact that both of them interrupt the sequence of the narrative marks them as later additions. The narrative about Ulpian stands between the martyrdoms of the brothers Apphianus and Aedesius; it is appended rather awkwardly to the former with the connecting particle δέ; and it might be omitted without the alteration of a single word of the preceding or following text. Eusebius actually apologizes for its introduction at this part of the treatise on the ground that, like Apphianus, Ulpian was cast into the sea. The reminiscences of John are intruded into the middle of the story of Silvanus, bishop of Gaza, and others who dwelt in a place by themselves and suffered martyrdom. John does not seem to have been one of them, though he was a companion of Silvanus. Eusebius tells how he saw him for the first time in the midst of a large assembly repeating the Scriptures by heart. This must have taken place after the time of which he was writing in the context, and probably in Egypt.

The simplest explanation of the presence of these two sections in the shorter recension only is based on the hypothesis that they contain information which Eusebius had not acquired when the longer recension was written.

Schwartz holds a view of the relation between the two recensions of the *Martyrs* directly opposed to that of Lightfoot. But the reasons which he gives for his opinion do not appear sufficient to establish it. He maintains that the priority of the shorter recension is clearly proved by a comparison of the two in a single passage. At the end of the sentence in which it is stated that the bodies of Pamphilus and his companions were by the providence of God preserved from injury and were buried in a fitting manner, the longer recension adds that they were deposited in shrines and placed in churches.¹ On which Dr. Schwartz remarks that when the first edition was written—immediately (as he thinks) after the fall of Maximin—it would have been impossible to build a martyrium. But nothing is said about building a martyrium. It is only implied that some churches in the neighbourhood of Caesarea were still standing—which is quite credible²—and that the bodies, after having been exposed for some days, were buried in them. This might certainly have been done, if not at once, yet within a very short time, since within less than three weeks the last Caesarean martyr was put to death, and there presently came a lull in the persecution throughout the whole of Palestine, which lasted for some months, and during which even churches were built.³ Moreover, the detail about the depositing of the bodies in churches was just such a feature of the story as, though of much interest for Palestinian churchmen, might well be omitted in abridging the tract for the benefit of a wider circle of readers.

I confess that I am at a loss to understand an argument by which Schwartz seeks to support his inference from the passage just considered, and to prove that the longer recension dates from 323 at the earliest.⁴ I conclude, therefore, that on the whole probability is in favour of the hypothesis that the shorter recension was abridged from the longer.

¹ *M. P.* (Grk.) 11. 28; Cureton, p. 45. For the text see above, p. 200 n.

² See Optat. i. 14; *Gesta Purg. Felicis* (Gebhardt, *Act. Mart. Sel.* 205); *Pass. S. Theodoti,* 15 f.; *Pass. S. Philippi ep. Heracl.* 3-5 (Ruinart, pp. 342 f., 410 f.)—all referred to in Mason, *Persec. of Diocl.,* pp. 153, 160 f., 176, 179, 362-364.

³ *M. P.* (Grk.) 11. 30; 13. 1.

⁴ p. lxi: '...verrät die Art wie von Licinius gesprochen wird [p. ܠ : ܘܐܝܬ ܠܗ ܝܕܥܐ܂ ܗܘ=ὅς ἐπὶ τῶν καιρῶν τὴν ἐξουσίαν εἶχεν] die Zeit nach 323.' But surely it is Maximin, not Licinius, who is here spoken of, and neither from the Syriac nor from Schwartz's restoration of the

The shorter recension was regarded by both Lightfoot and Westcott[1] as a portion of a larger work. What then was the work of which it is to be regarded as a fragment? Westcott identified it with that 'in which Eusebius included the records of ancient martyrdoms, reaching back as far as the reign of Marcus Aurelius'. This theory is not mentioned by Lightfoot, and in truth it is untenable. For the references to the 'Collection of Ancient Martyrdoms' of Eusebius found in his *Ecclesiastical History*[2] clearly prove that it was already compiled when the fourth and fifth books of the *History* were written, that it referred exclusively to the *early* martyrs, and that it was not a composition of Eusebius but a collection of documents, some of them, at any rate, contemporary with the events which they described.

But Lightfoot's own account of the matter is not much more satisfactory. The Greek recension, he says, 'was part of a larger work, in which the sufferings of the martyrs were set off against the deaths of the persecutors.' And he proceeds to argue that the Appendix to the eighth book of the *History*, which 'contrasts the miserable deaths of the persecutors with the happy end of Constantius the friend of the Christians, crowned by the happy accession of his son Constantine', is another fragment of the same work.

It is plain that when the earlier recension of the *Martyrs* was composed Eusebius had a treatise *de mortibus persecutorum* in contemplation. And though his first design was merely to relate the deaths of some subordinate officials, the plan was afterwards enlarged so as to Greek can it be inferred that he was not alive and in power when the sentence was penned.

[1] *The Two Empires*, p. 4 f. It would seem that when Westcott's Essay on Eusebius was written the Syriac version had not been discovered.
[2] iv. 15. 47; v. Pref. 2; 4. 3; 21. 5.

include at least the Emperor Maximin. If this design was accomplished the Appendix to Book viii may well be a fragment of the projected work. But if so, it is not likely that the Greek *Martyrs of Palestine* also belonged to it. For it is one thing to contrast the happy end of Emperors who favoured the Christians with the miserable deaths of those who persecuted them, and another to 'set off' the sufferings of the martyrs against those of their enemies. Moreover, the passage in which he mentions it remains, with but slight alteration, in the shorter recension. The language there used does not suggest that he is referring to a second part of the work of which the *Martyrs* formed the first. And indeed Lightfoot regards the Syriac recension as a tract complete in itself. Further, I can find nothing in the Greek *Martyrs* any more than in the Syriac to suggest such a motive as Lightfoot conceived to have been that of the entire work.

I venture to suggest another hypothesis. It is perhaps worth considering whether the 'larger work' may not be the *Ecclesiastical History* itself.

The eighth book of the *History* is confessedly not an exhaustive account of the persecution. In it Eusebius designedly omits many facts of which he had first-hand knowledge, and he refers his readers for them to a forthcoming work which is certainly the *Martyrs of Palestine*.[1] The omissions in the eighth book are in fact much more serious than this reference would lead us to expect. They concern not only the conflicts of individual martyrs in one district, but leading incidents of the persecution as a whole. It is impossible, even with the eighth book in its present form, to gather from the *History* anything like an intelligible and consecutive account of the development

---

[1] *H. E.* viii. 13. 7. The sentence in *H. E.* viii is almost quoted in the Syriac recension, Cureton, p. 3.

of the persecution up to the palinode. Of incidents in
the dominions of Maximin we are given a good many,
but he is mentioned by name only in one chapter, and in
a single sentence elsewhere.[1] Of his career as a persecutor we are told only what may be gathered from a
single sentence. And in it stress is mainly laid on his
erection of a pagan hierarchy, which belongs to the
period following the Edict of Toleration.[2] In its earlier
form the book must have been still more unsatisfactory.
The *Martyrs of Palestine* is now, and always was, an
indispensable ancillary to the *Ecclesiastical History*.

Moreover, it was written, at least in its Greek form,
after the eighth book of the *History*. In proof of this
statement it is only necessary to quote a passage to which
reference has been already made: '[the conflicts] at which
I myself was present, these I shall make known to those
that shall come after us in another book ($\gamma\rho\alpha\phi\hat{\eta}s$).'[3]

But it would seem to have followed it after no great
interval. The text of the palinode with which it once
closed was introduced with words that still remain, in
part transcribed from the eighth book of the *History*,
which plainly imply that the edict ended the persecution
not only in Palestine but throughout the Empire. Such
a sentence could not have been written by a Christian
subject of Maximin after the year 311.[4]

The reasonable conclusion from these facts seems to be
that the *De Martyribus* was actually written as a supplement to the eighth book. It was in fact part of the
History in one of its forms.

We find some corroboration of this from other considerations. Lightfoot uses two arguments to prove that
the Greek recension is a fragment. The first is drawn

---

[1] *H. E.* viii. 13. 15; 14. 7 ff.　　　[2] Ibid. 14. 9.
[3] Ibid. 13. 7.　　　[4] Compare also 12 ad fin.

from the twelfth chapter. There Eusebius enumerates
certain things which he omits as unedifying. These
things, he remarks, he passes over 'as it was said by me
when I was beginning'. No such statement appears
elsewhere in the book. From this Lightfoot infers that
the Preface is lost. But a closely similar remark is found
in the introductory portion of the eighth Book,[1] and to
it no doubt Eusebius here refers.

Lightfoot's second argument is based on the omission
of the text of the edict of Galerius at the end of the book.
That can easily be explained on our hypothesis. The
edict was already copied at the end of Book viii. It was
an obvious saving of trouble if a scribe on coming to it
a second time in the same manuscript contented himself
with inserting in place of it a cross-reference in his margin.

But the Greek recension of the *Martyrs* is connected
with the eighth book of the *History* in another way. It
differs from the Syriac for the most part by omissions.
The narratives of the martyrdoms are abbreviated, and
the hortatory introduction and conclusion are removed.
There are, however, besides the notices of Ulpian and John,
already considered, four considerable passages in the Greek
to which there is nothing corresponding in the Syriac.
The first of these is the Preface, which gives an account of
the first two edicts. This is copied from *H. E.* viii. 2. 4 f.,
with some alterations, most of which are purely verbal
and wholly unimportant. The more significant are made
in order to adapt the passage to the circumstances of Palestine. They are the change of the date of the first edict from
March, and before Easter, to April, and at Easter,[2] the
insertion of the name of Flavian, the praeses of Palestine,
and the omission of the word βασιλικά before γράμματα,
indicating, no doubt, that the document referred to was

[1] *H. E.* viii. 2. 2 f. [2] ἑορτῆς ἐπιλαμβανούσης.

not the imperial edict itself, but the letter founded on it by the praeses.

The second is a passage of some length in chapter 1, which is a reproduction of *H. E.* viii. 3.[1] Here again are some changes, including both omissions and insertions. Where they are not trivial they are obviously intended to adapt the passage to its new environment. In Book viii the occurrences are described in general terms as an illustration of the results of the second edict. In the *Martyrs* the scene is laid at Caesarea, and most of the other larger changes seem to result from this one.[2]

The third is chapter 12, concerning certain things which Eusebius omits from his narrative. It is an expansion of *H. E.* viii. 2. 1–3, without much verbal resemblance, and, as we have seen, reference seems to be made in it to that passage.

The last is the closing paragraph of the book.[3] It takes a rapid survey of the course of the persecution outside Palestine, and originally ended with the text of the palinode, which has disappeared from this place. The palinode still remains at the end of Book viii, and the sentence which here leads up to it is copied from *H. E.* viii. 16. 1.[4] The preceding sentences, with additional matter, contain reminiscences of *H. E.* viii. 6. 10; 13. 10 f.

[1] *M. P.* (Grk.) 1. 3–5 a.

[2] In one case a change seems to have been the result of careless copying. In *H. E.* viii. 3. 2 f. we have ἄλλος ἡμιθνὴς αἰρόμενος ὡς ἂν ἤδη νεκρὸς ἐρρίπτετο, [καί τις αὖ πάλιν ἐπ' ἐδάφους κείμενος μακρὰν ἐσύρετο τοῖν ποδοῖν,] ἐν τεθνηκόσιν αὐτοῖς λελογισμένος. In *M. P.* (Grk.) 1. 4. the words καὶ ἀνίετό γε τῶν δεσμῶν are quite suitably added after ἐρρίπτετο, but the bracketed words are omitted. Thus two persons became one, and the sentence not very intelligible.

[3] *M. P.* (Grk.) 13. 11–14

[4] The intervening portion of Book viii—the remainder of chapter 16 and the first section of chapter 17—is omitted. It is chiefly concerned with the illness and death of Galerius. These would naturally be passed over, as irrelevant to the subject of the *De Martyribus*.

Thus four passages were introduced into the *Martyrs of Palestine* when that work was recast: two of them wholly, and one partly, transcribed from the eighth book, while the other is expanded from, and refers to, a passage in it. It is interesting to compare with this the way in which Eusebius sometimes connects a book of his *History* with the one that immediately precedes it. Thus the last sentence of Book ii is repeated as the first of Book iii. In like manner the last sentence of Book iv is identical with the earlier part of the first sentence of Book v. The sixth book closes and the seventh opens with a reference to the epistles which Dionysius of Alexandria 'has left'; and the Preface of Book viii is an abridgement of the last paragraph of Book vii.[1] So in the *Martyrs of Palestine*, which covers exactly the same period as the eighth Book of the *History*, Eusebius, as though desiring to connect it with that book, commences by extracting from it, with suitable modification, the first sentence of its direct narrative, and ends with a passage consisting of two extracts from its final chapters.

Finally the manuscripts give some support to the theory that the shorter recension of the *De Martyribus* was intended by its author to serve as a supplement to the eighth book of the *History*, and to follow it. The text is preserved in four primary manuscripts only, those which Schwartz designates as A T E R. In all of them it has a heading to the effect that it was found in a certain copy (R has 'certain copies') in the eighth book. This statement must therefore have come from the common ancestor of A T E R. We may infer that the *De Martyribus* was not in the codex from which the greater part of the text of the *History* in that ancient copy was taken, and that

[1] Other examples are given by S. Lee in his English translation of the *Theophania*, p. vi. See also above, p. 257.

in the only manuscript of it which the scribe knew it followed the eighth book of the History. That was a position in which it was most unlikely to be placed by later scribes or editors. In fact it was felt to be so unsuitable that, in spite of its heading, the tract has been removed to the end of the tenth book in T E. How, then, did it originally find its way to the close of Book viii? Not the only possible, but certainly the most obvious, answer to that question is that it was put there by Eusebius himself before the ninth book was added.

It remains to be said that on the theory which is here maintained one clause which is attested by all the manuscripts cannot belong to the original text. It is that already referred to in which Eusebius announces his intention of describing in the future the deaths of the persecutors, 'both of Maximin himself and of those who acted with him.'[1] The last words must have been inserted after Maximin's death, and probably when the ninth book was added.

To sum up. I conceive that the history of the composition of the *Ecclesiastical History* was this. Eusebius had probably nearly completed the seven books of the *History* which brought the narrative down to his own time, when suddenly the Edict of Toleration was issued by Galerius and his colleagues. This event, which appeared to have ushered in a period of peace to the Church, after the most cruel of the persecutions, was seized upon by him as the natural terminus of his story. He therefore wrote a sketch of the history of the persecution as the eighth and last book of his great work, and published the whole. Immediately after, or perhaps before this, he wrote the longer edition of his *Martyrs of Palestine*. Somewhat later he abridged this work and added a few paragraphs

[1] *M. P.* (Grk.) 7. 8.

THE *ECCLESIASTICAL HISTORY* 291

to it that it might serve as a supplement to the somewhat meagre record of his eighth book. No doubt it was inserted at the end of the *History* in the copies subsequently made. All these works were completed between May and November 311. The eighth book of the *History*, with the addition of the *Martyrs*, we may count as a second edition.

But the dream that a permanent peace had been inaugurated for the Church was rudely dispelled, as far as the East was concerned, by the resumption of the persecution by Maximin in the last months of the same year. Once again the final peace seemed to have begun with the edict of Constantine and Licinius at Milan. No sooner had it been proclaimed at Nicomedia than Eusebius began his preparations for a third edition of the *History*. He revised Book viii, and to a small extent also Book vii and the *Martyrs*, and wrote Book ix, bringing it to an end with the text of the letter of Licinius of June 13, 313. It may be dated about the end of 313.

Some eleven years later, after a temporary interruption of the peace by Licinius, a fourth edition was issued. The text of the ninth book was slightly altered and the tenth was added, the whole work in its present form being finished in 324, or early in 325. Whether the *De Martyribus* was included in this final edition I do not venture an opinion.

INDEX OF PASSAGES OF EARLY WRITERS QUOTED OR REFERRED TO

HOLY SCRIPTURES.
Genesis ii. 21 : 118.
Isaiah xxxiii. 15, 16 : 8.
Matthew xiii. 16 : 90.
  xxiii. 34 : 131.
  xxviii. 19 : 33.
1 Corinthians ii. 9 : 90.
Hebrews v. 7 : 15.

Acta Anthimi : 270.
Acta Iustini : 168.
Acta Phileae et Philoromi : 272.
Africanus, ap. Eus. H. E. i. 7. 12 : 16.
Anonymus, Adversus Montanistas, ap. Eus. H. E. v. 16. 3 : 118.
  v. 16. 7, 8 : 119.
  v. 16. 7 : 117.
  v. 16. 9 : 117, 119.
  v. 16. 12 : 131.
  v. 16. 14 : 113, 124.
  v. 16. 19, 20, 21 : 132.
  v. 17. 2 : 119.
  v. 17. 3, 4 : 118.
  v. 17. 4 : 16.
Apollonius, Adversus Montanistas, ap. Eus. H. E. v. 18. 2 : 120, 124, 127.
  v. 18. 3 : 113, 128.
  v. 18. 4 : 113, 124.
  v. 18. 5 : 113, 124, 133.
  v. 18. 6–9 : 123.
  v. 18. 6 : 113.
  v. 18. 7 : 113, 124.
  v. 18. 10 : 113.
  v. 18. 11 : 124.
  v. 18. 12 : 122.
  v. 18. 13 : 120.
Anthimus, Epistola, ap. Chron. Pasch. : 270.
Aurelius Victor, De Caesaribus, 39. 48 : 204.

Cedrenus, Compendium, p. 257 f. : 175.
Chronicon Paschale : 73.
Cicero, Epistola ad Atticam, viii. 14. 1, 2 : 235.
Clemens Alexandrinus, Hypotyposes, ap. Eus. H. E. ii. 1. 2, 3 : 17.
  Stromata, i. 11 (ap. H. E. v. 11. 3–5) : 20.
Clemens Romanus, Epistola, 54 : 9 f.
Codex Iustinianeus, 3. 28. 26 : 201.
  11. 58. 1 : 219.
Codex Theodosianus, 13. 10. 2 : 275.
Constantinus, Oratio, 25 : 204, 253.
Cyprianus, Epistolae, 55. 6 : 175.
  71 : 176.

Didymus Alexandrinus, De Trinitate, iii. 41 : 110.
Dionysius Alexandrinus, Epistolae, ap. Eus. H. E. iii. 28. 4, 5 : 20.
  vi. 40 : 169.
  vii. 5. 6 : 160.
  vii. 11. 2 : 164.
  vii. 11. 8 : 174.
  vii. 11. 18, 19 : 164 f.
  vii. 11. 18 : 174.
  vii. 11. 20–5 : 164, 169.
  vii. 11. 23 : 173.
  vii. 11. 24 : 170.
  vii. 21. 3 : 172.
  vii. 21. 4, 6 : 171.
  vii. 22. 4–6 : 173.
  vii. 23. 1–3 : 170.
  vii. 23. 4 : 163.
  vii. 25. 1–5 : 20.

INDEX OF PASSAGES 293

Dionysius Corinthiorum Episcopus, *Epistolae*, ap. Eus. *H. E.* iv. 23. 3, 9 : 177.
iv. 23. 12 : 244.

Epiphanius, *De Mensuris et Ponderibus*, 15. 1-5 : 28-34, 101 f.
Epiphanius, *Panarion*, xxiv. 1 : 73.
  xxvii. 5, 6 : 73-5, 76, 77-84, 106 f.
  xxvii. 6 : 9, 73, 76, 105, 106 f.
  xxix. 4 : 10, 14, 15, 82, 98, 99.
  xxix. 7 : 28-34, 73, 101 f.
  xxx. 2 : 28-34, 73, 101 f.
  xlviii. 2 : 127.
  xlviii. 3, 4 : 118.
  xlviii. 4 : 119.
  xlviii. 8, 9 : 127.
  xlviii. 8 : 129.
  xlviii. 11 : 111, 127.
  xlviii. 14 : 120.
  xlix : 113.
  xlix. 1 : 120, 122.
  xlix. 2, 3 : 120.
  lxviii. 1 : 273.
  lxxviii. 7 : 5 f., 11 f., 14, 16, 35, 82, 98, 102.
  lxxviii. 8 : 12, 98.
  lxxviii. 13 : 13, 98, 99.
  lxxviii. 14 : 6, 7, 13, 15, 99, 100 f.
Epiphanius Monachus, *De Vita B. Mariae*, 14 : 44 f.
Eusebius, *Chronica* : 24, 43, 151, 160, 170, 177, 181, 186, 187, 237, 244.
Eusebius, *De Martyribus Palestinae*, Pref. : 180, 181, 186, 188, 228.
  Cureton p. 3 : 57, 285.
  1. 1, Cureton p. 4 : 192, 200.
  1. 2, Cureton p. 4 : 192.
  1. 3-5a, Cureton p. 4 : 200, 288.
  1. 3 : 186.
  1. 4 : 288.
  1. 5, Cureton p. 6 : 189, 192.
  2. 1, Cureton p. 6 : 189, 192.
  2. 4, Cureton p. 8 : 192.
  3. 1, Cureton p. 8 : 196, 202.
  3. 3, 4, Cureton p. 10 : 195.
  Cureton p. 12 : 187.
  3. 4, Cureton p. 12 : 202.

Eusebius, *De Martyribus Palestinae*, 3. 5-4. 15, Cureton p. 12 : 185.
  4. 8, Cureton p. 13 : 205, 210.
  4. 15 : 190.
  5, Cureton p. 17 : 186.
  5. 1 : 281 f.
  Cureton p. 17 : 190.
  Cureton p. 19 : 206.
  6, Cureton p. 19 : 196, 206.
  6. 1, Cureton p. 19 : 191.
  6. 5 : 57.
  7. 1, Cureton p. 22 : 193, 196.
  7. 3, 4, Cureton p. 24 : 189.
  7. 3, Cureton p. 24 : 196, 273.
  7. 4-7, Cureton p. 24 : 196.
  7. 5, 6, Cureton p. 25 : 199.
  7. 6, Cureton p. 25 : 195.
  7. 8, Cureton p. 26 : 280, 290.
  8. 1, Cureton p. 26 : 183, 196.
  8. 4-13, Cureton p. 26 : 206.
  8. 10, 11, Cureton p. 30 : 57.
  8. 12, Cureton p. 31 : 184.
  9. 1, Cureton p. 31 : 207.
  9. 2, Cureton p. 31 : 208, 230.
  9. 5, Cureton p. 32 : 207.
  Cureton p. 34 f. : 183.
  10. 1, Cureton p. 34 : 184.
  10. 2, Cureton p. 35 : 189.
  11, Cureton p. 36 : 194, 273.
  11. 1, Cureton p. 38 : 57.
  11. 5, Cureton p. 40 : 195, 196, 199, 210.
  11. 24, Cureton p. 44 : 57.
  11. 28, Cureton, p. 45 : 200, 283.
  11. 30, Cureton, p. 45 : 209, 283.
  11. 31 : 278.
  12 : 286 f., 288.
  13. 1-3, Cureton p. 46 : 183.
  13. 1 : 183, 195, 210, 283.
  13. 3, Cureton p. 46 : 273.
  13. 4, 5, Cureton p. 47 : 273.
  Cureton p. 48 : 288.
  13. 5, Cureton p. 48 : 209.
  13. 6-8 : 281 f.
  13. 8 : 198.
  13. 11-14 : 288.
  13. 12 : 197.
  13-14 : 265.
Eusebius, *Demonstratio Evangelica*, iii. 5 : 7, 92.

INDEX OF PASSAGES

Eusebius, *Historia Ecclesiastica*,
i. 1. 1, 2 : 258.
i. 1. 1: 81.
i. 1. 3 : 4.
i. 9. 1, 2 : 198.
i. 9. 1: 17.
i. 9. 2, 3 : 267.
i. 12. 1, 3 : 36.
i. 13. 11 : 152.
ii. 1. 13 : 22.
ii. 2. 2 : 36.
ii. 16. 1 : 36.
ii. 17. 1 : 36.
ii. 18 : 138–145.
ii. 22. 2 : 22.
ii. 23. 1 : 17.
ii. 23. 2 : 24.
ii. 23. 3 : 2, 11.
ii. 23. 4–18 : 4–17, 27, 96.
ii. 23. 4–7 : 7 f.
ii. 23. 4, 5 : 98.
ii. 23. 4 : 15, 17.
ii. 23. 5 : 10, 12.
ii. 23. 6 : 99.
ii. 23. 7–18 : 100 f.
ii. 23. 7 : 6.
ii. 23. 8 : 10, 58, 91.
ii. 23. 9 : 25.
ii. 23. 10, 11, 16 : 57.
ii. 23. 18 : 24, 32.
ii. 26. 2 : 289.
iii. 1. 1 : 289.
iii. 5–10 : 27, 50.
iii. 5. 2, 3 : 29–34, 101 f.
iii. 11–20 : 50 ff.
iii. 11, 12 : 21, 23.
iii. 11 : 11, 24–6, 27, 32, 35 f., 57, 80, 93, 102.
iii. 12 : 26, 52, 59-62, 103.
iii. 13, 15 : 82.
iii. 16 : 65, 105.
iii. 17–20 : 41–9, 50–3.
iii. 17 : 52, 61, 103.
iii. 18. 1 : 80, 95, 104.
iii. 18. 2–4 : 43 f.
iii. 19 : 24, 44, 58, 104.
iii. 20 : 11, 54.
iii. 20. 1, 2 : 96, 104.
iii. 20. 1 : 44, 80, 104.
iii. 20. 3–5 : 104 f.
iii. 20. 6 : 105.
iii. 20. 9 : 95, 104.
iii. 23. 3 : 10, 11.
iii. 23. 8 : 10.

Eusebius, *Historia Ecclesiastica*,
iii. 24. 2 : 148.
iii. 24. 5, 7, 11 : 22, 36.
iii. 32. 1, 2 : 24, 52.
iii. 32. 1 : 22, 33.
iii. 32. 2 : 40, 57, 58, 103, 105.
iii. 32. 3, 4 : 56.
iii. 32. 3 : 40, 59, 103.
iii. 32. 4 : 54, 105.
iii. 32. 6 : 54, 55, 59, 96, 105.
iii. 32. 7, 8 : 37-9.
iii. 32. 7 : 86, 102.
iii. 36. 3 : 22.
iii. 37. 1 : 22.
iii. 38. 1 : 148.
iv. 5 : 64, 92 f.
iv. 5. 1, 2 : 22.
iv. 6. 3, 4 : 64.
iv. 7 f.: 76.
iv. 7. 9 : 76.
iv. 7. 15 ; 8. 1 : 2, 62.
iv. 8. 2 : 2, 3, 10, 68, 90, 98.
iv. 8. 5 : 147.
iv. 10 : 169.
iv. 11–13, 16–18 : 145–7.
iv. 11. 7–9 : 145.
iv. 11. 7 : 68, 71, 72, 75, 89, 106.
iv. 11. 11 : 73.
iv. 12 : 169.
iv. 13. 6 : 169.
iv. 14. 10 : 17, 137.
iv. 15 : 55, 136 f.
iv. 15. 11, 12 : 57.
iv. 15. 46-8: 137.
iv. 15. 47 : 137, 284.
iv. 16 : 22.
iv. 16. 2 : 147.
iv. 17. 1 : 147.
iv. 22. 1 : 3, 10, 66, 105, 106, 107.
iv. 22. 2, 3 : 96.
iv. 22. 2 : 66, 72, 105, 106.
iv. 22. 3 : 66, 70, 75, 76, 106, 107.
iv. 22. 4–6 : 39, 96, 103.
iv. 22. 4, 5 : 77.
iv. 22. 4 : 11, 18–20, 25, 27, 57, 61, 102.
iv. 22. 5, 6 : 38.
iv. 22. 5 : 58, 62, 76.
iv. 22. 7 : 58, 91, 98.
iv. 22. 8 : 8, 35, 96.
iv. 23 : 147 f.

INDEX OF PASSAGES 295

Eusebius, *Historia Ecclesiastica*,
  iv. 26 : 148 f.
  iv. 26. 2 : 176.
  iv. 27 : 149-151.
  iv. 28 : 22.
  iv. 30. 3 : 289.
  v. Pref. 1 : 289.
  v. Pref. 2 : 284.
  v. 3. 4 : 132, 151.
  v. 4, 5 : 95.
  v. 4. 3 : 284.
  v. 5. 1, 2 : 22.
  v. 5. 4 : 151.
  v. 5. 9 : 86.
  v. 10. 1 : 22.
  v. 12 : 64.
  v. 12. 2 : 87, 92.
  v. 19. 1 : 22.
  v. 20 : 177.
  v. 22 : 198.
  v. 28. 8-12 : 125.
  vi. 2. 1 : 36.
  vi. 4. 3 : 22.
  vi. 19. 16 : 73.
  vi. 20. 1 : 136.
  vi. 22 : 151 f.
  vi. 26 : 198.
  vi. 32. 3 : 136.
  vi. 33. 4 : 36.
  vi. 36. 3 : 136.
  vi. 43 : 152 f.
  vi. 43. 2, 3 : 175.
  vi. 44-6 : 154-8.
  vi. 46. 5 : 289.
  vii. Pref. : 289.
  vii. 1 : 163.
  vii. 2-9 : 159 f.
  vii. 2 : 160.
  vii 5. 3 : 160.
  vii. 9. 6 : 176.
  vii. 10, 11 : 163, 165.
  vii. 12 : 36.
  vii. 17 : 36.
  vii. 19 : 17.
  vii. 20-23 : 160-5.
  vii. 26 : 165 f.
  vii. 32. 28 : 198.
  vii. 32. 31 : 267.
  vii. 32. 32 : 259, 261, 289.
  viii. Pref. : 259, 261, 289.
  viii. 2. 1-3 : 288.
  viii. 2. 2, 3 : 287.
  viii. 2. 4, 5 : 287.
  viii. 2. 4 : 181, 188.

Eusebius, *Historia Ecclesiastica*,
  viii. 3 : 288.
  viii. 3. 2, 3 : 288.
  viii. 4. 2 : 253.
  viii. 6. 6 : 268-70.
  viii. 6. 7 : 230.
  viii. 6. 10 : 200, 288.
  viii. 9. 1-5 : 270-3.
  viii. 9. 4 : 271.
  viii. 7. 1-13. 7 : 270.
  viii. 13. 1-7 : 273 f.
  viii. 13. 1, 2 : 269.
  viii. 13. 1 : 239, 274.
  viii. 13. 2 : 218.
  viii. 13. 5 : 183.
  viii. 13. 7, 8 : 262 f.
  viii. 13. 7 : 274, 285, 286.
  viii. 13. 8 : 259.
  viii. 13. 10, 11 : 197, 288.
  viii. 13. 10 : 187.
  viii. 13. 11 : 204.
  viii. 13. 15 : 275, 286.
  viii. 14. 7-16 a : 276, 286.
  viii. 14. 9 : 206, 209, 286.
  viii. 14. 16 b, 18 : 276.
  viii. 15 : 276.
  viii. 16. 1 : 259, 264, 276, 288.
  viii. 16. 2-17. 1 : 288.
  viii. 16. 2 : 264.
  viii. 16. 2, 3 : 253.
  viii. 16. 7 : 254.
  viii. 17 : 209.
  viii. 17. 3 : 278.
  viii. 17. 5 : 246.
  viii. 17. 11 : 266, 278.
  viii. App. : 253, 265 f., 284 f.
  viii. App. 2 : 187.
  ix. 1 : 260.
  ix. 1. 1 : 213, 214.
  ix. 1. 3-6 : 214, 254.
  ix. 1. 5 : 232.
  ix. 1. 7-11 : 187, 214.
  ix. 1. 7 : 233.
  ix. 2-4 : 206, 216.
  ix. 2 : 217, 229, 230, 231.
  ix. 2. 1 : 187, 214.
  ix. 3 : 229, 231.
  ix. 4 : 230.
  ix. 4. 1 : 229.
  ix. 4. 2 : 209, 216, 223.
  ix. 4. 3 : 231.
  ix. 5 : 230, 231.
  ix. 5. 1 : 267.
  ix. 6 : 231, 269, 274.

INDEX OF PASSAGES

Eusebius, *Historia Ecclesiastica*,
  ix. 6. 2 : 267, 274.
  ix. 6. 3 : 218, 239.
  ix. 6. 4 : 264.
  ix. 7. 1 : 223, 231.
  ix. 7. 2 : 223.
  ix. 7. 4 : 231.
  ix. 7. 7 : 209, 231.
  ix. 7. 10 : 223.
  ix. 7. 12 : 209, 229, 231.
  ix. 7. 13, 14 : 223, 231.
  ix. 7. 15 : 231.
  ix. 7. 16 : 223, 224, 228.
  ix. 8 : 224, 276.
  ix. 8. 1 : 224.
  ix. 9. 1 : 245, 246, 256.
  ix. 9. 12, 13 : 218.
  ix. 9. 12 : 245, 247, 252, 256.
  ix. 9. 14–22 : 232–4.
  ix. 9. 15–17 : 187.
  ix. 9. 17 : 217, 229.
  ix. 9. 19 : 231.
  ix. 9. 23, 24 : 233.
  ix. 9. 25 : 247.
  ix. 10 : 189.
  ix. 10. 3 : 247, 256.
  ix. 10. 7 : 224.
  ix. 10. 8, 9 : 227.
  ix. 10. 8 : 198.
  ix. 10. 12 : 197, 223, 228.
  ix. 10. 13 : 226.
  ix. 10. 14, 15 : 253.
  ix. 10. 14 : 225.
  ix. 11. 4 : 272.
  ix. 11. 8 : 250 f., 253, 257.
  x. 1. 1 : 250, 253, 257.
  x. 1. 2 : 243, 261.
  x. 1. 3 : 262.
  x. 2. 2 : 245, 249, 251.
  x. 4. 16, 60 : 245, 255.
  x. 5–7 : 248 f., 251.
  x. 5. 4 : 218.
  x. 5. 14 : 251.
  x. 8. 1 : 254.
  x. 8. 3, 5–18 : 255.
  x. 9. 9 : 253.
  x. 16, 17 : 249.
Eusebius, *Theophania*, ii. 97 : 278.
  v. 45 : 92.
Eusebius, *Vita Constantini*, i. 18 : 204.
  i. 23 : 253.
Eutropius, *Breviarium Historiae Romanae*, ix. 27 : 204.

Firmilianus, *Epistola*, ap. Cypr.
  Ep. 75. 10 : 113, 119.

Gesta Purgationis Felicis : 283.

Hegesippus, *Hypomnemata* : 98–107.
  See also the references there given to Epiphanius, Eusebius, Irenaeus and Photius.
Hieronymus, *De Viris Illustribus*,
  22 : 1.
  40 : 126.
  66 : 152–4.
  69 : 156, 157, 158.
  80 : 237.
Hippolytus, *Refutationes*, v. 24, 27 : 90.
  viii. 19 : 112.

Irenaeus, *Ad Florinum*, ap. *H. E.*
  v. 20. 5 : 95.
Irenaeus, *Adversus Haereses*, i. 25. 6 : 75, 86, 106 f.
  i. 27. 1 (ap. *H. E.* iv. 11. 2) : 85, 87.
  ii. 22. 5 (ap. *H. E.* iii. 23. 3) : 64.
  iii. 1. 1 (ap. *H. E.* v. 8. 2) : 22.
  iii. 3. 3 (ap. *H. E.* v. 6) : 15, 81.
  iii. 3. 4 (ap. *H. E.* iv. 14. 3–8) : 86, 137.
  iii. 4. 3 (ap. *H. E.* iv. 11. 2) : 85, 86.
  iii. 12. 8 : 22.
Irenaeus, *De Ogdoade*, ap. *H. E.*
  v. 20. 2 : 147, 177, 244.

Josephus, *Antiquitates*, xviii. 2. 2 ; 4. 2 : 198.
  xx. 9. 1 (ap. *H. E.* ii. 23. 21–4) : 24.
Josephus, *De Bello Iudaico*, ii. 15. 2 : 24.
Julius Caesar, *De Bello Civili*, iii. 76 : 235.
Julius Caesar, *De Bello Gallico*, v. 47. 1 : 235.
  vii. 10, 11 : 236.
  vii. 40, 41 : 235.
Justinus, *Dialogus*, 80 : 121.

Lactantius, *De Mortibus Persecutorum*, x–xx : 239.
  x : 253.

INDEX OF PASSAGES

Lactantius, *De Mortibus Persecutorum*, xi. 8 : 203.
xii–xiv : 185.
xii, xiii : 181.
xii : 188.
xv : 269.
xvii : 185, 192, 201.
xvii. 1, 2 : 240.
xviii. 1–7 : 204.
xviii. 8–15 : 205, 240.
xviii. 15 : 204.
xix : 185.
xix. 3 : 204.
xx. 1 : 240.
xx. 4 : 203.
xxi–xxiii : 240.
xxiv : 238.
xxvi–xxx : 240.
xxxiii–xxxv : 241.
xxxv : 209.
xxxv. 1 : 213.
xxxv. 3 : 215.
xxxv. 4 : 221, 238.
xxxvi : 215.
xxxvi. 1 : 216, 221.
xxxvi. 3–7 : 231.
xxxvi. 3 : 216, 231, 259.
xxxvi. 4 : 209, 231.
xxxvi. 6, 7 : 214, 239.
xxxvi. 6 : 187.
xxxvii. 1 : 239.
xlii : 275.
xliii, xliv : 240.
xliii : 276.
xliii. 1 : 265.
xliv. 4 : 218.
xlv–xlvii : 241.
xlv. 1 : 218, 241.
xlv. 2 : 219, 220.
xlv. 5, 6 : 219.
xlv. 5 : 222.
xlv. 6 : 212.
xlvi, 8, 9 : 219.
xlvii–xlix : 224.
xlvii. 6 : 225.
xlviii : 256.
xlviii. 1 : 238.
xlviii. 2 : 218.
xlviii. 13 : 238.
Lucianus, *Apologia*, ap. Rufin. *H. E.* ix. 6 : 218.

Optatus, *De Schismate Donatistarum*, i. 14 : 283.

Origenes, ap. Eus. *H. E.* vi. 25. 4 : 22.

Panegyrici Veteres, vi. 9 : 203, 204.
vii. 15 : 203.
x. 33 : 218.
Papias, *Expositiones*, ap. Eus. *H. E.* iii. 39. 16 : 22.
Passio Achatii : 133 f.
Passio S. Philippi Episcopi Heracleae, 3–5 : 283.
Passio S. Polycarpi, 6, 7 : 57.
Passio S. Theodoti, 15, 16 : 283.
Photius, *Bibliotheca*, 48 : 144.
121 : 152.
232 : 3, 90, 107.
Pseudo-Clemens, *Recognitiones*, i. 43 : 18.
Pseudo-Tertullianus, *Adversus Haereticos*, 7 : 112.

Rufinus, *Historia Ecclesiastica*, ii. 23. 3 : 2.
ii. 23. 8 : 91.
iii. 16 : 52 f.

Socrates, *Historia Ecclesiastica*, iv. 28 : 126.
Sozomenus, *Historia Ecclesiastica*, ii. 32 : 134.
vii. 19 : 130.

Tertullianus, *Adversus Marcionem*, iii. 24 : 120.
Adversus Praxean, 1 : 133.
2, 8, 13 : 111.
30 : 112.
Apologeticus, 5 : 4.
De Anima, 9 : 114, 115, 118.
11, 21, 45 : 118.
55 : 114, 130.
De Corona Militis, 1 : 130.
De Exhortatione Castitatis, 10 : 128.
De Fuga in Persecutione, 9, 11 : 130.
De Idololatria, 15 : 114.
De Ieiuniis, 1 : 112.
2 : 129.
3, 12 : 118.
13 : 129.
De Monogamia, 2 : 112.
3 : 118, 127.

Tertullianus, *De Pudicitia*, 19, 21, 22: 123.
De Resurrectione Carnis, 63: 111.
De Spectaculis, 26: 114.
De Virginibus Velandis, 1: 118.
  9: 120.
  17: 114.

Vegetius, *Rei Militaris Instituta*, i. 9: 235.

Zonaras, *Annales*, xii. 21: 175.
  xii. 33: 266.
Zosimus, *Historia*, ii. 7: 202, 276.

GENERAL INDEX

Abdication of Emperors, 185 f., 195, 197, 239 f.
   date of, 185-8.
Achatius, bishop, 133.
Aedesius, martyr, 282.
Aegaeae, 213.
Aemilianus, 174.
Agabus, 118.
Agapius, martyr, 191, 196, 206.
Agathonice, Acts of, 136 f., 167.
Agedincum, 236.
Ainsworth, W., 220.
Albinus, 24.
Alexander, Montanist, 122 f.
Alexander, Bishop of Jerusalem, library of, 136.
Alexander Severus, 152, 198.
Alexandria, martyrdoms at, 271 f.
   pestilence at, 164, 171-4.
   sedition at, 171 f.
Alphaeus, martyr, 189, 192.
Ammia of Philadelphia, 118.
Ammonius, martyr, 273.
Anencletus, Bishop of Rome, 9, 77, 79, 82 f.
Anicetus, Bishop of Rome, 66, 68, 72, 74 f., 78-80, 83, 145.
   heresy at Rome under, 80, 85 f.
Anonymous writer against Montanism, date and place of, 117 f.
   his statements about martyrs, 131-3.
Anthimus, Bishop of Nicomedia, 239, 268-70, 273-5.
Antinous, 3, 90 f.
Antioch, 215, 219, 221, 271.
   Church of, 270.
   distance of, from Chalcedon, 216.
   Milan, 219.
   Nicomedia, 212 f.
   memorial from citizens of, 216 f., 222, 231.
   routes to, from Tyana, &c., 212.

Antioch, Synod at, 157.
Antonine Itinerary: *see* Itinerary.
Antoninus Pius, 137, 145 f.
   only one martyrdom under, 168 f.
Apocalypse, authorship and date of, 43, 51, 95 f.
Apollinarius, writings of, 149-151.
Apollonius, Bishop of Ephesus, 113, 122 f., 126-8, 133.
   date of, 122 f.
Apostles, 26, 28, 33 f., 38 f.
Apphianus (Epiphanius), martyr, 185-7, 190, 205 f., 282.
Arabia, 271.
Ardabau, 109, 119.
Ares, martyr, 183 f.
Aristides and Quadratus, Apologies of, resemblance of titles of, 178.
   volume containing, 178.
Aristo of Pella, 64.
Aristotle, 75.
Armenians, 157.
Arykanda, inscription at, 223, 229, 239, 259, 278.
Asclepiodotus, 125.
Ashkelon, 183.
Asia, Diocese of, 213, 215, 225.
Asia Minor, roads in, 212.
Asparagium, 235.
Assemani, S. E., 185, 189 f.
Asterius Urbanus, 111.
Astyrius, 36.
Aubé, B., 133.
Aurelius Victor, 204 f.
Avircius Marcellus, 117.
ἀρχή, 76 f.

Bardy, G., 110.
Basilides, 2.
Basilidians, 62.
Benson, E. W., 153 f., 158, 175.
Bernard, J. H., 95 f.
Bithynia, 216.

GENERAL INDEX

Blastus, was he contemporary with Florinus? 177.
Bonwetsch, N., 113, 123, 125-7, 129, 133.
Brandt, S., 237.
Bright, W., 171, 226.
Browne, H., 190 f., 193.
Brundisium, 235, 241.
Bruttius or Brettius, 43, 53.
Burkitt, F. C., 90.
Bury, J. B., 215, 237.
Butcher, S., 188.
Byzantium, 219, 222, 241.
βιβλίον, 147, 177, 261.

Caesarea, 180, 183, 185-8, 193, 196, 200, 203, 206, 210, 288.
   First edict published at, 186, 199, 228, 287.
   last martyr at, 209.
   library at, 136, 144.
Campus Serenus, Battle of, 219, 224-6, 241 f., 276.
Cappadocia, 224 f.
   Montanism in, 113.
Carleton, J. G., 188.
Carpocrates, 74, 79, 84, 86.
   the father of the Gnostics, 2, 76 f.
Carpocratians, 62, 74 f., 78 f., 85.
   called Gnostics, 75-7.
Carpus, Acts of, 136 f., 167.
Carthage, pestilence at, 175.
Cataeschinites, 112.
Cataproclans, 112.
Catholic Epistles, 113, 147.
Cemeteries, assemblies in, 217, 230.
Cenabum, 236.
Cerdon, 85.
Chalcedon, 213, 215, 221 f.
Chiliasm: see Millenarianism.
Christians, persecution of under Domitian, 52, 54, 61.
Chronological errors of Eusebius, 166-77.
Chrysophora, 147 f.
Chrysostom, St., 49.
Churches standing at Caesarea in 310, 200, 283.
Cilicia, Gates of, 212 f., 220, 225 f.
Cities, memorials from: see Maximin Daza.
City let down from heaven, 120 f.

Clement, Bishop of Alexandria, 10 f., 17, 95.
Clement, Bishop of Rome, 9, 77, 79, 83.
   Epistle of, 9 f., 50, 65, 67, 69, 73, 82 f.
Cletus: see Anencletus.
Clopas, 25, 34-7, 39.
Colon or Conon, Bishop of Hermopolis, 156.
Commodus, 198.
Commune Asiae, letter to the, 145, 168.
'Complete years': see ὅλα ἔτη.
Constantia, 218, 276.
Constantine, 205, 215, 251 f., 254 f.
   at Rome, 218 f.
   flight of, from Nicomedia, 238, 240.
   patron of Lactantius, 238, 241.
   reverse of, near Rome, 240.
   victory of, over Maxentius, 218, 240 f., 252.
Corfinium, 235, 241.
Corinth, beginning of monarchical episcopacy at, 69.
   Church of, commended for orthodoxy, 66 f., 87 f.
   notice of, by Hegesippus, parallel to that of Church of Jerusalem, 69 f.
   disturbance at, 50, 65, 67, 69.
   Hegesippus at, 64 f.
   origin of heresy in, 70.
Cornelius, Bishop of Rome, 152-4, 157, 175.
Cramer, J. A., 41 ff., 103 f.
Crispus Caesar, 237.
Culcianus, 272 f.
Cureton, W., 179.
Cyprian, 152-4.

David, descendants of, 50, 52, 54, 56, 59-61.
De Boor, C., 41 f., 48 f., 103 f.
Decapolis, 29.
Decius, 133, 161, 167, 169, 174.
Demetrius, Bishop of Alexandria, 198.
De Soyres, J., 110, 113, 115.
Desposyni, 11, 26, 33 f., 56, 59-61, 63 f., 71.
Didymus: see Domitius.
Didymus of Alexandria, 110.

GENERAL INDEX 301

Dindorf, 28.
Diocletian, 218.
  abdication of, 185-8, 195, 203-6, 240.
  at Rome, 201, 240.
  death of, 253, 265, 275.
  dominions of, 201.
  illness of, 201-3.
  persecution of, 197-210.
    date of commencement of, 181, 199.
    end of in Palestine, 209.
    First edict in, 181, 199, 228, 268, 287.
    Second edict in, 200, 268, 287.
    'Third edict' in, 200.
    Fourth edict in, 202, 205, 240, 271.
    Fifth edict in, 208 f.
    intermittent, 199-210.
    remission of, in 309, 206-9.
    rigour of, depended on local authorities, 200.
  rescript of, in August 304, 201.
  vicennalia of, 192, 201.
Dionysius, Bishop of Alexandria,
  letter of, against Germanus, 164 f., 169, 174.
  letter of, concerning Lucian, 159, 176.
  letter of, on discipline, 161 f., 173.
  letter of, on martyrdom, 155, 157 f.
  letter of, on the Sabbath, 161 f.
  letters of, Festal, 160-5, 169-74.
  letters of, on Baptism, 159 f.
  letters of, on Sabellianism, 165 f.
  letters of, on the Schism of Novatian, 154-8.
  Paschal Canon of, 161, 164.
  treatise of, *On Promises*, 166.
Dionysius, Bishop of Corinth, date of, 177.
  letters of, 147 f., 177 f., 244.
Dionysius, Bishop of Rome, 159 f., 166, 176.
Disciples of the Lord, 26, 28, 33 f.
Dittrich, 163.
Dius, martyr, 273.
Dodwell, H., 191.
Domitian, 37, 50-4, 56, 61, 95 f.

Domitius and Didymus, 161-4, 169-72, 174.
Domninus, martyr, 189.
Druzipara, 241.
Duruy, V., 203.
Dyrrhachium, 235.
δηλωθεῖσαι, 163.
διαδέχεται, διεδέξατο, 15 f.
διαδοχή, 22, 66, 70-3, 86-8.
διακονική, 157 f.
διὰ τοῦτο, 19, 37.
διατριβὴν ἐποιησάμην, 70-2, 87.

East, Diocese of the, 224.
Ebionites, 28.
Ecstasy, 109, 117-19.
Egypt, 198, 225.
  martyrs in, 273 f.
Eleutherus, Bishop of Rome, 66-8, 72, 75, 85.
Elias, martyr, 183.
Empire, division of the, 197.
Ephesus, St. John at, 51, 53, 54, 64, 95 f.
Epiphanius, Bishop of Constantia,
  carelessness of, in quotation, 74, 78, 127.
  date and place of work on Montanism used by, 127.
  mutilation of authorities by, 35, 84.
  quoted the *Hypomnemata* of Hegesippus, 5-11, 14, 73-84.
  unsatisfactory method of citing authorities of, 35, 82.
Epiphanius, martyr: *see* Apphianus.
Episcopal succession: *see* Succession.
Ethiopia, 174 f.
Eubulus, martyr, 209.
Eusebius, Bishop of Caesarea,
  at Caesarea till 311, 271.
  Book of Martyrdoms of, 137, 148, 284.
  Ecclesiastical History of—
    Eighth Book of—
      appendix to, 265 f., 284.
      date of, 260, 275, 290.
      later additions to, 268-78.
      originally the last, 261.
      unsatisfactory character of, 285 f.
      manuscripts of, 243.

Eusebius, Bishop of Caesarea,
Ecclesiastical History of—
  Ninth Book of, a supplement, 257-66.
    date of, 255 f., 291.
    traces of revision in, 256 f.
    original end of, 259-66.
    purpose of, 258.
    Syriac version of, 18, 71.
  Tenth Book of, a supplement, 243.
    date of, 243, 255, 291.
    faulty construction of, 254.
    supposed earlier edition of, 243-55.
  father of Church History, 1, 4.
  habit of, of beginning a book with closing words of preceding book, 253, 257, 289.
  honesty of, 245, 252 f., 255.
  in Egypt, 198, 271, 282.
  libraries used by, 136.
  Martyrs of Palestine of, clause inserted in short recension of, 280 f., 290.
    corrupt text of passage in short recension of, 288.
    date of, 286, 290 f.
    date of long recension of, 179, 279-283.
    form of dates in, 182 f.
    Greek fragments of long recension of, 185, 190, 199 f., 206.
    inaccuracies of dates in, 189-94.
    manuscripts of, 289.
    passages in short recension of, derived from *H. E.* viii, 287-9.
    passages peculiar to short recension of, 281 f., 287-9.
    referred to in the *History*, 262 f., 285.
    relation of, to *H. E.* viii, 279, 285-90.
    two recensions of, 179 f., 185, 190, 279-83.
  method of, of paraphrasing Hegesippus, 47.
  method of, of using volumes of tracts, 137, 145 f., 152, 165.
  omissions of, in quotation, 18-20, 25, 36 f., 65-9, 96 f.

Eusebius, Bishop of Caesarea,
  projected work of, *de mortibus persecutorum*, 280 f., 284.
  work of, on Metonic cycle, 188.
  ἐγκατείλεκται, 148.
  ἐν ταὐτῷ, 147.
  ἐν τούτῳ, 185.
  ἐπὶ πᾶσιν, 176.
  ἐπιστολαί, 152 f.
  ἐπὶ τούτοις, 26, 142, 144.
  ἐπὶ τῷ αὐτῷ λόγῳ, 61.
  ἔτι δέ, 148 f.
  ἑξῆς, 142 f.

Fabius, Bishop of Antioch, 152-6.
Fasting, laws of, 129 f.
Faustus, martyr, 173 f.
Feltoe, C. L., 157-9, 162 f., 170, 173.
Festus, 24.
Ficker, G., 110.
Fires at Nicomedia, 268 f.
Firmilian, Bishop of Caesarea, 113, 119.
Firmilian, praeses, 199, 206.
Flavia Domitilla, 43 f., 51.
Flavian, praeses, 193, 200 f., 287.
Flavius, 161 f., 170.
Florinus, 177.
Friedländer, L., 213.

Galerius, 203-5, 218, 238, 240, 268.
  death of, 215, 221, 241, 288.
  dominions of, 213, 215.
  toleration edict of, 209, 213-15, 232, 241, 246, 251, 263 f., 286-8.
    believed to be the beginning of peace, 214, 259 f., 263 f.
    issued in the name of the four emperors, 259 f., 278.
    referred to at the beginning of the *History*, 264 f.
    the originator of the persecution ? 253.
Gallienus, 161, 163, 174.
  toleration edict of, 161, 172.
Gallus, 160, 174.
Gates of Cilicia : *see* Cilicia.
Gaul, 237, 240, 242.
Gaza, 196, 206.
Gebhardt, O. von, 133, 167, 223, 283.
Gergovia, 235.

GENERAL INDEX 303

Germanus, 163 f., 169.
Gnosticism, introduced into Rome, 77, 80.
Gnostics, 2 f., 75 f., 90, 129.
Gobarus, Stephanus, 107.
Gwatkin, H. M., 95, 115, 129, 174, 202 f., 205, 226, 232, 256.
Gwynn, J., 200.
γραφή, 136.

Hadrian, 3, 64, 92, 178.
Harnack, A., 9, 21, 71 f., 79, 81 f., 85-7, 95 f., 113, 117, 122, 135, 178.
Harris, R., 114, 178.
Hebrews, Gospel of the, quoted by Hegesippus, 8.
Hefele, C. J., 175.
Hegesippus, account of Jewish heresies by, 40.
  date of, 2, 68, 95, 145.
  date of arrival of, at Rome, 89.
  did he write a second treatise? 81.
  ends historical sketch of the Church of Jerusalem with Symeon, 64.
  father of Church History? 1, 3.
  Hypomnemata of, argument of, 62 f., 90.
  fragments of, 98-107.
  purpose of, 2-4.
  quoted by Epiphanius, 5-11.
  quoted by Irenaeus, 75 f.
  various texts of, 5-9, 44 f.
  journey of, to Rome, 64-73, 84, 86-90.
  misinterpretation of, by Eusebius, 24, 28, 38 f.
Heinichen, F. A., 19, 26.
Heraclea: see Perinthus.
Heresies referred to by Hegesippus, 58, 62.
Heresy, recent origin of, 63.
Hermammon, letter of Dionysius of Alexandria to, 161-3, 170, 172.
Hesychius, Egyptian bishop, 273.
Hierax, 161 f., 164, 170.
Hippolytus, 127, 157.
  Canons of, 158.
  Syntagma of, 112.
  works of, 151 f.
Holmes, Rice, 236.

Hort, F. J. A., 23.
Hunziker, O., 192, 269 f.
Hyginus, Bishop of Rome, 85, 87.

Ignatius, 22.
Images of Christ, 75 f.
Interpretatio Hebraicorum nominum, authorship of, 144.
Irenaeus, 43, 53, 83, 95, 244.
  his list of Roman bishops, 81.
  quotes Hegesippus, 75 f.
  volume containing letters of, 177.
Italy, persecution in, 197.
Itinerary, Antonine, 212 f., 219.
Iustum iter, 235.
ἱστορεῖ, 23.

James the Just, Bishop of Jerusalem, 1, 3-18, 27, 31 f., 93.
  appointment of, 15-17, 45, 63.
  converts of, 25.
  date of martyrdom of, 24, 28.
Jerome, St., 1, 144, 153 f., 237.
Jerusalem, bishops of, 22, 64, 92 f.
  history of Church of, given by Hegesippus, 64.
  library at, 136.
  sieges of, 24, 28, 64.
'Jerusalem', a name of Pepuza, 110, 120, 122.
Jewish war, 24, 27 f., 31.
Jews, heresies of the, 62, 91.
  persecution of the, 52, 54.
  tradition of the, 35, 82.
John, Egyptian confessor, 281 f.
John, St., apostle, alleged martyrdom of, 63, 96.
  at Ephesus: see Ephesus.
  banishment of: see Patmos.
  death of, 64.
Joseph, 12-14, 25, 34-7, 39.
Josephus, 24, 27, 31, 198.
Judas, 118.
Jude, grandsons or sons of, 42, 44, 51, 54 f., 60-4.
Julian, 209.
Julius Caesar, 235, 241.
Jupiter Philius, 281.
Justin Martyr, 2.
  date of, 145.
  date of *Second Apology* of, 168.
  MSS. of Apologies of, 146.

Justin Martyr, origin of Eusebius's mistakes about, 168 f.
Second Apology of, quoted by Eusebius, 146 f.
writings of, 145–7.
Justinian, Code of, 192.

Khatha, martyr, 184, 206.
καὶ ἔτι, 140.
κατάλογος, 78–80, 84–6.
κατείλεκται, 148.

Lactantius, 181, 185, 187 f., 211–13, 215 f., 224 f., 231.
at Rome, 241.
at Sardica, 242.
De Iustitia of, 238.
departure from Nicomedia, 237–9, 242.
in Gaul, 241 f.
Institutiones of, 237 f.
mistakes of, 238 f.
supposed mistake of, 192.
teacher of rhetoric, 237.
tutor of Crispus, 237 f.
Laodiceans, 156 f.
Lee, S., 289.
Legio Fulminata, 151.
Libraries to which Eusebius had access, 136, 144.
Licinius, 215, 222, 226, 241 f., 246–8, 255 f., 276, 278, 283.
at Rome, 218.
contest of, with Constantine, 244, 251, 255 f., 259.
dilatory tactics of, 226.
letter of, issued at Nicomedia, 224, 238, 251 f., 256 f., 291.
marriage of, 218 f.
treaty of, with Maximin, 215, 217 f., 221 f.
victories of, over Maximin, 219, 224, 241, 246, 276.
Lightfoot, J. B., 9, 10, 18 f., 21, 43, 57, 74, 79–81, 86, 96, 117, 144, 152, 167, 179 f., 255, 280, 282 f., 284 f., 286 f.
Linus, Bishop of Rome, 9, 77, 79, 82.
Little Labyrinth, 125.
Lucian, letter of Dionysius of Alexandria about, 159, 176.
Lucian, martyr, 218, 239, 269 f., 275.

Lucian, martyr, *Apology* of, 218.
letter of, 268, 270.
λεῖπον, 266.
λόγος, 262.
λόγος κατέχει (ἔχει), 21 f., 26, 36, 51 f., 92 f., 268.
λύσεις γάμων, 127 f.

McGiffert, A. C., 1, 21, 86, 131–3, 181, 257, 273.
'Mansionibus geminatis', 219.
Marcellina, 74 f., 79–81, 83, 85 f., 89.
Marching, rate of, 211 f., 216, 219–21, 235 f.
Marcion, 86.
Marcus Aurelius, 132, 137, 145 f., 167 f.
Martianus, 133.
Martyrdom of Polycarp, 55, 137 f., 165, 167.
Martyrs, honour given to, 63.
prerogative of, 123.
Martyrs of Lyons, 132.
Mary, B.V., 13 f., 35.
Mason, A. J., 187, 192, 200, 202, 219, 225 f., 232–4, 283.
Maxentius, 218, 240, 276.
Maximian, 203, 205, 240.
abdication of, 185, 240.
author of the Fourth Edict, 202.
public memorials of, destroyed, 275.
Maximilla, 109 f., 113, 119 f., 127 f., 131.
oracle of, 111.
Maximin Daza, 185 f., 205, 213, 215, 218–20, 241, 267, 276, 280 f., 283, 285 f., 291.
army of, collected in Cappadocia, 225 f.
at Nicomedia: *see* Nicomedia.
birthday of, 191, 206, 210.
death of, 225–9, 256.
defeat of: *see* Campus Serenus.
did not persecute at first, 187, 206, 214 f.
dominions of, 215, 225.
letter of, to Sabinus, 217.
memorials from cities to, 216 f., 222 f., 229–31, 239.
name of, in the edict of Galerius, 259 f., 278.

GENERAL INDEX   305

Maximin Daza, pagan hierarchy of, 206, 208 f., 230 f., 276, 286.
  policy of, regarding religion, 209, 230.
  rebuilds temples, 206, 208.
  rescript of, set up on pillars, 197 f., 222 f., 228 f., 231.
  restoration of paganism by, 206, 208.
  resumes persecution in Egypt, 272.
  secrecy of movements of, 222.
  toleration edict of, 189, 197, 210, 224-7.
  treaty of, with Licinius, 215, 217 f., 221.
Meletius, martyr, 198.
Meletius, schismatic bishop, 272 f.
Melito of Sardis, date of *Apology* of, 176.
  works of, 148 f.
Menandrianists, 62.
Menology quoted by Matthaei, 16, 44.
Metonic cycle, 188.
Metrodorus, Acts of, 136 f., 167.
Milan, Constantine and Licinius at, 218 f., 241.
  distance of, from Antioch, 219.
  edict of, 218, 224, 247, 251 f., 256, 259, 291.
Military road in Asia Minor, 212 f.
Millenarianism, 120 f., 165.
Milligan, W., 90.
Miltiades, Montanist leader in Phrygian Pentapolis, 117 f.
Milvian Bridge, Battle of, 218, 240-2.
Mommsen, T., 192, 243.
Monarchy, various opinions of Montanists on, 112.
Montanism, asceticism in, 123-30.
  attitude of, towards martyrdom, 130-5.
  first steward of, 112, 124.
  in Rome, 132, 151.
  instances of difference between Phrygian and African, 117-35.
  later prophets of, 112 f.
  local centre of, 109, 120.
  Millenarianism of, 120.

Montanism, not homogeneous, 109-16.
  oracles of, 110 f., 121-3, 128-30.
  origin of, 109, 151.
  penitential discipline of, 122 f.
  place of women in, 119 f.
  prophetic succession in, 118.
  teaching of, on fasting, 129.
    on marriage, 127 f.
  true method of investigating, 116 f.
  virgins in, 119, 128.
Montanists, a majority among Phrygian Christians, 134.
  errors of, 111.
Montanus, 109 f., 113, 124 f., 127 f., 131.
Morin, G., 158.
μετά, 142 f., 150, 170 f., 176.

Natalius, 125.
Nazoraeans, 6, 28 f.
Nepos, 165.
Nero, 87.
Nerva, 51, 53-5, 95 f.
Nestorius, 49.
New prophecy: *see* Montanism.
Nicephorus, 71.
Nicomedia, 186, 201, 212 f., 216, 218, 221, 226.
  distance of, from Antioch, Chalcedon, and Tyana, 213.
  edict issued at, 213.
  fire at, 268 f.
  Lactantius at, 237 f.
  Licinius at, 224.
  martyrdoms at, 239, 268 f.
  Maximin at, 216 f., 218 f., 221 f., 224, 229 f.
  memorial from citizens of, 217, 229-31, 239.
  rescript issued at, 201.
Nilus, Egyptian bishop, 273.
Notes in manuscripts, 144, 147 f., 177, 244.
Novatian or Novatus, 155-7, 159.
  letters on the schism of, 152-4, 154-8.
νομοθεσία, 251.

Oracles, 30, 34.
  see also Montanism.
Ordinances, collection of imperial, 248 f., 251 f., 257.

GENERAL INDEX

Origen, 49, 144, 157 f.
   letters of, 22, 36, 136, 148.
   library of, 144.
Orleans, 236.
Otto, J. C. T. de, 146.
ὅλα ἔτη, ὅλοι μῆνες, 197-9, 214, 228, 267 f.
ὠβλίας, 6-9, 45.

Pachymius, Egyptian bishop, 273.
Pagan hierarchy: *see* Maximin Daza.
Palestine, last martyrs in, 209, 263.
Palinodia: *see* Galerius, toleration edict of.
Pamphilus, 194 f., 210, 273, 282.
   imprisonment of, 195 f., 199.
   library of, 136.
Pantaenus, 22.
Panther, James, 35-7.
Papias, 49, 95 f.
Papylus, Acts of, 136 f., 167.
Passion of Christ in accounts of martyrs, 57.
Patmos, St. John in, 51, 53-6, 60 f., 95 f.
Paul, St., 9, 80.
Paul, martyr, 206.
   see also Peleus.
Paul of Samosata, 49.
Paulinus, Bishop of Tyre, 243, 255.
Peleus, Egyptian bishop, 273.
Peleus (Paul), martyr, 183.
Pella, flight to, and return from, 28-34, 50, 72.
Pentapolis, Phrygian, 117 f.
Pepuza, 109, 119-22.
Peraea, 29, 33 f.
Perinthus, 212, 219.
Perpetua, Acts of, 114.
Pestilence under Decius and Gallus, 164, 171-5.
Peter, St., 9, 57, 80.
Peter Apselamus (Absalom), martyr, 183, 189, 194.
Peter, Bishop of Alexandria, 267 f., 272-5.
   letter of, 272.
Phileas, Bishop of Thmuis, 272-4.
   letters of, 272.
Philemon, presbyter of Rome, 159 f.
Philip, daughters of, 118.

Philo, writings of, 138-45.
Philoromus, martyr, 272 f.
Phrygia, 271.
Pichon, R., 237.
Pierius, 49.
Pilate, 75, 198.
   Acts of, 218, 230, 267.
Pilgrims' Road in Asia Minor, 213.
Pinytus, Bishop of the Cnossians, 148.
Pionius, Acts of, 136 f., 167.
Pius, Bishop of Rome, 74, 84 f.
Plato, 75.
Polycarp, 146.
   interview of, with Marcion, 86.
   martyrdom of, 55, 136 f., 167.
Pontus, 271.
   Diocese of, 213, 215, 225.
Post, Imperial, 213, 219, 221.
Praxeas, 111, 132.
Primus, Bishop of Corinth, 66, 69 f.
Primus, martyr, 183 f.
Prisca or Priscilla, 109 f., 113, 119, 128.
Procopius, martyr, 191 f., 199 f.
   Latin Passion of, 192 f.
Prophetic succession, 118.
Prophets, Montanistic, prerogative of, 123.
Protevangelium of James, 12 f., 35.
Publius, Bishop of Corinth, 178.
Purser, L. C., 212, 235.
Pythagoras, 75.
πάλιν, 18 f., 32 f.
παρὰ ταῦτα, 140.
παρέκστασις, 119.
πρὸς Γερμανόν, 163 f.
πρὸς τούτοις, 140, 142, 144, 148 f.
πρότερος, 147.
φασί, 22, 26, 36 f., 94.

Quadratus, apologist, to whom was his *Apology* presented? 178.
   was he Quadratus the bishop? 177.
   see also Aristides.
Quintilla, 113.
Quintillians, 119.

Ramsay, Sir W. M., 113, 134, 212 f., 220, 225.
Relatives of the Lord: *see* Desposyni.

Romanus, martyr, 189, 192. .
Rome, 201 f., 218.
 arrival of heretics at, 85 f.
 Hegesippus's history of Church of, ended with Anicetus, 85 f., 89.
  parallel with that of Church of Jerusalem, 80, 85, 89 f., 92.
 list of bishops of, by Hegesippus, 77-80, 88 f.
  used by Eusebius, 82.
  why not quoted by him, 81.
 list of bishops of, by Irenaeus, 81.
 Montanism in, 132, 151.
Routh, M. J., 218, 270, 272.
Rufinus, 2, 18, 53, 70 f., 91, 218.
Ruinart, T., 133, 193, 272, 283.
Rusticus, 168.

Sabellianism, 111, 165 f.
Sabinus, letter of, 214, 254.
 letter of Maximin to, 217-21, 223 f., 227-9, 232-4, 247.
Salaries of clergy, 124 f.
Salmon, G., 113.
Salona, Palace at, 203.
Sanday, W., 95.
Sardica, 213, 215, 221, 241.
Saturnilians, 62.
Saturninus, 2.
Saturus, 114.
Schürer, E., 138-44.
Schwartz, E., 5, 7, 32, 91, 149, 156, 199, 243-55, 258, 265 f., 268, 275, 281-3.
Sens, 236.
Septimius Severus, 167.
Severus, Emperor, 205.
Silas, 118.
Silvanus, Bishop of Emesa, 273-5.
Silvanus, Bishop of Gaza, 196, 209, 273, 282.
Simonians, 62.
Smyrnaeans, letter of the: *see* Polycarp, martyrdom of.
Soter, Bishop of Rome, 66-8, 72, 177.
Stephen, Bishop of Rome, 159 f.
Stroth, 19.
Succession of bishops, 63, 70, 77.
 of prophets, 117 f.
Susa, Battle of, 241.
Swete, H. B., 96.

Symeon, Bishop of Jerusalem, 18-26, 32-4, 40, 54, 56-61, 64, 93.
 accusers of, 40, 56, 60, 62.
 election of, 15, 19, 32 f., 50, 55, 63, 93.
 electors of, 19, 26, 34, 38, 63.
Symmachus, quoted by Hegesippus, 8.
Synods regarding the Schism of Novatian, 152 f., 157, 175.
Syria, 219, 225, 230.
σύγγραμμα, 261.
συνῆπτο, 137, 152.

Tarsus, 212 f., 225.
 distance of, from Tyana, 220.
 road from, to Tyana, 220.
Taurus mountains, 220, 224-6
 passes of, fortified, 224 f.
Tax removed by Maximin, 221.
Telesphorus, Bishop of Rome, 169.
Temples, rebuilding of, 230.
Tertullian, 4, 51, 53.
 counted as main authority for Montanism, 108.
 De Ecstasi of, 126.
 did not admit absolving power of martyrs, 123.
 did not hold the Phrygian view of the Parousia, 120 f.
 did not recognize a prophetic succession, 118.
 does not mention Pepuza, 120.
 influence of, on African Montanism, 114-16.
 on unpardonable sin, 123.
 protest of, against women exercising clerical functions, 120.
Thebaid, 207, 210.
 martyrs of the, 270-4.
Thebuthis, 25 f., 58, 63, 70, 77, 80, 91.
Themiso, Montanist, 113, 124, 133.
Theodorus, Egyptian bishop, 273.
Theodosia, martyr, 193, 196.
Theodotians, 125.
Theodotus, a banker, 125.
Theodotus, first steward of the New Prophecy, 112, 124, 131.
Theotecnus, 222, 231.
Thmuis, 273.
Tiberius, 198.

Timolaus (Timothy), martyr, 195, 203.
Timothy, martyr, 195 f.
see also Timolaus.
Toleration, edicts of: see Galerius, Gallienus, Maximin, Milan.
Tradition of the Jews, 35–7, 82.
Trajan, 37, 54, 56, 64.
Trier, 238, 242.
Turin, Battle of, 241.
Turner, C. H., 17, 24, 92 f., 182, 221, 228.
Tyana, 212 f., 220, 224.
distance of, from Tarsus, 220.
Tymion, 110.
Tyrannion, Bishop of Tyre, 273 f.
Tyre, 228, 271.
inscription at, 223.
panegyric at, 251, 254 f.
Tyrrell, R. Y., 235.
Tzurulum, 219, 241 f.
τὰς διατριβὰς ἐποιεῖτο, 73, 87.
τόμος, 261.
τῶν ἀνωτέρω, 74, 84.

Ulpian, martyr, 281 f.
Urban, praeses, 186, 196 f., 199, 202, 205 f., 280.
ὑπομνήματα, 1, 10.
ὑπομνηματισμοί, 10–13, 82.

Valentina, martyr, 184, 206.
Valentinus, 85 f.
Valerian, 160, 164 f., 169 f., 173 f.

Valois, 2, 19, 39, 61, 167, 272.
Verona, Battle of, 241.
Vespasian, 50, 52, 59–61.
Vicennalia of Diocletian, 192, 200.
Virgin, a description of the Church of Jerusalem, 19, 37–9, 69.
Virgins among the Montanists, 119, 128.
Visions of Montanists, 114–16, 119.
Volumes of tracts used by Eusebius, the principle of the formation of, 166.

Westcott, B. F., 255 f., 284.
Wolseley, Lord, 236.

Xystus, Bishop of Rome, 159 f., 176.

Year, beginning of, 221, 227 f.
Years, complete : see ὅλα ἔτη.
of persecution, 181–4, 194–7.
relation of, to years A. D., 184–9.
regnal, 182.

Zacchaeus, martyr, 189, 192.
Zahn, Theodor, 4, 9, 17, 19, 24, 26 f., 35 f., 38 f., 44, 68, 71, 78, 80, 83, 86–8, 91, 93.
Zenobius, martyr, 273 f.
Zocer and James, 42, 44 f., 54–6.
Zoticus of Otrous, 118.

www.ingramcontent.com/pod-product-compliance
Lightning Source LLC
Chambersburg PA
CBHW030757230426
43667CB00007B/1000